Wings for the Navy

Naval Institute Press
Annapolis, Maryland

WILLIAM F. TRIMBLE

Wings for the Navy

A History of the Naval Aircraft Factory, 1917–1956

Library of Congress Cataloging-in-Publication Data

Trimble, William F., 1947–
   Wings for the Navy : a history of the Naval
  Aircraft Factory, 1917–1956 / William F. Trimble.
     p.   cm.
  Includes bibliographical references and index.
  ISBN 0-87021-663-5
   1. Naval Aircraft Factory (Philadelphia, Pa.)—
History.   2. United States. Navy—Aviation—
History.   I. Title.
VG94.5.N62T75   1990
338.7′623746′0974811—dc20   90-41959
                                CIP

Printed in the United States of America on acid-free paper ⊗

9 8 7 6 5 4 3 2
First printing

To William and Michael

Contents

Illustrations

Acknowledgments

This book, like others dealing with the histories of large and complex institutions, is the result of long-term collaborative effort. From the start of my work, J. Hartley Bowen, Jr., a former civilian engineer at the Naval Aircraft Factory (NAF), provided insight into the personalities and organization of the factory. He read with a sharp, critical eye early drafts of the manuscript and in ways too numerous to mention gave invaluable assistance and encouragement. Another NAF veteran, William J. Cox, helped with the material on catapults and arresting gear. Forrest S. Williams critiqued my coverage of the NAF's metallurgical research and laboratory activities. There was no more delightful person to talk to than the late Captain Ralph S. Barnaby, who knew many of the old-timers from the NAF and participated in guided weapon and glider projects at Philadelphia and Johnsville.

Among fellow historians deserving specific acknowledgment, Richard K. Smith stands almost alone. He read the entire manuscript and proferred advice and assistance based on his impressive knowledge of airplanes and aeronautical engineering. William J. Armstrong at the Naval Air Systems Command headquarters supported this project from its inception and located documents pertaining to specific NAF projects and aircraft. Eric Schatzberg of the University of Pennsylvania helped bring balance and perspective to my treatment of the factory's development of the metal airplane. Dean C. Allard, Forrest Barber, Archie DiFante, Robert A. Gordon,

James R. Hansen, Eden Harriss, Wesley P. Newton, Albert L. Raithel, Jr., Matthew E. Rodina, Jr., Howard Smeltzer, Jacob Vander Meulen, Louis M. Waddell, and Ray Wagner all contributed time and advice. Trudie Calvert expertly edited the completed manuscript, and Paul W. Wilderson of the Naval Institute Press helped guide the book through the maze of the publication process. When needed Tom D. Crouch was always there as a friend, booster, and confidant.

With much gratitude I thank the staffs of the Historical Society of Western Pennsylvania, the National Archives and Records Administration, the Naval Historical Center, the Library of Congress Manuscript Division, the Franklin D. Roosevelt Library, the Harry S. Truman Library, the United States Air Force Historical Research Center, the United States Naval Aviation Museum, the United States Naval Institute, and the Nimitz Library of the United States Naval Academy for making the research for this book an enjoyable experience. A grant from the Johnson Fund of the American Philosophical Society in 1982–83 helped get my research off the ground, and the Naval Historical Center's award of a Vice Admiral Edwin B. Hooper postdoctoral fellowship in 1987–88 facilitated its completion. *Business History Review* and the President and Fellows of Harvard College permitted me to reprint portions of my article "The Naval Aircraft Factory, the American Aviation Industry, and Government Competition, 1919–1928," which appeared in the *Review*'s Summer 1986 issue, pages 175–98 (© 1986 by the President and Fellows of Harvard College).

My good friends Paul and Harriet Sirovatka welcomed me into their home on more visits to Washington than I can count. My debt to them for this and other books goes far beyond anything words can express. Finally, to my wife, Sharon, and my sons, William and Michael, go thanks for many years of forbearance and unwavering support.

Introduction

In Philadelphia on 9 May 1956, the Naval Aircraft Factory became the Naval Air Engineering Facility (Ship Installations). At the time there was a sense that an important chapter in the chronicles of naval aviation had come to an end. Under its new name, the factory shifted its mission from specialized manufacturing to developmental work with catapults, arresting gear, and related equipment.[1] Yet despite these changes, there was a feeling that the factory had left a deep impression on naval aviation. In 1941, the NAF created and spun off the Aviation Supply Office, which continues to the present as a major component of the navy's aviation logistical support network. Two years later, the NAF spawned the Naval Air Material Center (NAMC), a major command responsible for aircraft production, modification, testing, and research and development. From the NAMC's laboratories came the Naval Air Development Center at Johnsville, Pennsylvania, and the Naval Air Engineering Facility went on to become the Naval Air Engineering Center at Lakehurst, New Jersey. Finally, the aero engine research that had been at the NAF since 1924 merged in 1967 into the Naval Air Propulsion Test Center at Trenton, New Jersey. Although the cavernous old NAF assembly buildings stand vacant, and the cracked asphalt runways at Mustin Field have long since been turned over to parked cars and weeds, the NAF lives on, albeit under other names, as a vital part of naval aviation.

The Naval Aircraft Factory was unique. It was one of the largest naval aviation installations in the United States, and it was for nearly thirty years the only government-owned and operated aircraft production facility in this country. For a time, it was the only major aircraft plant that also manufactured engines. Those distinctions alone merit its attention by the historian, but there is more to the story of the NAF than simply its exceptionality. Its history in many ways mirrored that of the formative years of naval aviation. Some of the key figures in naval aviation either worked at the NAF or their careers meshed in some way with the factory and its people. Henry Mustin, Jerome Hunsaker, William Moffett, George Westervelt, Ralph Weyerbacher, H. C. Richardson, Ernest King, and John Towers were only some of the officers whose names were linked in one way or another with the Naval Aircraft Factory.

In other ways, too, the NAF was representative of growth and change in naval aviation. During the hectic first year of American involvement in World War I, the factory was an important source of the long-range flying boats needed for patrols in the Atlantic and the approaches to the British Isles. To produce these airplanes, the NAF turned to large numbers of subcontractors for components, heralding a fundamental structural change in the American aircraft industry that enabled it greatly to expand its output in both world wars. After World War I, the NAF played a key role in the development of improved flying boats for the fleet and in experiments with metal airframe construction. The catapults and arresting gear so crucial for the advance of fleet aviation between the wars were largely the responsibility of the NAF. The factory was at times the navy's chief aviation overhaul and repair facility, and its supply department was the major disbursing agency for parts and equipment. Perhaps most significant in light of the changes in weapons technology that overtook the navy after World War II, the factory was one of the service's principal centers for the development of pilotless aircraft and guided missiles.

On several occasions, the Naval Aircraft Factory was caught in a vortex of controversy involving navy aircraft and engine procurement. The navy had always regarded itself as having special requirements, one of which was the need for airplanes to perform unique missions. That sense of privilege carried over into aircraft production. To guarantee an autonomous source of airplanes, naval officers argued forcefully and successfully for retention of the aircraft design and manufacturing capabilities of the NAF. At times, the navy's attitude coincided with that of political leaders and the general public, who castigated arms makers for unconscionable profits in the sale of weapons and who considered the NAF and other government facilities vital to maintaining a truly competitive environment and as a "yardstick" in the accurate determination of the costs of privately supplied material.

It is tempting to draw parallels between the Naval Aircraft Factory and other government forays into supposedly private enterprises. The most frequent comparison has been with the federal Tennessee Valley Authority (TVA) power complex. The authority did have distinct yardstick functions growing out of Franklin D. Roosevelt's advocacy during World War I of a government armor-plate factory, but the TVA as a concept and a reality went far beyond simply providing a guideline of the costs private utilities charged their customers.[2] The NAF was more narrowly directed toward extending and retaining military control over production for exclusively military purposes. Naval officers had no social agenda in the manufacture of aircraft at Philadelphia.

There was another compelling reason for the design and manufacture of aircraft at Philadelphia. As an integral unit within a technical bureau—in this case, the Bureau of Aeronautics (BuAer)— the NAF provided a valuable opportunity for "dirty hands" engineering. BuAer officers moved freely between Washington and Philadelphia and while at the factory learned firsthand what components went into an airplane and how it worked. Many officers considered that experience vital in drawing up specifications, designing aircraft, negotiating contracts with private firms, and providing technical verification of airplanes, engines, and components.

Regardless of the motives, the civilian aviation industry, especially during periods of business crisis, regarded the NAF as anathema and the elimination of the factory's design and production functions a panacea that would immediately heal all wounds. Their public importunities caught the NAF in political crossfire in the 1920s and 1930s. More perceptive naval officers understood that the real or imagined plight of the industry could not be ignored and that the private sector would have to be called upon for aircraft and engines in the event of war. This understanding led to a delicate balancing act whereby for much of its history the design and manufacturing missions of the NAF were greatly circumscribed, though it managed to preserve a significant proportion of its expertise in these areas.

The Naval Aircraft Factory was a component of what President Dwight D. Eisenhower in his 1961 farewell address labeled the "military-industrial complex." Broadly speaking, and at the risk of oversimplification, the military-industrial complex is that group of private corporations engaged in weapons development and production and the military services that buy their products. It encompasses, as well, corporate executives and military officers who represent those private and public institutions. There has always been a pejorative connotation to the term *military-industrial complex*, with hints of scandal, "double-dipping," and unseemly and dangerous influence in the nation's public affairs. In another sense, though, the term is a descriptive one that aptly represents the interactive nature of weapons procurement.[3] A close look at the NAF and its history can be especially revealing about the dynamics of weapons acquisition in the twentieth century.

Possibly as a result of industry propaganda or as a consequence of an innate abhorrence of anything even vaguely resembling socialism, there was a strong undercurrent of sentiment that the NAF was less efficient than civilian aircraft or engine manufacturers and that somehow its products were inferior. It would be revealing to compare the results of the production of aircraft from private manufacturers with that of the NAF, but it is impossible to do so. First, *efficiency* is a relative term; second, there is no agreement as to what criteria should be applied to determine efficiency. If cost is the major factor in computing efficiency, the results are inconclusive. Some of the airplanes built at Philadelphia were more expensive than those obtained from private industry; others were less expensive. Moreover, direct cost comparisons between aircraft manufactured at the NAF and similar ones produced by private industry (the much-touted yardstick) are not possible because of unavoidably divergent means of records management, accounting, and bookkeeping.

If relative productive efficiency is impossible to ascertain, so also is it impossible to determine whether the quality control standards at the NAF were below those of private industry. The impression persists among some naval officers, particularly, that the NAF put out a bad product. Operating personnel sometimes complained about the material condition or the design of aircraft obtained from the NAF. These cases may have been more numerous for NAF-built airplanes than for similar aircraft acquired from private manufacturers. But so far as is known, there was no attempt to amass technical orders, trouble reports, or BuAer bulletins on airplanes manufactured at the NAF or to compare these data with those of similar aircraft from other sources. Like the question of efficiency, the issue of quality is inherently unanswerable.

Some critics have denigrated the factory for never having designed or produced a front-line combat aircraft equivalent to or better than those of civilian manufacturers. Regarding this alleged failure, the point must be made that the principal objective of the navy in retaining aircraft design and production at Philadelphia was not to outdo the private sector. Had the NAF consistently bettered its private counterparts, it would have been symptomatic of serious deficiencies in the industry as a whole. The NAF was there to manufacture representative models and to meet the navy's short-term or emergency production requirements for aircraft, engines, and other equipment.

This is not to say that there were no blemishes in the NAF's complexion. The factory manufactured some airplanes that did not have good reputations, there were lapses in quality control, and there were gross cost overruns. No attempt has been made to gloss over the wrong decisions at the factory or its occasional mistakes. At the same time, there were some remarkable achievements at the NAF, when the factory produced a good product and completed a project on time and at cost. They deserve recognition, too. But the problems and the errors and the roads not taken are often instructive, and for that reason, this study attempts to deal with them objectively.

Aside from the pros and cons of efficiency, quality, and objectivity, the Naval Aircraft Factory deserves consideration because it can demonstrate in microcosm much about the structure and function of the aviation industry in the United States. The history of the NAF shows how a complex institution undergoes administrative change. At least through its early years, the factory and its administration reflected the personality and style of its manager. Fred Coburn, the first NAF manager, favored a loosely knit administrative structure that left considerable initiative and responsibility with the individual departments. George Westervelt, who succeeded Coburn in the top NAF position, favored a more centralized organization. One approach was not right and the other was not wrong; both were the results of individual personality and style at a time when the design and construction of airplanes tended to be largely a personal endeavor.

Not only can a study of the NAF provide an understanding of institutional history, but it can also give insight into technological change. The history of the NAF is, to a certain degree, also the history of the development of navy flying boats, training airplanes, catapults and arresting gear, and guided weapons. It is, in another sense, a glimpse at how aircraft and related equipment were designed, manufactured, and tested. In a general way, what happened at the NAF also took place in other aircraft design centers and manufacturing plants for which not even the sketchiest records are available. This study, then, is a fairly narrowly focused institutional history, but its implications go far beyond the confines of League Island and encompass much of what transpired in the aviation industry as a whole during the period covered.

Curiously, despite the importance of the factory, it has received little attention from historians of naval aviation. Part of the reason for this oversight may be the concentration on operational history and the admittedly more romantic aspects of that subject. Everyone wants to read about the exploits of the the navy's fighter aces and the triumphant rise of carrier aviation, but few stop to think about the infrastructure that made naval aviation a reality. For every pilot and every airplane, for every aircraft carrier at sea, there are literally hundreds, and possibly thousands, of people on the ground or on shore playing vital support roles. The Naval Aircraft Factory and the people who worked there sustained naval aviation and helped make possible the more glamorous accomplishments of those who hazarded the sea or the air. They were the engineers, the craftspeople, the foremen, the mechanics, the painters, the seamstresses, and many others—mostly civilian—who provided the means to get the job done; they were heroes of a different sort, less visible, but heroes all the same. This is to a great extent their story.

Wings for the Navy

1

A New Industrial Establishment

Less than a decade after Wilbur and Orville Wright launched humankind into the air age on the windswept sand dunes of North Carolina's Outer Banks, the United States faced a dilemma in its infant aviation industry. Although distinctly an American invention, the airplane in this country underwent little development after 1910, and by 1913 Europe had taken the lead in aviation. Among the general public in America few were concerned, for most regarded the airplane as little more than entertainment at county fairs or as a toy for the wealthy. But in military and government circles there was apprehension because the European industry was actively pursuing the airplane's development as a weapon. In contrast, aircraft manufacturing in the United States hardly justified being called an industry; it was instead a loose collection of small shops doing specialty work on order. By 1914, there were perhaps twenty aircraft manufacturing companies, with annual sales of only forty-nine airplanes, most coming from the well-established Wright and Curtiss firms. The navy that year had only eight airplanes, five of which had been supplied by Curtiss.[1]

Alleviating this situation brought out contradictory views of the fledgling aviation business, its relationship with the military establishment, and the role of the federal government in stimulating technological change and industrial growth. There was a consensus that European aircraft builders had seized an advantage because of the active intervention of their respective governments. This under-

1

standing extended to a belief among Progressive reformers—whose ideology by 1912 had come to dominate all levels of government—that a lack of competition was at least partially to blame for the poor condition of the aircraft industry. Furthermore, the Progressives reasoned, Washington shared some responsibility for the well-being of the industry because in the absence of a commercial market for airplanes, the government was the only customer. Beyond that, however, there were wide differences among the Progressives about how best to stimulate the moribund enterprise.

At one end of the spectrum a group of reformers saw the problem in a relatively simplistic context. If competition were necessary to assure the growth of the industry and to foster aviation technology, the most efficient means of creating competition was to involve the government directly in aircraft development and construction. Secretary of the Navy Josephus Daniels, a curmudgeonly North Carolina newspaperman steeped in the Progressive tradition, had long supported antitrust legislation and was committed to equal opportunity and free market competition. If need be, he was willing to see government-owned factories supply all of the nation's requirement for an important product. This, he argued paradoxically, was in keeping with the need for competition, and he refused to "call a monopoly anything that the government owns." Furthermore, such public facilities were needed to promote economy within the government. He worried that "the Navy's dependence on private contractors with no real competition cost Uncle Sam many millions of dollars."[2] To Daniels efficiency and national security were intimately linked to direct government participation in aircraft manufacturing.

Some of Daniels's evangelistic devotion to government-owned industries stemmed from a deep-rooted perception that trusts, huge business combinations created to limit competition, had been reaping exorbitant profits from shipbuilding, armor, and armaments contracts. Scandals during the 1870s and 1880s had led to the revitalization of navy yards and, by the end of the first Grover Cleveland administration, to appropriations for setting up a gun factory in Washington. There was a sense of outrage in 1901 when shipbuilders revealed that the "armor trust," dominated by the Carnegie and Bethlehem steel interests, had allegedly colluded on their bids to supply armor plate to the navy, while the low bids of potential "outside" suppliers had been rejected.[3]

During his first year in office, 1913–14, Daniels vigorously struck back at the trusts. When bids from private contractors for warships came in too high, he determined to build the vessels at navy yards. He claimed that trusts were overcharging the navy and argued that collusion among steel producers had led to outrageous prices for armor plate. In his first annual report, Daniels included a statement in favor of a government-owned and operated armor plant, which he maintained could be used as a check on the costs of material obtained from private contractors.[4]

An undercurrent sympathetic to government intervention prevailed in 1914, when Congress began investigating the dilatoriness of the American aircraft industry in producing suitable airplanes for the navy. On 30 November, Congressman Lemuel P. Padgett, a Democrat from Tennessee and chairman of the House Committee on Naval Affairs, convened a series of hearings on naval appropriations for the fiscal year 1916. In spite of reassurances from several naval officers that they wished to see aviation advanced, it seemed to the committee that the navy was not vigorously pursuing the development of the aerial weapon. At the time, the navy inventory was twelve airplanes, and the service was having problems securing more from private manufacturers, largely because of difficulties in meeting the navy's stringent operating requirements. This struck Padgett and some of his colleagues as a deficiency that could be partially or wholly remedied by constructing airplanes in a government plant.[5]

In testimony before the committee in December, Daniels outlined some of the obstacles to the procurement of aircraft from private firms. He explained, "There is no demand for air craft for the Navy. . . . The demand has been so small that no manufacturer has felt like going into the business and taking the risk." When asked if, under such circumstances, it was "highly probable that we will have to undertake the construction of these flying machines ourselves," Daniels responded, "It begins to look that way."[6]

Although naval officers concurred with Daniels on the poor condition of the American aircraft industry and the need to stimulate competition, they were unenthusiastic about the immediate prospects for a government aircraft factory. Rear Admiral Bradley A.

Fiske, aide for operations to the secretary of the navy and often at loggerheads with Daniels, argued for the private sector. One of the navy's stormy petrels, Fiske had a strong technical bent and was the inventor of electric sounding devices, navigation equipment, controls, and engine room telegraphs. He said that neither the navy nor any other service had experience in aircraft manufacturing, feared that valuable mobilization time would be lost in erecting a factory, and forecast the stifling of inventive genius. Captain Mark L. Bristol, recently appointed director of naval aviation, insisted that the navy had made steady progress in 1914, particularly in the areas of power plants and aeronautical instruments. He concluded that nothing stood in the way either technically or legally if the government decided to initiate aircraft manufacturing, but he added that for now, "we should . . . encourage the private manufacturers to provide a large source of supply."[7]

Fiske's and Bristol's opinions typified the ideas of those officers whose bureaus would be most directly involved with the manufacture of aircraft. Rear Admiral R. M. Watt, the outgoing chief of the Bureau of Construction and Repair, and Rear Admiral Robert S. Griffin, chief of the Bureau of Steam Engineering, which had authority over the development of power plants for aircraft, prepared a joint memorandum on the subject in December 1914. They acknowledged that the rapid progress of European countries in aircraft design and construction was owing mainly to government assistance and that "there are only a few companies in this country that can at present be considered as competent designers and builders" of airplanes. But the two officers did not believe direct government involvement was the answer, suggesting that the number of aircraft manufacturers was "sufficient to stimulate competition and bring about great improvements in design, *provided* there is a reasonable amount of Government business in sight." Their recommendation was straightforward: "The Bureaus believe it would be a great mistake for the Department to undertake at the present time the manufacture of air-craft except on an experimental scale."[8]

The Watt-Griffin memorandum was consistent with then-current beliefs that "standard" aircraft and engine types were sufficient to meet the needs of the military and that government manufacturing should be limited to "one or more" experimental types of aircraft and perhaps to a single type of engine. But Watt and Griffin did anticipate a larger facility capable of turning out two or three airplanes a month. "If the Department directs the establishment of a plant for the manufacture of aircraft," the officers continued, "it is recommended that the work be done either at the Navy Yard Philadelphia or the Navy Yard, Norfolk, these yards having a moderate amount of space for testing work. . . . [and] a considerable portion of the necessary plant . . . already available."[9]

Because of the opposition of some naval officers to a full-scale production facility and Daniels's apparent willingness to defer action for the time being, the navy's direct involvement in aviation in 1915 was limited to research and development and engineering. That year the Navy Department established a small aeronautical experiment laboratory at the Washington Navy Yard. Albert F. Zahm, a professor at Catholic University and one of the pioneer aerodynamicists in America, had operated a wind tunnel at the yard since 1913. Flying boat hulls and seaplane floats had also been tested in the yard's model basin. In April 1915, after a request for a new aircraft engine design brought an indifferent response from the industry, Lieutenant Warren G. Child of the Bureau of Steam Engineering organized an experimental engine laboratory at the yard, which originated and evaluated various engine designs. That autumn, construction began at Washington on an experimental twin-engine seaplane, known simply as 82A, which was based on the design work of a young naval constructor, Lieutenant Holden C. ("Dick") Richardson.[10]

Richardson exemplified a new breed of naval constructor dedicated to aeronautical engineering. Born in Shamokin, in the hard-coal region of Pennsylvania, Richardson graduated from the Naval Academy in 1901 and received his bachelor's and master's degrees in engineering from the Massachusetts Institute of Technology in 1907. Typically, such men as Richardson pursued advanced degrees, which helped make naval constructors even more a breed apart from the usual line officers. The Construction Corps, organized within the Bureau of Construction and Repair, had responsibility for the design and fabrication of ship hulls, as well as other activities related to those functions. The corps flourished with the growth of the technically oriented New Navy of the 1880s and 1890s, but corps officers could not command ships at sea. In this unusual

atmosphere Richardson honed his skills in the fields of hydrody-
namics and aerodynamics. In 1909, he reported for duty at the
Philadelphia Navy Yard, where a year later he designed and built a
glider. In January 1911, he had the craft towed behind a car driven by
his friend, Lieutenant Commander Henry C. Mustin, one of the
navy's first aviators. Richardson transferred to the Washington
Navy Yard in 1912 to work with Captains David W. Taylor and
Washington I. Chambers at the yard's model basin.[11]

An officer of tremendous personal charm and superior intellect,
Taylor had graduated first in his class from the Naval Academy in
1885. He joined the Construction Corps and went to the Royal
Naval College in England, where in 1888, after posting the highest
grades of any student at the school, he received an advanced degree
in marine engineering. Taylor perceived the modern navy's need for
skilled and experienced engineering officers, especially in the new
field of aeronautics. Along with Richardson, he brought to the
Bureau of Construction and Repair the brilliant Jerome C. Hunsaker, an Annapolis graduate of 1908. Hunsaker had begun an
undergraduate curriculum in aeronautical engineering at MIT in
1913 and the next year established a master's program in the field.
He also translated into English Gustave Eiffel's classic study *The
Resistance of the Air*. He went on to complete his doctorate at MIT
before returning to Washington in 1916 to head the bureau's aircraft
design division.[12]

By its very existence, the aeronautical laboratory at the Washington Navy Yard helped sustain official interest in a government
aircraft factory. Construction of 82A proceeded slowly, but the
Navy Department promised that any succeeding airplanes built at
the yard would be completed more expeditiously. This was important because the navy was still having trouble getting satisfactory
results from private builders. During House Naval Affairs Committee hearings in March 1916, Daniels repeated the problems the navy
was having with private suppliers. His complaints prompted Democratic Congressman Frank Buchanan of Illinois to raise again the
idea of a government factory. Admiral William S. Benson, the first
chief of naval operations, testified before the committee that it
might be necessary for the service to establish such a facility but
was unwilling to make a positive commitment.[13]

There was a strong perception in Washington, too, that the

Secretary of the Navy Josephus Daniels (seated) with four bureau chiefs. At far left, standing, is R. Adm. Robert S. Griffin, chief of the Bureau of Steam Engineering. Next to him is R. Adm. David W. Taylor, chief of the Bureau of Construction and Repair. Daniels, a North Carolina newspaperman and staunch Progressive, strongly advocated aircraft production in a navy-owned and operated factory. Taylor, one of the navy's brightest and most capable officers, agreed with Daniels on establishing a navy aircraft manufacturing plant. (80-G-1025348, National Archives)

private sector of the industry was incapable of carrying out the needed experimental and engineering work that underlay all successful aircraft designs. Captain Bristol had expressed these doubts in testimony before Congress in 1915. A number of aircraft manufacturers, he said, had been taken to sea and given a firsthand impression of the navy's aviation requirements, but their engineers seemed not to comprehend the unique circumstances under which the navy had to operate and maintain its airplanes. Daniels concurred, telling the House Naval Affairs Committee in 1916 that the "manufacturers of seaplanes in this country are meeting with a good deal of difficulty in producing machines that are suitable for Navy use."[14]

Assuring an adequate level of competition within the private sector and guaranteeing a high degree of engineering expertise were among Daniels's objectives in advocating a government aircraft factory in 1916. Added to these rationales was the so-called yard-stick, which Daniels called for more frequently as the nation slid closer to involvement in the European conflict and munitions prices threatened to skyrocket. The huge Naval Act of 1916, authorizing the construction of ten battleships, six battle cruisers, and a host of lesser warships and auxiliaries, included approval for an armor-plate and projectile factory. The purpose of the plant was not to provide all of the service's needs but only to function as a yardstick for the navy to determine the prices of products from private sources.[15]

Although the Senate voted in favor of the armor and projectile plant in March 1916, the House did not give its assent until June. Ground was broken at a site in South Charleston, West Virginia, in August 1917, and the projectile factory went into operation in the spring of 1918. Construction of the armor-plate plant started in October 1918, and portions of the facility were in production by early 1921. Although the plants had little or no effect on wartime procurement, Daniels got what he wanted: a yardstick or means of enforcing the price of privately supplied armor and munitions.[16]

Not until after the American declaration of war on 6 April 1917 did the manufacture of aircraft by the navy assume immediate significance. The United States lacked an aircraft procurement policy. It was necessary to decide quickly what types of airplanes were needed to prosecute the war and then expeditiously standard-ize designs to begin production with a minimum of delay. To this end, Secretary Daniels created the six-member Joint Army-Navy Technical Board on 27 April. Using a French request for forty-five hundred airplanes for 1918 as a guideline, the board on 29 May presented a plan under which the United States would eventually establish a force of twelve thousand aircraft.[17] This staggering figure, and the massive appropriations it implied, graphically dem-onstrated the magnitude of the nation's aviation commitment.

The size of the aircraft program, coupled with confusion over the types of airplanes to be manufactured and high-level decisions regarding civilian control of the production effort, led to concern that the needs of the navy would be subordinated to huge army orders at private plants. It also remained unclear what types of airplanes would receive priority in the program, and the navy had to make decisions soon about the specialized aircraft it required for sea warfare. Anxiety about the coordination of aircraft production by businessmen who had no appreciation of the navy's mission or requirements crystallized when the civilian Council of National Defense passed a resolution on 16 May establishing the Aircraft Production Board. Headed by Howard E. Coffin, a vice-president of the Hudson Motor Car Company, the board consisted of prominent industrial executives and representatives of the services, including Rear Admiral Taylor. Gradually the status of the Joint Army-Navy Technical Board waned while that of the Aircraft Production Board was enhanced.[18]

By June, civilian and naval authorities concurred that the government should go ahead with plans for an aircraft production facility. Taylor, since December 1914 chief of the Bureau of Construction and Repair, assigned Lieutenant Commanders Fred G. Coburn and Sidney M. Henry to survey the aircraft industry and prepare recommendations for a government-owned and operated factory. As a guideline for their study, Coburn and Henry arbitrarily chose an output of one thousand Curtiss N-9 floatplane trainers per year and relied heavily on engineering and production data by the Curtiss Aeroplane and Motor Company, together with a physical examination of the firm's Elmwood plant in Buffalo, New York, the only factory in the country then producing airplanes in large quantities. In the brief time available to them, Coburn and Henry also toured several potential sites for a navy aircraft plant.[19]

On 5 July, Coburn and Henry presented their report to Rear Admiral Taylor in a two-page memorandum. They foresaw "difficulties incident to obtaining an assured supply of such number of machines as the [Navy] Department may consider necessary to meet its requirements." Not only would a government factory help to assure the quantity of aircraft needed by the navy, but, according to Coburn and Henry, it would also "permit the Department to carry on its development work more logically than if it is entirely dependent on the output of private establishments, and will afford a check on excessive costs."[20] Thus the report underscored the concern expressed as early as 1914 about the availability of specialized aircraft for the fleet and the perceived deficiencies in the engineering capabilities of private manufacturers. To these the report added the precept that a government aircraft factory would help hold private contractors' prices down by promoting competition and asserting the yardstick for comparing manufacturing cost and production data.

The report included specific suggestions about the cost, characteristics, and location of the proposed factory. Coburn and Henry estimated that an appropriation of $1 million would be necessary "for the prompt construction of a plant having the capacity of 1000 school machines per year, or an equivalent in other types: this plant to include . . . sufficient equipment for experimental work to permit the Department to push the development of its designs with greatest rapidity." Because approximately two thousand workers were to be hired, the officers anticipated a localized employment problem and singled out the Philadelphia Navy Yard at League Island as "the most advantageous location" for the factory. There was not only an ample supply of labor in the area, but the yard had available abundant materials and considerable unused acreage, and its location next to the Delaware River was ideal "for testing both land and water machines." This last consideration echoed the conclusions of the December 1914 Watt-Griffin memo about the Philadelphia location. Coburn and Henry conveyed a sense of urgency. If production were to begin before the end of the year, the Navy Department had to extend "the freest possible hand to such officer as may be selected to undertake the work, as irrespective of the location selected, it will mean essentially the creation of a new industrial establishment."21

For well over a century, Philadelphia had enjoyed close ties to the navy. In 1794, Congress voted to construct six large frigates, each to be built in a different city. One of the cities that benefited from the federal largesse was Philadelphia, where the government rented land at the foot of Federal Street in the Southwark district for the construction of the frigate *United States*. In 1800, the navy bought the eleven-acre Southwark tract, which became the navy yard's home the following year. During the early part of the Civil War, when it became apparent that the yard was too small to meet the navy's present or future needs, the city acquired League Island, a low-lying, marshy, 410-acre expanse just east of where the Schuylkill emptied into the Delaware. In 1867, Philadelphia turned League Island over to the federal government for development as a navy yard. Subsequently, as part of its development of the area, the navy filled in many of the marshes and waterways, connecting the island to the mainland and providing nearly 600 acres of additional space for shipbuilding and other activities.[22]

Coburn and Henry's recommendation of the Philadelphia Navy Yard as the site for an aircraft factory may also have been influenced by the sporadic aviation activities there. In November 1910, as part of an eight-day exhibition sponsored by the Aero Club of Pennsylvania, the English flier Claude Grahame-White flew a Farman from Point Breeze to League Island, dropping a "stage bomb" (probably a sack of flour) on the navy yard administration building. The first airplane to land at the yard was a Howard Wright biplane piloted by another Englishman, Thomas O. M. Sopwith. Later famed as an aircraft designer, Sopwith unexpectedly landed near the yard's marine barracks on the afternoon of 20 May 1911.[23]

The Marine Corps provided most of the early military interest in aviation at League Island. Lieutenant Alfred A. Cunningham, assigned to the yard's marine barracks in November 1911, rented a biplane from a local enthusiast. Nicknamed "Noisy Nan," the airplane was incapable of flight, despite Cunningham's entreaties to the "flighty old maid to lift up her skirts and hike." Cunningham befriended the Belgian aviator M. V. de Jonckhere when he visited Philadelphia for an exhibition in April 1912. On 4 April, de Jonckhere flew his Blériot monoplane at the yard, followed by a spectacular demonstration of night flying two days later. Taking off from the yard, de Jonckhere soared over several battleships, keeping just out of the range of their searchlights, before swooping down in a simulated attack on the *Massachusetts*. Later, Cunningham persuaded the Aero Club of Pennsylvania to lobby for a marine aviation facility at League Island, which led in October 1913 to a proposal by the marine commandant to assemble a flying unit attached to the advance base force assigned to Philadelphia. Not until February 1917, however, did the corps establish an aviation company under Cunningham's command. By the middle of the year it had evolved into the First Marine Aeronautic Company, whose fliers operated from a small field and a cramped temporary hangar.[24]

With some understanding of the aviation presence at League

Aviation at the Philadelphia Navy Yard began as early as 1910. A marine officer, Lieutenant Alfred A. Cunningham, attempted flights in November 1911. Cunningham (left) is shown here with the Belgian aviator M.V. de Jonckhere and his Blériot monoplane at the navy yard in April 1912. (80-G-463673, National Archives)

Island, Taylor forwarded the Coburn-Henry report to Secretary Daniels. In his covering letter, Taylor repeated the navy's requirements for more specialized aircraft than were needed by the army, adding: "This very fact renders it desirable that the Navy Department take steps to expand in the direction of manufacturing aeroplanes." He also endorsed the Philadelphia Navy Yard as the most suitable location for an aircraft manufacturing facility. Along with Coburn and Henry, Taylor comprehended that the nature of the plant's work demanded supervision by a competent officer with a degree of independence from the usual navy yard command structure. He proposed to Daniels that, although the officer selected by the Bureau of Construction and Repair to run the factory should be "under the general direction" of the yard's commandant, he should not be regarded simply as another department chief.[25]

Taylor's letter presented the bureau's conception of the proposed factory and his own philosophy of how it would be integrated into the existing Navy Department decision-making system.

A great admirer of Taylor, Daniels was receptive to the bureau's recommendation. He had viewed a government aircraft plant as a means of promoting efficiency in the industry, assuring an adequate level of engineering, and keeping a lid on costs. Now that the country was at war, he wanted to do all he could to curtail profiteering and to restrict the power of civilian "dollar-a-year" men, who were coming into government service from private industry to fill management slots. Considerable public opinion had been aroused against the civilian advisory boards appointed to oversee the war effort, many fearing that they would lead to additional competition-smothering trusts. Meanwhile, President Woodrow Wilson had created the War Industries Board (WIB), with extensive powers over the procurement policies of the various government agencies. Daniels thought the time was ripe to restrict the powers of businessmen appointees to the WIB and to extend the government's role in the procurement of naval aircraft. On 27 July he earmarked $1 million from the Navy Department's aviation appropriations for the construction of the Naval Aircraft Factory at Philadelphia.[26]

Rear Admiral Taylor lost little time implementing Secretary Daniels's orders. Surveyors staked out a site on vacant, low-lying land at the eastern extremity of the yard, where the assembly building and ancillary shops were to be erected. Contract awards went out on 6 August. The Austin Company won the largest of these—for the 160,000-square-foot main building and assembly bay—and separate contracts were let for heating and lighting installations, the lumber kiln, and the paint shop. Four days later, on the tenth, under bright blue skies, construction began. The urgency of the moment precluded any formal groundbreaking ceremonies. Daniels announced to the press that the plant "was necessary to increase the Navy Department's facilities . . . to supply a part, at least of its own [aircraft] needs. . . . and keep the navy in the forefront with the latest developments in aircraft." The estimated cost of the building project, plus machinery and tooling, was nearly $900,000.[27]

As the growl of heavy machinery reverberated over League Island,

Taylor and his bureau confronted the task of putting in place an organizational and management structure as quickly as possible. In a letter to the navy yard commandant, Daniels clarified Taylor's ideas about the place of the embryonic factory within the navy yard system. Because of the need to "save time in getting the plant started and producing machines," it was to "be operated independently of the present navy yard departments." A manager appointed by the bureau would "be responsible for the work of the factory," and "matters of ordinary routine and of operation pertaining exclusively to the factory should be handled direct" by him. The yard commandant's authority was strictly circumscribed to "important matters of policy, questions of military discipline," and questions jointly affecting the factory and the yard. The factory's extraordinary independence was necessary for its proper functioning and the maximum efficiency of its personnel.[28] Even the choice of the word *manager* carried a businesslike connotation distinct from more traditional forms of military organization.

Taylor and Daniels proposed a unique command setup with possibly contentious implications. The demarcation of responsibilities between the factory manager and the yard commandant was expressed in only the most general way, leaving a great deal open to interpretation by both officers. If the system were to function smoothly, it was necessary to appoint an individual with navy yard background as well as an appreciation of the service's aviation requirements. Fred Coburn was Taylor's choice, and on 27 August he reported to Philadelphia as manager of the Naval Aircraft Factory.[29]

The selection of Naval Constructor Frederick Gallup Coburn as the first manager of the NAF was felicitous. A 1904 Annapolis graduate, he was familiar with aircraft manufacturing as a consequence of his earlier survey of the industry and had, according to a contemporary, "outstanding" managerial abilities. Coburn was a spare man, with a thin, intense face, prominent nose, and jug-handle ears. Like many naval constructors, he had earned a master's degree in engineering from MIT and had an unobstructed vision of the problems of modern industrial management within a sometimes inflexible military system. Nine years of experience at the Mare Island, Philadelphia, and Boston navy yards had led Coburn to draw a clear distinction between the military and the industrial functions

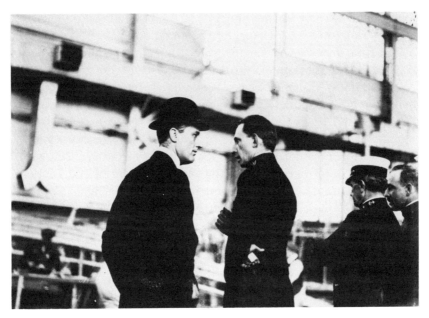

Lieutenant Commander Fred G. Coburn, shown here with Assistant Secretary of the Navy Franklin D. Roosevelt (left) in May 1918, was the first manager of the Naval Aircraft Factory. (80-G-48932, National Archives)

of naval construction facilities, and he advocated their organization into functional departments patterned after those in civilian factories. Yet Coburn saw that in this arrangement "the policy must be to observe the paramount interest of the individual" employee.[30] During its first two years, the NAF bore the unmistakable imprint of Coburn's philosophy and managerial style.

When he moved into his stark temporary office in Building 11 at the navy yard late in August, Coburn confronted an assignment of daunting proportions. Not a single building of the aircraft factory was ready for occupancy, yet a departmental organization had to be finalized, delivery schedules for machinery and plant equipment coordinated, and personnel recruited to oversee these myriad activities. And it all had to be done under strict deadlines and in an economy already dislocated by the exigencies of industrial mobilization. To minimize delay and to enhance flexibility, Coburn quickly departmentalized the organization along functional lines, giving wide latitude to individual department heads while keeping his finger directly on the pulse of the installation.[31]

The first department, engineering, came into existence in the middle of September in Washington, because space was lacking at Philadelphia. Within two weeks, Richard J. Tullar and G. A. Rathert arrived in Philadelphia to begin processing plans and generating the data needed before the first aircraft could be constructed. For organizing and building up the engineering department, Coburn turned to the automotive industry, specifically to Major George R. Wadsworth, a former manager and chief engineer of the Peerless Motor Car Company, who had come into the army's Signal Corps in June 1917. Wadsworth acted swiftly after he took over as chief engineer on 8 October to attract the necessary technical personnel and to complete production drawings.[32]

Other important departments at the Naval Aircraft Factory were production, headed by the general superintendent, which coordinated aircraft manufacturing, and supply, which administered parts flows and components deliveries. An inspection office, under the control of the chief engineer, had primary responsibility for quality control. It was soon obvious that large numbers of unskilled workers would be needed to fill out the contingent at Philadelphia; still another department, employment, took charge of recruiting personnel. Completing the early organization of the factory were the accounting and clerical departments.[33]

Adaptability to change was particularly important during the formative months at the Naval Aircraft Factory because there was still considerable uncertainty regarding the types and numbers of airplanes the navy needed. Coburn and Henry had given a figure of a thousand small floatplane trainers annually in their 5 July report in the absence of hard data on types and quantities. By mid-August, the navy had a clearer view of its future aircraft requirements. Naval Constructor Captain George C. Westervelt and Lieutenant Warren G. Child had accompanied a joint army-navy commission headed by Major Raynal C. Bolling to Europe in the summer of 1917. On 15 August, the commission issued its report on the status of the European aircraft industry and advised American officials on the best course to follow. Westervelt and Child saw a substantial role for large, long-range flying boats in suppressing the German U-boat offensive and called for an expansion of navy patrols in the eastern

Atlantic.[34] Requisite for such an operation was a multifold increase in the construction of big flying boats by American manufacturers.

But first the navy needed a satisfactory airplane. The Curtiss company had pioneered large flying boats in the prewar years, beginning with the *America* in 1914, an innovative three-engine biplane designed for a transatlantic flight under the sponsorship of Philadelphia department store magnate and aviation enthusiast Rodman Wanamaker. In 1916, the navy ordered an improved version of the *America* known as the H-12 and powered by twin Curtiss engines. In early 1917 Curtiss exported to England another model, the H-16, which was operated with Rolls-Royce Eagle engines. It was the H-16 (also known for a time as the C-1) that most interested the navy. With a maximum takeoff weight of 10,900 pounds, a wing area of 1,164 square feet, and a 95-foot span, the H-16 received its power from twin 400-horsepower 12-cylinder Liberty engines. Armament consisted of five or six 0.30-caliber Lewis guns and four 230-pound bombs. In October, the navy let contracts to Curtiss for the first H-16s and authorized the NAF to begin preliminary work on the airplane. On the twenty-second, the factory's engineers completed all manufacturing data for the H-16, and on 2 November NAF workers laid the keel of the NAF's first flying boat.[35]

By the beginning of November, the navy had decided what aircraft to build at the NAF, even if it did not yet have a complete plant in which to manufacture them. Coburn pressed hard for the earliest possible completion date for the factory, and his demands for urgency paid off. The main assembly building (number 59) had a four-hundred-foot-long "high" shop with fifty-one feet of overhead clearance for the manipulation of large components in the final assembly process. There was also a "low" shop for such ancillary activities as the preparation of subassemblies, fabric covering, and painting. A heating and ventilation system designed by Carrier included humidity control, used for the first time in an aircraft plant, although cotton mills had employed it earlier. The system justified its expense because it allowed the close regulation of the moisture content of wood parts and permitted their long-term storage. Workers enclosed Building 59 on 12 November, and on the twenty-eighth the structure was finished. This milestone came none too soon, not only because of the imminent onset of cold, wet weather, but because only eight days previously the NAF had received an order from the Navy Department for fifty H-16s. Employment statistics reflected the rapid progress being made at the NAF toward the end of the year. From 313 in the third week of November, the work force swelled to more than 700 by 28 December.[36] Much minor work remained to be done on the assembly building and other structures, and a fully trained work force was not yet in place, but those responsible for the NAF must have experienced a deep sense of satisfaction and relief to have an aircraft production plant completed only five months after Daniels's 27 July directive.

2

Flying Boats for the Fleet

When Admiral William S. Sims, the commander of American naval forces operating in European waters, arrived in London on 10 April 1917, one of his many urgent tasks was to determine for the Navy Department in Washington what types of airplanes and how many the United States required to bring the air war to the U-boat. Sims relied on his aide for operations, Captain Hutchinson I. Cone, and on Lieutenant Kenneth Whiting to formulate an aviation plan. The two concurred on the necessity of establishing bases in France and the British Isles and for equipping them with long-range flying boats to patrol the Atlantic and the North Sea. On that subject, Cone's and Whiting's ideas meshed with those of Westervelt and Child, but it soon became apparent that nearly everyone had underestimated the numbers of aircraft that should be sent abroad. This struck fully home in November, when Sims called for the construction of 864 flying boats in 1918.[1]

Sims's request created a flurry of activity in Washington. Secretary Daniels saw an opportunity to enlarge significantly the role of the Naval Aircraft Factory and welcomed the opportunity "to be able to build enough [airplanes] to add largely to our facilities." Although the yardstick had been largely negated by the need to maximize production regardless of cost, Daniels repeated his conviction that the government had to manufacture aircraft to "know exactly what it costs to make them" and to guard against unscrupulous profiteering. Rear Admiral Taylor was less sanguine than

19

Daniels about the implications of Sims's request. As he told Sims, "We had a program for our aeroplane building a month or so ago, and after strenuous exertions, have placed satisfactory contracts. Now the whole program is shot to pieces. . . . If we had known about this three months ago it would have been easy. But aeroplanes . . . can not be built over night by green people." Admiral Benson considered the expanded flying boat program important to the war effort and gave his assent on 26 December.[2]

Nearly quadrupling the flying boat construction program portended a significant reorganization of the Naval Aircraft Factory. Previous planning had envisaged building a relatively modest number of flying boats at the NAF in 1918. The original intention had been for an integrated plant at Philadelphia—that is, one able to handle all phases of aircraft construction. A joint committee, consisting of representatives from the Bureaus of Construction and Repair, Yards and Docks, and Steam Engineering, determined in January 1918 that the best way to achieve the new production levels was to reorient the factory as a final assembly plant with central control over civilian subcontractors, who would supply most of the major aircraft components. In this way expansion would occur in the shortest time with a minimum of disruption to existing aircraft manufacturers, whose resources were already stretched thin. Furthermore, it was expected that most subcontractors would be boatyards and metal- and woodworking shops, many of which had surplus capacity for this work.[3]

Taylor passed the committee's recommendation on to the Aircraft Production Board for approval before formally asking Daniels to set aside $3,250,000 for the work. Daniels quickly sanctioned the expansion, and an order for one hundred H-16s arrived at Philadelphia on 28 February. The contract was an interim one, intended only to keep the factory at maximum capacity until preparations were completed in anticipation of larger orders for H-16s and improved aircraft later in the year. Moreover, the H-16 contract allowed the NAF to line up its subcontractors and give them much-needed experience before the big orders started to pour in.[4]

Reorganization and expansion compounded Coburn's problems in getting production going at Philadelphia on the 1917 contract. On 18 December, work started on ten airplanes in addition to the first example begun in November. As historian Richard K. Smith has observed, the fabrication of large wooden aircraft during the World War I era "had more in common with cabinetmaking, boatbuilding, sailmaking, and piano manufacturing" than with modern aviation manufacturing. Wood, cotton, and varnish were the principal materials; metal appeared only in the fittings, screws, and bolts used to join one wooden part to another and in the omnipresent wire that when tensioned drew the structure of the airplane together into an organic unit. Wood was the critical material. Preferred for such major structural elements as wing spars was Sitka spruce, grown in stands along the Pacific Coast from northern California to Alaska. For longerons (longitudinal fuselage strength members) and for smaller parts in critical areas, white ash from second-growth forests in the Middle Atlantic states and the Midwest was used. The wood was kiln-dried to obtain the proper moisture content, then each piece was carefully inspected for defects, the most serious of which was cracking caused by spiral grain and knots. Lamination of smaller pieces of wood and balancing the grain patterns usually allowed aircraft builders to avoid the problems presented by spiral grain. Before and after working, the wood had to be stored under temperature- and humidity-controlled conditions.

The fabrication of wood parts demanded great skill and precision equipment. Waterproof glue, nails, screws, and bolts held assemblies together, while jigs and frames ensured proper alignment. Some components, notably ribs, webs, bulkheads, and hull planking, were built up of two or more plies of wood, usually separated by one or more layers of muslin and glued and pressed together. Metal fittings had to be precisely shaped and drilled, heat treated, and protected from corrosion by paint or varnish. An H-16 flying boat had fifteen different fittings for securing hull stanchions to one another and to the longerons. Internal wire bracing, situated diagonally and placed under tension, stiffened wings and hulls. Aerodynamic surfaces had fabric coverings, sometimes of finely woven linen, but as the war progressed and linen supplies became scarce, cotton was substituted. After cutting and sewing, the covering was tautly stretched over the frames and ribs, then painted with varnish or dope, which further tightened and sealed the fabric.[5]

Planking and covering the initial NAF H-16 proceeded in January when the factory received shipments of the airplane's Liberty engines for testing and installation. A cold snap that month over-

The first airplane manufactured at the Naval Aircraft Factory was the Curtiss H-16 flying boat. The factory built 150 H-16s in 1918–19. Here one of the aircraft is leaving the hangar in preparation for a test flight. (165-WW-187-H9, National Archives)

taxed the factory's steam plant and forced a brief shutdown, not so much out of concern for the comfort of workers as because of the adverse effects of low temperatures on the materials. Work soon resumed. By 27 March, when the factory's first H-16 (number A-1049) completed its inaugural test flight, Coburn was reasonably sure that he had command of a functional aircraft production plant.[6] Yet whatever satisfaction Coburn might have experienced when A-1049's twin Liberties roared to life on the Delaware was tempered by the uncertainties of the expansion program already under way at Philadelphia.

Coburn's chief tasks in early 1918 were to implement the NAF's reorganization and set up a system for coordinating the subcontracting work. The augmented responsibilities of the NAF led to changes in its departmental organization. The supply department now had to oversee the flow of parts not only within the factory but to and from a multitude of outside suppliers and subcontractors. A new contract manufacturing department was created to line up subcontractors for major aircraft components, to schedule deliveries, and to make sure that suppliers met all contractual obligations. The factory's inspection office had to bring together a field force to guarantee quality work by the various subcontractors. Representatives from on-site NAF branch offices inspected components to be sure they met rigid standards and sometimes worked closely with subcontractors in solving particularly thorny production problems.[7]

A survey of possible subcontractors for major components by Coburn underscored earlier conclusions about the need to bring in companies that were not already in the aircraft business. Among the factories previously supplying complete aircraft or components, only Curtiss Aeroplane and Motor, Ltd., of Toronto had the capacity to build wing and tail surfaces for NAF flying boats. In March, Curtiss Toronto received a contract to build fifty sets of H-16 wing and tail surfaces. Other subcontractors were new to aircraft component manufacturing. The Victor Talking Machine Company, a manufacturer of wind-up record players located across the Delaware in Camden, New Jersey, received an order for fifty H-16 hulls and a similar number of wing and tail surfaces. Victor was a logical subcontractor for aircraft structures because the company had woodworkers skilled in crafting record player cabinets. Following the order from Victor were contracts to four East Coast yacht builders. Charles L. Seabury and Company of Morris Heights, New York, received the biggest order—for fifty H-16 hulls. The Murray and Tregurtha Company of South Boston; the Albany Boat Company of Watervliet, New York; Henry B. Nevins, of City Island, New York; Mathis Yacht Builders of Camden; and the Herreshoff Manufacturing Company of Bristol, Rhode Island, one of the best-known names in the yacht-building business, each received a contract for ten hulls.[8] Like Victor, none of the firms had any background in aircraft production, but they did have experience in fabricating complex wooden structures, and all had excess manufacturing capacity and an adequate supply of skilled labor. The contracts followed standard wartime cost-plus-fixed-profit guidelines.

Coburn faced other problems besides reorganizing the NAF as an assembly plant with centralized authority over numerous subcontractors. In particular, he had the unenviable duty of prodding the principal contractor for the new main assembly building. Coburn had pleaded with Jerome Hunsaker to pressure the Bureau of Yards and Docks into selecting the Austin Company based on its proven record with the first plant structures. Even though Austin's bid on the new final assembly building was nearly $170,000 more than that of the lowest bidder, M. H. McCloskey and Company, Coburn warned that McCloskey's "record is not clear. They are filled up on navy contracts not one of which is *completed.*" But McCloskey had close ties to the Democratic party and, over Coburn's protests, won the contract in February with a bid of $839,557. Coburn's fears did not take long to materialize. When Daniels toured the factory in May, he expressed dissatisfaction with the lack of progress on the 135,000-square-foot facility. By June, Coburn estimated that Mc-Closkey was more than a month behind schedule and only by "extraordinary effort" had a portion of the building been occupied. "Draftsmen have been working at their tables," he wrote, "while painters were at work overhead."[9]

McCloskey admitted there were difficulties with the job but denied that they were the result of inefficiency. The firm blamed the protracted completion of the building on problems getting enough skilled labor at the navy yard and on unspecified obstacles that had not been anticipated in late 1917, when it had submitted its winning bid. Regardless of the reasons for the delays, the failure to complete the main assembly building on time threatened the new flying boat program. It was August before the structure (Building 77) was finished, three months later than the navy had wanted and $268,000 over budget. Intended for the final assembly process, Building 77's high shop was 100 feet wide and 680 feet long, 51 feet from floor to roof trusses, and had two 50-foot-wide bays on each side. The adjacent low shop accommodated fabrication of wing panels and floats and the varnish and dope rooms.[10]

In addition to the second major assembly building, the plant expansion involved the construction of a three-story office building (number 75, which also included a drafting room and a laboratory), a six-story concrete storehouse (number 76), another lumber kiln, and a boiler house. Workers completed new roads and rail lines and carried out minor improvements to the older assembly building. By the end of September 1918, the NAF covered forty-one acres and had a physical plant valued at $4.5 million.[11]

Thus far, the bustling plant on the Delaware had orders for only the twin-engine Curtiss H-16 flying boat. On 24 March, just three days before the first of the factory's H-16s took to the air, plans arrived in Philadelphia from England for a newer flying boat, the F-5. This aircraft bore a superficial resemblance to the H-16 but was superior to the older Curtiss design in all respects. Since 1916, the British, directed by John Cyril Porte, had updated Curtiss H-12s and H-16s at their naval air station at Felixstowe, designating each model with successive numbers (F standing for Felixstowe). Porte's Felixstowe flying boats incorporated a two-step planing hull, and their layout encouraged construction by relatively inexperienced workers. The most recent of the airplanes, designated F-5, when adapted to mount twin 400-horsepower Liberty engines, was a significant improvement over the H-16. Known as the F-5-L, the airplane had a maximum takeoff weight of 13,600 pounds and a wing area of 1,397 square feet within a span of nearly 104 feet. It carried up to eight 0.30-caliber guns and, like the H-16, four 230-pound bombs. Compared to the H-16, the F-5-L had improved ailerons, a balanced rudder, more than twice the range, and better rough-water takeoff characteristics. In the latter part of 1917, the navy determined that F-5-Ls would constitute the bulk of the 1918 flying boat construction program.[12]

The NAF assumed responsibility for transforming the British F-5 blueprints into detailed production drawings for American manufacture of the flying boat. As was the case with many European aircraft plans used by American builders during World War I, this took longer than expected. Although the F-5 was fundamentally a Curtiss design, it had been extensively modified, and the British drawings were meant for wholly different production techniques that emphasized a great deal of hand work. NAF draftsmen, working under Commanders Richardson and Hunsaker, pored over their tables for weeks tracing and retracing the innumerable details necessary for the mountain of production blueprints.

The finished plans retained the external dimensions and general lines of the F-5 but in almost all other respects diverged from British practice. The more robust hull incorporated ash longerons and two plies of cedar planking. Behind the wings, steel tubing reinforced the

The NAF's first F-5-L (no. A-3559) on 24 July 1918. An improvement on
the H-16, the F-5-L was larger, had better aerodynamics, greater payload
capacity, and longer range. (80-G-427566, National Archives)

hull of the NAF boat. One thousand metal fittings, 1,500 bolts,
50,000 screws, 4,500 square feet of cotton fabric, and 5,000 feet of
wire went into each airplane. Compared to the British F-5, the NAF
design had a revised engine installation, dual controls, solid wing
spars, and strengthened tail surfaces. On 26 April, work began on the
first F-5-L (number A-3559). After a gestation period of less than
three months, the big flying boat accomplished its maiden flight at
Philadelphia on 15 July with John Porte at the controls. He said the
airplane "balanced perfectly and the controls operated to my complete satisfaction."[13]

Determining the scope and distribution of F-5-L production
occupied Taylor as the first of the new airplanes took shape in
Philadelphia. Taylor's calculations showed that of the 730 airplanes
required under the 26 December program, 100 had been assigned as
H-16s to the NAF under the interim order of 28 February. This left
630 aircraft—all F-5-Ls—to be manufactured. Because its capacity
was limited, Curtiss Aeroplane and Motor in Buffalo could build no

more than 150. When even this number proved excessive, the bureau shifted orders for 50 F-5-Ls from Curtiss to Canadian Airplanes, Ltd., of Toronto. In late April, Taylor asked Daniels to approve construction of the remaining 480 F-5-Ls, along with 160 sets of spares, at the Naval Aircraft Factory.[14]

Daniels's authorization for the building of 480 F-5-Ls on 20 May signaled the start of furious activity in Philadelphia. To supply F-5-L hulls Coburn turned to the network of subcontractors he had woven earlier in the year, although the size of the program and the experience with the H-16 orders required some deviations in the pattern. The biggest contract—for 125 hulls—went to Charles L. Seabury, while Murray and Tregurtha, Mathis Yacht, and Robert Jacob Ship and Yacht Builders of City Island, New York, each received orders for 75 hulls. Henry B. Nevins and Herreshoff received orders for 10 hulls each. Pending an evaluation of the subcontractors' performance on the first 370 examples, 110 hulls were not yet assigned. Victor Talking Machine, which had experienced nagging problems with H-16 hulls, received no F-5-L orders. As with the H-16 orders, the new contracts were concluded on a cost-plus-fixed-profit basis. Largely because of quality control problems and late deliveries of H-16 wings and tail groups from outside suppliers, the NAF decided not to subcontract any of these components on the F-5-L.[15]

The tempo of flying boat production increased during the summer of 1918. The H-16 program hit full stride in June with the delivery of twenty-five aircraft, and the factory reached a milestone on 16 July when it shipped the fiftieth H-16 overseas. By the end of August, the NAF had turned out 50 percent more flying boats than it had in the previous two months combined. An increasing proportion of these were F-5-Ls, the first example of which (number A-3559) left the plant on 28 August for the Naval Air Station, Hampton Roads.[16]

Meanwhile, the seemingly insatiable appetite of the navy's patrol forces for aircraft led to a fresh order at the NAF for the advanced flying boats. In June, Daniels had authorized the production of 700 more F-5-Ls, with deliveries to carry over into July 1919. Citing anticipated excess capacity at the NAF after the first of the year, Taylor asked for and got authority on 12 August to assign 200 more

F-5-Ls and 66 sets of spares to Philadelphia.[17] This brought total F-5-L orders to 680.

Inevitably, problems accompanied the substantial production increases at the Naval Aircraft Factory. One difficulty was the discovery that two NAF H-16s had wings with "defective workmanship . . . in some of the spars." These wings had been manufactured by Curtiss Toronto, and the defective surfaces had slipped through the NAF's inspection office and the airplanes had been shipped to the operating base at Queenstown, Ireland. Hunsaker warned that the H-16s at Queenstown should be thoroughly inspected before they went into service.[18]

The two substandard H-16 wings were symptomatic of a fundamental dichotomy between the need to meet accelerated production schedules and to produce the highest possible quality of aircraft. The responsibility fell heaviest on the inspection office. As early as May, Lieutenant William J. Lee, an inspector at the NAF, wrote that meeting the new production quotas had raised questions about the ability of his office to ensure a minimum of defects in wood and other materials. A few weeks later, the Fourth Naval District learned through an anonymous informant that some flying boats had "been maliciously or through gross carelessness, seriously damaged, to the extent that will render them totally unfit for practical flying purposes." Based on this and other observations, the aide for information at district headquarters charged that "it would appear that there is a vast amount of defective workmanship carelessly, or knowingly, allowed to be shipped abroad," adding, "a serious condition exists in the Aircraft Factory."[19]

Three days after learning of the Fourth Naval District memorandum, Coburn appointed a new head of the inspection office in the engineering department. Lieutenant J. F. Williams, the new inspection officer, tightened inspection procedures and imposed closer personal supervision. Meanwhile, Lee investigated the charges and reported to Taylor that most of the accusations could not be substantiated; he did, however, acknowledge that there had been some lapses. Reasonably certain that Coburn had control of the situation, Taylor wrote to the chief of naval operations that steps had been taken to correct problems at the NAF and assured his superior, "In an undertaking of the magnitude of that being carried out in the Naval Aircraft Factory . . . some errors will unquestionably occur." There was no evidence, he said, of any "malicious or willful carelessness" at Philadelphia.[20]

These were potentially serious omissions in the otherwise smooth functioning of the NAF's inspection procedures. There is nothing in the record to indicate, however, that the inspection office's shortcomings were the result of anything more than overzealous attempts to meet or exceed production goals. But Coburn's personal management style left the organization vulnerable to such deficiencies, and he was forced to assume a more direct role in departmental operations to prevent a repetition of the problem.

If quality control within the plant were not vexing enough, Coburn had to grapple with the problems of inferior materials supplied by outside contractors. Much of the seamless steel tubing in stock for F-5-Ls was found to be below minimum requirements. But wood was the most troublesome raw material. When it arrived at Philadelphia, it varied widely in strength, density, and moisture content. The wood technology section of the factory had to carry out numerous tests on spruce and other woods and develop a system to determine how failure was related to temperature, stresses, and grain patterns. Over time, the factory built up a cadre of highly trained and experienced inspectors who spotted defects in lumber before shipment to the factory, which eliminated many of the difficulties that hitherto had not been evident until the assembly process.[21]

Design modification based on aircraft testing and in-service use also affected production at the Naval Aircraft Factory. Every change order arriving at Philadelphia meant a potential delay in the assembly and delivery of aircraft so it was incumbent on everyone to keep such changes to a minimum. The H-16 was fundamentally a sound design, but early NAF models did exhibit deficiencies. An H-16 (number A-1064) delivered to Hampton Roads in May developed cracks in its hull. Less serious defects were control wires that abraded the exterior of the hull and flight controls that were not sufficiently robust. Strengthening the hull with tougher spruce laminations and more attention to detail by production workers corrected these faults in subsequent aircraft.[22]

It was not enough for the factory to turn out large numbers of reliable, highly complex, and virtually defect-free aircraft; it must also deliver them to operating forces in the shortest possible time. The large dimensions of the flying boats precluded rail shipments because other manufacturers had found that aircraft so delivered were often damaged. The NAF crated the hulls, wings, and other components and shipped them by barge to their destination. Overseas shipment meant reloading the crates on oceangoing vessels. Coburn pointed with justifiable pride to the NAF's record of delivering its aircraft without damage caused by inferior shipping procedures.[23]

Coburn was proud, too, of the efficiency of his shop-floor workers. The usual procedure in aircraft manufacture was to have as many workers as possible performing a variety of tasks on a single airplane simultaneously. One crew worked on one airplane from start to finish, and no single worker became proficient in any one job. Output was low and material flows bogged down because the crews needed to have a large quantity of parts and components on hand for extended periods. Coburn changed this system. Taking his cue from the automobile industry, he divided the assembly process into sixteen separate operations and assigned those tasks to work gangs who went from airplane to airplane carrying out their specialized jobs. This change led to a dramatic reduction in the time needed to complete an airplane; eventually, the NAF required less than a day for finishing an F-5-L.[24]

With increased production came a sizable multiplication of the NAF work force. The Philadelphia area had been attractive in the first place because of the anticipated ready availability of labor. By January 1918, however, localized labor shortages caused by the expansion of the shipbuilding and locomotive industries and by the increased demands of the armed forces reduced the pool of skilled workers from which the NAF drew its personnel. Employment at the factory jumped as the H-16 program peaked in the spring and summer of 1918. From 1,360 workers on 22 March, employment went up to 2,000 by the beginning of April and to nearly 2,400 in June. To meet current labor needs and those forecast as a result of the new flying boat programs, the NAF set up apprentice training schools to instruct unskilled workers in aircraft manufacturing.[25]

These efforts notwithstanding, the NAF suffered throughout 1918 from a chronic labor shortage. Coburn estimated in September that industry in Pennsylvania as a whole was deficient by three hundred thousand workers and that the problem was most acute in the southeastern corner of the state. To attract more employees, he asked the Navy Department to allow an increase in pay from forty to sixty cents an hour for workers doing such critical jobs as lumber handling, which, although it sounded menial, involved the skillful manipulation of the factory's most important raw material. Insisting on uniformity of pay scales, Washington refused Coburn's request.[26]

The Naval Aircraft Factory could not have kept up its production schedule in 1918 without employing women in substantial numbers. In December 1917, Marion Elderton, a secretary, became the factory's first female employee. Others followed Elderton into clerical jobs and similar positions, especially after the employment department began a training program for women in May 1918. By June 218 women were employed at the NAF, making up 9.4 percent of the force of 2,392 workers; by September, 590 women were on the payroll at the plant, or 17.9 percent of the work force. Three months later, when NAF employment reached its zenith at 3,640 workers, 890 of them, or 24.5 percent, were women. Most of the tasks performed by women required some training, especially in the cutting and sewing of fabric, covering wings and other aerodynamic surfaces, and painting; a few women's jobs demanded considerable skill, such as drill press operation and some machinist positions. Only three women achieved supervisory status; there were forewomen in the inspection office, paint shop, and in charge of drill press operators. Coburn said forewomen had been tried in other areas of the plant, but he found the experiment "not practical as women have not yet acquired sufficient mechanical proficiency."[27]

Discrimination against female employees at the NAF was most apparent in pay scales. Although women put in the same forty-nine-hour workweek as did men, the assumption was that "their output had not equalled" that of their male counterparts and, consequently, they received only helpers' wages. Coburn's attitude toward the issue was contradictory. On one hand, he expressed a philosophical commitment to equal pay for equal work, but on the other, he refused to put women up to mechanics' wages. The war ended with the question unresolved.[28]

As if to compensate for the evident disparity in pay, the navy tried to accommodate the special needs of women at the factory. Acting

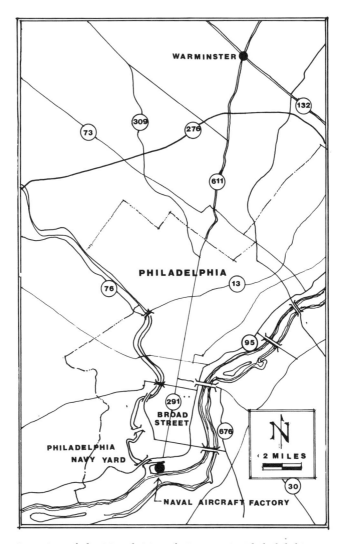

Location of the Naval Aircraft Factory in Philadelphia

on a request by Assistant Secretary of the Navy Franklin D. Roosevelt, the Committee on Women in Industry of the Advisory Commission of the Council of National Defense reported on the status of women at the NAF in September 1918. The committee was critical of pay inequities and the lack of women in supervisory roles and stressed the need for more attention to the unique requirements of women at the factory. Ignoring the pay and supervisory issues, the factory expanded separate washrooms and toilet facilities, brought in female nurses to attend to the women's health needs, and implemented tests to determine whether women suffered any adverse effects from working in the dope rooms. To enliven the lunch break, a navy brass band struck up the popular tunes of the day. By the Armistice, women had cultivated a certain esprit, evidenced by their adoption of a distinctive uniform—forest green coveralls with a brown belt and shoes, topped off with a jaunty aviator's cap.[29]

The experience of female employees at the NAF was representative of that of women aircraft production workers as a whole during World War I. By the end of the war, women made up more than 23 percent of the total work force in aircraft manufacturing. Sixty percent of them occupied positions normally reserved for male workers. But the war did not mark any significant shift away from the home and the woman's traditional place in the domestic environment. Women who took wartime manufacturing jobs for the most part left occupations outside the home, coming mostly from domestic service, textile mills, and the clothing industry. Rather than breaking new ground, women followed paths already well trodden during the prewar years.[30]

Women were not the only group that faced discrimination at the Naval Aircraft Factory; blacks also found the avenues to economic equality strewn with formidable obstacles. When the NAF advertised for people to fill skilled positions, a significant number of blacks applied for jobs as carpenters and woodworkers. Coburn thought that blacks were "unsuited to the work of this Factory," and all were shunted into menial jobs as janitors, helpers, and general laborers. A group of black workers approached Coburn in July 1918 to register their complaints. They said, "We believe that this factory is run by you in interest of the government, and that all employees who faithfully discharge their duties are entitled to a fair deal." They pointed out that "there are a number of men who are rated as woodworkers' helpers, general helpers, etc., who on account of their color are absolutely denied the right to work in the various shops." The black employees entreated Coburn to investigate instances of racial discrimination and trusted that he would rectify the situation, but they came away disappointed. Coburn did not budge from his and the Navy Department's policy of refusing to hire blacks for skilled trade positions.[31]

In August, Coburn faced a potentially serious racial problem when black women at the factory complained that white women refused to allow them access to all toilet facilities. They charged specifically that the whites had set aside three toilets for use "by colored women only." Coburn mentioned that this caused "quite a little protest among the colored women," but he refused to pursue the matter or rectify an obviously blatant case of de facto segregation. He added that "any persons who do not like the employment . . . can leave the Factory" and recommended to the yard commandant "that no action be taken" in the matter of the "alleged discrimination" of the women's toilet facilities.[32]

Neither the navy nor Coburn exhibited enlightened views about equality for women or blacks during the war. That should not be surprising, given the prevailing social consciousness of American society and the toleration of Jim Crow by the Wilson administration. It was unrealistic to expect a government-owned and operated aircraft plant to be in the forefront of social change during a period of national emergency. Yet Coburn was in a unique position to effect some reforms in the treatment of women and blacks, and he could have done so without seriously jeopardizing production schedules or provoking a backlash among white workers. Whites, too, could "leave the Factory" if they found pay or working conditions unsatisfactory. Coburn and the navy missed an opportunity to improve social and economic conditions, at least among the NAF's minority employees.

Employee morale remained generally high at the Naval Aircraft Factory during the war years. Most workers endured with good spirits the daily tedium of riding the Philadelphia Rapid Transit subway to the end of the Broad Street line and transferring to a trolley to complete the commute to League Island. Then there was the occasional pungent whiff of the marshes along the Delaware, punching the time clock, sorting and resorting parts, checking tolerances, and typing and filing seemingly endless forms. The bland institutional fare and mediocre service at the cafeteria drew complaints, but most of these were of the long-suffering, good-natured variety. After lunch, employees clustered around the bulletin board to read, as one put it, "the old news of yesterday," or found a place to "match" for silver dollars or half-dollars. Many looked forward to a cigarette or cigar during the daily smoking hour. Not even the deadly influenza epidemic of the fall of 1918 had much effect on morale. It is often forgotten, but the outbreak killed far more Americans than the German artillery and gas on the western front. At one point influenza killed more than seven hundred Philadelphians a day. One of the jokes at the time concerned an NAF worker named Mike who succumbed following a bout with "the flu." When he arrived at the "Pearly Gates," Saint Peter greeted him: "Hello, Mike. How did you get up here?" "Oh," he replied, "flu." In a more serious vein, Fred Coburn forged personal links between management and employees through informal talks with worker groups. And the workers created the Naval Aircraft Association, an informal, clublike organization intended to generate fellowship and a patriotic commitment to the war effort.[33]

That effort mostly concentrated on the production of proven types of aircraft during 1918, but experimentation with new designs—or research and development—was not completely ignored. For some time, the navy had looked for a means to provide airplanes with more firepower in duels with surfaced submarines, only to be stymied by the weight and bulk of conventional light artillery. The answer was an entirely new airplane designed to carry the Davis gun. In 1911–12, Commander Cleland Davis had invented a lightweight recoilless rifle that seemed to offer exactly what the navy wanted in airborne artillery. The weapon fired a six-pound projectile, counterbalancing it with a blank discharged in the opposite direction. A 0.30-caliber Lewis gun mounted on top of the Davis gun facilitated aiming. Work began in February 1918 at the NAF on the N-1, an airplane specifically intended to mount and fire the Davis gun.[34]

Designed by Jerome Hunsaker at the NAF, the N-1, rather prosaically named the Davis Gun Carrier, fell considerably short of expectations. An ungainly looking twin-float biplane with a maximum takeoff weight of 5,900 pounds, a wing area of 694 square feet,

The N-1 Davis Gun Carrier, four of which were built at the NAF in 1918, was the first airplane designed by the factory. (80-G-410384, National Archives)

and powered by a 360-horsepower Liberty driving a pusher propeller, the first N-1 (number A-2282) narrowly avoided catastrophe on its initial test flight, 22 May, when both pontoons collapsed. Investigation showed that the floats were too weak for service use, and new ones had to be fitted. Not until 27 July was the main armament successfully fired. The factory built only four N-1s, two of which were seriously damaged in accidents, before the navy canceled the project. Considering the money and time expended on the N-1, the project made little sense under the factory's wartime production demands.[35]

Far more significant than the N-1 in setting the course for naval aviation was the preliminary development work at the NAF on air-launched torpedoes. Bradley Fiske, one of the navy's most vociferous supporters of aeronautics in the prewar years, took a personal interest in developing equipment and methods for delivering torpedoes from aircraft. Fiske's work on an air-launched torpedo had begun in November 1914, but the weapon failed to gain much support in the service even after the country's entry into the war in 1917. Coburn and Taylor, however, showed more foresight. In January 1918, Coburn told Fiske that the NAF would assist him in building the airplanes necessary to carry and launch the weapon. Later, Taylor concurred that a dummy torpedo should be sent to Philadelphia for tests. After a visit to the factory in June, Fiske was convinced that he had his airplane—an F-5-L modified to carry a thousand-pound torpedo attached to each side of the hull—but he still faced persistent inertia in Washington. Not until 5 November did Benson approve the project. Once the NAF received the go-ahead, work proceeded rapidly, with the first test drop of a four-hundred-pound dummy torpedo from an F-5-L on 22 November.[36] It was far too late to have any effect on the naval war effort, but the air-launched torpedo project stayed alive at the NAF and bore fruit in the 1920s.

All this experimental activity and the test flying that went along with it, combined with the expectation that larger aircraft would be built and flown at Philadelphia, made it crucial to upgrade the factory's limited hangar space. It had been contemplated that only a minimum of flying would be done at the NAF, and in 1917 the navy considered the small hangar of the marine aeronautic company sufficient. In July 1918, Coburn reported to the Bureau of Construction and Repair that a new hangar was badly needed, but he had to wait until 20 September to receive authorization for the building. Work began later that month on the $238,000 steel structure, which was completed in August 1919, well after the Armistice.[37]

The Duke of Wellington is said to have lamented the "melancholy nature of victory," but there was only rejoicing in Philadelphia when news reached the city of the signing of the Armistice on 11 November 1918. Within hours of receiving notification that the pall of war had been lifted, NAF workers joined in an impromptu victory parade and gathered outside for a brief speech by Coburn, who later sent everyone home for the afternoon. Well before this, however, the navy had reevaluated its flying boat programs in light of the expected conquest of the German U-boats. Production at the NAF had attained a peak of eight F-5-Ls weekly before the Navy Department ordered cutbacks. These initially took effect on 1 November, when Coburn canceled 235 hull orders from subcontractors. Most of the yacht builders were behind on hull deliveries

An aerial view of the Naval Aircraft Factory in 1919. Building 59 (Plant No. 1) is left center and Building 77 (Plant No. 2) is to the far right. Building 76, a storehouse, is still under construction. Building 75, the NAF office building, stands beside the storehouse. (165-WW-184C-9, National Archives)

anyway so the effect on production schedules was minimal. A day later, Daniels annulled the August order for two hundred F-5-Ls. This spurred Coburn to halt all subcontracting on hulls less than half finished and to make arrangements to transfer all subcontracted hull work beyond that state of completion to the factory proper.[38]

The full effect of the end of the war descended on Coburn and the NAF on 12 November. Taylor sent orders stopping all work on the F-5-Ls "as soon as possible" and with "the least number of boats possible produced," although he understood that this would "leave 100 to 135 F-5 boats to be completed and delivered." Experimental work on the four N-1s and the airborne torpedo was to be finished. Taylor recognized that peace would place new pressures on the NAF, and he hoped that deliveries of the remaining F-5-Ls could be postponed until the middle of 1919 so as to retain a nucleus of the factory's organization.[39]

In the brief span of sixteen months since Daniels's directive of 27 July 1917, a physical plant valued at more than $4 million had been built at Philadelphia and aircraft and parts worth an estimated $5 million had been manufactured. This output included 137 H-16s, 31 F-5-Ls, and the 4 N-1 Davis Gun Carriers, in addition to 17 sets of H-16 and 8 sets of F-5-L spares. At the end of the war the NAF was a larger organization than the navy yard alone had been before the conflict. More than six thousand men and women had been hired and trained, and another six to eight thousand employees worked for companies subcontracting parts and components for the factory. Sixteen million board feet of lumber had been handled and stored, of which 7,759,000 board feet were used in aircraft production, most going into wings and tail groups.[40]

Although there was a sense of relief and jubilation on 11 November, for the NAF the war had ended too soon. The elaborate system of subcontractors, the training program, and the plant-floor organization effected by Coburn were just starting to show results by the fall of 1918. Those results were obvious to the knowledgeable observer: more than one F-5-L per day was leaving the plant for shipment overseas, and those aircraft that went into service were taking their toll of U-boats in the Atlantic. Now that apparatus had to be dismantled, if only in part, to adjust to the peace that had come so suddenly. Yet for the long term, the war had vindicated those who had advocated the concept of a government aircraft factory to supply the special needs of the navy, and the plant itself had been built and placed in operation in record time despite the economic dislocations of the wartime emergency. In the years to come, many basic issues concerning the country's aircraft industry would revolve around the NAF. Taylor, perhaps inadvertently, set the stage for controversy as early as November 1918, when he wrote, "It is desired to maintain intact the establishment of the Naval Aircraft Factory in all its departments as the principal future source of Naval aircraft."[41] For the present, there was sufficient work to be done winding up the war contracts, closing out the subcontracting work at minimal cost to the government, reducing the work force, and securing experimental aircraft and production orders.

3

If You Produce,
I'll Get the Work to You

Peace in November 1918 elicited pride among the people at the Naval Aircraft Factory in having been part of a magnificent victory, but the end of the war also brought anxiety about the future. The Philadelphia plant had been established to carry out a trifold mission: to assure a reliable source of specialized aircraft for the navy at reasonable cost (by its own production and by stimulating competition); to maintain a level of engineering expertise through aeronautical design and development; and to tabulate production cost data as a check on private manufacturers (the yardstick). As manager of the NAF, Coburn had been granted wide latitude over the factory and its functions; under his command, the plant responded to the wartime challenge and became one of the nation's largest aircraft production centers, supplying a significant percentage of the navy's flying boats. The service continued this and the factory's other principal roles as a means of ensuring the place of the NAF in the framework of postwar naval aviation.

On 12 November 1918, Coburn stood before workers in the new assembly building to inform them about changes in hours and the future of the plant. He was frank about the necessity for cutbacks, but he was also confident that there would be plenty of work for the time being. To guarantee this, Coburn wanted to complete as many H-16s and F-5-Ls as possible. Toward the end of the month, he reported to Taylor that only thirteen H-16s remained to be built, and they "could be wound up and completed and shipped on very short notice." The F-5-L program had not advanced nearly as far. No work had been done on the 200 F-5-Ls in the 12 August order, and the navy had canceled the contract on 2 November. Of the 480 flying boats ordered from the factory on 30 April, 33 had been finished. Another 32 hulls were ready at the NAF, and 73 hulls were nearing completion by subcontractors. Because considerable expenditure of time and money had been made on these airplanes, Coburn urged the bureau to make a decision regarding their ultimate disposition.[1]

Taylor authorized the completion of as many H-16s and F-5-Ls as was reasonable under the circumstances. In early December, he ordered Coburn to finish the remaining 13 H-16s and 105 F-5-Ls on which extensive hull work had been done, bringing the total number of F-5-Ls to 138. (This figure included 2 F-6-Ls, which were advanced models of the F-5-L with greater load-carrying capacity and redesigned vertical tail surfaces.) Production of the big twin-engine flying boats went ahead smoothly at the NAF in 1919. Twenty-five F-5-Ls had been completed by 27 May; less than two months later, all but 9 were ready for delivery. The F-5-L order wound up on 18 September with the completion and delivery of the last flying boat.[2] The preservation of a significant portion of the F-5-L program was an important victory for Coburn, but merely stretching out wartime business was at best a stopgap measure. New orders were also necessary for the factory to remain a primary manufacturer of aircraft in the immediate postwar years.

Coburn and Taylor were helped in their quest to ensure the NAF's status as a production plant by the availability of a quantity of materials and aircraft parts at Philadelphia. In June 1918, the navy had decided to procure three hundred flying boat trainers from Curtiss Engineering in Garden City and the Aeromarine Plane and Motor Company in Keyport, New Jersey. By November that number had been drastically reduced, but Taylor persuaded the chief of naval operations that a significant proportion of the Curtiss aircraft should be built at the NAF, largely to use up the accumulated surplus material and parts. On the twenty-first, Taylor informed Coburn that the factory had been selected to produce eighty modified Curtiss F-boats (or MFs) and twenty sets of spares for delivery in the summer of 1919. Closely resembling the old F-model pusher biplane, the new aircraft had a maximum takeoff weight of 2,488 pounds, a wing area of 402 square feet, and a span of 49 feet, 9 inches. The MFs featured two-step hulls with sponsons for better takeoff performance and stability in the water. A 100-horsepower Curtiss OXX provided power. Construction of the first four MFs began in January 1919, but unexpected snags in obtaining engineering data and working drawings from Curtiss prevented the NAF from meeting its original production schedule. Although the first MF (number A-5483) flew in the middle of March, the remaining aircraft were not delivered until well into autumn.[3]

Along with the MF program, the Naval Aircraft Factory received an order for twenty Vought VE-7s on 27 September 1919. Designed in 1918 by the new Lewis and Vought Corporation of Long Island City, New York, as an advanced trainer, the VE-7 was a biplane with a maximum takeoff weight of 2,100 pounds and a wing area of 284.5 square feet within a span of 34 feet. The VE-7s were powered by 180-horsepower Wright-Hispano E-2 V-8 engines. Armament consisted of a Vickers gun firing forward through the propeller and a 0.30-caliber Lewis gun mounted on a scarf ring in the rear cockpit. The VE-7GF series airplanes had emergency flotation gear.[4]

One of the most widely used naval aircraft in the immediate postwar years, the VE-7 was a major element of the factory's production during this period. Deliveries began in September 1920. Authorization for an additional thirty VE-7s came from Secretary Daniels in November 1920. Of these, sixteen were to be standard two-seat trainers and the remaining fourteen were to be VE-7SF models with emergency flotation gear. An order for twenty more SF versions followed on 27 January 1921. Subsequently, however, Taylor transferred ten of the factory's VE-7SFs to Lewis and Vought, citing "delays and rush jobs" on other projects that prevented the NAF from completing all fifty aircraft by the 30 June deadline. Nevertheless, the NAF had requisitioned enough parts to complete nine more aircraft in 1922.[5]

Had either Taylor or Coburn been inclined to cite the MF and VE-7 programs as examples of what the Philadelphia plant could do in comparison with private manufacturers of similar aircraft, they would have been disappointed. NAF assembly workers had great difficulty properly aligning the tail surfaces of the MFs to the hulls without the use of additional internal wire bracing. Curtiss had none of these problems, or at least did not admit to any of them.

Difficulties with the VE-7s appeared when the commander of a squadron in San Diego complained about aircraft he had received from the NAF. "Generally speaking," he wrote, "the condition of these new planes, particularly as regards workmanship, is far below the high standard ordinarily found in the product of a private builder." A prompt tightening of the factory's quality control and predelivery inspection procedures rectified both problems.[6]

In addition to the Curtiss and Vought designs, the Naval Aircraft Factory manufactured sizable quantities of other airplanes. In 1919, the navy ordered ten M-81s (or M-8-1s) from the NAF, followed by a contract for twenty-six more in 1920. Conceived by the pioneer aeronautical engineer Grover C. Loening, the M-81 was a monoplane with a maximum takeoff weight of 2,068 pounds, a wing area of 229 square feet, and a span of 32 feet, 9 inches. A 300-horsepower 8-cylinder Hispano-Suiza gave the airplane a top speed of 145 miles per hour. The NAF delivered its first M-81 in September 1920 and by the end of the year completed another thirteen; the remainder followed in 1921. The M-81 was not a success. Pilots intensely disliked the airplane, largely because of its poor cockpit visibility, and, even worse, the craft exceeded its specified weight limits.[7]

Another order in August 1919 was for the assembly of surplus De Havilland DH-4s to be used by the marines. In 1922, the NAF brought in eighty more DH-4s for reconstruction as DH-4Bs, which had relocated fuel tanks and plywood-covered fuselages. Fairly typical of the use of surplus materials and components was the PT-1. A big twin-float patrol-torpedo plane powered by a 330-horsepower Liberty, the PT-1 had a maximum takeoff weight of 7,075 pounds. The wings, from the Curtiss HS-1L, had an area of 652 square feet and a span of 62 feet. Secretary Daniels authorized the construction of fifteen PT-1s in January 1921. Supplementing these were eighteen PT-2s, which had Curtiss HS-2L wings, areas of 803 square feet and spans of 74 feet, improved seats, and fuel-tank modifications. The factory completed these airplanes by mid-July 1922.[8]

Production of NC flying boats also kept NAF shop workers busy. The NC (for Navy-Curtiss) originated in 1917 when Admiral Taylor called for a patrol plane with significantly greater endurance than existing aircraft, which could, in addition, ferry itself across the Atlantic. Because of problems at Curtiss, the first of the 25,000-

pound aircraft, NC-1, did not fly until October 1918, too late to take
part in the conflict. Yet NC-1 and her three sisters were ready by the
spring of 1919 to fly the Atlantic, and NC-4 accomplished this
notable aviation benchmark when she landed in Lisbon on 27 May.[9]

A priority in 1919 and 1920 was continuing the development of
the NC type and providing enough of the airplanes for scouting
duties with the fleet. Consequently, the NAF received an order for
four NCs in mid-1919 and, despite congressional rumblings that the
airplanes ought to be built by private concerns, gained two more in
July 1920. Various delays pushed back the delivery of NC-5 and
NC-6 into May 1920, with NC-7, NC-8, NC-9, and NC-10 following
in the spring of 1921. Because the first two flying boats had only
three engines and were badly underpowered, the NAF and the Naval
Air Station, San Diego, modified the remaining four to the four-
engine configuration. The NCs never had a good reputation with the
fleet, and complaints were heard about their poor construction and
reliability. NC-5 and NC-6 were lost in accidents in January 1921,
and NC-7 sank later that year under circumstances that underscored
skepticism about their suitability for general patrol work.[10]

Severe reductions in the size of the work force at Philadelphia
alarmed Coburn and others who were concerned about the future of
the plant. The first cuts were the most extensive. From the peak of
3,640 in late October 1918, employment fell to 2,345 by the end of
November and to only a little more than 2,000 by 1 January 1919. In
June, the figure leveled off at about 1,650 workers. Coburn warned
that "unless steps are now taken to avert it, the major portion of the
Naval Aircraft Factory may be lost to aviation purposes." He
indicated to the various bureaus that the NAF had space available
for the manufacture of both experimental and production aircraft. If
these facilities were "not put into service for aircraft manufacturing,
as the accumulations of aircraft and material are consumed the
space will undoubtedly be taken over for general Navy purposes."
On 27 August, Coburn promised the plant's workers that there
would be no further layoffs and insisted, "If you people will produce,
I'll get the work to you. That's my business."[11]

Aircraft production was considered vital for maintaining a nucleus of skilled workers at the NAF, but it was also thought crucial
to the factory's yardstick function. To correlate cost data with those
of private manufacturers, the NAF kept close track of the unit costs

of H-16s and F-5-Ls throughout the war. The last 30 of the 150 H-16s built at the NAF cost $22,000 apiece, compared with $22,775 for similar airplanes from Curtiss. F-5-Ls from the NAF averaged about $24,000 each, while those from Curtiss cost about $1,000 more. Most dramatic was the differential between the NAF and Vought on costs of VE-7s; the factory delivered its airplanes for $7,100 each, compared to Vought's unit price of $12,300. Only for the MF flying boats were the factory's cost figures more than those of Curtiss— $8,700, compared to $8,000 from the private manufacturer.[12]

Before the House Naval Affairs Committee in February 1920 Hunsaker explained unit costs at the Naval Aircraft Factory in comparison with those of outside manufacturers. He said that on small orders, a private plant had to make so many changes that it almost always ended up with higher costs than the NAF. But with "quantity production of standard machines it is much cheaper to go outside to the man who is making that type." To illustrate his point, Hunsaker said the Curtiss plant in Buffalo at full capacity "could make a world's record on low cost for any small plane in quantity production." For smaller numbers of large aircraft, or if an entirely new type were to be designed and built, Hunsaker admitted that "it is a toss-up as to which way it would come out the cheapest."[13]

As Hunsaker's testimony implied, it was moot whether it was less expensive to build aircraft in government plants than to procure them from private manufacturers. It all depended on the types of aircraft, the quantity ordered, and how much development work was called for. Vought's costs may have been inflated because of the considerable expense it put into the VE-7 development and the low output possible from its small plant in Long Island City. For similar numbers of identical models, the navy cost figures show the NAF's costs were close to those of private industry. The navy was particularly conscious that its cost-accounting procedures at the NAF closely followed those of the private sector. Of major concern was reducing overhead. As the work force fell off at the NAF in 1919–20, expenditures for wages and salaries declined, bringing about significant cuts in the plant's overhead. With steady production of proven types of aircraft at the NAF it was also possible to hold down costs; it looked better on the books to turn out large numbers of standardized types than to employ the same number of workers to manufacture a few specialized aircraft. In later years, Captain Emory S.

Land, the assistant chief of the Bureau of Aeronautics, insisted that the NAF's accounting procedure was "very accurate" and compared favorably to that of civilian aircraft plants.[14]

Those who championed the NAF for its potential as a check on costs of privately supplied aircraft regarded such careful attention to accounting and overhead as proof of the viability of the yardstick. In truth, other factors such as rent, taxes, insurance, civil service employment, and depreciation of equipment were involved in the calculation of direct cost comparisons. Nor was it possible to determine with certainty whether competition from the NAF forced Curtiss and other firms to keep their costs down or by how much. The yardstick may have had some validity during the rapid wartime expansion of the industry, but in 1920, with the commercial and military market glutted by surplus airplanes and the navy's aircraft requirements reduced to a minimum, there was little private industry for the yardstick to measure. To a large extent these were merely questions of academic interest to Congress and military officers and of little concern to private manufacturers as long as there was ample business for everyone, but as the market evaporated over the next year and a half, they served to fuel a burning controversy between the government and private industry.

For a variety of reasons, production was a vital activity of the NAF in the postwar years, but a realistic appraisal of the situation in 1919 led Coburn to believe that the factory had to pursue its other functions with equal vigor if it were to keep its place within the industry. In an article in the *Transactions of the Society of Automotive Engineers*, Coburn wrote that the factory in the postwar years should complement private industry in the development of experimental aircraft designs.[15]

A major wartime requirement was for a long-range fighter to escort H-16s and F-5-Ls on their Atlantic and North Sea patrols. Following a report by the British Air Ministry establishing the basic performance criteria for the new airplane, the Bureau of Construction and Repair began preliminary design work on the fighter in August 1918. To achieve the necessary combination of speed and range in the 8,846-pound airplane, the bureau decided to employ twin 400-horsepower Kirkham engines. The hull configuration closely resembled that of the NC flying boats, although the 930-square-foot wing area was much less than that of the big NC craft.

General plans were completed shortly after the Armistice, and the bureau advertised for bids on four aircraft in January 1919. Because the NAF had not been involved with bidding procedures during the war, it set up a committee to furnish estimates from which a formal bid could be derived. The factory's bid of $84,680 earned the contract on 9 April.[16]

No sooner had the NAF received the contract for the new fighter than it faced formidable obstacles in meeting the design requirements. Because the Kirkham engine proved unsatisfactory, NAF engineers decided to use two 300-horsepower Hispano-Suizas, mounted in tandem between the wings aft of the cockpit. Dick Richardson, the NAF's chief engineer, was at the controls on 13 October 1920 for the first test flight of the new airplane, which was by now designated TF for Tandem Fighter. Everything went smoothly until the engines overheated. Richardson made a successful emergency landing on the Delaware near the Hog Island shipyard, only to avoid disaster when the craft's right wing was badly damaged after a tip float carried away during takeoff. Richardson's experience and skill as a pilot were all that prevented the total loss of the first TF.[17]

The tandem location of the TF's engines made it impossible to provide adequate cooling for the rear engine, and its propeller, working as a pusher in the slipstream of the forward engine-propeller combination, could not function at maximum efficiency. Hunsaker oversaw experiments with several different propeller designs, and considerable effort went into radiator improvements to resolve the overheating problem. On one of the four airplanes the Hispano-Suizas gave way to twelve-cylinder Packards as the NAF attempted to overcome the persistent difficulties with the TFs. By 1923, Hunsaker had decided it was fruitless to go on with the project. "The job is now 3 years old & shows no signs of being useful," he wrote at the end of a project report on 1 January 1923. "It has had many of the bugs taken out and no doubt another year's work would be enough to perfect [the airplane]. But the tandem props are always bad, the type is not needed, & we can't afford to devote [the] energy of our best men & money on a losing proposition." Within days, the navy wisely halted all work on the TF.[18]

Another NAF design to come out of the war period was the SA, or ship's airplane. The SA was a small monoplane built to test the

The TF Tandem Fighter was the result of an effort to design an aircraft to escort flying boats on long-range patrols. Persistent troubles with the twin 300-horsepower engines mounted in tandem led the factory to abandon the design after building four airplanes in 1920–22. (80-G-431547, National Archives)

feasibility of flying either from carrier decks or from platforms on the gun turrets of battleships. Simplicity, light weight, and ease of handling in the air were the primary design requirements in these diminutive airplanes. Deriving its power from a 55-horsepower, three-cylinder Lawrance radial engine, the SA-1 had a maximum takeoff weight of only 695 pounds and was fitted with a skid-type undercarriage. In contrast, the SA-2 had conventional wheeled landing gear, a maximum takeoff weight of 810 pounds, and a wing with a revised airfoil section. The NAF delivered two each of the SA-1 and SA-2 models in 1919, but no production orders ensued despite initial plans to build twenty of the airplanes.[19]

A craft larger and with better performance than the SA-1 and SA-2 would be needed aboard existing battleships and the aircraft carriers planned in the early 1920s. To meet this need, Admiral

Taylor wrote the chief of naval operations in April 1921 that designs for a convertible land- and floatplane were to be prepared and "turned over to the Naval Aircraft Factory for development and construction." Jerome Hunsaker assumed responsibility for drawing up plans for the new aircraft, which was to be known as the TS-1. An overriding consideration was simplicity and ease of operating and maintaining the airplane within the confines of a ship. Hunsaker came up with a compact, clean-looking design that is considered a classic by some aviation historians. Hunsaker did away with the unsightly and aerodynamically inefficient interplane wire braces and located the fuel tank in the center section of the lower wing. The TS-1 had a maximum takeoff weight of 2,133 pounds and a wing area of 228 square feet within a span of 25 feet. Power came from a nine-cylinder, 200-horsepower Lawrance J-1 air-cooled radial engine.[20]

With the TS-1 design finalized, contracts for thirty-four of the airplanes went to Curtiss Aeroplane and Motor, and the Naval Aircraft Factory received an order for five. The first examples joined the carrier *Langley* late in 1922 and operated with the fleet through the middle of the decade. Moreover, the NAF made progressive improvements to the airplane in 1922–23. Two versions, designated TS-2s, had 240-horsepower Aeromarine engines, and two more (TS-3s) flew with Wright-Hispano E-2s.[21]

The shipboard airplanes represented one side of an emerging pattern of naval aviation's role in the projection of offensive airpower at sea, combined with the more traditional scouting and patrol missions. Advocates of the latter wanted more long-range flying boats, exemplified by the NC craft and their smaller sisters, the H-16 and F-5-L. But the NC boats had obvious limitations, and navy planners envisioned a much larger airplane with considerably augmented range and payload capacity.

On 30 July 1918, the chief of naval operations issued a letter based on the recommendations of the General Board for the development of "Giant types of Flying Boats" weighing approximately twenty-five tons. Later that year, Jerome Hunsaker and Commander Lew Atkins in the Bureau of Construction and Repair began preliminary design studies, but nothing coalesced until 1919. Curtiss, experienced with the NC boats as well as with a large four-engine triplane that had been designed for the British in 1915, submitted drawings to the bureau for a 45,000-pound triplane flying boat with six engines arranged in tandem.[22] Although the Curtiss design progressed no farther than these preliminary renderings, it inspired Hunsaker and Dick Richardson to forge ahead with their own plans for a large flying boat.

Working most of the summer, Richardson devised general specifications for a flying boat that he hoped would be a major advance over the NCs. He still wanted the airplane to be within the state of the art in 1919 and warned that "any radical or unusual departure from previous practice must be demonstrated as practical and based on sound engineering." Staying within these parameters, however, introduced complications, especially in the arrangement of the airplane's power plant. The aircraft was to be multiengined, but there were to be at least two engines per propeller, linked by a drive shaft and a clutching system that permitted the engines to be disengaged for minor in-flight repairs and maintenance. Rarely have such multiengine installations been practical, and it has been axiomatic among aeronautical engineers that no airplane with a drive shaft has been an operational success. Richardson emphasized that when wood construction might drive up weights to prohibitive levels, metal should be substituted as the primary fabrication material. The maximum radius of action for the airplane was to be no less than eighteen hundred nautical miles (approximately the distance from Newfoundland to the Azores) at a cruising speed greater than eighty miles per hour. Richardson imposed no dimensional restrictions, although he did caution that excessive size "to obtain only a slight gain in performance will not be considered favorably."[23]

The bureau had hoped that Richardson's specifications would spur "individual initiative" among private contractors to submit detailed proposals for the large flying boat. The response to the design competition that opened in November 1919 was disappointing; only one company, Curtiss, submitted a proposal, and it was considered unsatisfactory. Therefore, the Bureau of Construction and Repair, working with the Bureau of Steam Engineering, prepared its own design for a triplane, by then commonly referred to as the Giant Boat. With a maximum takeoff weight of 70,000 pounds—more than twice the weight of the NCs—the Giant Boat was truly monstrous; the bureau acknowledged that it "represents the maxi-

Hull assembly of the Giant Boat at the Naval Aircraft Factory in March 1921. A seventy-thousand-pound triplane, the Giant Boat was meant to be a successor to the NC-series aircraft, but the project was canceled late in 1921. (Robert A. Gordon and Connecticut Aeronautical Historical Society)

mum size which seems practical making use of American engines." Power came from nine 400-horsepower Liberties linked together in three huge nacelles and geared to a shaft driving 18-foot-diameter tractor propellers. Each engine could be disengaged for repairs in flight. The top and middle wings of the Giant Boat had 150 foot spans and areas of 2,100 square feet; the lower wing had a 121-foot span and an area of 1,694 square feet. Because of their size, the wings incorporated metal construction, except for their covering, which was to be conventional doped fabric.

The specifications for the rest of the Giant Boat are a study in superlatives. The hull, similar in appearance to that of the NC boats but much larger, was nearly sixty-five feet long, had girder-type longerons, and was divided by five semiwatertight bulkheads. Designers gave some consideration to using metal for the hull construction, but in view of the extra engineering work involved, the bureau chose wood as the principal hull material. The bottom of the hull was built up of two plies separated by cotton sheeting and joined by waterproof glue, while the top had a single layer of planks laid longitudinally. There were accommodations in the hull for nine crew members, but ten cylindrical four-hundred-gallon aluminum fuel tanks occupied much of the internal volume. Armament was five 0.50-caliber machine guns and six 1,000-pound bombs. At a cruising speed of 78 miles per hour, the airplane had a range of 1,630 nautical miles. On 7 June, Secretary Daniels, despite some reservations about the range deficiency, authorized the construction of two Giant Boats, one to be built by a private firm and the other by the Naval Aircraft Factory to provide cost comparisons.[24]

To supply the power plants for the Giant Boat, the navy turned to the Gallaudet Aircraft Corporation in East Greenwich, Rhode Island. This firm, founded by Edson F. Gallaudet, had experimented with geared propellers on the D-1, D-2, and D-4 aircraft in 1916–18 and had already submitted plans under a previous engineering contract for a three-engine Giant Boat nacelle. On 12 March 1920, Gallaudet received a $40,000 award to build one of the power units; the navy later assigned two more nacelles to the company, completing the power plant contracts for the Giant Boat. Delivery of the first nacelle to the NAF came on 21 November 1921, with the remaining two to follow in February 1922. In keeping with the scale of the Giant Boat project, the nacelles were massive 23-foot-long, 5,885-pound streamlined duralumin structures mounted on the middle wing of the triplane.[25]

As Gallaudet concentrated on the power plants, the NAF went ahead in the summer of 1920 with work on the hull and wings of the first Giant Boat. Primary responsibility fell upon the project engineer, J. A. Christen, who had been with Curtiss in 1918–19 and had considerable experience with the NC boats. Chronic shortages of draftsmen hampered progress on the detail drawings of the hull structure, which were not sent to the bureau until August. Actual construction, begun later that year, went slowly and was not finished until the end of 1921. The wings, however, were another matter. Experiments in the wind tunnel at the Washington Navy Yard had resulted in a suitable design by the beginning of 1921, despite Hunsaker's reservations about the viability of the triplane configuration. High-strength alloy steel imported from Sheffield, England, went into the wing spars, which were built up from lattice box beams, and duralumin, an aluminum-copper alloy developed in Germany, was used for the ribs. Yet just when wing construction had started at the NAF, it became apparent that in the interval since the project had begun, European advances in the fabrication of duralumin rendered the Giant Boat wing design obsolete.[26]

The prospect of delay and expense to create a new wing design, coupled with the need for other aircraft types, killed the Giant Boat project in the summer of 1921. Appropriations for naval aviation since 1919 had hardly been generous and had already forced the navy to cut back from two Giant Boats to one, but in 1921 the situation became acute. Admiral Taylor estimated that at least $200,000 more would be needed to complete the lone airplane and that it would pull an inordinate number of draftsmen and engineers away from ship's aircraft and experimental work at the NAF. Taylor recommended that the Giant Boat project "be held in abeyance" until the fleet had sufficient fighters and observation aircraft. Following Taylor's suggestion, Captain William A. Moffett, the director of naval aviation in the Office of the Chief of Naval Operations, ordered hull construction and nacelle deliveries to be completed but that no further work be done on the Giant Boat.[27]

When work stopped on the Giant Boat and under what circumstances are not entirely clear. *Aviation* magazine reported in January 1922 that it had been rumored for several months that the project had been suspended and that expenditures had been cut off. The hull, wing spars, interplane struts, and power units went into storage at the NAF and were probably disposed of sometime after 1925.[28]

It is tempting to dismiss the Giant Boat and other unsuccessful or incomplete experimental work at the Naval Aircraft Factory as largely wasted effort. The Giant Boat was an aberration; it stretched the technological capabilities of the day, especially in the areas of propulsion, aerodynamics, materials, and drag reduction. Flying boats weighing as much as 70,000 pounds would have to await the development of larger, more powerful, and more reliable aircraft engines, better airfoil designs, and greater facility in the use of metal to increase wing loadings and weight-carrying capacity. Not until

1934 and the advent of the four-engine Sikorsky S-42 and the Martin M-130 did the United States have flying boats with ranges exceeding one thousand miles, and not until 1938 did the Boeing 314, with a maximum takeoff weight of 82,500 pounds, get into the air.[29] Unquestionably, greater numbers of smaller flying boats could have (and later did) fulfill the Giant Boat's intended mission. Yet the project was significant in providing NAF engineers with hands-on experience with large metal aircraft structures, weight-control measures, and managing long-term experimental programs. This work heralded much of what was to come for the Naval Aircraft Factory as it moved into the changed political and economic circumstances of the 1920s.

In part, those changed circumstances involved top-level administrative shifts at the NAF. Fred Coburn stepped aside as manager during the height of the factory's immediate postwar production and experimental programs. For some time, Coburn had considered leaving the navy and joining a private engineering firm. On 6 October 1919, he saw Secretary Daniels and requested permission to resign his commission. Daniels refused; instead he granted Coburn an extended leave of absence, during which time a new manager would take over at Philadelphia and Coburn's resignation could be effected at a more leisurely pace. Two days later, Coburn spoke to the employees of the NAF. He told them that "the future of the factory is assured" and that "there is in mind steps for the development of the plant" to guarantee its continued role in naval aviation. Genuinely moved, he added, "It is not an easy thing to leave you. . . . I will always be here in spirit." His last day on the job was 15 October.[30]

Coburn's managerial philosophy, which had relegated considerable responsibility to department heads and had depended heavily on personal accessibility and loyalty, worked well under the extraordinary pressure imposed on the factory during the war years. His successor, Captain George C. Westervelt, who arrived at the NAF on 28 October, brought with him a distinctly different style and personality. Offsetting his short stature and gruff demeanor with a lightning-quick mind and bulldog tenacity, "Scrappy" Westervelt came to Philadelphia with wide experience in naval aviation. Three years after graduating tenth in his class from Annapolis in 1901, Westervelt went into the Construction Corps and then on to MIT, where he took advanced engineering courses. In 1915, while serving at the Puget Sound Navy Yard in Bremerton, near Seattle, Washington, he joined William E. Boeing in designing and building two small floatplanes—the first in an illustrious line of Boeing aircraft. Westervelt accompanied the Bolling mission to Europe in the summer of 1917 and became an early advocate of the long-range flying boat. Together with Hunsaker and Richardson, he assisted in the design and construction of the famous NC boats.[31]

In December 1913, Westervelt published an article in the *U.S. Naval Institute Proceedings* in which he elucidated his ideas about industrial management in the navy. He believed that discipline, motivation, and an esprit de corps—all distinctly military in connotation—were the key ingredients for efficient manufacturing at naval facilities. Coburn's management style had worked well under the stress of war; the NAF had "responded by delivering the goods," Westervelt acknowledged. But adjustment to peacetime conditions required belt-tightening and a commitment to productivity if the NAF were to retain its place as an aircraft manufacturing center. Within two weeks of taking over as manager, Westervelt cut back the number of department heads and instituted a procedural system with strictly delineated avenues of responsibility. Further to systematize the factory's organization, Westervelt assigned Lieutenant Ralph S. Barnaby in 1920 to prepare a manual that outlined department functions, chains of command, and the entire production system from design and procurement through manufacture and delivery.[32]

A confirmed believer in heavier-than-air flight, Westervelt, ironically, found not long after assuming command in Philadelphia that much of his time was devoted to the design and construction of a large rigid airship. In 1919, the rigid airship, with its unique combination of payload capacity and endurance, appeared to offer a cost-effective alternative to large numbers of cruisers for scouting with the fleet, particularly in the vast reaches of the Pacific. German experience with Zeppelins in combat seemed to verify this assessment. In 1919, Secretary Daniels called upon the navy to move more aggressively in lighter-than-air experiments and suggested that the NAF was an appropriate venue for naval airship work. Admiral Taylor doubted if there was enough room at the factory but admitted

Captain George C. Westervelt took over as factory manager from Lieutenant Commander Fred Coburn in October 1919. Westervelt's formidable personality shaped the NAF for nearly eight years. (U.S. Naval Aviation Museum)

that there were no alternative sites for a lighter-than-air development facility, which he considered "essential."[33]

Lighter-than-air work was already under way at the NAF when Daniels and Taylor spoke on Capitol Hill. In November 1918, the factory undertook the construction of five two-engine control cars for 189,000-cubic-foot D-series nonrigid airships (commonly known as blimps). The cars were to have been delivered in June 1919 but were not completed until later that autumn. Additionally, the NAF built improved D-series tail surfaces that in October were retrofitted to several C-series blimps stationed at the Naval Air Station, Cape May, New Jersey. Further activity at the factory in 1920 centered on the construction of an enclosed D-series control car with integral fuel tanks.[34]

On 9 August 1919, less than a month after Congress had appropriated $1.5 million for building a large Zeppelin-type rigid airship, Secretary Daniels authorized the work to be done at the Naval Aircraft Factory. According to the scheme devised by Admiral Taylor, the Bureau of Construction and Repair would supply basic engineering information for the rigid, known at first as Fleet Airship

1, while the NAF was responsible for detail design and fabrication of parts and components. Erection of the 2-million-cubic-foot craft would take place in a huge hangar built expressly for the purpose at the Naval Air Station, Lakehurst, New Jersey. Naval constructor Commander Ralph D. Weyerbacher, Fred Coburn's assistant during the war, learned later in August that he had been assigned to manage the airship project.[35]

Detail drawings for the hull structure, control car, and power units of the airship, which was now designated ZR-1, occupied a major portion of the staff in the engineering department at the NAF from the end of 1919 through early 1921. The Bureau of Construction and Repair did not furnish complete data for the hull frame members until July 1920, and further delays ensued while the bureau prepared information relative to the control car. The power units were the responsibility of the Bureau of Steam Engineering, which made at least one false start on a preliminary design before permitting detail plans and construction of a mockup to go ahead at the NAF. Some savings of time and expense occurred when it was decided not to erect a complete test section of the airship, consisting of three transverse frames and gas cells.[36]

Delivery of materials proved to be another bottleneck to the rapid prosecution of work on the big dirigible. Before 1916, no one in the United States had any experience with duralumin so it was necessary to lean heavily on German and British experience with this important structural material that combined the light weight of aluminum with the tensile strength of mild steel. Alcoa, the nation's largest producer of aluminum, had experimented with duralumin for the navy during the war and received the contract in December 1919 to manufacture the large quantities of the alloy required for the airship. Deliveries from Alcoa's New Kensington and Munhall, Pennsylvania, plants were originally to have started in February 1920, but the company was unable to stamp or roll the duralumin to the specifications demanded by the navy. To accommodate the aluminum company's limitations, the bureau instituted design changes that imposed further delays in the construction of ZR-1. In September, Alcoa promised the navy that duralumin production was "well established and the difficulties previously encountered in fabricating this material have been overcome." Still, no duralumin arrived in Philadelphia. Westervelt expressed his

The *Shenandoah* (ZR-1) under construction in the hangar at Lakehurst, New Jersey, in December 1922. The Naval Aircraft Factory fabricated the airship's duralumin girders and frames in Philadelphia, with final assembly at Lakehurst. (80-G-441991, National Archives)

annoyance in January 1921: "As is well known by the Bureau, the actual date for starting the fabrication of hull members has been and still is, one of wide conjecture due to the fact that the deliveries for the material for hull fabrication can not be scheduled." Not until February did some duralumin begin to reach the NAF; another three months slipped by before the factory had enough of the metal to begin preliminary construction of girders.[37]

Once girder fabrication started in mid-1921, the factory made more satisfactory progress toward the completion of the airship. NAF assembly workers cut the complex duralumin members to length and fitted them together into transverse frames on a thirteen-sided radial jig laid out on the floor of the high shop in Building 77. The first midship frames came off the jig in the spring of 1922, followed by main and intermediate frames for the fore and aft sections of the craft. Fabrication was substantially complete by September 1922. Meanwhile, delivery of the frames to Lakehurst had begun, allowing Weyerbacher to get on with the actual erection in the new airship hangar. Most of the duralumin structure, totaling twenty-five tons of material, arrived at Lakehurst by rail, the remainder by truck. Assembly of the power cars and control car was more leisurely. By June 1922, a portion of one of the power cars had been finished, but nothing had been done on the control car pending completion of the detail drawings. The factory did not ship these units to Lakehurst until late July 1923, barely a month before the airship's commissioning as the USS *Shenandoah*.[38]

The *Shenandoah* was the first and only rigid airship built by the Naval Aircraft Factory, and her career was tragically brief, ending in a severe thunderstorm over Ohio in September 1925. Notwithstanding the operational and structural limitations she and succeeding navy rigid airships exhibited, the *Shenandoah* further expanded the NAF's reputation as a leader in metal aircraft construction, as well as its position in the industry as an aviation development and production facility. The *Shenandoah* also occupied scores of engineers, draftsmen, and shop workers for more than 160,000 man-hours over a period of years when the factory otherwise would have had to dismiss a substantial portion of its work force. The *Shenandoah*, the stillborn Giant Boat, the Tandem Fighter, and continued production of established aircraft indicated the navy's commitment to the retention of the NAF as a major aviation center in the postwar years.

4

Controversy and Compromise

In the caldron of world conflict, there was plenty of business for everyone, and few in the American aircraft industry had any misgivings about a government-owned and operated aircraft factory during the war. Moreover, there was a cooperative attitude among suppliers of naval aircraft, exemplified by the intimate wartime association between the NAF and Curtiss. Amplifying that sense of common purpose were the number of subcontractors linked to the NAF, all of which were private concerns that directly benefited from orders for parts and components. Samuel Stewart Bradley, general manager of the Manufacturers Aircraft Association, which had been formed during the war to hold patents and supervise cross-licensing agreements, expressed a common sentiment when he wrote that the navy's needs for flying boats had been met "by the cooperation of the manufacturers and the creation of the naval aircraft factory at Philadelphia."[1]

But the immature and exceedingly volatile aircraft industry could depend on only one customer—the federal government. Decisions made along the Potomac affected the allocation of resources for, and the immediate viability of, the nascent enterprise. From an output of only 2,148 aircraft in 1917, the industry had expanded to manufacture nearly 14,000 airplanes by November 1918. Capacity at the end of the war was estimated at 21,000 airplanes annually. But the collapse of the German armies caught everyone by surprise and precipitated a dilemma. Some of the estimated 1919–20 aircraft

production was needed to meet the military's postwar requirements; the remainder, valued at as much as $100 million, had to be
liquidated. A crisis of major proportions ensued as companies
desperately sought to preserve what was left of a rapidly shrinking
market. Even the NAF, which had maintained relatively stable
production and employment into 1921, did so by shedding itself of
subcontractors, most of whose orders were canceled within days of
the Armistice.[2]

American aircraft manufacturers struggled to survive in the midst
of a maze of government restrictions concerning competitive bidding procedures, design rights, and the lack of a long-range aviation
policy. Their complaints often focused on what they considered
unfair competition from the Naval Aircraft Factory. The manufacturers' attack on the plant highlighted many of the problems facing
the postwar aircraft industry and forced navy and civilian authorities to evaluate how the factory could best fit into naval aircraft
procurement needs.[3]

Official evidence that the navy intended to retain the Philadelphia
factory as a major potential source of aircraft compounded industry
worries. In July 1919, the American Aviation Mission, appointed by
Secretary of War Newton D. Baker to investigate postwar commercial and military aviation, strongly recommended that "competition
of the government with industry should be avoided; the only
allowable exception being cases where, either on account of expense
or other cause, [the services] cannot obtain needed material or
design from existing sources." Half the mission's members were
prominent business representatives: Howard E. Coffin, former chairman of the Aircraft Production Board; George H. Houston, president
of the Wright-Martin Airplane Company; Clement M. Keys, vice-
president of Curtiss Aeroplane; and Samuel Stewart Bradley of the
Manufacturers Aircraft Association. Captain Henry Mustin was
the sole navy spokesman on the mission. In two addenda to the
mission's report, he upheld the navy's long-standing view that its
needs were exceptional. He particularly stressed the requirement
"of an organization and facilities for carrying on experimental
aviation work of a class that is exclusively of a Naval character."[4]

The place of the factory in the postwar aircraft industry attracted
the attention of the House Naval Affairs Committee in February
1920. Before the war, members of the committee considered a

government plant crucial to expanding the navy's sources of aircraft. Now some wondered what effect the factory would have on private suppliers. Congressman Frederick C. Hicks, a Republican from Long Island, said American aircraft production capacity had been cut back "95 percent" at the end of the war, with devastating results for most aircraft builders. In reply, Captain Thomas T. Craven, the director of naval aviation in the Office of the Chief of Naval Operations, claimed that the war had significantly increased the number of aircraft manufacturing firms and argued that a shakeout was inevitable: "I think that the commercial business in the country at the present time will be sufficient to keep certain of these corporations in operation; probably, certain of them will be liquidated."[5]

Craven adhered to the navy's policy of keeping the right procurement mix to ensure a continuous and predictable source of aircraft, but Congress persisted in wanting all navy production concentrated at Philadelphia. When Congressman Lemuel Padgett asked if it would be advantageous to obtain the navy's total 1921 requirement—156 airplanes—from the NAF, Craven disagreed. He said that the navy had always wanted to distribute some of its orders among private manufacturers, not only because it was less expensive to obtain airplanes used by the army from the same source but also because it was imperative to have that capacity available in the event of war. Congressman Patrick Henry Kelley of Michigan, however, did not want the taxpayers' investment to go to waste, stating that "we have a plant of our own, and we must keep that running full blast, and if there is any [aircraft requirement] left, we will let the outsiders have it."[6]

Jerome Hunsaker provided the committee with a lucid summary of the navy's position regarding the NAF and private industry. Maintaining that "we have made no estimates" of the size of the factory, he said the navy did not prefer "to do all the work in our own plants." He saw the need for balanced procurement programs that included purchases from private manufacturers: "We want to get the ideas of outside people. We must keep the outside stimulated, and give them work. . . . We want to make use of outside facilities and outside engineers and inventors." Cooperation between the navy and private enterprise was especially critical at the design stage. Hunsaker knew the advantages of collaboration from his work with the NC boats and told the congressmen, "By that means we have been able to have machines developed which have broken world records." Hunsaker assured those who wanted to make full use of the costly Philadelphia installation that it was now at maximum capacity. The factory could continue at this pace by filling only one-third of the service's aircraft manufacturing orders and keeping its present level of overhaul, maintenance, and experimental activities.[7]

Private aircraft manufacturers suffering through the postwar doldrums were not pleased to have to concede one-third of their navy business to a government-owned and operated plant. Nor were they happy about the army air service's Engineering Division at McCook Field in Dayton, Ohio, which also built aircraft in the immediate postwar period, although in numbers less worrisome than the quantity in production at Philadelphia. Samuel Stewart Bradley and the Manufacturers Aircraft Association acted quickly to meet the threat in 1920. Bradley offered a proposal to the National Advisory Committee for Aeronautics (NACA) and the War and Navy departments: if the government directed 100 percent of its orders to the private sector, the industry would put all its profits into research and development and give the army and navy "the best flying machines in the world."[8]

Bradley's bold statement had a hollow ring. The control of patents by the Manufacturers Aircraft Association had tended to benefit the larger builders during the war at the expense of smaller firms. It is highly unlikely that he would have been able to bring all the companies into line to make good on his offer of a total plowback of profits into research and development. In addition, the modified cost-plus contracts of the war years had yielded comfortable—some said exorbitant—profits for selected firms, which had shown no inclination to use their windfall to generate advanced designs. Nor was it realistic to expect businessmen in the 1920s, especially those responsible for such battered industries as aircraft manufacturing, to commit all their earnings to research and development, the benefits of which would materialize, if at all, years in the future.[9]

But because of its substantial institutional stake in the NAF, the navy could not abandon aircraft production. Hunsaker and other officers had been instrumental in steering contracts to Philadelphia that ensured production well into 1922. In March 1921, Josephus Daniels repeated his belief that the NAF was a national asset "supplementing private aircraft construction by building special types of planes for Navy use." He estimated that the NAF could manufacture up to one thousand airplanes a year. This exceeded the navy's postwar requirements and seemed to Bradley to be rubbing salt into the wounds of private aircraft manufacturers.[10]

The status of the NAF depended not only on how the navy integrated its functions into aircraft procurement programs but also on the postwar administrative changes that occurred in naval aviation. Hitherto responsibility (or "cognizance" in navy jargon) for the NAF had resided primarily in the Bureau of Construction and Repair, with the Bureau of Steam Engineering playing a lesser role in matters concerning aircraft power plants. This situation had not caused major problems for the NAF in large measure because of the strong advocacy of Admiral Taylor, but the potential for discord was always present. Higher up, in the Office of the Chief of Naval Operations, the director of naval aviation had no administrative authority; his prerogatives were limited to requests to the bureaus for materials and personnel.[11]

A combination of external and internal pressures finally resolved this anomalous situation. From outside the service intense criticism of naval aviation came from General William ("Billy") Mitchell, an outspoken and often intemperate apostle of land-based airpower. His strident demands in Congress and the public for a unified air force, which threatened to eliminate the navy's air arm, helped naval officers close ranks and press for the centralization of naval aeronautics under a separate administrative unit.[12]

Building on this foundation, Congressman Hicks introduced a measure to create a bureau of aeronautics in April 1921. The Naval Aircraft Factory was one of the questions brought up when the House Naval Affairs Committee considered the bill later that month. Captain William A. Moffett, who had replaced Captain Craven as director of naval aviation on 7 March, told the committee that overall responsibility for the NAF would rest with the new bureau, which would disburse funds, originate aircraft designs, and detail personnel to the factory. The Bureau of Construction and Repair, however, would retain authority over the day-to-day functioning of the plant. This joint control affected those in the Construction Corps who opted for aeronautical engineering duty officer (AEDO) status; by moving over to the new Bureau of Aeronautics and the NAF, they effectively eliminated themselves from advancement within their own corps.[13]

With broad-based congressional support and the backing of the White House, the Hicks bill moved easily through the legislative mill and received President Warren G. Harding's signature on 12 July 1921. Captain Moffett, temporarily promoted to flag rank, became chief of the Bureau of Aeronautics on 10 August. A native South Carolinian, William Adger Moffett graduated from the Naval Academy in 1890 with an undistinguished record that seemed to portend an equally undistinguished career. That changed when he received the Congressional Medal of Honor for heroism during the landings at Vera Cruz in 1914. Command of the huge Great Lakes Naval Training Station during World War I provided him with valuable administrative experience. He oversaw the expansion of the facility from sixteen hundred to more than fifty thousand trainees and instituted a school for aviation mechanics and flight instruction. After the war, Moffett commanded the battleship *Mississippi* before coming to Washington at the behest of Admiral Robert E. Coontz, the chief of naval operations, to take over Craven's job as director of naval aviation. Although Moffett was a relative latecomer to naval aviation, he took to it with the characteristic zeal of a convert and his enthusiasm was bolstered by an acute political sensitivity.[14]

Even before he assumed his new duties, Moffett faced the prickly question of government competition from the Naval Aircraft Factory. Admiral Taylor concurred with the decision giving BuAer administrative control over the NAF but warned that private industry would attempt to curtail aircraft production at Philadelphia. "The Aircraft Factory," Taylor said, "is one of the things the Manufacturers' Aircraft Association has been gunning for, and there will be constant pressure from the manufacturers to have it closed or restricted. The truth of the matter is that . . . it is the best aircraft factory in the country and is doing work more cheaply than any private concern."[15]

In a five-page memorandum to Moffett, Taylor elaborated on the advantages of retaining aircraft production at the NAF. Just as the navy procured a number of ships from navy yards, so should it acquire some of its airplanes from the NAF. Arguing that "money spent at the Factory is economy to the government," Taylor used the Vought VE-7 order as an example of the benefits that could accrue by building such airplanes in a government plant. He estimated that Vought charged $12,000 for each airplane, whereas one from the NAF cost about $6,800. Aside from such direct savings, the factory's yardstick function was a check on the cost of airplanes from private suppliers. Taylor confidently added, "It is not necessary to point out what a valuable resource the NAF is likely to be to you."[16]

Moffett turned to Jerome Hunsaker for his opinion of the possible consequences of eliminating aircraft manufacturing at Philadelphia. Hunsaker responded that doing so would mean that "the organization which has been built up over a period of years will be disbanded with no hope of ever reassembling [it]." Moreover, current stocks of material would have to be sold at huge losses and a considerable number of personnel retained just to store the inventory of unfinished airplanes, parts, and other items. He echoed Taylor's concern about the navy having to rely entirely on private builders and asserted that the NAF could carry out its activities "more economically than most private contractors." To Hunsaker it was even desirable, if aviation appropriations were to undergo further cuts, to place "a minimum of work or no work with outside contractors and of building up the Naval Aircraft Factory . . . to the point where it can take care of all the Navy Department's requirements."[17]

What was Moffett to do? He had to establish a political base with an industry begging like a blind mendicant for any handout, yet the navy would have to rely on that industry in time of national crisis. He also had within the navy a substantial organization that could meet anywhere from a third to all of the service's peacetime aircraft production needs, depending on how many airplanes were required and the relative looseness of congressional purse strings. Against these conflicting points of view was a body of opinion within the navy that the NAF should be reserved for building only a few representative production aircraft and experimental models. Thus Moffett confronted a dilemma and he would have to take into account, if not accede to, at least some of the demands of private aircraft manufacturers. He also had to weigh the yardstick function of the NAF, which involved enough production to allow the navy to determine fair unit prices, against experimental construction, which in the aviation business was characteristically a high-cost, low-efficiency undertaking.

The answer was a compromise. Initially, Moffett assured the Manufacturers Aircraft Association that the NAF would no longer undertake major production runs. Henceforth, the plant would "be employed primarily for experimental work" intended to prove designs promulgated within BuAer. Moffett also emphasized "cooperative efforts between the Bureau, the Naval Aircraft Factory, and the outside manufacturers." In January 1922, Moffett clarified his perception of the factory's new role: "The Naval Aircraft Factory is to all intents and purposes no longer an aircraft factory, but a combination of naval aircraft base, naval aircraft storehouse, naval aircraft experimental station, and in general a naval aircraft establishment. . . . It is not the policy of the department to go into production of aircraft at the Naval Aircraft Factory." A variety of experimental projects would continue, as would the factory's yardstick function. Moffett proposed to build at the NAF such production models as were needed "to keep a check on costs, time of construction, together with a general line on commercial activities." Because Moffett considered the term *factory* "objectionable to commercial concerns," he suggested that the name of the installation be changed to Naval Aircraft Establishment.[18]

One of Moffett's main strengths as a bureau chief was his ability to gauge shifts in the usually capricious political winds of Washington. He understood that the Harding administration and the Republican Congress leaned toward cooperation rather than confrontation between business and government. By eliminating major production at the NAF, Moffett expected to defuse the issue of government competition and preserve the nucleus of a manufacturing facility by retaining the plant's capacity to design and build new and experimental aircraft. He hoped, too, that diverting attention from the NAF would help generate the cooperation of politicians and influential private individuals in building up a strong and independent naval air arm.[19]

Moffett recognized the fragility of his compromise and rarely missed an opportunity to defend it. In December 1923, he told Secretary of the Navy Edwin Denby: "The Naval Aircraft Factory bears the same relation to the Naval Air Service that Navy Yards bear to the Fleet. The services rendered are such that their duplica-

The Naval Aircraft Factory as it looked in December 1924. One of the
largest aircraft plants in the country, it was a target for attack from private manufacturers. At the bottom of the photograph is a large pier with
two turntable catapults. The open area to the right became Mustin Field.
(80-CF-712812–19, National Archives)

tion by outside contract could not be satisfactorily obtained"
because of the frequent changes called for in the development of
experimental aircraft and the delays created by bidding procedures.
He emphasized limited production as a yardstick for gauging the
costs of private suppliers. The bureau's policy was "to give out
practically all new construction to the trade," directing only the
barest minimum of such work to the NAF as a "check and
safeguard." In conclusion, he said, "the Naval Aircraft Factory
represents one of the most important and vital functions of the
aeronautical organization of the Navy Department. This aeronautical organization could not function satisfactorily without the Naval
Aircraft Factory."[20]

The design work and experimental aircraft manufacturing at the

NAF continued to disturb private industry. Although major production had ended by 1923, the Philadelphia plant still employed about thirteen hundred people in 1923–24, more than were working at any other aircraft factory in the country at that time. Moreover, the NAF was assuming responsibilities that indicated an expansion rather than a contraction of its activities in design development. In December 1922, Moffett authorized the transfer of the Aeronautical Engine Laboratory from the Washington Navy Yard to the NAF, and the move was almost completed by the spring of 1924. The factory's request for a wind tunnel in late 1923 served as further proof that the navy did not plan to limit its design and engineering activities at Philadelphia.[21]

At stake, as far as the manufacturers were concerned, was the nettlesome issue of proprietary rights over aircraft design. It had been common practice for the military to acquire the design rights to an airplane and then invite other manufacturers to submit bids for its production. Sometimes the company that had invested in the original design increased its bid to recoup its development costs and therefore lost the production competition to a rival firm. The manufacturers contended that it was ruinous competition, for it deprived the most innovative companies of profitable production runs and inhibited them from pursuing additional research and development.[22] The navy's retention of a large design and engineering staff at the NAF exacerbated this problem because the service could turn to Philadelphia for all its new aircraft designs, and the industry would eventually lose all control over design rights. If and when that happened, the more inventive firms that previously had counted on their superior designs to outdistance their competitors would find themselves at a distinct disadvantage.

Clement Keys emphasized this problem on 8 March 1924 in a report to the stockholders of his company, in which he cited "a sharp increase in the direct competition of our government" in the aircraft industry. He said there was "a strong tendency toward a Government monopoly of engineering and development work and the consequent elimination of private initiative." Lester D. Gardner, publisher of the influential trade weekly *Aviation*, also saw the danger. He wrote that the only way to cure the ills of the industry was by giving private manufacturers "responsibility for the design, engineering development, and manufacture of all service aircraft

and [by] giving rewards in the form of production orders for successful competitive products."[23]

Gardner called a meeting in New York in December 1924 to study
the problems created by the Naval Aircraft Factory. From the
gathering emerged a special committee to determine what could be
done to improve relations with Washington and to enhance the
stability of aircraft manufacturing. The group was headed by
Charles L. Lawrance of Wright Aeronautical and included Samuel
Stewart Bradley and representatives from twenty-three other companies, among them such aviation pioneers as Chance Vought and
Glenn L. Martin. The committee met with President Calvin
Coolidge, Secretary of Commerce Herbert Hoover, and Secretary of
the Navy Curtis D. Wilbur (a Naval Academy graduate and friend of
Moffett's) to determine what could be done to alleviate the situation. The committee projected a simple resolution of the problem:
the federal government should do everything possible to "encourage
and promote the design and manufacture, by other than Government agencies, of aircraft, aircraft engines, and equipment. The
Government shall not engage in such work in competition with the
aeronautical industry."[24]

Industry representatives had an opportunity to air their grievances before a special House committee that convened in March
1924. Charges of corruption in the air services during the war and
allegations that an "aviation trust" was in collusion to stifle
competition provided the initial impetus for the investigation, but
the committee probed virtually all phases of the nation's aeronautical establishment. Congressman Florian Lampert, a Progressive
LaFollette Republican from Wisconsin, chaired the panel.[25]

Aircraft manufacturers appeared before the Lampert Committee
in January 1925. Stung by the navy's reaction to his M-81 monoplane fighter, Grover Loening lashed out at the service for its
involvement in design and experimentation at the NAF. Loening
maintained that if private industry were given a free rein in these
areas, the navy could count on consistently first-rate aircraft for the
minimum expenditure. But, Loening concluded, "It is pretty hard
for an individual to compete with a rich man like the Government."[26]

Charles Lawrance and Clement Keys expressed many of the same
ideas before the Lampert Committee. Lawrance attacked the policy

of assigning design and engineering work to the NAF, contending that "design or construction of aircraft by governmental agencies . . . has never equaled the contemporary products of private initiative, either in performance or price." There was a place, Lawrance said, for government experiment stations, but they should "carry on experiments of such a nature that no private manufacturer can afford to undertake it, and they should also be capable of testing the planes and engines brought out by the industry, so that corrected data can be developed for those different products." Any greater government involvement would be "disastrous."[27]

Keys was equally explicit about the inherent threat presented by the continuation of design and engineering work at the NAF and the construction of experimental aircraft. These functions, he argued, "are the airplane industry." Keys regarded the so-called yardstick, which Moffett had cited as a reason for continued limited aircraft manufacturing at Philadelphia, as irrelevant because "we have never been able to find out on what basis the naval aircraft factory costs are calculated." The NAF was, he said, "a subsidized industry" that outmatched private manufacturers in competing for aircraft production orders.[28] Like Loening's testimony, the statements of Lawrance and Keys were a direct challenge to the compromise that Moffett had hoped would settle permanently the controversy over how the Naval Aircraft Factory could be integrated into the navy's procurement programs.

Naval officers appeared before the Lampert panel to answer the charges that the design and experimental activities of the NAF represented a threat to private industry. Although Commander Dick Richardson, formerly chief engineer at the NAF, could see no advantage in having the factory engage in the major production of aircraft, he defended experimental construction at Philadelphia as especially costly work that few private enterprises could sustain. Richardson was emphatic "that it is not competition where we are developing a design. I believe that to that extent we ought to be permitted to manufacture in our research department." Once the design had been perfected at the Naval Aircraft Factory, it would be put out for production by private firms. Richardson considered this a nearly ideal arrangement, but because it imposed what the industry perceived as intolerable restrictions on proprietary design rights it was not acceptable to private aircraft manufacturers.[29]

Captain Emory S. Land, the assistant chief of BuAer, did little to calm the anxieties of the aircraft industry when he spoke to the Lampert Committee. Although he said the navy should do all it could toward "encouraging an aircraft trade," he disagreed with Moffett and Richardson that the NAF should surrender its capacity for quantity aircraft production. Because the factory did not have to account for profit margins in calculating costs, it could successfully "compete with outside concerns." But for the present it was sufficient to maintain only limited production at the factory to provide data for contract negotiations.[30]

Land expanded on these views in a memorandum to Theodore Robinson, the assistant secretary of the navy. Land saw no immediate need for series production at the NAF, and he certainly wanted to "assist the trade in every reasonable manner." But "to safeguard the Government's interests," a "nucleus" of a production facility had to remain at the factory, not only for the yardstick but also to serve as a reminder to the industry that if its prices became "exorbitant," the navy could on its own design, develop, and produce the aircraft it needed. He dismissed criticism of the Naval Aircraft Factory as "without foundation and much of it is caused on account of the entire misapprehension of the facts."[31]

By early 1925, Moffett's compromise was in jeopardy. The private sector of the industry was assailing the design and experimental functions of the factory, which Moffett and other naval officers wanted to preserve to keep the plant active and to provide the specialized aircraft the navy needed. Within Moffett's own bureau, Land had further muddied the waters by confusing the yardstick principle, which was based on the sample production of a few aircraft, with the imminence of quantity production at the factory as a means of forcing private manufacturers to reduce their prices. If either the industry or Land were completely victorious, the results could be disastrous. Without some control over design, the navy could not guarantee that it would get the aircraft it required, and without the cooperation of a healthy private industry, it could not obtain them in the quantities necessary in wartime. An effective balance had to be struck between extreme centralization of procurement at the NAF and the maximum encouragement of free enterprise.

When the Lampert Committee issued its report on 14 December

1925, the vulnerability of Moffett's position was obvious. The committee concluded that the aircraft industry was "dependent on Government contracts" and was "rapidly diminishing under present conditions." It suggested that the government should "cease competing with the civilian aircraft industry in the construction of aircraft, engines, and accessories." The committee was extremely critical of the design and experimental work at the NAF and other government-owned facilities. Since 1920, both services had spent more than $30 million in these areas, which had no direct benefit to the private sector and had resulted in only a bare minimum of production orders. "They have spent a large part of their appropriations in attempting to do things that ought to be left to private capital, all with the result that the aircraft industry is languishing." Significantly, though, the Lampert Committee did not call for closure of the NAF, recommending only that its manufacturing, design, and experimental functions be sharply curtailed or eliminated altogether.[32]

The Lampert Committee was not the only body to deal with the problems of the aircraft industry in 1925. On 12 September, in the aftermath of the disappearance of the navy's PN-9 flying boat on a flight from San Francisco to Hawaii, the crash of the rigid airship *Shenandoah*, and the increasingly shrill criticism of American aviation policy by General Mitchell, President Coolidge appointed an investigating board of his own. The board, like the Lampert Committee, explored all aspects of aeronautics in the United States but did so in the full glare of media attention. Chaired by Dwight Morrow, a friend of Coolidge's from their college days at Amherst, the board included such notables as Howard Coffin; retired Rear Admiral Frank F. Fletcher, an expert on wartime industrial controls; Senator Hiram Bingham of Connecticut; Democratic Congressman Carl Vinson of Georgia; and William F. Durand, a Naval Academy graduate, professor of engineering at Stanford, and member of the NACA. The panel was to hear witnesses, study the pertinent data accumulated by other committees, and arrive at a decision that was politically acceptable. Because of the guaranteed publicity and the certainty that the president would accept its recommendations, the Morrow Board was an ideal forum for examining the NAF and its place in navy aircraft procurement policies.

Moffett stated his case for the NAF before the Morrow Board, emphasizing the cooperative rather than competitive nature of navy-industry relations and stressing that quantity production was not a part of the factory's mission. The NAF, said Moffett, "is open at all times to representatives of the airplane manufacturers and when matters of special interest are under way manufacturers are invited to inspect them." Research and development and testing at Philadelphia, which the industry wanted to eliminate, were necessary "to coordinate the interests of the Navy Department with the interests of manufacturers. . . . An interchange of information is constantly occurring, and the lines of development followed prevent unnecessary duplication." Moffett reassured the board that BuAer "has a definite policy of encouraging design and invention outside the naval service to the fullest extent."[33]

A parade of officers followed Moffett to the witness table, all presenting much the same arguments about the navy and the aircraft industry. George Westervelt supplied the most comprehensive overview of the NAF's work and an eloquent challenge to those who wanted to do away with aircraft design, experimentation, and construction at the factory. Some specialized manufacturing was needed because it was too complex and expensive to bid out to private firms, and at the NAF was restricted to originating designs that filled particularly demanding naval requirements. Large flying boats were a case in point; they were essentially seagoing craft, and few companies had extensive experience with them. Moreover, the navy had been quick to cooperate with private companies in such specialized work whenever possible; the transatlantic NCs and the Giant Boat were two examples of such harmonious collaboration.[34]

Morrow set aside one day of the hearings to listen to the complaints of the industry. In the meantime, the manufacturers girded for another round in the controversy. On 30 September, at a meeting in New York, twenty-four members of the Aeronautical Chamber of Commerce (ACOC), an offshoot of the Manufacturers Aircraft Association, had agreed upon a statement to be presented to the Morrow Board. The second recommendation of the statement was straightforward: "Stop direct competition of Government-owned plants with the industry." Lawrance and Keys were the ACOC spokesmen before the board. They repeated their arguments against the NAF, asserting that the manufacturing, design, and experimental work there had been highly detrimental to private industry. Morrow questioned Lawrance about how the manufacturers regarded government competition in the construction of experimental aircraft. Lawrance replied, "It is the opinion of everybody . . . that that should not be done." Even small numbers of experimental models threatened the industry's vital proprietary design rights.[35]

Jerome Hunsaker delivered a carefully reasoned rebuttal to the ACOC's arguments. The NAF and government competition were more symptoms than causes of the industry's woes, he said. What the industry needed most to assure stability was "the enunciation of a far-sighted and sound policy by the Navy Department as to what it wants." A four- or five-year program of aviation development would provide the continuity of orders necessary to turn the industry around, as well as meet the navy's long-term needs. The experimental manufacturing at the NAF that had been excoriated by the ACOC could not provide the uninterrupted flow of orders necessary for the well-being of the trade. Hunsaker concluded that maintaining a large measure of design and technical control in BuAer and offering guidance to the industry through the NAF would in the final analysis work in the best interests of both the navy and the industry.[36]

The Morrow Board finished its hearings and rushed to print its report on 2 December before Congress reconvened and the Lampert Committee issued its findings. The Morrow Board recommendations, as expected, carried considerable weight. They led, for example, to congressional action establishing the Aeronautics Branch in the Department of Commerce, a federal commitment to aviation regulation, and the recognition of proprietary design rights. The board accepted Hunsaker's argument that most of the industry's ills could be traced to the failure of the two services to establish continuity in orders for new aircraft. Based on the board's proposals, the army and navy set up five-year aircraft procurement programs that were funded by Congress in 1926. Naval aviation also benefited in 1926 by the appointment of an assistant secretary of the navy for aeronautics. The most important item in relation to the Naval Aircraft Factory was the Morrow Board's general acceptance of Moffett's compromise. The NAF would continue to function as it had since 1922. Although the board warned that "government competition with the civil industry in production activity" was unacceptable, it agreed that design and experimental work and limited production to obtain yardstick data should go on.[37]

With the resolution of the controversy, it remained to be determined how the Naval Aircraft Factory would fulfill its mission in light of the circumstances of 1925–26. In one sense, little changed as a consequence of the investigations of the Lampert Committee and the Morrow Board. The work force at Philadelphia remained stable at approximately twelve hundred; the experimental work and aircraft construction continued. Nor were any drastic transformations looming on the horizon. Yet it was now obvious that private industry, public opinion, the chief executive, and Congress would significantly affect the activities and personnel of the factory. No longer would the NAF enjoy the relative autonomy it had had since its inception in 1917.

The independence of the NAF was something of a triumph for those in the Construction Corps who had become aeronautical engineering duty officers under BuAer, and it had helped to attract and retain in the service such brilliant individuals as Jerome Hunsaker. Westervelt understood that the restrictions imposed on the NAF would adversely affect both the factory and the careers of those specialist officers who had left the Bureau of Construction and Repair to work under BuAer. He expressed his concern to the Morrow Board in October 1925 that aeronautical engineering could become a dead end for such career officers: "If anything should develop to cause the people who are at the present time in charge of designing and other engineering specialties to drop it, it would place our Air Service in a very serious position." He admitted that he and others were considering leaving the navy because they could see "nothing beyond our present positions."[38]

Westervelt's pessimistic assessment of his and other officers' circumstances as AEDOs was borne out when the navy passed him over for promotion to flag rank in February 1926. The action made it clear to Westervelt that the aeronautical engineering officer would always have limited career opportunities in the service. Westervelt continued his watch as NAF manager for another year before retiring from the service on 14 April 1927. Another loss that year was Hunsaker, who quit the navy for greener pastures at Bell Telephone Laboratories.[39]

To succeed Westervelt as manager of the Naval Aircraft Factory,

Commander Ralph D. Weyerbacher took the helm as the NAF's third manager in September 1927, when he succeeded Captain George C. Westervelt. Weyerbacher had previously served as assistant to the manager under Fred Coburn and had handled the ZR-1 construction at Lakehurst. (72-AF-24049, National Archives)

Moffett in September 1927 selected Commander Ralph D. Weyerbacher, who had been serving as chief engineer at the plant. Weyerbacher was a good choice. Born in Indiana, he had graduated from the Naval Academy in 1909 and, after transferring to the Construction Corps, had received a master's degree in aeronautical engineering from MIT in 1914. During the war years, Weyerbacher had been Fred Coburn's right-hand man at the NAF, responsible as assistant to the manager for many details of the H-16 and F-5-L construction programs. Afterward, he had ably overseen the complex ZR-1 airship project at the NAF and Lakehurst and had earned his naval aviator's wings. Like Moffett, Weyerbacher had a keen political sense, making it reasonably certain that his and the navy's aviation voices would be heard in the cacophony of the late 1920s.[40]

Weyerbacher saw new opportunities for the NAF following the Morrow Board report. In December 1926, he published an article in the *U.S. Naval Institute Proceedings* in which he outlined the service's aviation needs and suggested how the factory could best meet them. A healthy private industry and a busy factory at Philadelphia were not mutually exclusive. The competitive aircraft procurement procedures favored by the industry meant that manufacturers had to provide not only designs but flying prototypes as well. This could be exceedingly costly to the builders and to the government. With no guarantee of production orders, manufacturers had to commit large numbers of skilled workers to the design and construction of prototypes, and the navy sometimes had to pay for the development of airplanes it would never use.[41]

As a solution Weyerbacher proposed a plan that he hoped would satisfy both private industry and the navy while ensuring adequate work for the NAF. He suggested that the manufacturers submit competitive type designs only, the most promising of which would be selected. The NAF would then prepare detailed designs, build prototypes, and oversee the experimental and developmental programs leading to the selection of the contractor for the production order. In this way, Weyerbacher reasoned, the aircraft industry would be relieved of expensive design and prototype responsibilities and still reap the profits of series production. In turn, the NAF would be able to retain its technical staff and expand its experimental and research facilities. Equally important, it would become, under Weyerbacher's proposal, the navy's central flight test installation.[42]

In retrospect, it is easy to see that Weyerbacher's scheme, attractive as it was in many respects, was unworkable. Clement Keys's earlier protest to the Lampert Committee that design, engineering, and the construction of prototypes "are the airplane industry" was indicative of the deep-seated opposition of the industry to any infringement on its proprietary design rights. Nor was there much encouragement from within the service itself. When Weyerbacher sought to consolidate all flight testing at the NAF in June 1928, his superiors agreed that centralizing this activity was an excellent idea, but they disagreed that the NAF was the best place to do so. Emory Land thought the naval air station at Anacostia should remain the principal navy test field because of its proximity to BuAer in Washington. In denying Weyerbacher's request, he said current plans did not "warrant the increase of the Navy Aircraft Factory as recommended."[43]

Intraservice opposition to expansion of the Naval Aircraft Factory's activities came also from the commandant of the Philadelphia Navy Yard, Rear Admiral Thomas P. Magruder. The delineation of responsibility between the navy yard commandant and the NAF manager had always been murky, and it was generally understood that the former was to deal only with matters of policy affecting both installations. Magruder had written to Secretary Wilbur outlining his efforts to eliminate the separate accounting, supply, and transportation organizations at the NAF. Because Westervelt had consistently rejected Magruder's overtures, the commandant concluded that personal obstinacy was the chief impediment to rationalizing at least some of the overlapping functions of the cotenants at League Island. Magruder concluded by asking Wilbur for specific authority to combine the accounting offices of the navy yard and the NAF.[44]

Magruder's request touched off a feud with Moffett over the independence of the NAF within the bureau system. Although Moffett had been willing to make concessions on the factory for the sake of harmony with the aircraft industry, he was absolutely against surrendering any of its responsibilities to the navy yard. Moffett pointed to investigations in 1922 and 1923 that had explored the question of merging the functions of the two organizations and had recommended against doing so. He defended the separate management of the NAF as essential for the continued development of naval aviation and worried that any consolidation would lead to a loss of critical funds. Distinct accounting procedures were needed at the NAF if it were to continue its yardstick function, and the factory's supply department had evolved to the stage where it was vital to maintaining and equipping the navy's air arm.[45]

Moffett emerged victorious in the struggle with Magruder when the Navy Department decreed in March 1927 that consolidation of the accounting and supply departments was unwarranted. But the fight was not over. Magruder next objected to the assignment of Weyerbacher as manager of the NAF and made his own recommendation to the Bureau of Navigation of an officer to replace Westervelt. Moffett responded in a strongly worded letter that as chief of the Bureau of Aeronautics he had a "decisive" role to play in naming the officer in charge of the NAF and that any suggestions the navy yard commandant might have for the position should be routed through the bureau chief's office: "I think you will agree with me that the Manager of the Factory should be a man who has as much knowledge of Aviation as possible as well as experience in Navy Yard work and Aviation technical matters. . . . I think, considering everything, that Weyerbacher is the best of those available for the position at the present time." Magruder apologized for failing to consult Moffett and reluctantly assented to Weyerbacher's appointment.[46]

Moffett's success in preventing any dilution of the functions of the NAF and the authority of his bureau over the appointment of key personnel, combined with the reconciliation of private aircraft manufacturers and the government to his 1922 compromise, secured the place of the factory in the naval aviation establishment. By 1928, a balance had been achieved in naval aircraft procurement, and there was little incentive on the part of either naval authorities or private industry to upset it. Equilibrium came from the confluence of several factors: the 1925 Kelly Air Mail Act providing for the establishment of contract airmail routes stimulated sales of aircraft to private carriers; congressional appropriations for the army and navy 1926 five-year programs substantially restored the military aircraft market; and the Bureau of Air Commerce, created within the Department of Commerce in 1926, encouraged normally cautious businessmen to invest in aviation enterprises.[47] With the return of prosperity, private industry was more willing to tolerate a continued role by the NAF in limited production, design, and experimental aircraft construction. At the same time, it served little purpose to risk setting off a new round of debate by adding to the factory's activities, especially in sensitive areas that appeared to threaten the understanding that had been reached on design rights. In the climate of 1928, such ideas as Weyerbacher's could not be seriously considered.

Moffett was able to preserve the basic functions of the Naval Aircraft Factory during the 1920s primarily because of a general comprehension in Washington that the installation was important to ensuring long-term control over the navy's aircraft requirements. Moffett and others believed that the public good—that is, the acquisition of suitable aircraft at the most reasonable cost—was best served by integrating the NAF's activities with those of the private aircraft industry. The degree of that integration and the scale and nature of the work at the factory led to charges by the manufacturers of government competition, but during the 1920s and through succeeding decades the Naval Aircraft Factory continued to operate in uneasy partnership with private enterprise to meet the navy's aviation procurement demands.

5

Charting New Courses

Rear Admiral Moffett had reached an accommodation with private industry that was secure as long as the Naval Aircraft Factory concentrated on activities that seemed not to be in competition with private industry. The VE-7, DH-4, and PT projects, part of the highly visible and much-publicized production role of the NAF, ran down in 1922, giving way to the design and development of airplanes for production by civilian manufacturers. Central to the NAF's new mission, and oriented toward cooperation with the private sector, was a long-term and technically demanding program to perfect metal aircraft construction. Equally noteworthy were a multiplicity of other activities, including the factory's participation in racing, and its testing, supply, storage, and support functions.

It is important to understand that Moffett's policy did not preclude the manufacture of airplanes at the Naval Aircraft Factory. Rather, the emphasis was on assisting private aircraft builders with modifications and augmenting their production, particularly if those manufacturers were new to the business or had limited plant capacity. Representative of this policy was the Douglas DT-2 torpedo bomber. Designed and built by the fledgling company established by Donald Douglas in Santa Monica, California, the DT-2 was powered by a 400-horsepower Liberty, had a maximum takeoff weight of 7,293 pounds and wings 50 feet long encompassing an area of 707 square feet. In February 1922, the Bureau of Aeronautics authorized the NAF to manufacture half a dozen of the airplanes. A year later, the factory engineered a folding-wing system for landplane versions of the DT-2, and twenty-four of the aircraft underwent such conversion at Philadelphia. In 1924, the NAF modified four DT-2s as DT-4s with 525-horsepower Wright T-2 engines. Although better than the Liberty, the T-2 was inferior to the air-cooled radials then gaining favor in the navy. Still, the NAF persisted with variations of the engine in the DT aircraft; one DT-4 became a DT-5 when it received a geared Wright T-2.[1]

As the need arose by 1925 for an improved torpedo bomber, BuAer designed a convertible biplane powered by twin Wright 525-horsepower R-1750 engines. Designated the XTN-1, the airplane had a maximum takeoff weight of 9,760 pounds with conventional landing gear and 10,535 pounds with floats. The wing area was 886 square feet within a span of 57 feet. A $130,000 order for the prototype of the airplane went to the Naval Aircraft Factory in May 1925, with delivery coming in early 1927. Meanwhile, Douglas had received a contract for three of the airplanes, designated T2D-1, after which the company received orders in 1927 and 1930 for twenty-seven more.[2] The arrangement whereby the NAF bore the burden of bringing the torpedo plane design through the prototype stages, leaving a private manufacturer to profit from production orders, set a pattern for other aircraft.

The NAF also constructed small numbers of airplanes to fill specific training and operational requirements. By the beginning of November 1923, the factory had shipped three N2N-1 twin-float primary trainers to the navy's principal flight instruction center at Pensacola, Florida. Another airplane was the TG single-float biplane gunnery trainer, of which the factory manufactured five in 1924. Three NO-1s, designed and built at the factory in 1924, conformed to a BuAer requirement for a three-seat observation aircraft.[3]

Not only did the NAF direct its attention to torpedo bombers, it also played a major role in the design and development of dive bombers. After the marines had demonstrated the effectiveness of dive bombing against guerrillas in Haiti in 1919 and Nicaragua in 1927, the navy determined to adopt similar tactics using heavy bombs against large warships. The concept for the airplane originated in 1927 at BuAer, emerging as a dive bomber capable of carrying a thousand-pound bomb or torpedo and able to withstand the aerodynamic stresses of vertical dives and pullouts. BuAer

The XTN-1 twin-engine torpedo plane as it appeared during flight tests in 1927. The Douglas company produced a version of this airplane, designated the T2D-1. (80-G-460607, National Archives)

invited both the Glenn L. Martin Company and the NAF to submit detail designs for the airplane based on general designs promulgated by the bureau. On 18 June 1928, the NAF received a $60,000 project order for the construction of a prototype, powered by a 525-horsepower Wright R-1750 and given the designation XT2N-1. The aircraft had a maximum takeoff weight of 5,282 pounds, a wing area of 416 square feet within a span of 41 feet, and carried two Lewis guns mounted on a scarf ring aft and two machine guns fixed to the upper wing. The design featured an all-metal monocoque fuselage.[4]

Problems might have been anticipated with an aircraft that broke new ground, but the XT2N-1 seemed to have more than its share. Shortly after the project began, wind tunnel tests at the NACA's Langley Memorial Aeronautical Laboratory revealed that dive bombers had to have horizontal stabilizers and elevators stressed for much higher G loadings than had previously been considered necessary. As a result, the NAF had to redesign the tail group of the XT2N-1. A long series of change orders followed approval of the

A view of the NAF's XT2N-1 dive bomber in 1930. A large, single-engine aircraft with an all-metal monocoque fuselage, the XT2N-1 was designed to deliver a one-thousand-pound bomb against naval targets. (80-G-462291, National Archives)

mockup in March 1929. Change orders are the bane of an aircraft manufacturer. Coming from the "customer"—that is, BuAer—they often require redesign of parts and components and have a snowballing effect on other aspects of the total development project. The original July completion date of the XT2N-1 passed, as did subsequent deadlines. In March 1930 the airplane at last got into the air, and then it suffered from engine cooling problems, leaks in the integral fuel tanks, and structural weaknesses in tail components that limited the angle of dive and pullout loads. Further tests at Anacostia reaffirmed these defects, as well as problems with the position and feel of the cockpit controls. Although the bureau invited the NAF to submit estimates for producing twelve airplanes, Martin won a contract for twelve BM-1s, based on the company's XT5M-1 prototype.[5]

A critical element in the design and construction of the XT2N-1 was its all-metal monocoque fuselage—it was the first NAF-built airplane with this important structural innovation. The NAF's background in metal aircraft structures included the Giant Boat in 1920–21, which was to have had steel wing spars and duralumin ribs, and the fabrication of the *Shenandoah* in 1921–23. Equally important, experimentation of this sort meshed with Moffett's perception of the factory as the navy's principal aviation development installation and did not appear to constitute direct competition with private industry.

To many it seemed obvious by the 1920s that steel and aluminum alloys were superior to wood and other materials in aircraft manufacture, but metal presented difficult technical problems, and its application to aircraft came slowly. Ralph Weyerbacher argued for the use of metal in the construction of flying boat hulls. Not only would the material bring immediate weight savings, but metal-hulled flying boats would not have the water-soakage problems of aircraft with wooden hulls. A wooden-hulled flying boat absorbed a considerable amount of water under normal operating conditions. Flight Lieutenant D. Lucking, a Britisher, said that he had weighed an eighteen-thousand-pound flying boat after it had spent several months in a shed; following a short time in the water, the airplane weighed six hundred pounds more. After even more time, a flying boat could absorb up to 10 percent of its weight in water, an intolerable increase that could seriously degrade the airplane's performance. Metal wings and floats offered additional weight economies in flying boats.[6]

But weight was not the only reason for turning to metal for aircraft construction. Cost also had to be taken into consideration. Dick Richardson argued that though the initial cost of metal was six or seven times greater than that of wood, the service life of a metal airplane was up to five times that of its wooden counterpart. Weyerbacher added that the price of spruce had skyrocketed by the end of World War I and would go much higher in the event of another major conflict. Nor could a reliable supply of the material sustain the voracious appetite of a wartime industry. Wood rotted, warped, split, and could not be joined or formed as easily as light alloys; there was considerable wastage in the shaping of finished wood aircraft parts; and because of variation in different stocks of wood and difficulties testing their strengths, engineers had to design in higher safety factors than were necessary with metal.[7]

This is not to say that metals were an unqualified boon to aircraft design and construction. High material cost was an obstacle, and another was the need for expensive tools, jigs, and dies. Especially important was close attention to protection from corrosion and avoiding contact between dissimilar metals where an electrical potential could lead to deterioration. Metal fatigue was trouble-some, and thin metal sections, especially in wings, were prone to compressive buckling and failure.[8]

Not only were there cost penalties and other factors that had to be taken into consideration, but it was not clear to engineers in the early 1920s what type of metal aircraft construction was best. One possibility was mixed construction whereby welded steel tubes replaced wooden members in the fuselage and aerodynamic surfaces of airplanes; doped fabric covered the airplane in the conventional manner. A second alternative was mixed steel and aluminum alloy construction. In this case, the fuselage and other major components were steel while the covering and other less stressed portions of the airframe were light alloy. The major problem with this method was electrolytic action and corrosion in areas where the two metals came together. All-aluminum construction was the most attractive method of fabrication to the navy, but it pushed the limits of metallurgy at the time, and because aluminum could not readily be welded, designers had to make allowances for large numbers of riveted joints.[9]

For all these reasons, the NAF took a methodical approach to the design and construction of metal aircraft. The factory saw the most possibilities in all-aluminum construction and borrowed heavily from the German and British experience. Between 1903 and 1914, German and British metallurgists had made significant progress in the development of duralumin, an aluminum alloy containing 3 to 5 percent copper, 0.4 to 1 percent manganese, and 0.3 to 0.6 percent magnesium. This remarkable material could be cut, pressed, forged, or cast into many shapes. Then it was heat treated and aged to yield a tensile strength comparable to that of mild steel. German and British rigid airships incorporated duralumin in their construction, and the Germans pushed ahead with the use of the material in airplanes. The experience of the Dornier, Junkers, and Rohrbach companies during and shortly after World War I most influenced the course followed by the Naval Aircraft Factory with metal aircraft design and construction.[10]

The exchange of information on metal aircraft fabrication between the factory and German builders began in earnest in January 1921 when Jerome Hunsaker reported on the advances that had been made abroad. In May 1921, Admiral Taylor authorized the purchase of a Dornier CsII all-metal flying boat. The Dornier, a single-engine cabin monoplane, underwent extensive flight tests and structural analyses at the NAF in 1921–22. The factory maintained its connections with the Dornier company through the end of the decade. A D.1 *Falke* (Falcon) all-metal, high-wing monoplane fighter was tested at Philadelphia in March 1922, and in September 1929, the NAF completed the assembly of two 31,120-pound, all-metal Dornier Super Wal flying boats from components shipped from Germany. Both airplanes were flown at Philadelphia before being leased to William B. Stout's Detroit and Cleveland Airlines. This arrangement, which Commander Ralph Weyerbacher had concluded with Stout, provided a graphic demonstration of cooperation between the NAF and industry and gave the factory valuable exposure to the latest advances in German all-metal aircraft construction.[11]

Some of the earliest experience with metal construction at the NAF came as a result of the work of Dick Richardson with duralumin floats. Richardson reported in 1924 that few private firms in the United States had done much with the material, and he thought the NAF could play an important development role. Under Richardson, the factory designed and constructed a series of duralumin floats for the Curtiss N-9. In the course of the work, Richardson and his colleagues learned of the need to concentrate loads in the bottom plating of the floats and to distribute those forces equally through the structure. Another lesson was keeping the form of construction as simple as possible to hold the line on costs and to facilitate corrosion protection and inspection.[12]

In the course of his work with duralumin floats, Richardson found that the considerable weight savings (seventy pounds compared to a wooden N-9 float) came at a premium. Typically, a metal float cost about $7,000, whereas a wooden float was only about $900. With more experience in design and construction, the cost of metal floats could be significantly reduced, but Richardson cautioned that because of materials and fabrication costs, metal units would always be more expensive. He also admitted that saltwater corrosion caused "some difficulty" with the floats. This observation proved to be portentous, but at the time Richardson was confident that better methods of applying protective coatings would solve the problem.[13]

In addition to floats, the Naval Aircraft Factory explored the potential of duralumin in the design and construction of wings. One of the first efforts by the NAF was an experimental wing built around a box section fabricated from duralumin sheet. Weighing 239 pounds, excluding the aileron, the wing easily bore up under the weight of a 200-pound man walking on its upper surface. As the NAF progressed in its experiments with metal wings, there was close liaison with Charles Ward Hall, a graduate of Cornell University and president of Charles Ward Hall, Inc., of New York City. In May 1920, Hall contracted to manufacture two sets of metal wings for an HS-3 single-engine flying boat. In their final configuration, the Hall wings incorporated steel spars, but all other parts, including the ribs and leading and trailing edges, were of stamped duralumin sheet. Hall shipped one set of wings to the Naval Aircraft Factory for evaluation in January 1922, with another set following in April. The saving in weight was considerable. A wooden HS-3 wing weighed 1,314 pounds, whereas the Hall wing weighed 851 pounds. After static tests of the wings, the factory fitted them to one of its HS-3s and immediately found that the wings contributed to a significant increase in the airplane's performance.[14]

Yet it was a big step from floats and cooperative ventures with private manufacturers of metal wings to a complete duralumin airplane. Work on the factory's first all-metal aircraft began after the NAF received orders from Admiral Moffett in April 1922 to design and build two marine expeditionary airplanes, one with conventional landing gear and the other with twin duralumin floats. Moffett emphasized that the job was experimental and "primarily initiated for the purpose of developing metal construction for naval airplanes." The two-seat aircraft, known as the NM-1, had a maximum takeoff weight of 4,190 pounds in its landplane version and 4,440 pounds with floats. Powered by a 325-horsepower Packard, the NM-1 made its first flight in December 1924. The design closely followed that of Dornier, with transverse duralumin bulkheads braced by stamped structural members reinforcing the fuse-

The NM-1 of 1924–25 was the Naval Aircraft Factory's first effort to design and construct an all-metal airplane. Note the beaded duralumin covering of the fuselage and vertical tail surfaces. (72-AF-34211, National Archives)

lage, the beaded duralumin covering of which provided additional strength. Wings and tail surfaces also featured metal skins.[15]

The NM-1 was not successful, although the surviving material does not make it clear why. Most likely there was a problem with the duralumin covering of the fuselage and aerodynamic surfaces of the airplane. By 1924, the Junkers company had found that great care had to be taken not to overstress duralumin while it was being cold worked because the metal could become brittle and prone to corrosion. The firm warned that corrugating duralumin sheet often created this problem and consequently the company had had to develop special machinery to stamp the corrugations without damaging the metal. If the NAF stamped the duralumin parts or the beads in the sheet used for the fuselage of the NM-1 without knowledge of the Junkers experience, it is possible that corrosion developed within a short time that could have been severe enough to jeopardize the structural integrity of the airplane.[16]

At first considered a "miracle metal," duralumin as an aircraft material began to exhibit such alarming deficiencies by 1926 that Lieutenant Commander Lawrence B. Richardson of BuAer said, "Grave doubts were raised in many quarters that the use of the alloys was justified at all." The most immediately worrisome of these problems was surface corrosion. In some airplanes, areas of the fuselage where duralumin sheets joined one another showed signs of severe surface corrosion after only a year. Duralumin wing ribs, which had many crevices where moisture could accumulate, also deteriorated so that sometimes the entire wing had to be scrapped. A saltwater environment magnified all these problems. C. G. Grey, the outspoken editor of the British journal *Aeroplane*, summed up the situation in 1924: "We have had a belief in England, and I think it is general in most of Europe, that duralumin could not be trusted within smelling distance of seawater."[17]

At the NAF, technicians under Roy G. Miller developed improved means of protecting duralumin from surface corrosion. Most important was thorough cleaning of the surface to remove grease or other contaminants and roughening it so the paint would adhere better. Every part had to be so treated, usually before assembly, to ensure complete protection. Ordinary varnishes or paints were usually inadequate for duralumin. Instead, the metal had to be coated with an anodic primer containing red lead or zinc chromate, followed by a baked enamel finish. For interior surfaces, a bitumin-based paint pigmented with aluminum powder adhered well and provided excellent long-term protection.[18]

Surface corrosion was only one form of deterioration to which duralumin was prone. Another was intercrystalline embrittlement. This insidious phenomenon penetrated deep into the metal, tracing the microscopic crystalline patterns of the material. Usually the corrosion first manifested itself in small paint blisters or surface discolorations; by the time these made their appearance, the duralumin had already seriously corroded. Thin duralumin sheets were most susceptible to this form of deterioration, which could quickly destroy the ductility and tensile strength of the metal. Researchers at the NAF, led by T. Watson Downes and Horace C. Knerr, tackled this difficult metallurgical puzzle in 1925. They found that some of the duralumin girders of the *Shenandoah* had corroded, and they concluded that the culprit was intercrystalline embrittlement. Some suspected that this deterioration had contributed to the crash of the airship in 1925, but tests by the Bureau of Standards revealed that it was not sufficient to weaken the structure of the aircraft. Upon inspection, girders in the *Los Angeles* were found to exhibit some of the same problems. In connection with this work, the NAF hosted a meeting of the Committee on Materials of the NACA in 1925 that outlined a research program intended to solve the problem. Over the next two years, the NAF and other research organizations found that prevention of such deterioration involved proper heat treatment of the duralumin and more attention to quality control at the manufacturer's plant.[19]

Ultimately a material known as Alclad provided the corrosion resistance sought by the navy. Introduced by Alcoa in 1927 as a result of the work of Edgar H. Dix, Jr., a metallurgist in the company's Pittsburgh research laboratory and formerly chief of the metallurgical branch of the army air service's engineering division at McCook Field, Alclad was a metallurgical tour de force. It consisted of duralumin 17ST sandwiched between layers of 99.9 percent pure aluminum. The Alclad ingot was rolled under heavy pressure to assure a permanent chemical and physical bond between the two metals, and the resulting material could be forged, drawn, cut, and formed into any shape, and it still retained its protective coating of pure aluminum. Remarkably, Alclad was "self-healing." Electrolytic action between the pure metal and the alloy extended the corrosion protection to areas where the metal had been sheared, rivet holes cut, or the pure aluminum coating had been scraped off. Alclad 17ST had about 10 percent less tensile strength than ordinary 17ST duralumin, and it was marginally more expensive, but those were small sacrifices to make in return for the material's superior corrosion resistance.[20]

The most dramatic representation of the progress made at the Naval Aircraft Factory in the design and development of metal airplanes during the 1920s came with the PN flying boat program. The PN series of aircraft evolved from progressive improvements to the F-5-L. NAF engineers worked out modifications to the original design, including a new, larger vertical fin, a balanced rudder, and weight-saving detail improvements. Two F-6-Ls incorporating these changes left the factory in late 1918 and early 1919; subsequent tests of these craft demonstrated the superiority of the new tail surfaces, and F-5-Ls in service later received the modifications. Under a new designation system in 1921, the F-5-Ls and F-6-Ls became PN (Patrol, Naval Aircraft Factory)-5s and PN-6s respectively, although the airplanes retained their old designations in practice.[21]

In January 1923, BuAer authorized the NAF to construct two new flying boats (numbers A-6616 and A-6617) based on the F-5-L. With Henry S. Cocklin as project engineer, the new aircraft, which were designated PN-7s, took shape in the NAF shops. Outwardly these airplanes differed little from their predecessors, but there were important modifications. Their maximum takeoff weight was 14,203 pounds and their wing area was 1,217 square feet within a span of 72 feet, 10 inches. Wright T-2 engines with capacities of 525 horsepower replaced the obsolescent Liberties, and a more efficient USA 27 high-lift airfoil design was used in the wings. Though still of fabric-covered wooden construction, the wings were thicker and shorter than those of the F-5-Ls, and there were fewer drag-inducing external braces and wires.[22]

By mid-November 1923, preliminary test flights of the first PN-7 had been made at Philadelphia, with official trials following in December. Other than minor engine troubles and adjustments to the airplane's tail surfaces, the tests proceeded smoothly and the craft went into service with the Scouting Fleet at Hampton Roads in early 1924. Material shortages, however, delayed the completion and delivery of the second PN-7 to Hampton Roads until August 1924.[23] Although the PN-7s had much better all-round performance than the F-5-Ls, the airplanes broke little new technical ground and were largely transitional to more advanced types.

Of significance in follow-on PN aircraft was the increased employment of metal in the hulls and wings. BuAer authorized the NAF in August 1923 to construct a PN-type hull of welded steel tubing covered by duralumin. When the factory received orders in early 1924 to build the airplane, Westervelt decided it was "a major alteration" of the original model and recommended a new designation—PN-8. The bureau concurred, and in June authorized a second example of the airplane.[24]

Less than two months passed before BuAer decided that the PN-8s should be extensively modified to augment their range and payload.

Moffett explained to Westervelt that the bureau had been drawing up plans incorporating the changes and wanted to know how these would affect the work at Philadelphia. Westervelt, who understood how disruptive such late change orders were, answered that "it would be extremely bad policy" to alter the airplanes at that juncture because it meant scrapping a considerable amount of material and delaying completion of the two aircraft. To Westervelt, it made more sense to complete the PN-8s substantially as is and to work the desired changes into a third airplane, built from the keel up as a PN-9 model. Dick Richardson worked out an understanding whereby the first airplane (number A-6799) would be finished as originally intended, and the second (number A-6878), on which construction had not gone as far, would be completed as a PN-9. After brief service tests, the PN-8 could be rebuilt to PN-9 specifications.[25]

Westervelt pushed through the completion of the PN-8 by early 1925. The airplane had a maximum takeoff weight of 13,925 pounds. This was only a 2 percent weight savings over the PN-7, but Dick Richardson estimated that the metal hull resulted in a 500-pound weight reduction in comparison with the standard wood hull. When trials began at Philadelphia, however, the airplane "was subjected to a great deal of vibration" from the twin Wright 525-horsepower T-3 engines. Rather than try to solve the engine problems and prolong tests of what was basically an interim aircraft, the factory converted number A-6799 to a PN-9. One of the most important changes was fitting the airplane with 525-horsepower Packard water-cooled V-12s. The Packard, with an output equal to that of the Wright T-3, was more than 300 pounds lighter and considerably more compact. Installation of the new Packards involved new radiators and extensively redesigned engine nacelles, which caused postponement of flight tests until April.[26]

Tardy delivery of engines from Packard and a variety of minor though annoying problems held up work on the second airplane, number A-6878. This aircraft had a maximum takeoff weight of 19,600 pounds within the same overall dimensions as the PN-7 and the PN-8. Flight tests, which Westervelt had hoped to begin in late March, finally took place in April, and they were disappointing. The factory technicians wrestled with persistent oil line problems, and during a short flight on 15 April a broken fuel line caused a small fire. On another flight three days later, ignition problems forced a hazardous night landing on the Delaware. Later tests revealed shortcomings in the Packards' NAF-designed and built cooling systems. Dismayed, Westervelt told Moffett, "The date which the Bureau has assigned for the shipment of these planes cannot be met."[27]

Under ordinary circumstances, the troubles with the PN-9s would not have been of major consequence, but Moffett and others in the bureau had made a commitment earlier in the year for a flight from the West Coast to Hawaii to demonstrate publicly the importance of naval aviation and the capabilities of the service's long-range flying boats. It became imperative to have the PNs tested and ready for delivery to San Diego by early June if the transpacific flight was to come off as scheduled in late August or early September.[28]

The critical factor was endurance. The PN-9s had been built to achieve an eighteen-hundred-nautical-mile range; the distance to Hawaii was twenty-one hundred nautical miles, which was the longest continuous overwater stretch on the globe. To span this distance, the PN-9s needed to stay in the air for thirty hours. Therefore, in late April Westervelt concentrated on a thirty-hour test flight with number A-6878. After half a dozen failed attempts because of a profusion of mechanical ills, on the morning of 1 May, Lieutenants Clarence H. ("Dutch") Schildhauer and J. R. Kyle, Jr., with L. M. Woolson of the Packard company aboard to monitor engine performance, took the big flying boat up for another try. Through the rest of the day and into the night the airplane droned up and down the Delaware. Shortly before 1400 hours on 2 May, the craft alighted on the river after spending twenty-eight hours and thirty-five minutes in the air and setting a new endurance record for flying boats.[29]

Although the flight had fallen short of the thirty-hour goal and had revealed deficiencies with the PN-9's cooling system and excessive fuel consumption, most were certain the mission would succeed. Noting that the 1,930 nautical miles covered was "not sufficient in still air for the [Hawaii] flight," Emory Land said modifications would be effected and was "confident . . . the success of the flight is assured." Dick Richardson added his belief that with a favorable tail wind there would be an adequate "margin of safety on this flight" to reach Hawaii. Still, he cautioned, the attempt

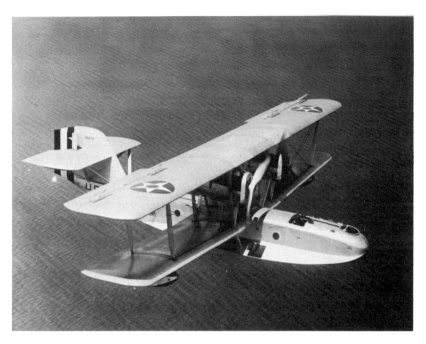

PN-9 (no. A-6878). First flown in April 1925, this airplane was the first
NAF flying boat with an all-metal hull. In May 1925, the airplane accom-
plished a twenty-eight-and-a-half-hour endurance flight at Philadelphia.
Three months later, John Rodgers commanded A-6878 on the failed West
Coast–Hawaii flight. (80-G-4302, National Archives)

would not be without risk and would demand the utmost in flying
skills.[30]

Buoyed by this optimism, the NAF crated the two PN-9s and
shipped them to San Diego in June for the West Coast–Hawaii flight.
During reassembly and testing, Commander John Rodgers, who had
been selected to lead the flight, struggled to get the aircraft into
shape and expended great energy speeding up the delivery of spare
parts from Philadelphia. Chronically leaky radiators were his major
worry. Those supplied by the NAF were too lightly constructed to
withstand sustained engine vibrations, and Rodgers decided to
replace the NAF units with radiators from the Flexo Company in
Los Angeles. With their new radiators, the PN-9s took off for San
Francisco, the jumping-off point for the flight. On 31 August, the
flying boats departed from San Francisco for Hawaii. Number

A-6799 went down with engine problems less than five hours into the flight; Rodgers, commanding number A-6878, pressed on for twenty more hours until his fuel gave out 1,840 nautical miles from the West Coast and more than 200 nautical miles short of Hawaii. He and his crew survived nine days at sea before making landfall on Kauai.[31]

In retrospect, the attempted West Coast–Hawaii flight was premature, even foolhardy, given the known range limitations of the PN-9s and ignorance of the weather patterns over the route. Yet the airplanes themselves earned the praise of nearly everyone; especially impressive was the toughness of their duralumin hulls, which stood up to days of pounding at sea without major damage. BuAer continued the PN development program at the NAF, emphasizing the use of metal construction and employing more powerful and efficient engines. Emory Land made it clear in June 1925 that the bureau's primary objective was the "development for service use of the PN-9 type" as a replacement for the venerable F-5-L.[32]

As the PN-9s were getting into the air in April 1925, BuAer took the first steps toward the all-metal flying boat when it authorized the NAF to design and manufacture a set of duralumin wings for a PN-type aircraft. Six weeks later came a project order from the bureau for two new airplanes to be designated PN-10s. These were to be of duralumin construction throughout, except for the conventional fabric covering of the wings and tail surfaces. Considerable weight savings resulted. Weyerbacher estimated that the PN-10 hull, at 1,810 pounds, was 530 pounds or 23 percent lighter than the hull of the PN-7, and that figure did not take into account the additional weight of the PN-7 hull caused by soakage. The PN-10 wings, weighing 1,465 pounds, represented a further savings of 24 percent over the wings of the PN-7.[33]

Expectations in Washington that the Naval Aircraft Factory could move swiftly toward production of the all-metal flying boat in 1925–26 were soon dashed. Westervelt reported in early 1926 that "our metal work in connection with [the] PN-10 . . . has not been going so very well." Delays in the delivery of duralumin from Alcoa and specification changes by the bureau had created "a very bad jam" in the metal shop at the NAF. The factory also encountered difficulties with fabrication and assembly of the thin metal ribs and other parts of the PN-10 wings, further setting back the completion date of the aircraft. When it became apparent that there was no hope of completing the PN-10s by the original deadline of 1 June, BuAer, with a great deal of reluctance, allowed the NAF to fit wooden wings to the PN-10s "in order to get the planes in the air . . . at the earliest practicable date." One officer conceded that this was "a step backward," but it was necessary to flight test the new geared Packard engines and other components of the aircraft while the factory sorted out its difficulties with the metal wings.[34]

The bureau's decision to go ahead with the PN-10s, even though they would have to fly with wooden wings, proved justified. PN-10 number A-7029 was finally test flown on 21 June 1926. It and a companion, number A-7028, had numerous teething problems. Their Packards suffered gearing breakdowns, and it took weeks to achieve the optimal settings for the three-blade adjustable-pitch Standard Steel propellers. Meanwhile, Westervelt had to postpone completion of the PN-10 metal wings from late March to late June 1927.[35]

Westervelt's concern that he might have to lay off skilled workers unless the factory received more flying boat work led to the authorization of two more PN-10s in the summer of 1926. These airplanes, numbers A-7383 and A-7384, were to have metal wings and were to be finished by the middle of July 1927. Delays ensued when Packard announced it could not deliver the four engines until September, thus setting back the maiden flight of A-7383, the factory's first all-metal flying boat, until 30 November 1927.[36]

All four PN-10s put in extended service as flying test beds. Numbers A-7028 and A-7029 completed a flight from Hampton Roads to the Naval Air Station, Coco Solo in the Canal Zone, in November 1926, stopping only in Cuba along the way. In August 1927, A-7028 spent more than twenty continuous hours in the air. There was no question about the ruggedness of the airplanes' duralumin hulls and wings, but their liquid-cooled engines never matched expectations in service. When BuAer decided to compare the performance of liquid-cooled and air-cooled engines, the NAF fitted two 525-horsepower Wright R-1750 Cyclone radials to A-7384; in May 1928, A-7383 received a pair of 525-horsepower Pratt and Whitney R-1690 Hornet radials. The radials offered a 130-pound weight advantage over the Packards, but more significant, they promised deliverance from the persistent cooling system troubles

The NAF built four PN-10s in 1926–27. The first pair had wooden wings;
the second batch were the factory's first flying boats with metal wings.
When fitted with radial engines, the PN-10s were redesignated PN-12s.
This photograph shows a PN-12. (80-G-4870, National Archives)

that had plagued the liquid-cooled engine installations. Subsequent
service convinced BuAer that the air-cooled radial power plant was
superior to the liquid-cooled inline for large patrol flying boats and
other aircraft.[37]

In its infinite wisdom BuAer redesignated all the PN-10s as
PN-12s when they underwent modifications and received radial
engines in 1928–29. Contemporary naval aviators and latter-day
historians were confused because the designation PN-11 went to a
more advanced aircraft. The PN-12s continued to put in exceptional
performances. At Philadelphia on 3–5 May 1928, Lieutenant Arthur
Gavin, a veteran of the 1925 Hawaii flight, along with Lieutenant
Zeus Soucek, shattered all previous flying boat endurance marks
with a thirty-six-hour flight in the Wright R-1750-powered A-7384.
More records fell. On 26 June 1928, the Pratt and Whitney R-1690-
powered A-7383 lifted a two-thousand-kilogram payload to 15,426

feet and the following day reached nearly 19,600 feet with one thousand kilograms.[38]

The PN-12 was still not the definitive design for a flying boat to succeed the F-5-L. On 19 April 1927, BuAer authorized the NAF to build another flying boat incorporating changes brought to light thus far by the experimental program. The bureau designated the new aircraft as PN-11 and assigned it number A-7527. This airplane was, like the later PN-10s (PN-12s) of all-metal construction, but it had a longer and wider hull without the broad sponsons of the previous models, and its maximum takeoff weight was 16,870 pounds, compared to the 18,069 pounds of the PN-10 (PN-12) Moreover, the PN-11 fuel tanks were integral with the hull structure, and the airplane featured a 1,154-square-foot wing with a revised airfoil section. Visibly the most distinguishing feature from earlier PNs was the airplane's twin vertical tail surfaces and rudders.[39]

At the bureau's urging, Ralph Weyerbacher, the new manager of the Naval Aircraft Factory, spurred construction of the airplane, but its estimated completion date slipped from March to September 1928 despite Washington's importunities. When the aircraft finally began flight tests on the Delaware during the second week of October, it suffered from inadequate oil cooling of its Pratt and Whitney R-1690 Hornets, and some time passed before the NAF corrected a severe propeller vibration problem. At Anacostia for more trials, the airplane developed fuel leaks and its engines overheated, much to the exasperation of those like Dick Richardson in the bureau who wanted to move quickly into production of the flying boat.[40]

Gradually the NAF overcame the growing pains of the PN-11. At Weyerbacher's insistence, the factory received an order for a second example (number A-8006) in January 1928, and the airplane, designated XPN-11, made its initial flight in early April 1929. With a maximum takeoff weight of 17,900 pounds, this aircraft flew first powered by Wright R-1820–64 Cyclones, but under the new designation XP4N-1, it received a variety of engine and propeller combinations. Two more PN-11s (redesignated XP4N-2s) followed under an order in May 1929, bringing the total of the type built at the NAF to four.[41] For information on the entire PN series see Table 1.

Table 1. PN-Series and PN-Based Flying Boats, 1923–1931

Model	BuNos.	Years	No. Mfrd.	Engines	MTOW* (pounds)	Wing area (square feet)	Speed (miles per hour)
PN-7	A-6616-A6617	1923–24	2	2 525 hp. Wright T-2s	14,203	1,217	113
PN-8	A-6799	1925	1	2 525 hp. Wright T-3s	13,925	1,217	106
PN-9	A-6878	1925	1	2 525 hp. V-1500s Packard 1A-1500s	19,600	1,217	115
PN-10	A-7028-A-7029 A-7383-A-7384	1926–27	4	2 525 hp. V-1500s Packard 2A-1500s A-7384 (as PN-12): Wright R-1750s A-7383 (as PN-12): P&W R-1690s	18,069	1,217	114
PN-11	A-7527	1928	1	2 525 hp. P&W R-1690s	16,870	1,154	128
XPN-11	A-8006	1929	1	2 575 hp. Wright R-1820-64s	17,900	1,154	128
XP4N-2	A-8583-A-8484	1931	2	2 575 hp. Wright R-1820-64s	17,595	1,154	128
PD-1	A-7979-A-8003	1929	25	2 525 hp. Wright R-1750s	14,837	1,162	121
XPH-1	A-8004	1929	1	2 537 hp. Wright GR-1750s	13,228	1,180	124
PM-1	A-8289-A-8313 A-8477-A-8481	1930–31	30	2 525 hp. Wright R-1750s	16,117	1,236	119
PK-1	A-8507-A-8524	1931	18	2 575 hp. Wright R-1820-64s	17,074	1,226	120
PM-2	A-8662-A-8686	1931	25	2 575 hp. Wright R-1820-64s	17,284	1,236	119

*MTOW = Maximum takeoff weight.

Private aircraft manufacturers were the beneficiaries of the PN development program when the navy placed orders for the new flying boats. In December 1927, the navy awarded a contract for twenty-five PD-1s to the Douglas Aircraft Company and a single XPH-1 to the Hall Aluminum Aircraft Company in Buffalo, New York. The PD-1s closely resembled the NAF's PN-12; the Hall had a hull similar to that of the PN-11. To assist Hall, the NAF forwarded detailed drawings of the hull, wings, and engine installations. The Glenn L. Martin Company earned a production order for twenty-five PM-1s in May 1929 and a month later received an order for another five airplanes. These were of the PN-12-type; in fact, the NAF's A-7029 went to Baltimore for use as a "dog ship" in working out the detailed design for the first PM-1. A contract for eighteen PK-1s went to the Keystone Aircraft Corporation in Bristol, Penn-

The definitive NAF flying boat design was the PN-11, of metal construction throughout. Four aircraft of the PN-11 type were built by the NAF. Number 8006, shown here at Anacostia in 1931, flew for the first time in April 1929. This airplane was redesignated XP4N-1. Douglas, Hall Aluminum, Martin, and Keystone produced flying boats similar to the PN-12 and PN-11 during the 1930s. (80-G-4683, National Archives)

sylvania, in November 1929; the flying boats differed from PN-12s in having twin tails and fully cowled Wright R-1820-64s. Finally, in June 1930, Martin received an order for twenty-five PM-2s, which were nearly identical to the Keystone model.[42]

Having the navy bear the expense and assume the responsibility for a costly decade-long research program in the application of new materials to the construction of airplanes meshed nicely with Moffett's blueprint for the Naval Aircraft Factory. The metal aircraft projects helped preserve the navy's considerable investment in the factory's physical plant and kept intact the engineering and technical work force at Philadelphia. Furthermore, the development of metal aircraft made the best use of the NAF's laboratory personnel and facilities. For the NAF the metal airplane was an ideal mission, accomplished for the most part with skill and efficiency.

The private sector of the industry also gained from the arrangement. Aircraft manufacturers avoided many of the risks inherent in the development of the metal airplane and, perhaps most important, received major new production orders that helped bring their industry out of its depressed state. All told, between 1919 and 1930, the NAF spent in excess of $1.5 million, exclusive of engines, overhead, and depreciation, to bring the PN to maturity.[43] Could the private sector, especially during the austere early and mid-1920s, have marshaled the capital and engineering talent needed for such a massive undertaking, and would the navy have acquired the airplane it wanted and needed? Possibly they could have. But such industry representatives as Clement Keys, who in January 1925 had told the Lampert Committee that design, engineering, and prototype work "are the airplane industry," were convinced the PN program was another means of cheating private industry of its just due. Given the permanent place of the NAF within the naval bureaucracy and the concomitant need to support and mollify civilian aircraft manufacturers, the metal aircraft program was a workable compromise that introduced a new technology while giving the navy a much-needed flying boat for its far-flung patrol squadrons.

Racing also demonstrated the cooperative nature of the NAF's activities during the 1920s. Ironically, the first effort of the NAF in racing came not with an airplane but with a balloon. As the National Elimination Races leading up to the Gordon Bennett contest neared in 1922, BuAer turned to the NAF to supply one of the navy's two entries. In contrast to the other balloons scheduled to take part in the races in Milwaukee, which were filled with coal gas, the one built by the NAF was inflated with helium. Lieutenant Commander Joseph P. Norfleet flew the eighty-thousand-cubic-foot balloon in the competition on 31 May but found that it leaked a considerable quantity of helium. Westervelt attributed the balloon's poor performance to the NAF's lack of experience with the proper methods of varnishing to ensure the impermeability of helium balloon envelopes.[44]

Early racing airplanes from the NAF were modifications of existing service or competition aircraft. The factory converted a TS-1 shipboard fighter and fitted out a Wright-powered TS-3 as a TR-3 for the Curtiss Marine Flying Trophy Race at Detroit in October 1922. A second TS-3 equipped as a TR-3A with a Wright E-4 had engine problems that prevented it from starting in the prestigious Schneider Trophy Race in Cowes, England, in September 1923. The NAF's participation in the 1926 Schneider Trophy races, which were held at Hampton Roads, was more disappointing. In preparation for the November contest, the NAF rebuilt one of the 1925 Curtiss R3C-2 racers as an R3C-3. During a practice flight the R3C-3 landed heavily in the choppy water of Chesapeake Bay, somersaulted, and sank upside down. Fortunately, the pilot escaped uninjured from the submerged wreck.[45]

After the conspicuous failure of the NAF's entry in the 1926 Schneider contest, Secretary of the Navy Wilbur expressed his opposition to direct navy involvement in racing. He was, however, agreeable to a joint effort with private industry. The impetus came from Moffett's close friend and special aide, Lieutenant Alford J. Williams, Jr., who through a nonprofit organization, the Mercury Flying Corporation, began to raise money in 1926 to design and build a Schneider racer. Mindful of the public relations benefits of a successful private-navy venture, Moffett agreed to have BuAer supply Williams with two 500-horsepower Packard engines. In early 1927, the Mercury company signed a contract with the Kirkham Products Corporation of Garden City, Long Island, to build the airplane. The results were discouraging; the aircraft was overweight and its top speed was considerably less than expected.[46]

Williams, displeased with Kirkham, received approval to have a new racer built at the NAF. Work on the airplane began in September 1928 under the direction of the factory's chief engineer, John S. Kean. A bespectacled, scholarly looking civilian who had come to the plant during the height of the World War I flying boat programs, Kean had studied at the University of Pennsylvania and at the Drexel Institute of Art, Science and Industry (after 1936, the Drexel Institute of Technology and now Drexel University). He had broad experience in wooden aircraft construction and had overseen the design and manufacture at the NAF of hundreds of floats for VE-7 and other naval aircraft. His work in modifying a Curtiss F6C-3 Hawk with a supercharged engine and glycol cooling system provided him with practical experience in high-performance aircraft.[47]

Because the races were set for early September at Cowes in England, a sense of urgency pervaded the entire Mercury project. Though the actual design and construction of the wooden, midwing monoplane presented no insurmountable problems, the twenty-four-cylinder twelve-hundred-horsepower, X-configuration Packard engine and its installation did. Kean found that even the use of glycol coolant and covering the entire surface area of the wings with skin radiators did not prevent overheating of the enormous engine at taxiing speeds. To correct this, he rebuilt the duralumin floats with double bottoms, through which coolant circulated while the airplane was still on the water. Nevertheless, no one seemed able to resolve satisfactorily recurrent gearing and other difficulties with the big Packard before the deadline arrived for flight tests.[48]

Time was clearly running out when the sleek blue racer finally entered the water for preliminary trials at Philadelphia in late July 1929. Only limited taxi tests were possible before Kean and Williams shipped the airplane to Annapolis for more extensive evaluation on the broad reaches of Chesapeake Bay. Amid great publicity and with Moffett anxiously monitoring the tests, the airplane failed to overcome severe engine and propeller problems. There was some hope that a new Packard engine could be installed, but in August, with the Schneider races only two weeks away, Williams reluctantly decided to forgo the competition. He still expected to make an attempt on the absolute speed record, but mounting public and congressional criticism of the abortive $175,000 project led Assistant Secretary of the Navy for Aeronautics David S. Ingalls to cancel further work on the airplane and order Williams to return to sea duty in March 1930. Moffett, in England as a technical adviser with the American delegation to the London Naval Conference, agreed with Ingalls's decision.[49]

Less glamorous but potentially more significant than the Naval Aircraft Factory's participation in racing during the 1920s was laboratory work in materials, structures, and power plants. In conjunction with inspection and quality control of its World War I aircraft production, the NAF had experimented with improved fabrics, dopes, manufacturing techniques, and evaluation of the physical properties of wood, metals, and other materials. In 1920, these functions coalesced into a single organization, the Physical Testing Laboratory (PTL). As the industry moved away from wood and into the use of metals in aircraft construction, the laboratory was reorganized. In 1928, it split into two divisions, one of which concentrated on materials while the other emphasized structures. The structural division carried out static and dynamic tests of

The Mercury racer, built by the NAF in 1929. Powered by a twenty-four-cylinder X-configuration Packard, the airplane was to carry Lieutenant Alford J. Williams, Jr., to victory in the Schneider Trophy races. Instead, it had seemingly endless engine, propeller, and cooling problems. (80-G-464877, National Archives)

wings, tail surfaces, fuselages, and other aircraft components, measured shear strengths of metal aircraft parts, evaluated new welding processes, and studied the effects of vibration. The materials engineers and scientists primarily worked on corrosion resistance and protection, paints, finishes, and cleaning agents. The laboratory produced and distributed numerous reports on these subjects in the late 1920s and early 1930s.[50]

The transfer of the Aeronautical Engine Laboratory (AEL) from the Washington Navy Yard to Philadelphia in 1924 further augmented the research and testing activities of the Naval Aircraft Factory. The laboratory had been in Washington since its establishment in 1915, but its location—an old storehouse at the yard—gave it no room to expand. "The lack of proper facilities of this nature is already an embarrassing handicap to our aircraft development," insisted Moffett in December 1922. Philadelphia, he reasoned, was "indubitably the best location" for the engine laboratory. The NAF offered advantages of propinquity to aircraft and engine manufacturers, had plenty of space in a suitable building, and was in Moffett's mind the "recognized workshop for experimental aircraft construction."[51]

Moffett hoped to effect the move of the laboratory as soon as possible after receiving authorization to do so from the secretary of the navy in February 1923. He dispatched officers from Washington to inspect the factory and draw up procedures for transferring material and personnel. But bureaucratic inertia and unanticipated delays in buying and setting up new equipment delayed Moffett's schedule for having the AEL in operation at Philadelphia at the end of 1923. Early in 1924, a group of about twenty engineers and machinists arrived at the factory from Washington, followed by the rest of the laboratory personnel later in the year. It was not until April that the AEL was fully functioning in Building 77 at the factory.[52]

The Aeronautical Engine Laboratory was exceptionally well equipped to perform a wide range of tasks. It had ten dynamometer rooms for both liquid-cooled and air-cooled engines, seven of which were in use by the spring of 1925. A large refrigeration unit supplied air at temperatures down to minus 58 degrees Fahrenheit to simulate engine operating conditions at extreme altitudes. In another building there were four torque stands used for testing engine-propeller combinations. The AEL also had machine and overhaul shops, instrument and electrical laboratories, and a facility for testing engine accessories. Under Lieutenant Commander Charles G. McCord, the AEL conducted reliability tests of new and reconditioned engines under a variety of conditions as well as evaluating their lubrication, carburetion, and electrical systems. Furthermore, the laboratory developed new components and systems to improve existing and future engines and drew up specifications that served as guidelines for manufacturers and for those determining future procurement policies. A project that occupied a considerable proportion of the AEL's staff was the development and testing of water recovery apparatus for the airships *Shenandoah* and *Los Angeles*.[53]

The NAF met the diverse needs of naval aviation in the 1920s in other areas. With the Armistice ending World War 1 the armed services found themselves with vast quantities of surplus aircraft, components, and parts. Both the army and the navy sold much of this equipment at bargain-basement prices, with dire consequences for the aviation industry. But the navy also decided to keep a proportion of its aviation inventory, handing out stocks as needed by the fleet and using up spare parts to keep its airplanes flying. Storage and supply thus became Naval Aircraft Factory functions in the 1920s. At the end of the war, the NAF completed a $444,000 storehouse (Building 61) for production materials, and within days of the Armistice, Coburn learned that a large storage facility planned for New York would be erected instead at the NAF. Costing in excess of $650,000, this building (number 86) was ready by early 1920. Although some members of Congress questioned the wisdom of keeping large stocks of aircraft and material in storage, the navy's policy remained unchanged. In time, large numbers of Curtiss HS-1L, HS-2L, and MF flying boats, along with wings, tail surfaces, and engines, poured into Philadelphia from Hampton Roads, Cape May, Far Rockaway, and Gloucester City, New Jersey.[54]

The manipulation of these huge stocks was an administrative headache for Coburn and his successor Westervelt. Maintaining up-to-date inventories and issuing items from storage to the fleet in the preelectronic era required enormous quantities of paper. Items had to be inspected periodically; even so, material deteriorated through water damage, rot, and corrosion. A clever means of reducing the number of surplus HS-1L and HS-2L wing sets was to incorporate them into the NAF's PT-1s and PT-2s, but it was impossible to use up all such stocks in this fashion. Moreover, Moffett, ever conscious of the precarious relationship between the NAF and the aircraft industry and unwilling to do anything that might further aggravate private manufacturers, put off dumping these materials on an already glutted market. Not until well into 1923 did he allow the NAF to begin the wholesale disposition of obsolete airplanes and components.[55]

Part of Moffett's conception of the NAF as a support facility rather than an aircraft manufacturing plant was linked to the increasing emphasis on repair and overhaul work at the factory. It served Moffett's purposes to consolidate as much of this work as possible at the NAF, for doing so helped maintain the nucleus of the plant's

A view of the NAF's landing field in 1925, with hangars in the background. Increased traffic and larger airplanes rendered the field inadequate. In 1926, Mustin Field was dedicated on the site. (80-CF-712812–20, National Archives)

production work force while not adding fuel to the controversy over competition from a government factory. By the mid-1920s, the NAF had become the navy's principal repair and overhaul center for aircraft and engines. One of the biggest projects at the factory was rebuilding eighteen H-16 flying boats with improved ailerons, balanced rudders, new radios, and strengthened hulls. The cost, estimated at $16,000 per airplane, was perhaps $4,000 less than it would have been for a new aircraft, and the rebuilt H-16s, though less capable than newer models, adequately served the fleet's needs through the remainder of the decade.[56]

These activities, plus the navy's increased reliance on land planes, placed a considerable burden on the limited flying facilities at the NAF during the 1920s. In response to the need, inquiries began as early as 1921 into the possibility of establishing an airfield at League

Island that could be used by both the NAF and the city of Philadelphia. In 1922, a 136-acre site east of the factory was chosen as the best location for a new airfield. Acting Secretary of the Navy Theodore Roosevelt, Jr., approved the construction project on 3 June, and work began immediately. Within a year, about a quarter of the land had been prepared, and airplanes began to operate from the field. In addition to the flying that was done in conjunction with the experimental activities of the NAF, the Navy Department in 1924 authorized the use of the field by the aero squadron of the Pennsylvania National Guard, and before the end of the decade a naval air reserve unit was using the field for training purposes.[57]

The navy was generous in allowing civilians to use the field at League Island. In June 1926, the Navy Department granted permission to Thomas E. Mitten, president of Philadelphia Rapid Transit, to use the field to provide air passenger and mail service between Washington and Philadelphia in connection with Philadelphia's 1926 sesquicentennial celebration. Marking the nation's 150th birthday was an international exposition that opened on 31 May at a site on Broad Street in South Philadelphia near League Island. Highlights of the celebration were pageants, parades, exhibits, and, in September, the National Air Races. Even though the agreement with Mitten to use the NAF airfield was consistent with Moffett's policy of cooperation with the private sector, it did not always sit well with commercial operators. C. Townsend Ludington and Harold Pitcairn, owners of other Philadelphia-based airlines, complained that it was unfair to allow one commercial operator to use the field but to exclude competitors. They also thought the navy's action would be detrimental to the city's new municipal airport, which was located on Island Road not far from the sesquicentennial grounds and which they hoped would get extensive use during the festivities.[58]

Despite this opposition, the Navy Department allowed Mitten's Philadelphia Rapid Transit (PRT) airline to use the NAF flying field. Wilbur said, "This line . . . will not be in competition with other civilian aviation activities already undertaken in the vicinity of Philadelphia," assuring the interested parties that Mitten would provide the necessary support facilities and that Mitten's "object . . . in establishing this line is primarily to test the practicality of a commercial air line under the best possible conditions." Wilbur added: "The Aeronautical Organization of the Navy is directed to give the project its hearty cooperation." Mitten began his service on 6 July and continued it through the end of the sesquicentennial celebration. It was, as anticipated, a model of efficiency, but the experiment showed that such commercial operations demanded substantial subsidies in the form of airmail pay to guarantee their long-term success. Mitten ended the service on 30 November.[59]

Coincident with the PRT air service flights between Philadelphia and Washington was the formal dedication of the NAF's flying field on 17 September 1926 in memory of Captain Henry C. Mustin. Mustin was a Philadelphia native who had experimented with a glider at the Philadelphia Navy Yard in 1911 with Dick Richardson. He had gone on to make his first solo flight in 1913 and had established the naval air training facility at Pensacola in 1914. Following the war, Mustin served as the assistant chief of the Bureau of Aeronautics until his sudden and untimely death in 1923. It was particularly fitting that the NAF field should be named for him.[60]

As dignitaries gathered for the dedication of Mustin Field on that September day, the *Philadelphia Inquirer* observed that "leaden clouds" hung over League Island. Among the notables present were W. Freeland Kendrick, the mayor of Philadelphia, Rear Admiral Thomas P. Magruder, the commandant of the Philadelphia Navy Yard, Admiral Moffett, Captain Westervelt, and Assistant Secretary of the Navy Theodore D. Robinson. The ceremonies included addresses by Moffett and Westervelt and the unveiling of a granite monument and bronze tablet commemorating Mustin's achievements in naval aviation. An air show followed, with navy, marine, and army pilots putting on a display of aerobatics and a bombing demonstration.[61]

In the dedication of Mustin Field, naval aviators were commemorating one of their own, and the attendant fanfare was consistent with Admiral Moffett's strategy of showcasing the accomplishments of naval aviation. But the celebration also symbolized the new directions taken by the Naval Aircraft Factory since the promulgation of Moffett's 1922 compromise. As long as the NAF's mission was in support of, and not in competition with, private aircraft manufacturers, the factory was acceptable to both the navy and industry, especially in the relative prosperity of the late 1920s. Nevertheless, there were those who were less confident about the enduring nature of the Moffett compromise and the security of the niche the admiral had carved out for the factory within the naval aviation establishment.

6

The Vinson-Trammell Act and After

On the eve of a new decade, Ralph Weyerbacher had reason to doubt the future of the Naval Aircraft Factory. Although the nearly thirteen hundred workers under his charge in May 1929 were busy with the PN flying boats, the ill-starred Mercury racer, the XT2N-1 dive bomber, and a plethora of experimental programs, he was worried about the NAF over the longer term. The new chief executive, Herbert Hoover, had strong pacifist leanings and was ideologically opposed to direct government involvement in economic activities traditionally associated with private business. Hoover was not likely to be sympathetic to increased appropriations for the NAF, especially if they came at the expense of private aircraft manufacturers.

Aside from his concerns about Hoover and the long-range prospects of the Naval Aircraft Factory, Weyerbacher feared short-term reductions in the engineering and production force at Philadelphia. Weyerbacher told Admiral Moffett that new engineering projects were necessary "to keep the flow of design and experimental work up to the established level" at the plant. He wanted the Bureau of Aeronautics to authorize the NAF to begin designing an advanced all-metal, monocoque-fuselage fighter and a new flying boat as a follow-on to the PN-11. Furthermore, he said, the factory should be permitted to begin production of PN-11-type aircraft alongside that of private manufacturers.[1]

112

Weyerbacher's letter precipitated another review of the NAF and its place in naval aviation. Assistant Secretary of the Navy David S. Ingalls, a World War I naval aviator and the navy's only ace, asked Moffett for a "study . . . of the past, present, and future activities" of the factory. One of the major issues Ingalls wanted BuAer to explore was aircraft production. Should the NAF manufacture airplanes in quantity, and should the factory's output be of the most modern designs? Conversely, should the factory confine its production to older models or merely to spare parts and components? Ingalls called, too, for an examination of the research and development activities at Philadelphia, particularly as they might duplicate those of the army and commercial firms. Finally—and ominously—he made it clear that the bureau's summary and recommendations should be made "with a view of reducing the cost of operation" of the Naval Aircraft Factory.[2]

Moffett also had heard rumblings from the Hoover administration about fiscal economy and knew that there was little sympathy for the NAF among representatives of the aircraft industry, which anticipated the end of the five-year production programs and shortly would be reeling from the effects of the stock market collapse in October. He recognized the dilemma inherent in the situation at Philadelphia. If the factory built older-model aircraft in numbers, it would deprive the industry of its "bread and butter." Yet if the NAF concentrated on more modern designs, it would have to reinforce its design staff, trespassing in the uncertain territory of proprietary design rights and taking away what Clement Keys had considered to be "the aircraft industry." Unhappy about the outcome of recent design projects at Philadelphia—particularly the Mercury racer— Moffett had some sympathy for the industry's opposition to aircraft design at Philadelphia, but he could not recommend a policy that was likely to result in a significant diminution of the Naval Aircraft Factory's activities or a reduction in its work force.

Moffett found sanctuary in the status quo. He told Ingalls that NAF production was limited to the number of aircraft needed for development purposes and the yardstick: "to obtain information on civil production costs." Quantity production, Moffett understood from experience, "whether . . . of new or of old types, would be greeted by protests from the trade." The production of spare parts at the NAF was also likely to stimulate a negative reaction among private manufacturers, who found the sale of spares to be highly lucrative long after the initial aircraft contract had been completed and who depended on spares to carry them over to the next major order. Nor did Moffett find any "undue amount of duplication" between the research and development at Philadelphia and that at McCook Field or at private facilities. Because the factory's work was specialized and generated "fairly high" overhead figures, the only way to effect real economies was to increase production output, thereby arousing the ire of private aircraft manufacturers, who would surely dispatch a gaggle of angry lobbyists to Capitol Hill.[3] It was best to leave well enough alone.

Having restated his conception of the NAF's role, Moffett still had to divert enough business to the factory to maintain its operations at an acceptable level. Weyerbacher was insistent about the inevitability of laying off employees unless more work came through, stressing that a reduction in the number of people at the factory would be followed by an increase in overhead costs. Moffett replied that he did not foresee any new experimental aircraft projects "for some time to come." To safeguard the nucleus of an engineering and production staff at the NAF, he guaranteed that the factory would be given a six-month work load. He backed this up by assigning to the factory a mixed bag of jobs, including wooden floats, wing surfaces, and major aircraft and engine overhauls.[4]

The negative publicity attendant to the Mercury racer influenced Moffett's decision to deprive the NAF of new experimental aircraft projects. Few NAF airplanes had received the front-page coverage the Mercury racer did, and its failure was conspicuous, reflecting adversely on the factory. Moreover, subsequent developments cast a dark shadow over the NAF as Congress and the press subjected the racer to merciless scrutiny.

Al Williams had been bitterly disappointed by the navy's decision to write off the Mercury racer as a failure. But another calamity befell him in 1930, when he was ordered to sea duty with the carrier *Lexington*. Rather than accept an assignment that would have removed him from further aircraft development projects, Williams resigned his commission on 7 March. Amid rumors that the navy was pushing Williams aside, Senator Millard E. Tydings of Maryland introduced a resolution to have a subcommittee of the Senate Naval

Affairs Committee investigate the racing airplane program and the navy's policy on high-performance aircraft. [5]

Shortly after the subcommittee convened its hearings, attention shifted to the Naval Aircraft Factory. Williams stunned his audience with testimony that he planned to wreck the Mercury racer in England rather than reveal serious defects caused by slipshod practices at the NAF. Despite assurances to the contrary, the airplane had been delivered nearly 18 percent overweight. When he learned of the problem, he admitted it "was quite a setback," but because of the press of time he decided to go ahead with the Annapolis tests anyway. Ingalls countered with a defense of the factory. He said that more than six hundred pounds of extra weight was in the form of equipment supplied by outside firms. Moreover, Ingalls pointed out, Weyerbacher and Kean had argued that "the difficulty [was] more with the engine than with anything else." If responsibility for the failure of the Mercury racer had to be relegated to anyone, Ingalls said, Williams himself should bear the principal burden because he had been in charge of the entire project.[6]

Williams and the Mercury project were only one of many of the Naval Aircraft Factory's worries as the nation sank deeper into the economic morass of the Depression. An overwhelming concern was fiscal economy. Deep cuts by the Bureau of the Budget in 1930–31 limited appropriations for the acquisition of new aircraft and restricted fleet operations. Some retrenchment occurred in personnel at the Naval Aircraft Factory in late 1930, but for the most part the installation escaped major layoffs. There was, however, constant pressure from BuAer to trim overhead costs and step up productivity at the factory.[7]

Into this uncertain situation stepped Commander Sydney M. Kraus as the new manager of the Naval Aircraft Factory. Weyerbacher ended his three-and-a-half-year tour of duty on 7 January 1931, a little less than a month before Kraus assumed command. "Moe" Kraus was a forty-three-year-old Indianan who had graduated from the Naval Academy in 1908, one of two Jews in his class. It is hard to determine how Kraus's religion may have affected his career, but it is safe to assume that in the conservative naval establishment Jews were a rarity and that they were not welcomed into the commissioned ranks. Understanding this prejudice, Kraus may have been driven to excel in his profession. He joined the Construction

Commander Sydney M. Kraus took over as manager of the Naval Aircraft Factory in February 1931, succeeding Commander Ralph D. Weyerbacher. Kraus headed the factory during the lean years of the early 1930s, when the plant depended heavily on overhauls and miscellaneous projects. (72-AF-25230, National Archives)

Corps, completed postgraduate work in mechanical engineering, and trained as an aviation observer at Pensacola. One of his assignments had been as an officer aboard the airship *Los Angeles* in 1925. Since July 1926 he had been BuAer's officer in charge of aircraft procurement.[8] Although bright and capable, Kraus lacked much of the aircraft development experience of either Weyerbacher or Westervelt, and he was under nearly constant pressure to justify every penny spent at the NAF. He did not begin his watch under the most auspicious circumstances.

Fortunately for Kraus, there was more than enough overhaul and repair work to make up for the lack of experimental aircraft construction. By the middle of 1931, the plant was averaging one major overhaul per week. Captain Arthur B. Cook, the assistant chief of the Bureau of Aeronautics, said in November 1931 that plans for the following year called for overhauls of seventy-nine aircraft, including flying boats, trainers, fighters, and observation planes. One of the more unusual jobs in 1931–32 was the Plane-

Trap, a V-shaped float designed for the under-way recovery of floatplanes by cruisers and battleships. Another in 1932 was the overhaul of six skyhook-equipped Consolidated N2Y-1s to be used as trainers for the heavier-than-air units of the new airships *Akron* and *Macon*. The NAF also rebuilt the airplane hook-on device (or "trapeze") used aboard the smaller airship *Los Angeles* for installation in the *Akron* in February 1932.[9]

Despite efforts to steer as many projects as possible to the NAF, there was continuing insistence on economy. Moffett wrote to Secretary of the Navy Charles Francis Adams pleading the NAF's case. Moffett said that "through cost records maintained at the Factory, information has been obtained which has made possible a very material reduction in costs of aircraft and accessories." But the yardstick was not enough for the budget-minded Hoover administration. Orders came down through Captain Cook in October 1932 that it was time for the factory to "cut its cloth to fit the pattern and gauge the size of its force on the amount of work the Bureau [of Aeronautics] can legitimately and economically assign" to it. Because it was impossible to increase the number of aircraft and engine overhauls at the plant without diverting some of this work from private firms, personnel reductions had to be seriously considered.[10]

Whether Moffett would have acceded to Cook's suggestion to decrease the size of the work force at the Naval Aircraft Factory will never be known. On the night of 3–4 April 1933, in the turbulence of a cold front off the coast of New Jersey, the airship *Akron* crashed into the sea, carrying to their deaths Moffett and seventy-two others.[11] With Moffett's death naval aviation lost one of its strongest and most vocal advocates. He was a consummate politician who had seen the fleet's air service through some of its most critical years. And he had left an indelible mark on the Naval Aircraft Factory. His decision to end production there had not satisfied everyone—not the least being those critics in private industry whose voices could have been silenced only by closing the factory altogether. But Moffett had effected a workable compromise in a statesmanlike manner, thereby preserving the NAF as a potential supplier of aircraft and consolidating it as one of the navy's foremost aviation installations.

Exactly a month after Moffett's death, Rear Admiral Ernest J. King became the new chief of the Bureau of Aeronautics. King's background had been in submarines, but at Moffett's urging he had taken command of the aircraft tender *Wright* in 1926. In early 1927, he reported for flight training at Pensacola and received his wings in May of that year. In 1928, he replaced Emory Land as the bureau's assistant chief before leaving that post to become commanding officer at Hampton Roads. In 1930, he assumed command of the carrier *Lexington*.[12] Acerbic, opinionated, and ramrod straight, King was every inch the professional. His dynamic leadership and sense of duty offset his relative inexperience in aviation; he was an excellent choice to succeed the nearly legendary Moffett.

In the interval, a new administration took office in Washington. Promising to make war on the Depression, Franklin D. Roosevelt unleashed a kaleidoscope of emergency programs aimed at restoring the nation's economic health. The future looked bleak for the aircraft manufacturing industry, which had been staggering since 1931, when the 1926 five-year procurement programs had run out. Well aware of the industry's dependence on favorable treatment from Washington, the Aeronautical Chamber of Commerce stated that the only way "to maintain design staffs and up-to-date construction facilities [was] through the medium of a reasonable number of military orders" and called upon Congress and the president to clarify aviation policy in regard to experimental design competition, bidding procedures, and proprietary design rights. Yet among the American public and in Washington there was a different attitude concerning the acquisition of potential instruments of war, which complicated the development of a new and viable procurement policy. The popular literature of the day assailed munitions makers as "merchants of death" for the profits they allegedly had made supplying the nation's armed forces during World War I.[13]

Congressman Carl Vinson, a Georgia Democrat and chairman of the House Naval Affairs Committee, introduced legislation in January 1934 to build sufficient numbers of warships and aircraft to bring the navy up to its treaty ceilings. When Vinson's committee began hearings on the bill, some voiced concern about what they thought to be a lack of competition among aircraft manufacturers, resulting in high prices charged to the government.[14] In an atmosphere heavy with public criticism of war profiteers, the committee began a reexamination of naval aircraft and engine procurement that often centered on the role of the Naval Aircraft Factory.

In February, Vinson appointed a special subcommittee chaired by John J. Delaney, a confirmed New Dealer from Brooklyn, to conduct a detailed investigation of naval aircraft and engine procurement. The committee began its hearings with two days of testimony from Admiral King. King carefully detailed the navy's aircraft and engine procurement policies, followed by an explanation of why manufacturing—even of experimental models—at the Naval Aircraft Factory was not in the best interests of either the navy or the public. Convinced that "manufacture at the Naval Aircraft Factory . . . costs more than it does to have it done by private firms," King believed the nation's interests were best served by tapping a deeper pool of engineering talent than was available at Philadelphia. "With the method we now pursue [in developing new aircraft] we make available all the ingenuity and skill and engineering ideas of the entire aircraft industry of the United States."[15]

Admiral C. J. Peoples, chief of the Bureau of Supplies and Accounts, said that King's views on the Naval Aircraft Factory were not universally accepted. When asked by George P. Darrow, a Republican from Philadelphia and a strong supporter of the NAF, if the factory should be allowed to do any manufacturing, Peoples responded that the plant "had a very useful purpose" even if it were not the sole source of the navy's aircraft and engines. He went on to assert that the yardstick had been of "great value" in negotiating contracts with private concerns and that the NAF could be used to prevent private manufacturers from making excessive profits from aircraft and engine contracts.[16]

David Ingalls, who had lost his position as assistant secretary of the navy for aeronautics in an economy move in March 1932, saw a definite connection between industry profits and "the continued threat the Navy held over all manufacturers, that we would go in and build planes ourselves, unless they came down to prices we thought fair and reasonable." Because the NAF had no comparable capacity to build engines, it had been impossible to use the factory as leverage to hold down power plant prices. But Ingalls could see no reason for the navy to go to the great expense of producing significant numbers of airplanes or engines at the NAF as long as the "threat" to do so remained. He considered the yardstick inaccurate because of differences in calculating overhead and expressed opposition in principle to government aircraft manufacturing.[17]

The strongest statement against the Naval Aircraft Factory came from Edward P. Warner, an engineer who had served as assistant secretary of the navy for aeronautics until March 1929 and in 1934 was editor of the influential trade journal *Aviation*. Because the aircraft industry was undergoing rapid change, Warner doubted if the navy could muster the needed engineering talent to keep pace and consequently thought it undesirable to have the factory construct experimental types. He also questioned the yardstick, arguing that there were more economical means of checking manufacturers' prices than involving the factory in expensive production runs. "I am opposed to quantity production of naval aircraft in Government plants," Warner said, "unless it is to be undertaken as a part of a general program of complete socialization and State operation of the whole military aircraft industry." That, obviously, was out of the question.[18]

In its report of 8 March, the Delaney Committee was unswayed by the arguments against manufacturing aircraft at the NAF. Although the committee could find no evidence of collusion among manufacturers, it did make a connection between the relatively low profits of the airframe industry and the capacity of the Philadelphia plant to produce airplanes in quantity: "The existence of the Naval Aircraft Factory at Philadelphia has probably served as an effective brake on the price of airplanes." The NAF's lack of a comparable facility for manufacturing engines was a contributing factor to the high profits of such firms as Pratt and Whitney and Wright Aeronautical.[19]

Unstated but implicit in the Delaney report was acknowledgment that aircraft engine manufacturing was by far the most lucrative aspect of the aviation business. Because possibly half a dozen different airframes used the same type of power plant over periods of several years, engine manufacturers could standardize their designs and amortize their considerable investment in tooling and other equipment. This was something few aircraft manufacturers could do. Additionally, for each batch of four single-engine airplanes—or for every two twin-engine airplanes—there had to be five engines. Engine production was inherently a profitable enterprise, and there was nothing to convince members of the Delaney Committee that the manufacturers were passing those profits on to the navy.[20]

Unswayed by the testimony of King, Ingalls, or industry representatives, the Delaney Committee vigorously recommended quantity aircraft and engine production at the Naval Aircraft Factory. The chief reason given was the yardstick: "to determine accurately what are reasonable prices to pay for aircraft, their engines, and aircraft appliances." The NAF was an excellent place to prepare officers and other personnel "not only in the mechanical operations connected with the manufacture of airplanes but in the general administration of all phases of manufacturing." In conclusion, "It seemed to the committee that the Naval Aircraft Factory can, and should, be utilized for a greater amount of production activity and for such confidential work, experimental construction, [and] emergency fabrication work . . . as will keep this establishment alive and abreast of the best progress that the aircraft industry as a whole is able to show."[21]

It was clear from the Delaney Committee report that the sentiment in Congress was favorable to moderate restrictions on navy aircraft and power plant contractors and that the Naval Aircraft Factory would provide at least some of the service's airplane and engine needs. On 20 February, a Democrat from Washington, Senator Homer T. Bone, incensed by the aviation industry's "unholy and unconscionable profits," introduced an amendment to the Vinson bill calling for the construction of 50 percent of the navy's aircraft and engines in government plants. Later, Park Trammell, a Democrat from Florida and chairman of the Senate Naval Affairs Committee, suggested 25 percent as a point of discussion. Bone and Trammell then concurred that the president should be given broad discretionary powers to determine how many airplanes and engines should be manufactured at the Naval Aircraft Factory up to the percentage limit required by Congress. The naval construction measure, now firmly linked with Vinson and Trammell, went to a House-Senate conference committee, which after two weeks of deliberation reported out the compromise legislation.[22]

The conference report determined that "not less than 10 percent" of total navy aircraft and engine production must come from the Naval Aircraft Factory. President Roosevelt was given authority to establish the exact number of aircraft and engines to be built as permitted by the available facilities. At the same time, and to ensure that the NAF could get started on production, the report called for the navy to initiate planning to expand the physical plant at Philadelphia and to hire and train the necessary personnel.[23]

Passing with substantial majorities in the House and the Senate, the Vinson-Trammell Act became law with the president's signature on 27 March 1934. It provided blanket authorization to build the fleet up to its treaty limits and to replace vessels as they reached the age limits delineated by the Washington and London agreements. The legislation was specific about aircraft procurement: "Not less than 10 per centum of the aircraft, including engines therefor . . . shall be constructed and/or manufactured in Government aircraft factories." The president could employ government plants whenever there was sufficient evidence of collusion among bidders on aircraft and engine contracts or whenever bids were in excess of the cost of production "plus a reasonable profit." The act authorized appropriations "for the enlargement and expansion of such existing plants and facilities now owned by the Government for the construction and manufacture of naval aircraft." Finally, the act restricted profits on navy aircraft and engine contracts with private suppliers to no more than 10 percent.[24]

Because estimates of the number of airplanes needed by the navy ran as high as twelve hundred, with five hundred called for in 1934–35, the private sector of the industry should have understood that there would be enough work for everybody despite the imminent renewal of production at the Naval Aircraft Factory. Yet representatives of aircraft manufacturers were uniformly critical of the Vinson-Trammell legislation. Edward P. Warner attacked the 10 percent requirement in an editorial in *Aviation* in April 1934: "The scheme of putting a substantial part of the construction of service aircraft into government-owned plants [was] almost certain to be bad." He doubted the navy's ability to put together a corps of aeronautical engineers capable of conceptualizing and carrying through innovative design projects. And he thought it a basic conflict of interest to have BuAer officers weighing the merits of the NAF aircraft designs against those of private competitors. For Warner, the outlook was gloomy: "The trend of procurement policy, and especially of the thought of Congress upon procurement matters, seems to be toward the adoption of practices sure to retard progress and to slow down an improvement in military aircraft performance which has been extraordinarily rapid over the past three years."[25]

Although there remained vocal foes of government competition in aircraft manufacturing, the Vinson-Trammell Act secured the new place of the Naval Aircraft Factory as a production center. In the interval, Kraus began preparing for the expansion of the NAF. During and after the Delaney Committee proceedings, he generated data on the history of the plant, lists of current projects, comparative costs, and aircraft production estimates. He followed up with information regarding a new hangar, storehouse, engine manufacturing facility, and miscellaneous alterations and equipment. Kraus estimated that more than $3.1 million would be necessary for producing 125 aircraft and an equivalent number of engines annually. In May, Kraus made the rounds of the Wright, Pratt and Whitney, and Packard engine factories to familiarize himself with their work and to gather data to determine the optimal layout and tooling for the new plant at Philadelphia.[26]

At a cabinet meeting on 17 August, President Roosevelt authorized the allocation of $2.7 million to expand the Naval Aircraft Factory and to institute the production of airplanes and engines. Months passed, however, before a final determination was made regarding the types of aircraft and power plants to be manufactured and the facilities completed for producing them. A. D. Bernhard of BuAer's Plans Division recommended against going ahead with the development of new aircraft designs for production by the NAF. In view of the continued restrictions on funds and "the intent of Congress that we manufacture service types in order to establish comparative costs," Bernhard advocated concentration on models already in production by private manufacturers. Regardless of whether a new or an existing aircraft design was produced at the NAF, Bernhard wanted the factory to lay out a five-year program in which it specified its programs and estimated expenditures year by year.[27]

Rear Admiral King correctly perceived that producing engines was technically more difficult than manufacturing airplanes. No one at Philadelphia had any experience in engine production, and, although there were some officers who could supervise the preparation of a new engine design, none had specialized in such work. Two alternatives presented themselves: buy the design and manufacturing rights for an engine already in production, or design a new engine and manufacture it in quantity. The first course of action ran the risk of ending up with large numbers of obsolescent or obsolete engines, while the second involved the creation of a wholly new design staff at Philadelphia, with attendant delays and expense. King decided to do both, initiating a program whereby the factory went ahead with the production of a proven engine while simultaneously designing a new engine model. It would not be easy, King insisted, "but the project is feasible and can be made successful."[28]

The assistant chief of BuAer, Captain Frank R. McCrary, investigated the matter of aircraft and engine design and construction before reporting to King in October 1934. McCrary disagreed with Bernhard that the NAF should forgo a new aircraft design in favor of production of existing types. There was sufficient expertise, he asserted, in the factory's design section to develop a good observation airplane or trainer. To save time and money, he recommended that the NAF acquire several established designs from private firms and incorporate the best features of each into a new airplane. In this manner, the factory will "obtain valuable experience in design, and the prospect of the Navy obtaining a satisfactory plane from the first attempt . . . will be at least promising."[29]

A new engine design was a different matter. McCrary cited the retention of competent and experienced engineers as a problem the army had run into with its power plant work at McCook Field. The highly successful Pratt and Whitney radial engine and the Hamilton Standard variable-pitch propeller were largely the consequence of the labors of former McCook Field engineers who had been lured to East Hartford by significantly higher salaries. "The Navy could not hope to employ men of such experience," McCrary averred. He went on: "The present aircraft engine manufacturers are so far ahead of us, or any civilian designers that we may obtain, that the efforts to accomplish a new design look hopeless. We will save a large amount of money and grief if we can steer clear of this labyrinth." If that were not possible, McCrary urged BuAer to obtain rights to manufacture suitable engines for trainers and observation aircraft.[30]

After several conferences and much deliberation, King outlined the factory's new responsibilities on 19 October. Henceforth the NAF would be organized and its personnel prepared to "conduct the following new and *additional* major functions: (a) *Manufacture* and development of airplanes; (b) *Manufacture* and development of airplane engines." As production of aircraft and engines gained momentum, overhauls were to be phased out. In accordance with BuAer directives, the factory should plan for the production of no more than sixty training airplanes and eighty engines. The power plants were to be of a proven design for which the manufacturing rights could be bought from private concerns. But "at some future time, the Bureau will authorize the development of airplane engines of Navy design."[31]

Production at the NAF, according to King, "must be conducted on commercial principles" to establish the yardstick called for by Congress in the Vinson-Trammell legislation. King elaborated: "The Naval Aircraft Factory must thoroughly realize that. . . . the basic principle involved in the law requiring 'manufacture' is the procurement of 'yard-sticks' wherewith to compare the costs of purchase of similar articles (airplanes, airplane engines, aircraft parts) from commercial sources." To accomplish this, careful accounting procedures had to be followed that computed not only direct manufacturing costs but all "indirect charges" and overhead. King stressed, "The costs will be the subject of report to Congress, which makes it mandatory that the . . . costs contain every item of actual costs, to the end that there may be no grounds whatsoever for questioning their accuracy, whether by the Congress or by the aircraft industry."[32]

The responsibility for carrying out Admiral King's orders rested with forty-four-year-old Commander Samuel J. Zeigler, Jr., who had replaced Kraus as manager of the NAF on 8 June 1934. A handsome and ambitious native of South Carolina, Zeigler graduated fourth in his class from the Naval Academy in 1912. Zeigler served at the American naval air station at Brest during World War I and came to the NAF during the early 1920s to work as production superintendent. During his tour of duty he had studied and written about industrial planning, scheduling, and production. His philosophy stressed organizational flexibility and the encouragement of a maximum of incentive and initiative among foremen and shop workers.[33]

Zeigler was particularly concerned that cost accounting procedures at the NAF were in conformity with accepted methods.

Commander Samuel J. Zeigler, Jr., served two tours as NAF manager —in 1934–36 and 1943–44. This photograph shows him when he took over from Commander Kraus in June 1934. Zeigler's major responsibility was instituting aircraft and engine production at Philadelphia as part of the mandate of the Vinson-Trammell Act of 1934. (72-AF-29435, National Archives)

Responding to criticism that the NAF's overhead and depreciation calculations were too low to permit accurate cost comparisons, Zeigler recommended the inclusion of all operations expenses and costs of developing new designs in manufacturing cost figures. Added to these would be the salaries and wages of all personnel and an equivalent of plant depreciation costs arrived at by charging off housing expenses and the outlays for the installation of new tools and equipment. Zeigler wanted to be certain that design and shop work were "as nearly as possible under the same conditions as the similar work in private commercial plants." The problem here was that although a private firm might have only one or two projects ongoing simultaneously, the NAF usually had several hundred. As priorities shifted, personnel and money were transferred from one project to another, usually resulting in delays and inflated cost figures. Zeigler wanted to keep the same priority for a given project until it reached completion. From BuAer Zeigler received assurance of 100 percent priority for aircraft and engine production orders and guarantees that once production got under way at Philadelphia, major overhaul work would cease, thereby eliminating conflicts with manufacturing projects.[34]

To expand the physical plant at the Naval Aircraft Factory in preparation for the production of aircraft and engines Congress allocated $2,708,000 in June 1934. Although it was hoped that construction would begin before the end of the year, it was not until January 1935 that satisfactory low bids were in hand for the expansion of the administration building and the construction of the engine shop, a new test building, a hangar at Mustin Field, and an enlarged maintenance facility. The initial work totaled more than $1 million, and the successful bidder, the Philadelphia firm of Irwin and Leighton, promised completion within eight months.[35]

The smell of fresh paint and the organized confusion of construction were everywhere at the factory in 1935 and 1936. Building 75 was enlarged to house the expanded engineering and drafting staff, and work began on the engine shop, test facilities, and the new hangar. Mustin Field also received attention. Aircraft production required more space to test airplanes, and the quay next to the Delaware was filled in to provide room for expansion of the airfield. A separate $800,000 allotment provided for additional hangars, asphalt paving for the southeast and southwest runways, and improvements to existing structures. Painting, new window sash, upgraded lighting, and elevators went into many of the factory buildings, and $700,000 in new tools, jigs, and other equipment completed the renovations.[36]

While the factory was readied for aircraft and engine production, BuAer determined in October 1934 that the NAF was "to design and construct an experimental primary training airplane." "The major purpose," the directive continued, "is to develop in this type of airplane maximum ruggedness and ease of maintenance consistent with general stability for primary training purposes and meeting the specified performance." King ordered Zeigler to prepare cost estimates for a prototype and forty-five production airplanes.[37] This was consistent with earlier decisions to have the factory start with a relatively simple airplane and restrict its production to no more than sixty examples.

Within a month, Zeigler submitted an estimate of nearly $42,000 to manufacture the prototype, which would be fitted with either conventional wheeled landing gear or floats. He thought it reasonable to expect flight tests by 1 November 1935. An initial production order for forty-five airplanes, including engines and propellers, would cost another $583,200, with the first airplane delivered within ninety days of authorization and the remainder manufactured at a rate of one per week. In December, BuAer approved the prototype, designated XN3N-1, powered by a 220-horsepower Wright R-790-8 (or J-5) engine; the bureau authorized production of forty-five R-790-powered airplanes at the end of the month.[38]

BuAer's aircraft design section drew up the preliminary plans and specifications for the new trainer, while the factory's draftsmen and engineers concentrated on the detail drawings. There was some urgency because BuAer faced a critical shortage of primary trainers at the navy's principal flight school at Pensacola. To ensure "the greatest possible dispatch," King exempted the NAF from the sometimes long process of seeking preliminary bureau approval of the design. He also accorded the project 100 percent priority. Zeigler, in turn, said the "work will be prosecuted vigorously," adding that the 1 November completion date of the prototype "will be anticipated as much as possible." As project engineer, he selected Charles E. Kirkbride, a forty-year-old civilian who had come to the factory in 1921 as a draftsman and had previously worked for the Victor Talking Machine Company.[39]

Zeigler committed virtually the entire engineering and drafting force of the NAF to the XN3N-1 project. In March, he reported that "progress to date has been excellent," an observation borne out by the rapid completion of the mockup. On 19–20 March, officers from the Board of Inspection and Survey went over the mockup, finding it "excellent," although the board did recommend various minor changes that the NAF incorporated into the final design. There was nothing pathbreaking in the XN3N-1 design, but NAF engineers did incorporate several unusual features reflecting their experience with aluminum aircraft structures. The two-place, dual-control, open-cockpit biplane had a maximum takeoff weight of 2,636 pounds when fitted with conventional landing gear and 2,770 pounds with floats. Wing area was 305 square feet within a span of 34 feet. Beneath the fabric covering of the fuselage the main structural members were built up of riveted aluminum extrusions rather than the more typical steel tubing. The entire tail assembly of the airplane was an aluminum monocoque structure fastened to the main fuselage structure with four bolts; it had the advantage of quick and economical replacement in the event of damage. Along the left side of the fuselage were three removable panels that permitted ready inspection of the airplane's interior. Extruded aluminum I-beams made up the main wing spars, and the ribs were one-piece aluminum stampings. Both cockpits had complete instrumentation and controls.[40]

On 23 August 1935—fully two months ahead of schedule—crews rolled airplane number 9991 out of the hangar at Mustin Field for its first test flights. With Lieutenant Commander Henry R. Oster, the factory's chief engineer, in the forward cockpit, Captain H. P. Becker of the Marine Corps piloted the craft. It was immediately apparent that the airplane was tail heavy, and neither a heavier adjustable-pitch propeller nor adjustments to the rear stabilizer alleviated the problem. Moreover, the airplane responded sluggishly during spin tests, leading the factory's engineers to increase the airplane's rudder area. After modifications, there were further tests at Anacostia, but these were not any more encouraging about the poor spin-recovery characteristics. Captain Rufus F. Zogbaum, commandant of the Naval Air Station, Pensacola, added his concern about the lack of "crush space" forward of the front cockpit and considered the midship location of the fuel tanks a hazard for instructors.[41]

These defects had to be corrected before production of the airplane could begin. NAF personnel labored feverishly in January 1936 to fix the rudder and tail surfaces and extend the engine mounts forward to improve the aircraft's balance. Because poor weather prohibited extensive trials at Anacostia, these were transferred to Pensacola in February. By early April, the bureau was satisfied that the modifications had solved the worst problems of the prototype and that further improvements would be made in production versions of the airplane. Foremost among those changes was relocation of the fuel tanks to the upper wing, thus largely eliminating the crash hazard and assuring positive gravity feed of fuel to the engine.[42]

By April 1936, the factory had received two project orders for eighty-five N3N-1s (without engines) worth nearly $800,000: the first, issued on 30 April 1935, called for the completion of twenty-five airplanes with wheeled undercarriages by 31 August 1936; the second, dated 29 June 1935, specified the completion of sixty aircraft

The XN3N-1 (no. 9991), the prototype for a long series of NAF-built trainers, flew for the first time in August 1935. This photograph shows the airplane during evaluation at the Naval Air Station, Pensacola. (80-G-646804, National Archives)

with float gear by 30 June 1937. To meet anticipated delivery dates, the factory planned to manufacture between two and three airplanes per week through the middle of 1937. On 22 May 1936, the first production model went to Anacostia for service trials. By 8 October, the NAF had delivered thirty-three N3N-1s, and the rate of production had reached three airplanes per week. In the meantime, the bureau had issued project orders for 105 more airplanes, 80 of which were to be powered by 235-horsepower Wright R-760-2 engines manufactured at the NAF.[43]

A $175,000 cost overrun on the first eighty-five aircraft marred Zeigler's otherwise remarkable achievement with the N3N-1 program. The total seems insignificant by more recent standards, but it amounted to more than 20 percent of the estimated N3N-1 program costs, and it led the bureau to cancel the June 1936 order for twenty-five additional airplanes. At a conference in July, the new bureau chief, Rear Admiral Arthur B. Cook, who had taken King's place in mid-June, determined to employ the resulting savings of nearly $200,000 to maintain the production schedule for the original eighty-five airplanes ordered in 1935.[44]

With the start of N3N-1 production came another change of command at the Naval Aircraft Factory. Zeigler left Philadelphia on 7 July 1936 and returned to duty at BuAer; his replacement as manager of the NAF was Captain Walter Wynne Webster. Genial, well liked by his fellow officers and workers, and respected for his engineering knowledge, Webster assumed his new post less than a month before his forty-eighth birthday. Born about as far from the sea as imaginable—in Fargo, North Dakota—in 1888, Webster had graduated third in his class from Annapolis in 1911 and had gone on to receive a master's degree in naval architecture from MIT in 1916. He became a naval aviation observer in 1922 and qualified as a naval aviator in 1933. Webster had previous experience at the NAF as production superintendent and chief engineer from 1925 to 1929.[45]

Captain Webster harbored no illusions about the N3N-1 as a

Final assembly of N3N-1 trainers at the NAF in November 1937. (72-AF-214474, National Archives)

primary trainer. Notwithstanding the various "fixes" of early 1936, the trainer still suffered from shortcomings in handling and control. Cognizant of the problems with the prototype, BuAer in October 1935 had authorized the construction of a second experimental trainer. It had a 240-horsepower Wright R-760-98 engine, new engine mounts, and a longer cowling, and some equipment was moved forward to correct the tail heaviness of the XN3N-1. The airplane, designated XN3N-2 (number 0265), flew for the first time at Mustin Field on 11 August 1936, but trouble with the rudder delayed the next flight for more than a month. Finding the XN3N-2 to be "no real improvement" over the N3N-1, BuAer canceled its further development.[46]

N3N-1 production ended at Philadelphia in the spring of 1938 with 179 examples delivered over a two-year period. But the need for more trainers again arose after the summer of 1938, as successive crises in Europe threatened to break out into war and spurred the expansion of naval aviation in the United States. The logical solution was to renew N3N production, at the same time correcting the deficiencies that had beset the airplane since its maiden flight. Webster wrote to Rear Admiral Cook that the NAF planned to redesign the tail surfaces to remedy the poor spin characteristics, upgrade the landing gear and brakes, and provide a more satisfactory arrangement of cockpit controls. He recommended returning an N3N-1 to the factory and rebuilding it incorporating the various modifications. Webster estimated that once the airplane had flown and the factory had received production orders, the NAF could deliver the first fifty airplanes by the end of September 1940 without disrupting other programs.[47]

Based on Webster's recommendations, BuAer issued a project order to the NAF on 21 June 1939 to manufacture fifty trainers with the model designation N3N-3, later adding another one hundred airplanes to the order. Including floats and complete sets of spare parts, but minus engines, the first fifty airplanes were estimated to cost nearly $12,000 each. In late July, the bureau assigned N3N-1 number 0020 to the factory for prototype development, and Webster ordered a civilian, John F. Horrisberger, to the job as project engineer. Using the N3N-1 as a "dog ship," the factory's engineers worked various improvements into the new design. The airplane, when completed by the factory as the XN3N-3, had a revised vertical tail surface, more rugged single-strut landing gear, and lacked the distinctive engine cowling of the N3N-1. Less visible were the alterations to controls and the replacement of some fabricated structural members with aluminum forgings. Maximum takeoff weight was 2,802 pounds for the airplane with conventional landing gear and 2,940 with floats.[48]

The new trainer was exactly what the navy needed. Webster reported to BuAer in January 1940 that the XN3N-3 had completed tests as a landplane at Philadelphia and that floatplane trials were under way. Webster concluded, "All tests conducted indicate that the XN3N-3 airplane meets the requirements of the specification." Subsequent test flights at Pensacola in February and March bolstered Webster's confidence in the NAF's product. Lloyd Harrison, the senior member of the informal flight test evaluation team at Pensacola, had nothing but praise for the craft, which, he said, "has been materially improved over . . . the N3N-1 airplane, in both landplane and seaplane conditions." He specifically noted the airplane's superior short-field takeoff characteristics, climbing capability, and cockpit visibility. In combination with other changes, Harrison said that the N3N-3 promised "increased ruggedness and convenience" in operation. There were some minor annoying defects—most notably in the brakes and rudder controls—and the airplane had persistent vibration problems, but they did not adversely affect the nearly universal admiration for the airplane.[49]

Such glowing recommendations from the people who had to live with the new trainer inspired confidence that the N3N-3 would easily negotiate the hazards of the formal evaluation process. The first production version (number 1759) had already made preliminary flights at Philadelphia in early February 1940 and the next month went to Anacostia for consideration by the bureau's trial board. Once again, the results were satisfactory. The board thought the navy had an extremely good primary trainer in the N3N-3; it was fully capable of meeting the increased requirements for these types of aircraft, and the NAF was in an excellent position to go ahead with a major production run.[50]

On 17 May 1940, the bureau informed the factory that it should begin preparations for manufacturing a "considerable number" of N3N-3s. The NAF was to provide time and cost estimates and submit requisitions for material for the production of 75 airplanes

Possibly the best-known, and certainly the most ubiquitous, NAF-built airplane was the N3N-3. This is the prototype (no. 1759), derived from N3N-1 number 0020, and shown at Anacostia during tests in March and April 1940. The NAF produced 816 N3N-3s in 1940–42. (80-G-1001403, National Archives)

per month. On 28 May a project order was issued for 500 N3N-3s, plus 20 percent spares and sixty sets of floats, costing a little more than $5 million. The figure did not include engines. Captain Marc A. Mitscher, the assistant chief of BuAer, stressed that the airplanes were "urgently needed to meet the needs of the Service" and that "it is essential that work . . . be started at the earliest practicable date." On September 18, BuAer issued a project order for another 166 of the trainers, raising the total number of N3N-3s to 816, worth nearly $7 million.[51]

The NAF stepped up N3N-3 production. BuAer had originally wanted a rate of seventy-five aircraft per month, but it agreed that fifty would be sufficient, starting with thirty in November. Fortunately, no major retooling was needed for the N3N-3, and the existing plant space was adequate, although some additional storage sheds had to be erected. Through 1941 the factory maintained the preliminary delivery schedule worked out with the bureau, and the last N3N-3 was delivered in January 1942.[52]

No sooner had the NAF completed the N3N-3s in early 1942 than it appeared the factory would be called upon to fill another large production order. Captain Ernest M. Pace, Jr., at BuAer and Webster at the NAF discussed over the telephone the possibility of manufacturing twelve hundred N3N-3s worth more than $7.7 million. The navy's air arm, along with the army and the British, needed about two thousand new trainers, equivalent to about three months of total American aircraft production. It seemed for a time that the NAF was in the best position to meet these demands, but in the end the bureau decided against placing any fresh orders with Philadelphia. The rationale was that a new order would interfere with the manufacture of spares for the just-ended N3N-3 production run and that by the time the NAF got quantity deliveries going again, the Stearman firm would be turning out enough N2S-3 trainers to fill the requirement. Consequently, on 21 March, Rear Admiral John H. Towers informed Webster: "It has been decided that the manufacture of additional N3N-3 airplanes is unnecessary."[53]

The N3N-3, sometimes known as the Yellow Bird for its distinctive, high-visibility paint scheme, or less kindly, Yellow Peril for the jeopardy in which student aviators often found themselves, showed itself to be rugged, reliable, and generally forgiving to student pilots. Some of the early airplanes sent to Pensacola experienced landing gear failures, but the NAF came up with replacement fittings that solved the problem. Late in 1942, the Naval Air Station, Corpus Christi, reported cracks in the main floats of some of its N3N-3s, but the defects were minor and easily fixed. On the whole, the aircraft had a reputation for great structural integrity and could be put through maneuvers that would overstress the airframes of other primary trainers. There were no obvious handling quirks, although the N3N-3s did have a tendency to "float" on landing, and some documents indicate potential difficulties in pulling the airplanes out of inverted spins.[54]

Robert R. Rea, a naval aviation student in the War Training Service, flew N3N-3s at Lawrence, Kansas, in 1943 and recalled that the airplanes were smooth and responsive to control inputs. He wrote at the time: "I have a great deal of respect for the N," which probably summarized the feelings of most neophyte naval aviators toward the NAF-built aircraft. Remarkably, the N3N-3s remained in the navy inventory until 1959, the last ones being retired in the summer of that year after having been used for flight indoctrination of midshipmen at Annapolis.[55]

The N3N-3 was the last production airplane for which the NAF had total design responsibility. Other designs would originate at the factory, but they would not be placed in production, and subsequent quantity manufacture at Philadelphia would be limited to aircraft designed by private firms. The little biplane trainer therefore marked, subtly to be sure, a change in the role of the NAF toward the specialty manufacture that largely dominated the factory's World War II activities. The N3N-3 had another distinction, however, that helped set it and the NAF apart; unlike all other quantity-built airplanes in the United States, it was powered by an engine manufactured in the same factory that produced the airframes.

Aircraft production was only part of the NAF's mission; the factory, according to King's directives in the autumn of 1934, was also charged with the development and manufacture of aircraft power plants. In early October, BuAer determined that the NAF should manufacture under license a relatively low-horsepower engine for a trainer or observation aircraft. The Wright Whirlwind series offered possibilities. Either the five-cylinder R-540 version or the seven-cylinder R-760 (J-6-7) would be satisfactory for trainers, while the more robust nine-cylinder R-975 (J-6-9) could be used to power an observation airplane. Other choices might be two inverted air-cooled inline engines manufactured by the Ranger Engineering Corporation (a subsidiary of the Fairchild Engine and Airplane Corporation) with which the NAF's Aeronautical Engine Laboratory had had considerable experience.[56]

By the beginning of November, BuAer had decided that because of the pressing need for training-plane engines, the NAF should concentrate its first efforts on a less powerful power plant. Commenting on a survey by the factory of domestic and foreign engine manufacturers that had been completed by the NAF in October 1934, Lieutenant Commander T. C. Lonnquest, head of the bureau's power plant design section, said that an engine of "proven but moderate performance" was preferable. This, he maintained, would "reduce the manufacturing difficulties in the initial attempt" to build engines and offer the best early chance of meeting the 10 percent requirement of the Vinson-Trammell Act. Most promising were two Wright radials, the five-cylinder 165-horsepower R-540 or the seven-cylinder, 240-horsepower R-760 (J-6-7) and the 150-horsepower Ranger 6-390. Initially the NAF favored the Ranger because it had less frontal area than the radial designs and it appeared to have more room for growth into higher-powered derivatives.[57]

Yet the Wright prevailed in the end. By the third week of March, BuAer had decided that the R-760-2 was "somewhat more suitable" for application in the trainer and that Wright had presented a satisfactory licensing proposal. The NAF received official notification in March 1935 of the selection of the R-760-2 for the trainer and the nine-cylinder R-975 for possible use in an observation airplane. When an order for one hundred R-760-2s followed later in the year, M. A. McCullough took charge as project engineer.[58]

More than two years went by before the first flight test of an NAF-built Whirlwind. Numerous changes were needed in the Wright-supplied drawings before fabricating and production tools could be acquired and parts lists put together. The modifications by the NAF were so extensive the Wright engine was virtually redesigned, and the work was not completed until September 1936. Manufacturing started in the spring of 1937, and the first R-760-2 flew in an N3N-1 in May. Altogether, the factory manufactured 155 R-760-2s for use in the N3N-1 aircraft.[59]

When major orders for N3N-3s began to arrive in 1940, the factory was in a good position to supply the necessary engines. On 28 May 1940, the same day the NAF received the order for 500 N3N-3s, BuAer notified the factory that it was to produce 532 R-760-8s, plus spares, worth more than $2.5 million. A subsequent order for 235 R-760-8s and spares, estimated at nearly $1.2 million, followed on 18 September. An upgraded version of the R-760-2, the R-760-8 had some detail differences that required the acquisition of new tools. To prevent production delays, BuAer determined that Wright should supply the crankshafts for the first hundred or so NAF engines. For a while, Wright seemed unable to meet the delivery dates, but production began as scheduled in February 1941, and the NAF manufactured about 45 engines per month through the remainder of 1941.[60]

Despite problems in beginning engine production at the NAF, the choice of the Wright over the Ranger was fortuitous. Although the

Production of Wright R-760-2 seven-cylinder radial engines began at the Naval Aircraft Factory in the spring of 1937. This photograph shows some of the machine tools and workers in the engine shop in November 1937. (72-AF-215072, National Archives)

Ranger proved to be an adequate engine and was used in thousands of Fairchild trainers, manufacturing the engines in quantity would have pulled the factory out of the mainstream of power plant technology, for by the mid-1930s the emphasis in American naval aviation was definitely on air-cooled radial engines. Moreover, the choice of a radial for production placed the factory in a better position to exercise its yardstick function vis-à-vis the major navy engine suppliers. Rumors persisted that once the NAF began man-ufacturing the R-760 in quantity, Wright significantly reduced its prices on these engines.[61]

By the end of the decade, the will of Congress had become BuAer policy in regard to the Naval Aircraft Factory. In addition to research and development, the NAF was once more a factory—not as it had been during World War I principally to supply the specialized needs of the navy for flying boats—but as a yardstick or check on the costs of aircraft and engines procured from private sources. The decision to return quantity production to the NAF was a political signal that the chief executive and Congress were committed to the principle of direct government intervention in an industry deemed vital to America's defense. This compared with Moffett's policy in the 1920s that restricted aircraft production at Philadelphia to allay private industry's fears of government competition. Yet these policies were really only different means to the same end—to integrate the Naval Aircraft Factory into an effective aviation procurement program that met the requirements of the service. Which method was best and whether the results of renewed aircraft and engine manufacturing justified the expense and the diversion of personnel from other activities remained open to debate. In any case, the factory was fully committed to production and continued to be so as naval aviation faced the prospect of having to fight another war.

7

Projects and Production

As the decade of the 1930s waned, the Naval Aircraft Factory once again pulsed with activity. The navy had accepted the factory as a source for at least a portion of its aircraft design and production and deemed the NAF essential to fulfilling the intent of the Vinson-Trammell legislation. At the same time, there were faint indications that the factory's days as an aircraft design and production center were limited, as the navy's requirements for testing, research and development, and special weapons took on higher priority.

Although the manufacture of N3Ns occupied center stage at Philadelphia, the Bureau of Aeronautics assigned to the NAF the design and production of other aircraft under the aegis of the Vinson-Trammell Act. As early as the fall of 1934, the service considered acquiring significant numbers of new observation airplanes for use with the fleet and subsequently opened a design contest to select a manufacturer for the aircraft. Following an August 1936 conference at BuAer, Captain W. W. Webster initiated preliminary work at the NAF on the design of an observation airplane to be submitted in the competition. In less than two months the NAF presented a design proposal to the bureau. The factory planned an all-metal biplane with streamlined interplane struts and full-length flaps on the upper wing to reduce landing speeds. The airplane was also to be convertible between conventional landing gear and floats. Considering the factory's design "of sufficient promise, when compared with all other designs submitted . . . to rate it as one of the best," BuAer approved the manufacture of a prototype, designated XOSN-1.[1]

The factory completed the observation airplane in early 1937. Powered by a 550-horsepower Pratt and Whitney R-1340, the XOSN-1 had a maximum takeoff weight of 5,167 pounds with wheels and 5,412 pounds with floats. The total wing area was 378 square feet within a span of 36 feet. The airplane competed with entries from Stearman and the Vought-Sikorsky division of United Aircraft and outperformed both of its rivals in landing speed and water-handling characteristics. But it was less satisfactory in other respects, and the navy awarded the production contract to Vought-Sikorsky in March. The Vought aircraft, a monoplane designated OS2U and known generally as the Kingfisher, went into service in 1940 as the standard fleet observation airplane and was one of the most successful aircraft in the navy's inventory. The NAF's XOSN-1 put in long years of service as a utility airplane at Annapolis.[2] Though adequate, the XOSN-1 demonstrated that the NAF could not compete with private firms in the design of modern aircraft, even those demanding such modest performance as observation airplanes. One of the major shortcomings of the NAF's XOSN-1 was its biplane configuration. Although biplanes were adequate in the trainer role in the late 1930s, monoplanes were superior for virtually all other applications. The factory had to do much better if it was to keep pace with the latest advances in aeronautical engineering.

Possibly recognizing that they needed to promulgate a more advanced design, engineers at the factory followed the XOSN-1 with a monoplane primary trainer intended to supplement or replace the N3N-3 and similar aircraft. The project had its origins in April 1938, when Rear Admiral Cook, chief of BuAer, indicated to Webster that the bureau wanted a single-engine, two-seat airplane of rugged construction that would not have any tendency toward flat, uncontrolled spins. "Ease of maintenance shall be a primary characteristic," too. The bureau wanted cost and time estimates for the construction of the airplane and suggested that one hundred examples could be procured in the next fiscal year.[3]

Webster responded with commendable alacrity, submitting a projected design for a low-wing monoplane on 22 April. He contended that the airplane would fulfill the primary flight instruction

The XOSN-1 in early 1938. The airplane was completed by the NAF
early the previous year. Although a sound design, the biplane proved inferior to the Vought OS2U Kingfisher monoplane in the observation role.
(72-AF-214941, National Archives)

role and permit the "ready transition" from primary to more
advanced training. The airplane was to have an aluminum monocoque fuselage, low cantilevered wings with metal-covered leading
edges, and fixed landing gear. NAF engineers considered flaps
essential to reduce landing speeds. Power came from an R-760
engine, which, with 320 horsepower, provided a significant performance increment over the N3N-3. One airplane, less engine, would
cost $154,000, and the cost for five additional examples would go
down slightly to $149,000 each.[4]

Not everyone at BuAer concurred on the merits of the NAF's
suggested features for the new airplane, thinking that the proposed
aircraft was too costly and had more performance than was desirable
in a primary trainer. Some engineers were critical of the use of flaps
in the NAF design, preferring instead greater wing area and reduced

loading to increase the rate of climb and improve takeoff character istics. Nor were they entirely ready to accept a monoplane in the role of primary instruction, an area in which both the army and the navy had relied exclusively on biplanes. The proposed monocoque fuselage also elicited debate, particularly over whether it was easier to maintain than a steel-tube fuselage. It made little sense to give a student pilot an expensive airplane with advanced technical features if there was a good chance it would be wrecked.[5]

The NAF had a great deal at stake with this airplane, which the navy had by now designated the XN5N-1. NAF designers, unwilling to reduce the wing loading or abandon the monoplane configuration, decided to fit a more powerful version of the R-760, or possibly even a 440-horsepower R-975, a split flap, and a special propeller to the aircraft to improve its takeoff and climb characteristics. Webster told Admiral Cook that "regardless of what assumptions or conditions are prescribed, I feel confident that the Naval Aircraft Factory can design and build a low wing monoplane trainer fully as good" as could be obtained from private competitors. He urged the bureau to authorize construction of the new airplane "immediately," warning, that "if this is not done now, our airplane design staff will be almost entirely disbursed [sic] and the Factory will not be in a position to proceed expeditiously with the design four or five months from now."[6]

Webster's mild ultimatum brought the desired results. Commander A. C. Davis at BuAer acknowledged that the XN5N-1 with the changes suggested by the factory would take off and climb better than the N3N or the roughly comparable Stearman NS. Davis said the "big stumbling block" that still remained was the "relatively high cost estimate" and urged the bureau to see if the NAF could reduce it. Upon learning that cost was the only real objection, Webster sharpened his pencil and responded with an estimate of $136,700 for the prototype, a reduction of more than 10 percent from the previous cost figures. Commander Frederick W. Pennoyer reviewed the latest proposal from the NAF. The factory's ability to meet the "previous inadequacies" of the aircraft while adhering to the same basic configuration impressed Pennoyer, who raised "no objections of a fundamental nature" to the airplane. He recommended that BuAer issue a project order for the design and construction of the airplane.[7]

The XN5N-1 moved through the detail design phases to the mockup stage in the fall of 1938 and winter of 1939. The factory received the project order for the design and construction of the airplane in August 1938, and work began almost immediately under John F. Horrisberger as project engineer. Although detail specifications showing minor weight increases resulting from modifications of the engine cowling and oil cooler caused some concern, BuAer received assurances that the airplane would meet the original performance criteria and that the weights were still "reasonable." An inspection board convened at the NAF on 3–4 April 1939, reporting a month later: "The mock-up in general was excellent . . . and it is above average in completeness of detail." The board did not recommend any major changes.[8]

The early momentum of the XN5N-1 project quickly dissipated in the spring of 1939 when Webster reported to BuAer that fabrication had not yet started and that the airplane's completion date would be delayed. This turn of events had come about because the factory did not have enough engineers and draftsmen to handle higher-priority projects in addition to the new trainer. Another problem, Webster pointed out, was that the bureau in recent months had siphoned off six of the NAF's "best engineers" for duty in Washington. Still, Webster was confident that when the engineering work load leveled off, the factory would "prosecute with one hundred percent priority" the XN5N-1 project.[9]

Not readily apparent to most observers in 1939 was a distinct shift toward research and development that inexorably drove the NAF away from the design of aircraft into other activities. The XN5N-1 was caught in this unfolding trend. In November 1939, Webster once again had to tell BuAer that all work on the trainer "has been suspended, due to other important projects." The project, which had now been held up for nearly a year, had reached something of a crossroads. Some in the bureau said that the navy needed a monoplane trainer and recommended that if the NAF could not complete it, the job should be given to Waco, Spartan, or some other private manufacturer. Commander Leslie C. Stevens, however, did not see another airplane builder "picking up this job where NAF leaves off." "It would seem more satisfactory," Stevens concluded, "to let NAF finish the job." Thus the XN5N-1 was safe for the present, but the factory would have to perform a delicate balancing act as it juggled the trainer project and higher-priority research and development programs.[10]

Work on the trainer proceeded sporadically from late 1939 through 1940. Wind tunnel tests at the NACA's Langley Aeronautical Laboratory in the fall of 1939 indicated that the airplane was likely to have some undesirable spin characteristics and might also be subject to flutter at higher speeds. NAF and Langley people collaborated on changes to the design, one of which was to reposition the vertical tail slightly. When at last the XN5N-1 got into the air in the spring of 1941, it had a maximum takeoff weight of 3,370 pounds and a wing span of 42 feet. Preliminary demonstrations, completed by the second week of April, showed the airplane to be "very satisfactory," with "excellent" stability in all three axes. The only black mark was the unreliable vacuum operation of the flaps, which was solved when the factory substituted an electrically actuated system.[11]

From Philadelphia the XN5N-1 went to Pensacola in May for more than ten days of test flights. The flaps still caused problems, but nothing severe enough to detract from the nearly universal impression that the XN5N-1 was well designed and well built. In fact, the people at Pensacola found the airplane superior in nearly every respect to the N3N-1, N3N-3, and the Stearman biplane trainers. Captain Albert C. Read, the commandant of the naval air station, recommended that the factory be authorized to produce a limited number of the aircraft.[12]

Despite the XN5N-1's many admirable qualities, no production contract for it resulted. In July 1941, the factory learned that "it had been definitely decided . . . not to go into production on N5N-1 airplanes." The XN5N-1 underwent modifications over the years, one of which was an enclosed cockpit, and was used in early 1943 for glider towing tests at the NAF. Part of Naval Aircraft Factory lore is that the XN5N-1 was too good an airplane and that its easy handling characteristics made it unsuitable as a primary trainer. Dan Smith, one of the test pilots on the XN5N, said the airplane had a "built-in three-point landing."[13] There is a grain of truth in this, for the performance of the airplane tended to put it in the category of an intermediate trainer. But the reality is that by 1941 BuAer had determined that it did not need any more primary trainers, that it could use versions of army airplanes as intermediate trainers, and,

Designed and constructed to meet the navy's demand for an improved primary trainer, the NAF's XN5N-1, shown here during preliminary trials in the spring of 1941, fell victim to priority problems and changes in the navy's trainer requirements. (80-G-1040981, National Archives)

most important, that aircraft production at the NAF would be curtailed.

The priority problems besetting the XN5N-1 showed that BuAer considered the design of new aircraft only part of the NAF's mission. Under the Vinson-Trammell mandate, the factory was legally bound to establish the yardstick, which compelled the NAF to manufacture a quantity of privately designed aircraft to establish cost guidelines. During hearings on the navy's appropriation bill for 1938, the question of the yardstick arose. Admiral Cook testified in February 1937 that the $2.7 million allotted to the factory had been spent on the expansion of its physical plant to handle the production of airplanes and engines under the Vinson-Trammell provisions. Sydney Kraus said that the factory could manufacture 450 airplanes and 250 engines per year—more if it went to a second work shift. This information piqued the curiosity of Congressman William

Bradley Unstead, a Democrat from North Carolina, who asked Kraus if he had "an adequate and helpful yardstick in connection with the manufacture of airplanes commercially."[14]

Unstead's question ignited a dialogue with Kraus that revealed some of the prevailing attitudes about the yardstick as a principle underlying aircraft and engine production at the NAF. Responding to Unstead, Kraus said that the navy probably already had enough aircraft production capacity at Philadelphia to provide an accurate measure of what private manufacturers were doing. But the NAF needed more time, equipment, and experience before it would be able to give the navy firm guidelines on the costs of engines supplied by outside firms. Kraus was certain "the yardstick will be of use. It has resulted, insofar as we can see now . . . [in] fairly dependable information on the cost of aircraft constructed by contract."[15]

Unstead wanted further explanation. He told Kraus that it was his understanding that NAF's unit costs exceeded those of private companies. Admitting that "the indications are that the cost of airplanes [from the NAF] will exceed the cost of a corresponding airplane built in a commercial shop," Kraus said this was "due to the cost of getting started on the project of manufacturing, and of training an organization for the purpose of quantity production." That explanation seemed reasonable to Unstead, who agreed "that is to be expected, certainly until operations have proceeded long enough to eliminate or reduce a good many items of expense that would not thereafter reoccur in your production operations."[16]

The foregoing exchange, ending with an apparent understanding of at least part of the yardstick mechanism, obscured the problems inherent in cost comparisons. Though simple in its conception and logical given the prevailing political and economic climate of the late 1930s, the yardstick as implemented at Philadelphia illustrated many of the difficulties associated with the accumulation and interpretation of comparative data. These comparisons were not made any easier when the factory undertook quantity production of other manufacturers' airplanes.

Curtiss had submitted and BuAer had accepted a design for a biplane scout-observation aircraft in 1933. Designated the SOC and known as the Seagull when it went into service in November 1935, the airplane was convertible, meaning that it could be readily shifted from conventional landing gear to floats. The aircraft was similar in many respects to the NAF's XOSN-1. In conformance with the stipulations of the Vinson-Trammell Act, the NAF submitted estimates in May 1937 for the manufacture of airplanes identical to the SOC-2, a slightly improved version of the original Curtiss model. BuAer issued project orders to the NAF on 10 June 1937 for the manufacture of forty-four of the airplanes, which received the designation SON-1.[17]

Delays set back the start of SON-1 production. NAF engineers first planned to produce one airplane to check the accuracy of the drawings and the fit of the various parts and components. Before starting work on the production drawings, however, the factory received an SOC-2 landplane from storage at Norfolk that was disassembled and inspected. In addition, the SON project engineer, Charles Kirkbride, journeyed to Buffalo to familiarize himself with the Curtiss operation in general and the assembly of the SOC-2 in particular. One of the chief problems early in the SON program was the decision in July to make the NAF airplane identical to the SOC-3 rather than to the SOC-2. Ordinarily the switch would not have caused too many difficulties, but in this case the factory was already well along with the preparation of plans and drawings based on the SOC-2. And the SON, as it resulted, was not identical to the SOC-3, for it incorporated numerous detail changes, each of which involved more time at the drafting table. Among the modifications were different wing tip floats, a redesigned radio installation, and changes to the covering of the horizontal stabilizer.[18]

Strained relations with Curtiss further complicated the situation. Webster explained to Admiral Cook that NAF engineers and draftsmen had found discrepancies between the dimensions given on the drawings obtained from Curtiss and the aircraft parts themselves. Thus each part had to be checked individually to ensure absolute interchangeability with the Curtiss airplanes. All this would have been frustrating enough had the Curtiss people been fully cooperative. But they were not. Lawrence B. Richardson of BuAer commented that trips to Buffalo to consult with Curtiss engineers were to no avail: "Curtiss gave no information about errors until they were asked, and it was not feasible to refer every discrepancy to them. All data received from Curtiss were replete with errors. The bills of material were practically useless; this alone caused a loss of three months' time." Not everyone agreed with this assessment of the situation, but obviously much had changed since 1919, when the factory had closely collaborated with Curtiss on such designs as the NC boats and MF seaplanes, and there was evidently some resentment in Buffalo that a portion of the SOC production was being siphoned off to Philadelphia.[19]

Such problems should not have been entirely unanticipated, for during World War I, aircraft and engine manufacturers, including Curtiss, had discovered that foreign designs required a great deal of extra drafting work before production could begin. Additionally, it was not uncommon for a manufacturer to complete an entire aircraft production contract using only partial drawings and then to submit finished plans some time after delivery of the last airplane. Although many have assumed that aircraft design and manufacture are precise and scientific, in reality there is considerable "art" in the process of making an airplane. Airplane design and manufacture are not readily amenable to quantification or reduction to a neat pile of data and drawings. Nowhere was this more apparent than in the experience of the NAF with the SON-1.[20]

Originally planned for June 1938, the first test flights of the SON-1 (number 1147) in its floatplane configuration did not occur until 15 September. Powered by a 550-horsepower Pratt and Whitney R-1340, the airplane had a maximum takeoff weight of 5,287 pounds, a wing area of 342 square feet, and a span of 36 feet. The Anacostia tests were not particularly auspicious. During the preliminary flight demonstrations, held at Anacostia, the fabric on the upper side of one of the top wing panels showed a tendency to pull away from the ribs. The NAF had to rework the fabric attachment points before returning the airplane to Anacostia in November for further trials. Although Webster assured Cook that "the strength and stability of the . . . airplane have been definitely established," the tests at Anacostia revealed some potentially alarming spin characteristics. Changes to the rudder trim tab alleviated the problem, and further tests of the aircraft in both its floatplane and landplane versions proceeded without major incident.[21]

Deliveries of production aircraft began early in 1939 and continued on a regular schedule through the late summer, with parts production extending into October. Half the airplanes went into service as landplanes, some of which flew from the carriers *Wasp* and *Hornet*, and half were shipped as floatplanes, equipping cruisers and battleships in the fleet. Units operating the SON-1s found them to be generally satisfactory, but the airplanes did appear to suffer from more than the usual corrosion problems, requiring the replacement of some fittings with ones fabricated from stainless steel. Because the original SON-1 fixed-pitch propellers developed cracks in some of the early production models, the bureau altered the specification in April 1939 to incorporate adjustable-pitch propellers.[22]

From the inception of the SON-1 project, the NAF maintained complete records and supplied cost data to the bureau for comparative purposes. Webster noted with pride that the NAF had done considerably better than had Curtiss in materials purchases for the aircraft. Whereas the NAF bought a selection of products for a little less than $23,000, Curtiss had paid more than $42,000 for the same quantity of goods. In the final accounting, the factory completed the production of the forty-four airplanes and spares for a little more than $1.1 million, which was $220,000 less than project order estimates. Each airplane cost $22,000, compared to the unit cost of approximately $21,000 from Curtiss. Captain Marc A. Mitscher, the acting chief of BuAer, was almost effusive in his praise of the NAF's performance, stating that "the Bureau is very much gratified by the Factory's efficient execution of the SON-1 airplane project." The bureau directed that the NAF could keep $70,000 of the savings and use it to buy new equipment for the factory's engine shop.[23]

Certainly the NAF's performance was creditable, demonstrating, as did the N3N program, that it could efficiently undertake quantity manufacture of specific airplane types. The NAF's unit costs were higher in part because of the shorter production run of the SON-1s, and the airplanes themselves were more complex than the SOC-1s and SOC-2s that made up the bulk of the Curtiss order. Yet, the NAF was able to buy virtually complete fuselages from Curtiss, a procedure that involved considerable shipping expenses but saved the factory some tooling and assembly costs. The yardstick, then, despite all the efforts of BuAer and the NAF, was at best an inexact measure of the private company's performance.[24]

Cost comparison was consistent with the objects of the Vinson-Trammell legislation, but the navy also had to uphold the provisions of the law requiring that 10 percent of total aircraft procurement be derived from the NAF. This stipulation led to a peculiar application of the Vinson-Trammell Act whereby the Naval Aircraft Factory assumed responsibility for the entire production run of a privately designed airplane. In October 1934, the Brewster Aeronautical Corporation of Long Island City, New York, received a contract to manufacture a prototype scout bomber. Brewster was a newcomer to the design and construction of complete aircraft, having previous experience only with subcontracting components and assemblies for other builders. But the firm had been reorganized by James Work in 1932 and was moving aggressively to obtain navy contracts. The scout bomber, designated XSBA-1, was an all-metal two-seat monoplane with internal bomb stowage. Upon delivery in April 1936, the airplane was overweight, and the company did not receive a production order. Nevertheless, the navy saw enough potential in the Brewster design to return the airplane to the company, where it was refitted with a more powerful Wright XR-1820-22 engine and accepted into service after trials in 1938.[25]

Still, Brewster received no production contract. Citing the priority of the company's other work for the navy, chiefly the development of the F2A fighter, BuAer determined to shunt quantity manufacture of the scout bomber to the Naval Aircraft Factory. The real reason was to satisfy the 10 percent provision of the Vinson-Trammell Act. Rear Admiral Cook wrote in June 1938 that "maintaining 10% production at the [Naval] Aircraft factory is a pain in the neck, and political pressure to maintain the force there is continuous." Brewster seemed willing to sacrifice the production order. Both Work and Dayton T. Brown, the company's chief engineer, had been employed at the NAF and presumably still had close connections with Philadelphia. Moreover, it was critical to cooperate with BuAer should Brewster be considered for future manufacturing orders.[26]

In late June 1938, Commander Ernest M. Pace, Jr., of BuAer directed the NAF to submit estimates for the production of a scout bomber based on the XSBA-1 prototype. Pace emphasized that the bureau would demand certain design changes, among them flush riveting on the leading edges of the wings, a more aerodynamically efficient engine cowling, improved rear cockpit layout, and revisions to the landing gear. The NAF itself determined to use magnesium in some small parts and to use forgings in place of many of the stampings and miscellaneous fabricated components on the XSBA-

1. On 29 September 1938, BuAer issued a project order for the production of thirty airplanes, which received the designation SBN-1.[27]

Many of the same delays that accompanied the SON-1 program during its early phases also afflicted the SBN-1 project. After brief flight tests of the XSBA-1 prototype (number 9726) in the spring of 1939, NAF technicians, working under project engineer Charles Kirkbride, disassembled the aircraft to study its construction details and to take measurements. No problems surfaced until NAF engineers and draftsmen began to grapple with Brewster-supplied drawings of the XSBA. They found these to be incomplete and in places illegible, requiring more drafting work and additional mockups of important components. During assembly of the first SBN-1, other difficulties arose, which further delayed the project. Perhaps a worse problem was the growing shortage of personnel in 1939–40. The need to meet the schedule for deliveries of higher-priority N3N-3s drew workers away from the SBN-1 project, and officers at the NAF despaired of recruiting additional workers from outside because of the demands placed on the industry from rapidly increasing British and French aircraft orders.[28]

Plagued from the start with problems, the SBN-1 program never seemed to recover. The completion of the first SBN-1, originally to have occurred in the middle of May 1940, slipped to the first week of November. As delivered, the SBN-1 had a maximum takeoff weight of 6,759 pounds and a wing area of 259 square feet within a span of 39 feet. The airplane had a 950-horsepower Wright R-1830-38 and was armed with a 0.50-caliber fixed gun, a 0.30-caliber flexible gun, and a 500-pound bomb carried internally. Flight tests of the SBN-1 proceeded until early January 1941, when engineers found that dives exerted sufficient air pressure loads on the windshield to cause it to crack. Minor "fixes" did not work, and the NAF had to develop an entirely new windshield design. Engine deficiencies postponed completion of the airplane's carrier acceptance trials until the autumn, and an assortment of other defects drove costs of the SBN-1 up more than $300,000 in 1941. Not until June 1942 was the last of the thirty aircraft delivered, roughly seven months later than originally planned. In service, the ill-starred airplane's troubles continued. Twenty-two SBN-1s with Torpedo Squadron 8 and the Advanced Carrier Training Group at Norfolk suffered from fuel tank

Derived from the Brewster XSBA-1 scout bomber, the NAF's SBN-1 was one of the factory's least successful airplanes. This photograph shows the first example (no. 1522) in November 1940. (72-AF-218940, National Archives)

leaks, blown tires, overheated cockpits, and hydraulic system failures during operations in the fall of 1941. Some of these problems—the tires, for example—were caused by operational deficiencies beyond the control of the NAF, but the SBN-1 did nothing to enhance the factory's reputation for manufacturing good airplanes.[29]

The SBN-1 program telescoped many of the difficulties that had to be overcome in carrying an aircraft production effort through to a successful conclusion. Initially, the XSBA-1 design was apparently too much for the inexperienced Brewster organization to handle. After transferring production to the NAF, BuAer insisted on numerous change orders, a considerable number of which had to be executed after SBN-1 production had already begun. These added to the costs and delays. One of the advantages often cited for aircraft production at the NAF was the flexibility of the factory and its receptiveness to design changes based on operational experience. That may have been true with some of the manufacturing programs at Philadelphia, but it was not the case with the SBN-1. Finally, the SBN-1 project became mired in the welter of priority conflicts and personnel shortages that affected the aircraft industry as a whole in 1940–41. Though not all of the factory's making, these problems were similar to those encountered by many aircraft production programs, and they demanded the utmost managerial skills to hurdle. Sadly, that talent seems to have been lacking at Philadelphia throughout the SBN-1 program.

Engine manufacturing continued at the NAF alongside aircraft production. Despite some parts shortages and the need to acquire specialized machine tools, the factory stepped up the production of Wright R-760-8s in 1941, completing 69 of the engines in April alone. R-760-8 output from the NAF in 1941 was 557, followed by another 239 of the engines in the first half of 1942. All told, the factory delivered 995 R-760-8s before production ended in June 1942, most of which went into the factory's N3N-3 trainers. These engines added to the 155 R-760-2s completed earlier for N3N-1s.[30]

From the beginning it was understood that the Wright R-975 nine-cylinder radial was the best engine for the factory to produce once enough experience had been gained with the R-760. With about 440 horsepower, the R-975 was a rugged and reliable power plant mainly used in scout and observation aircraft. In February 1941, Commander Ernest M. Pace, Jr., the manager of the NAF, requested a new engine order, suggesting that the R-975 would require a minimum of additional machine tools and urging BuAer to make a decision as quickly as possible to preclude the "possible serious disorganization of productive effort." Unfortunately, authorization for the manufacture of R-975s still had not arrived in Philadelphia by August 1941, necessitating the temporary layoff of about two-thirds of the engine shop work force.[31]

The NAF finally received project orders for the manufacture of 63 R-975s, broken down into 37 R-975-11s and 26 R-975-28s. Supplementing these was an order for 371 R-975-30s. The first two of the engines—R-975-11 models—left the factory's engine shop in August 1942. Of the 371 R-975-30s called for, the NAF had delivered 216 by August 1943 and projected that it would complete the remainder at a rate of 30 per month, despite continued nagging parts shortages, especially of Holley carburetors. Monthly output reached 53 in October and 47 in November 1943; the engines delivered in November were the last complete aircraft engines manufactured by the NAF.[32]

The Naval Aircraft Factory also became a major center for the production of parachutes in the 1930s and early 1940s. Parachutes became standard aviation safety equipment after World War I, and the navy's requirements for them increased throughout the 1920s. The NAF inspected all parachutes returned from overseas in 1919 and 1920, surveying their condition and sending those that were still serviceable to the Follmer-Clogg Company in Lancaster, Pennsylvania, for repairs and return to the navy inventory. In 1929, as part of an ongoing effort to find an alternative to silk as a parachute fabric, the factory began investigations into a lightweight, chemically treated cotton cloth. The fabric had to be of the right consistency to allow air to flow through the parachute and assure stability. The factory completed 450 parachutes in 1931 and 1932 but received no additional major orders until 1941, when BuAer assigned to the factory a contract for 2,900 parachutes, worth more than $300,000. In April 1942, the bureau assigned a $1.2 million project order to the factory to manufacture 12,000 seat-type parachutes at a rate of 1,000 per month. To fill these and other orders, which led to a total production of 30,000 parachutes during the war, the factory converted the low shop of Building 77 for layout, cutting, assembly, and inspection of parachutes. Austin Joy was the civilian shop master in charge of NAF parachute workers, many of whom were women.[33]

To a degree, these production programs overshadowed the laboratory work at the NAF, which steadily expanded in size and scope through the late 1930s and into the 1940s. The Aeronautical Engine Laboratory, led by Senior Engineer Kermit J. Leach, undertook studies using the new dynamometer that had been installed in the early 1930s. The dynamometer put the AEL in an excellent position to conduct experimental programs with the latest and most powerful aero engines, but equipment still imposed some limitations on the lab's activities. By early 1935, the AEL had under its wing modifications and improvements to the Pratt and Whitney R-1535 and R-1830 radial engines planned for use by the navy in new patrol airplanes and the Douglas XTBD torpedo bomber. Because of the volume of testing at the AEL, it was apparent that new equipment and more space would be needed. Lieutenant Commander Thomas L. Sprague, superintendent of the AEL, pointed out in the spring of

1935 that the existing propeller test stands were insufficient to keep up with the testing schedule and posed a danger for aircraft approaching Mustin Field. "The building of an adequate engine-propeller test house is considered an absolute necessity," concluded one memorandum. BuAer conveyed the urgency of the AEL's space and equipment limitations to the Office of the Chief of Naval Operations (CNO), which in April 1936 approved money for an extension to Building 533 to house eight new engine-propeller test stands.[34]

Still needed was a comprehensive, long-term plan for the expansion of the AEL to meet the navy's increased requirements for power plant research and development and testing. Captain W. W. Webster provided that plan in a message to the chief of BuAer in March 1937. Reporting that the NAF had completed a "thorough study" of the engine lab and the "present unsatisfactory conditions" there, Webster said: "The work done at the Engine Laboratory never has been so great as at present and it is constantly increasing." He recommended that the bureau approve new construction in stages, starting with a new dynamometer building and followed by new office and shop space. This, he argued, would make the estimated $1.1 million AEL expansion program more palatable to Congress.[35]

But Congress was not prepared to commit major funds to the expansion of the AEL at that time, and more than two years passed before the money was forthcoming. In the meantime, the NAF raised the ante, requesting an additional $175,000 in 1938 for a seven-by-ten-foot wind tunnel. BuAer saw this request as reasonable, and Commander Pennoyer commented: "The necessity for a moderate size wind tunnel at the Aircraft Factory has arisen in connection with the airplane building program which that organization must undertake in accordance with a Congressional directive that 10% of the new aircraft procured annually must be manufactured by the Factory." Furthermore, Pennoyer argued, "New designs require a considerable amount of wind tunnel testing and a substantial saving of time and cost can be effected if such testing can be done under the immediate supervision of the responsible designers. Solutions to aerodynamic problems can thus be obtained and applied in practice with minimum delay."[36]

The wind tunnel, plus other equipment and additions to the physical plant, increased the NAF request to $2,175,000 by the end of 1939. When it at last got around to appropriating money for the AEL, however, Congress placed a $2 million ceiling on spending. Reluctantly, planners shelved the wind tunnel, although as late as November 1940 it remained on the NAF's "wish list." Construction of the new AEL building (number 599) got under way on Rowan Avenue in 1940, and the facility became fully operational before the end of 1941. The loss of the tunnel must have been a bitter pill to swallow for some at the NAF, for wind tunnels had considerable prestige in the tightly knit aeronautical engineering community. Yet it was a good decision, for it avoided duplication of facilities already present at the NACA's Langley laboratory and built on the strengths of the NAF rather than taking it in new directions where its personnel had little experience.[37]

One of the NAF's strengths in the 1930s was the Physical Testing Laboratory, the senior lab at Philadelphia. Lieutenant N. A. Drain visited the factory in the middle of August 1934 to observe and report on the research and testing activities of the laboratory. He submitted a twenty-nine-page memorandum to the Material Branch of BuAer in which he stressed that the lab's work load had increased since the previous year and that there was every indication it would continue to do so. Much of the research involved experimentation with dopes and aircraft finishes, especially those containing zinc chromate and that had anticorrosion properties. Metallurgical experts at the lab tested failed aircraft parts and passed judgment on the quality of parts supplied from private fabricators. They also spent a great deal of time with vibration testing and examining the properties of aluminum and various alloys thereof. Drain praised the lab for the "variety and excellence of the test equipment and apparatus."[38]

Among the metals and alloys that involved researchers at the PTL was magnesium, which attracted aircraft designers and builders because of its lightness and strength. Lieutenant Drain noted in his 1934 memorandum that the lab had been investigating the use of magnesium in the fabrication of various aircraft parts and components. The results of the tests were not encouraging. Magnesium proved difficult to shape, it had a tendency to crack easily when stressed, and it presented an ever-present fire hazard, but these limitations did not deter further investigations. In December 1937, BuAer held a conference at which it was agreed that magnesium

The machine shop of the NAF's Physical Testing Laboratory as it appeared in September 1937. Laboratory work continued alongside aircraft and engine production as part of the factory's mission in the pre–World War II years. (72-AF-214095, National Archives)

warranted more attention and use as an aircraft material. The Dow Chemical Company, maker of a magnesium alloy known as Dowmetal, offered to help set up a test program with the NAF to determine whether the material could be used in aircraft structures.[39]

BuAer seized the initiative and pressed for an ambitious research program into magnesium's potential applications. Following a survey in 1939, the bureau expressed concern that other countries were making more progress with the metal than the United States was. The bureau directed the NAF to prepare cost estimates and plans for the construction of two N3N-3s using substantial quantities of magnesium. Captain Webster, the NAF manager, responded in October with a proposal to build two of the airplanes with magnesium wings, ailerons, tail surfaces, fuselages, and landing gear. If the bureau wished, the factory could also use magnesium propellers in the aircraft. The cost estimate for the two aircraft was $339,500, which included tooling, tests, and actual construction.[40]

Webster urged, however, that BuAer should adopt a cautious approach in using magnesium as an aircraft material. Before the N3N-3s could be completed, there would have to be extensive tests of all the structural components and, because of the difficulty in forming magnesium sheets and other shapes, fabrication would take much longer than usual. He recommended that BuAer consider limiting experiments with magnesium to one component at a time rather than committing to an entire airplane. "The problems involved in the construction of an airplane of magnesium alloy at this time are such that the engineering effort, the cost of dies, forms and shop experimentation represent a disproportionately large cost for the relatively small amount of information that will be obtained," Webster said. Finally, the severe corrosion problems associated with magnesium remained to be solved and did not offset whatever weight advantage the metal had. Dow and BuAer remained optimistic about the metal, and experiments continued throughout the late 1930s and early 1940s, but in the end, Webster's pessimism about magnesium proved justified and the material did not find a major place in the aircraft industry.[41]

The Physical Testing Laboratory also worked with plastics. The trend in the late 1930s toward more airplanes with enclosed cockpits led the lab to begin investigations into transparent plastics for use as canopies and windows. Cellulose nitrate had long been used, but this material constituted a fire hazard and yellowed with age. The PTL's research led in 1936 to a determination that a clear acrylic plastic manufactured by the Philadelphia firm of Rohm and Haas best met the requirement. Known generally by its trade name Plexiglas, it came to be the preferred material for aircraft windows and canopies. Later, the lab expanded its studies of plastics as substitutes for more traditional materials in aircraft construction and with epoxy resins as bonding agents.[42]

In 1935, the PTL became the Aeronautical Materials Laboratory (AML), headed by an officer who also held the position of assistant chief engineer at the NAF. A year later the lab relocated to Building 59, the old assembly shop, where there was enough room for both structures and materials testing. The work load increased. By the end of 1936, the lab was experimenting with spot welding of stainless steel for aircraft applications and had under way the construction of a stainless steel float for flying boats. Testing continued, too, on corrosion prevention, and the lab took on experiments with textiles and flight equipment. The latter included sleeping bags, wing covers, flotation bags, flight clothing, parachutes, harnesses, tapes, webbing, and cord. There was concern that appropriations for the lab were not sufficient to keep up with the demands for increased testing; it was evident as well that there was a need for more specialized engineers as the AML diversified its activities.[43]

To meet the staffing requirement, the Aeronautical Materials Laboratory, under Commander Raymond D. MacCart until 1940, attracted and retained experienced scientists and engineers. One of them was Richard R. Moore. A specialist in light alloys and fatigue problems, Moore was well known for his invention of the Moore rotating beam fatigue testing machine. He held degrees in civil engineering and metallurgical engineering from Columbia University. Before coming to Philadelphia in 1935, Moore had been chief of the materials laboratory of the army's Engineering Division at McCook Field and chief metallurgist for the Wright Aeronautical Corporation. Another key person was John F. Hardecker, an NAF veteran who had received a degree in civil engineering from Cornell University before starting work at the factory in October 1917 as an aeronautical draftsman. Hardecker was the author of several important technical articles on materials testing, and he served as project engineer for the Army-Navy Standardization and Specifications program at the materials lab from 1936 through 1940.[44]

With two laboratories already in place at Philadelphia, the navy, seeking to concentrate as much experimental and testing activities as possible, decided to locate a third such facility at the NAF. On 13 January 1938, BuAer established the Aircraft Navigational Instruments Development Section under Lieutenant I. E. Hobbs as a part of the NAF's Engineering Department. According to the directive from the bureau, the section was to evaluate instruments developed by the military, the Bureau of Standards, and the various private suppliers of such equipment. The instruments included drift sights, octants, compasses, navigation plotting devices, and Pelorus and azimuth circles. Because many of the instruments would have to be tested in the air, the factory received additional aircraft dedicated to the section's mission. At about the same time that the navy established the Navigational Instruments Development Section, it created a separate laboratory in the inspection department of the factory devoted to inspecting all instruments procured from private sources. In later years, the inspection department lab broke off to join the Navigational Instruments Development Section as part of the new Instrument Development Section.[45]

As it had for the Aeronautical Engine Laboratory, space became critical for the Aeronautical Materials Laboratory in 1939. Accordingly, the NAF asked for and received money to construct two new buildings (numbers 600 and 601) adjacent to the AEL's building on Rowan Avenue. Work began in 1940, and the buildings were ready for occupancy the following year. With a high bay, traveling crane, and reinforced concrete floors, Building 601 was designed with structural research and testing in mind. Building 600 was mainly offices, but it also housed the instruments lab on its first floor and the paint and chemicals labs on its second and third floors.[46]

By the late 1930s, the Naval Aircraft Factory was generally accepted as an important source for the design and production of at least limited numbers of airplanes. The factory could and did fulfill the basic intent of the Vinson-Trammell Act in the late 1930s with aircraft and engine production. Yet it was obvious as well that design and production were only part of the factory's role in naval aviation. The AEL, the Aeronautical Materials Laboratory, and the instruments labs conducted important testing work for the navy. And when the service had to meet requirements for such specialized technologies as catapults, arresting gear, and pilotless aircraft, it turned to the NAF, which was positioned to take on long-term development projects that most private firms would have found technically difficult as well as uneconomical during the interwar decades.

8

To Sea on the Back of the Fleet: Catapults and Arresting Gear

As chief of the Bureau of Aeronautics, William Moffett often found himself in an advocacy role. In early 1922, he appeared before the House Naval Affairs Committee to defend aviation as an integral part of the fleet and its operations. He told the committee that the future offensive power of the navy rested on its ability to acquire as many aircraft carriers as were permitted under treaty obligations and to equip as many other vessels as necessary for launching and recovering aircraft at sea. In August of that year he amplified his concerns in a memorandum to the secretary of the navy: "The Navy is the first line of offense," he said, "and naval aviation as an advance guard of this first line must deliver the brunt of the attack. Naval aviation cannot take the offensive from shore; it must go to sea on the back of the fleet."[1]

The assimilation of aircraft into the fleet was easier said than done. In the 1910s and 1920s, the airplane was a fragile piece of machinery that required special handling and equipment aboard ships. Aviators had to convince line officers that the advantages of the airplane outweighed the attendant hazards and the inevitable interference with routine seagoing operations. Moreover, taking the airplane to sea involved complex technical puzzles, paramount among which were developing catapults to launch airplanes and arresting gear to decelerate aircraft safely within the confines of a carrier deck. Along with its production and other activities, the

162

Naval Aircraft Factory assumed major responsibility for the design, development, and installation of catapults and arresting gear, equipment vital to the realization of Moffett's goal of aviation as an organic part of the fleet.

Aircraft catapults are as old as aviation itself. Samuel P. Langley devised an overhead, spring-powered catapult to launch his steam-powered models from a houseboat in the Potomac River in 1896. Building on that success, Langley constructed a larger boat and mounted on it a fifteen-ton turntable catapult for his ill-fated human-carrying Aerodrome in 1903. At the Wright brothers' Huffman Prairie flying field outside Dayton in 1904, they used a simple but remarkably effective catapult consisting of a derrick with a line running over a pulley at the top. To one end of the line were attached six hundred pounds of metal weights, while the other end of the line ran through a pulley at the base of the derrick, under fifty feet of track, through another pulley at the end of the track, and back to a launching car resting on the track. Compared to Langley's launching mechanism, which had cost many thousands of dollars and had proved totally useless, the Wrights' was a model of cost-effective ingenuity. The Wrights' chief rival, Glenn Curtiss, experimented with an inclined wire cable in September 1911 that he hoped would permit launching hydroairplanes from ships' decks.[2]

While Curtiss conducted trials of his launcher at Hammondsport, Captain Washington Irving Chambers pursued a more fruitful avenue of investigation at the Washington Navy Yard. Working with the Bureau of Ordnance and the Naval Gun Factory nearby in Washington, Chambers developed a catapult consisting of a piston driven by compressed air and acting on a system of cables to propel a launching car or shuttle down a track. He installed the catapult on the *Santee* dock at the Naval Academy in Annapolis for tests in 1912. On 31 July, the first trial of the catapult, with Lieutenant Theodore G. Ellyson piloting the Curtiss A-1 Triad, failed when the airplane prematurely lifted off and was thrown into the water by a severe crosswind. Back at the Washington Navy Yard Chambers redesigned and rebuilt the catapult with the assistance of Dick Richardson of the Bureau of Construction and Repair. On 12 November 1912, the catapult, mounted on a barge at the navy yard, launched a Curtiss A-3 with Ellyson at the controls.[3]

The big lesson learned from the experiments at the Washington

Navy Yard was that future catapults required greater capacity, and Richardson worked toward that end in 1913. Much of the job was accomplished in the shops at the yard, with some of the parts fabricated by the Naval Gun Factory. Upon completion, the unit was sent to the Norfolk Navy Yard for preliminary tests, following which the catapult went to Pensacola, where it was fitted to a coal barge for additional experiments. The major obstacle was safely decelerating the launching car at the end of the track. When spring bumpers proved totally inadequate—destroying the car after a series of test shots—Richardson turned to friction brakes as a solution to the problem. Lieutenant P. N. L. Bellinger successfully flew from the catapult in November 1914 in the Curtiss AB-2 flying boat. This catapult had a track 65.5 feet long and accelerated the airplane to speeds of up to forty-six miles per hour.[4]

Captain Henry Mustin, the commanding officer at Pensacola, took charge of subsequent development of the launching device. He had the catapult disassembled and mounted aft on the armored cruiser *North Carolina*. Following tests with a timber dead load matching the weight of an airplane, Mustin flew the AB-2 from the catapult on 5 November 1915. This was the first time the navy successfully catapulted an aircraft from a ship, but the *North Carolina* was at anchor and not under way at the time. Mustin later devised a means of elevating the tracks of the catapult and using the after turret as a turntable to transfer aircraft from storage to the launching position. Mustin assembled a staff at Pensacola that continued work on catapult designs; much of the fabrication took place at the Norfolk and Washington navy yards.[5]

Operational use of catapults followed. The *North Carolina* received an improved catapult in July 1916, from which Lieutenant Godfrey deC. Chevalier flew while the ship was under way. The armored cruisers *Seattle* and *Huntington* had catapults installed in the fall of 1916 and early 1917 respectively. The catapults rested on stanchions that raised the tracks clear of the aft turrets; launching was over the stern. But a satisfactory method of bringing the launching car to a halt at the end of the track remained elusive. Friction brakes proved inadequate in the higher-capacity catapults so the common method was to let the car go overboard and recover it with a line from the ship. Although Mustin's elevated tracks could be stowed out of the way when not in use, they were cumbersome, and the cruisers' aviation detachments were never accepted as part of the day-to-day functioning of the ships. Therefore, when the two ships went on convoy duty during the early stages of American participation in World War I, they did so minus their catapults and airplanes.[6]

It was not until after the war that American planners again began seriously to consider launching aircraft from warships at sea. Instead of catapults, though, the secretary of the navy in July authorized flying-off platforms for battleships. Fitted to the number 2 and number 3 turrets of seven vessels, the platforms were about the same length as the main battery and had canvas hangars to protect the aircraft. The arrangement did not work, however, because the platforms interfered with the training of the turret guns, and they were subsequently dismantled.[7]

Together, Kenneth Whiting, Dick Richardson, Robert Stocker, and Clayton M. Simmers determined in early 1920 that a compressed-air catapult mounted on a turntable similar to that of a triple torpedo tube might be the best way to launch aircraft at sea. The catapult could be trained in any direction and if mounted on the weather deck would not significantly interfere with the functioning of the ship's armament. In late August 1920, the Bureau of Construction and Repair directed the NAF "to develop plans for a turntable catapult similar to deck torpedo tubes." Richardson, who at this time was the chief engineer at the NAF, took a direct interest in the job, assigning Lieutenant William Fellers, a highly capable naval aviator with a degree in mechanical engineering from Georgia Tech, as project engineer. By November 1920, he and his assistants had completed specifications for the launcher and, in April 1921, began its construction.[8]

The NAF moved ahead quickly with work on the turntable catapult. The major technical difficulty remained how to decelerate the launching car at the end of its run. Mechanically operated friction brakes might have been the best solution to the problem, but they were complicated and not wholly reliable; NAF engineers turned instead to a hydraulic braking system. With a minimum of fanfare (the entire program was confidential), the NAF conducted the first "live" tests of the prototype turntable catapult with a Curtiss N-9 seaplane on 26 October 1921. Richardson was the pilot.[9]

In the meantime, the Bureau of Construction and Repair had

A Curtiss N-9 being readied for launch from the NAF's first turntable catapult in October 1921. Compressed air provided the impulse. (80-G-651881, National Archives)

called upon the NAF in April 1921 to investigate a turntable catapult that could be fitted to battleships. The NAF's estimate of nearly $22,000 for its manufacture received quick bureau approval, and the factory completed the catapult by the middle of November. Designated Mark I, it weighed twenty-eight thousand pounds, had a sixty-foot-long track, and could accelerate a thirty-five hundred-pound airplane to forty-eight miles per hour. Following tests at Philadelphia, the catapult went to the New York Navy Yard before the end of the year for installation in the new battleship *Maryland*, from which the first live launching took place off Yorktown, Virginia, on 24 May 1921. The battleships *Nevada* and *Oklahoma* received Mark Is later in the year.[10]

The success of these installations provided the impetus for Moffett's crusade to make fleet aviation a reality. Henry Mustin presented the aviators' position before the General Board in 1922. By the 1920s the board had established itself as the chief advisory body to the secretary of the navy, and its findings and reports often formed the basis for Navy Department policy decisions. Mustin went before the board in March and November to state the case for fleet aviation. He called for aircraft on battleships, cruisers, destroyers, and auxiliary vessels and argued that the navy's complement of aircraft carriers had to be increased. One catapult would be needed on each battleship, cruiser, destroyer, and fleet train vessel, and two catapults would be fitted to each carrier, provided they did not interfere with airplanes using the flight deck. Some senior members of the board expressed skepticism, but younger flag officers, notably Rear Admiral William Veazie Pratt, were receptive to the idea of taking aircraft to sea. Budget restrictions prevented quick action. Not until 1928 did formal statements on naval policy include references to determining the practicality of equipping large numbers of ships with aircraft.[11]

The navy fitted compressed-air catapults to many of its battleships and cruisers in the late 1920s and early 1930s. The Philadelphia Navy Yard manufactured the first production run of the catapults, which were designated Type A, Mark II. Similar to the Type A, Mark Is, they had improved air valves, tracks seventy-nine feet long, and could propel a six-thousand-pound airplane at speeds of up to sixty miles per hour. One each of these catapults went into the battleships *New Mexico, California, Mississippi, Idaho,* and *Tennessee,* and two were mounted amidships in each *Omaha*-class cruiser. By 1925, the yard had produced thirty Type A, Mark Is and Mark IIs. Later in the decade, the NAF developed the Type A, Mark IV, with a slightly higher rating than the Mark II. Manufactured by the McKiernan-Terry Corporation, Mark IVs eventually replaced the Mark IIs in *Omaha*-class cruisers in 1931–33.[12]

Despite the operational success of the navy's compressed-air catapults in the 1920s, the technology remained in a state of flux. In the quest to increase the capability of the fleet's catapults, work began toward the end of 1921 on a launcher with a gunpowder engine, which promised greater simplicity and reliability of operation than existing compressed-air catapult engines. In January 1922, BuAer joined with the Bureau of Ordnance and the Coast Guard in the development of the first gunpowder catapult. Typically installed atop a battleship's number 3 turret, the catapult overhung the turret, barely clearing the after mast as the turret revolved. Because aircraft

The Type A, Mark IV compressed-air catapult developed by the Naval
Aircraft Factory in the late 1920s and manufactured by the McKiernan-
Terry Corporation. This catapult went aboard *Omaha*-class cruisers. (72-
AF-27976, National Archives)

stowed at the end of the track could be damaged when the turret was
trained, the catapult was designed to launch toward the aft end of
the turret and not forward over the guns. As quickly as they were
manufactured and tested, gunpowder catapults augmented or superseded compressed-air catapults on the navy's bigger surface vessels.
The first of the launchers, the Type P, Mark III, went into service in
the battleship *Mississippi* in 1924. Improved versions—Type P,
Mark IV and IV-1—followed, replacing some of the compressed-air
catapults on battleship turrets. A number of the navy's ten-thousand-ton, eight-inch-gun heavy cruisers also received gunpowder
catapults.[13]

   Gunpowder catapults generated questions of bureau responsibility. Following a conference in early 1923, it was agreed that BuAer
would develop the general design and specifications for such cata-

pults, as well as their launching cars, release mechanisms, and braking systems. The Bureau of Ordnance took the initiative for the guns themselves, while the Bureau of Construction and Repair dealt with the launching tracks, aircraft stowage, handling gear, and catapult installation. The Naval Gun Factory carried out the final assembly of the launchers, and most of the specialized components, including launching cars and miscellaneous accessories, came from the NAF.[14]

The Naval Aircraft Factory's largely peripheral role in the development of gunpowder catapults changed in 1926, when the factory undertook the design of a new turntable gunpowder catapult, designated Type P, Mark V. Installed first in the battleship *Colorado* in April 1927, the prototype performed well enough to encourage the navy to authorize the development of an improved model, the Type P, Mark V-1, in which the factory used high-test steel to save weight and increase strength. BuAer ordered four Mark V-1s by March 1928. Next came the Type P, Mark VI, also developed by the NAF and similar to the Mark V-1, except that it weighed less and had slightly greater capacity. Able to accelerate a seven-thousand-pound aircraft to sixty-five miles per hour, the forty-four-thousand-pound Mark VI became the standard gunpowder catapult during the 1930s. The Bartlett Hayward Division of the Koppers Company manufactured 165 catapults of this model, the bulk of which went aboard battleships, ten-thousand-ton, eight-inch-gun heavy cruisers, and six-inch-gun light cruisers.[15]

Gunpowder catapults never replaced or rendered obsolete compressed-air catapults. Although compressed-air launchers had to have large accumulators or air flasks and complicated valves, they offered a great deal of flexibility in operation. The air pressure, for instance, could be varied to accommodate different aircraft weights, and the catapults could operate continously without overheating. Gunpowder catapults, by contrast, had fixed-capacity charges and launched heavier airplanes at slower speeds. Moreover, after three successive launches the catapults overheated and had to be temporarily shut down. Cartridge charges had to be requisitioned from ammunition depots and presented handling problems on the ships themselves.[16]

Nevertheless, the relative lack of complexity of the gunpowder catapults suited them to installation on a variety of vessels, and

Moffett could forcibly argue once more for equipping significant numbers of the navy's ships with such equipment. In late 1928, he wrote to Secretary of the Navy Wilbur requesting approval for BuAer to develop and coordinate a comprehensive catapult program in cooperation with the Bureau of Ordnance and the Bureau of Construction and Repair. Under Moffett's plan, BuAer would receive all catapult money and would then distribute it among the three bureaus to eliminate the bottlenecks arising when one bureau or the other lacked adequate funds to complete its part of a given project. Moffett's proposal died when the Bureau of Ordnance, traditionally oriented toward the navy's "gun club," insisted on retaining its own prerogatives in requesting money for catapult development.[17]

Moffett's scheme would have gone a long way to streamline the development and procurement of catapults and would have helped speed up the integration of aviation with the fleet. Still, considerable progress was made toward that end during Moffett's years as BuAer chief. From 1926 to 1933, about $3.5 million was spent on development and procurement of catapults. Early-model compressed-air catapults had been superseded by such improved models as the Mark IV, and gunpowder catapults added to the navy's ability to launch aircraft from a large number of combatant vessels. The NAF was instrumental in the design, manufacture, and testing of shipboard catapults, and it instituted a training program in their operation. Lieutenant Lisle J. Maxson, an engineer who worked on several early catapult projects, claimed in 1931 that the United States was "far in advance in the design and operation of this means of launching aircraft at sea." Yet thus far the use of catapults on aircraft carriers had been minimal; in fact, the navy had authorized the removal of the *Langley's* catapults in 1928.[18]

As a first step in the development of a carrier catapult, experiments began at Philadelphia to determine what measures would have to be taken for the catapult launch of landplanes from battleships or aircraft carriers. In late 1931, the NAF began modifications of a Type A, Mark IV compressed-air catapult for test launches of a Vought O2U-3. The launching shuttle had two semicircular castings that thrust directly against the wheels of the airplane, thus eliminating the need for a bridle or special reinforcement of the aircraft structure. Lisle Maxson personally delivered the airplane to Mustin Field from Anacostia for the test shot on 25 October 1932. It was satisfactory, except that the tail wheel of the aircraft was badly damaged.[19]

The test demonstrated only the feasibility of launching conventional wheeled aircraft using catapults; it did not resolve many of the obstacles that remained in the way of a practical catapult for carriers. In carrier air operations the rate of launching was critical. As the weight and performance of airplanes increased, their takeoff rolls became longer, and the interval between launches consequently increased. Furthermore, longer takeoffs required more deck space, which limited the number of airplanes that could be ranged on the flight deck in preparation for launch. The catapult offered at least a partial solution to these twin dilemmas. Yet a catapult would have to be designed so that it would not hinder the routine handling of aircraft on the carrier's flight deck. The British attacked the problem by placing a catapult in a tunnel beneath the deck forward, launching over the bow. But this presented its own difficulties by effectively reducing freeboard, creating adverse wind conditions in the tunnel itself, and sacrificing hangar space.[20] Americans thought a better solution was a catapult mounted flush with the flight deck and situated forward, leaving the deck unobstructed and providing more room aft for aircraft awaiting takeoff.

The NAF's role in the project began when BuAer directed the factory on 13 November 1933 to study designs for a carrier catapult. Sydney Kraus, manager at the time, responded a month later with cost estimates for the work, and on 11 January 1934, the bureau issued a project order for $8,600 to get the job started. The assumption was that within a few months tests could begin with a Type A, Mark IV catapult and a simulated carrier deck, but the bureau also wanted the NAF to begin longer-term development of an improved compressed-air catapult of greater capacity than the Mark IV. A $17,000 project order for the experimental Type A, Mark V catapult followed on 15 March 1934.[21]

Construction and tests of the flush-deck catapult took most of 1934. The NAF erected a steel deck above the Mark IV catapult already in use on Pier 7 next to the river. The deck had a one-and-one-half-inch slot running its length, through which protruded a towing fitting that was fixed to the launching shuttle beneath. A Y-shaped bridle linked the towing fitting to open hooks on the landing gear of the aircraft. After a number of dead load tests, the

A flush-deck catapult suitable for use aboard aircraft carriers was developed at the NAF during the 1930s. This photograph shows a test of a Mark IV compressed-air catapult with a simulated deck above it in October 1934. The airplane is an O2U-3. (72-AF-29515, National Archives)

factory accomplished its first live launch—with an O2U-3—on 1 October 1934. Two days later, six different pilots, none of whom had any previous experience with catapults, made successful flights from the test device.[22]

These experiments were important in showing that a flush-deck configuration worked, but the compressed-air catapult used for tests at the NAF did not have all the characteristics necessary for a practical carrier catapult. With the Type XA, Mark V, the NAF incorporated a system of cables running through sheaves connecting the shuttle to the catapult engine located below the flight deck. This was the basic arrangement employed in subsequent flush-deck catapults. Yet the major stumbling block remained the relatively slow recycling time dictated by the need to replenish the catapult's compressed-air supply. To get around this problem, the NAF provided for twelve separate air flasks in the Mark V catapult, allowing as many launches in quick succession.[23]

At best, this was a clumsy solution, and the NAF soon abandoned the Mark V project and set in motion studies for alternative catapult engines. To this point in the development of the technology, compressed-air and gunpowder catapults had shown the most promise. A small number of flywheel-powered catapults (Type F, Mark II) were also manufactured in 1927 and one each installed in the carriers *Lexington* and *Saratoga*. Designed by Carl L. Norden, a consulting engineer better known for the bombsight that later bore his name, the catapults were not practical in service.[24]

BuAer began a preliminary investigation in January 1934 of a hydropneumatic unit that was more compact than the compressed-air or gunpowder catapults and had faster recycling times. The NAF produced detail drawings and specifications for the new catapult. Although the design lacked the sheer motive force of existing catapults, this was not considered a problem because carriers presumably would steam into the wind when aircraft were being launched. The catapult engine consisted of a hydraulic piston and cylinder linked to an oil accumulator and a pressure tank similar to that used in a compressed-air catapult. Oil under pressure drove the piston through the cylinder, while a rack-and-pinion return mechanism forced air back into the pressure tank and rapidly recharged the system. There was no need for continuous admission of air into the pressure tanks, which was one of the major reasons for the relatively slow recycling rate of compressed-air catapults. The factory built an experimental version of the hydraulic catapult (designated XH, Mark I) in 1935, but tests revealed that more work was needed to perfect the return mechanism, high-pressure oil pumps, and controls. Precision was vital in all hydraulic catapult parts and components, for the slightest amount of air in the system could cause combustion under high pressure, followed by an explosion and serious damage to the ship and its personnel.[25]

While the Type XH, Mark I was still under development, engineers at Philadelphia started design studies for the Type XH, Mark II catapult, a fifty-thousand-pound unit capable of launching a fifty-five-hundred-pound airplane at speeds of sixty-five miles per hour. The catapult, tested at the NAF in September 1936, led to the improved Type H, Mark II that could accelerate a seven-thousand-pound airplane to a velocity of seventy miles per hour. In place of the heavy and troublesome rack-and-pinion return mechanism was a lighter and more efficient system of cables and sheaves. By March 1936, the NAF had five of the improved Mark IIs in production. Later, BuAer issued project orders totaling nearly $250,000 for the manufacture at Philadelphia of four Type H, Mark IIs for the older carriers *Saratoga* and *Lexington*.[26]

The factory manufactured thirty-two Type H, Mark II catapults. Each new carrier—*Yorktown*, *Enterprise*, *Wasp*, and *Hornet*—received three of the catapults by 1940; two were installed in the flight decks forward of each ship, and one was fitted athwartship on the carriers' hangar decks. The athwartship catapults arose from a requirement that the ships be able to launch a scout while their flight decks were jammed with other airplanes awaiting launch or being recovered. Tests at the NAF showed that launches from the athwartship catapults were possible in crosswinds of up to twenty-six miles per hour. In August 1939, the *Yorktown* and the *Hornet* successfully launched O3U-3 and SBC-3 aircraft from their athwartship catapults while under way at sea. Nevertheless, the athwartship catapults were seldom used, and they were removed from some of the carriers in 1942.[27]

The Type H, Mark IV was significantly larger than the Type H, Mark II flush-deck catapult. In November 1939, in response to the advent of bigger and heavier carrier aircraft, BuAer instituted feasibility studies of a hydraulic catapult that could be mounted in the bow or athwartship on the hangar deck of the new *Essex*-class carriers. The NAF began the detail design for the catapult before the end of the year. Delays resulted from the need to have two versions of the catapult: one, the Mark IVA, had a track length of only 72.5 feet because of the limited width of the hangar deck; the second, the Mark IVB, had a track just over 96.5 feet long. The scale of the machinery created other problems. Both versions of the catapult weighed considerably more than two hundred thousand pounds, four times that of the Type H, Mark II. The Mark IVB, with four hydraulic pumps, could launch an eighteen-thousand-pound airplane at a velocity of ninety miles per hour, and the Mark IVA, with two pumps, accelerated a sixteen-thousand-pound airplane to speeds of eighty-five miles per hour. Recycling time for the Type H, Mark IVA was 60 seconds; for the Mark IVB it was 42.8 seconds. By December 1940, the NAF had completed plans for the catapult and began working with potential outside suppliers on cost estimates for the first twenty-three units.[28]

Because of the press of other work at the Naval Aircraft Factory and the anticipated demand for catapults as the nation edged closer to war, BuAer determined to cultivate private manufacturers as potential sources for Type H, Mark IV, and other catapults. In September 1940, Rear Admiral John H. Towers, the new bureau chief, wrote Captain Ernest M. Pace, Jr., manager of the NAF: "It is desired to initiate a program of catapult manufacture and procurement which . . . will establish reliable outside sources of design and construction for future needs." The NAF contacted the McKiernan-Terry Corporation, already a manufacturer of compressed-air catapults, about the possibility of producing Type H, Mark IVs. Although the firm lacked some of the equipment needed for catapult production, its vice-president replied that "it is our desire to co-operate with the Government so that they may secure proper facilities for the Defense Program," and he was confident that the company, with the support of the NAF, could meet the navy's requirements.[29]

McKiernan-Terry's certainty that it could do the job evaporated amid management inefficiencies and problems obtaining suitable materials for the Mark IV program. By early 1942, the delays were serious enough that people at the NAF expressed concern that the completion dates of the first *Essex*-class ships would have to be postponed. Sydney Kraus defended the company, arguing that the catapult was so complex that "any source of procurement would have encountered similar difficulties." That may have been true, but only direct intervention by the NAF and BuAer prevented a bad situation from getting worse. By forcing McKiernan-Terry to oust a number of plant executives and by bringing in more experienced shop-floor supervisors, the navy got the Mark IV program back on track. Catapult deliveries reached two per month before the end of 1942. No carrier completion dates had to be delayed by the unavailability of Mark IVs, although the *Essex* went to sea without catapults. The *Lexington*, the first of the class to receive the catapult, completed tests of the Mark IVB in March 1943; the first live shots of the Mark IVA occurred at sea aboard the *Yorktown* in May of that same year. McKiernan-Terry and the Wellman Engineering Company, of Akron, Ohio, a respected manufacturer of heavy machinery, produced 117 of the catapults before the end of the war.[30]

Despite the vicissitudes of their early production, the flush-deck carrier catapults turned out to be one of the NAF's outstanding accomplishments, but not all the NAF's catapult stories had such happy endings. A 1935 BuAer directive called upon the NAF to design and construct a portable catapult for launching and arresting the landings of shore-based aircraft. The factory responded the following year with the Type XHE, Mark I, which had a hydropneumatic engine similar to those under development for aircraft carrier catapults. Two platform runways separate from the catapult engine were to be used for takeoffs and landings, with the engine acting through cable systems in both the launch and arresting modes. Technical problems forced engineers to abandon the two platform runways for a single one and to add a second engine for arresting operations. Tests demonstrated the practicability of the catapult, which weighed only 12,750 pounds, and for a time the Army Air Corps engineers at Wright Field were interested in it, but production versions of the launcher never proved their worth in amphibious operations.[31]

Another singular failure was the Type XS, Mark I. As the search for alternatives to conventional compressed-air and gunpowder catapult engines continued in the 1930s, some outlandish proposals found their way into BuAer offices. Lisle Maxson offered a concept for a powerful and lightweight catapult in July 1933, suggesting the use of a compressed-air radial engine with four banks of nine cylinders to turn a screw. A nut rapidly advanced along the rotating screw, carrying the launching car with it and eliminating the cables and sheaves of conventional catapults. The proposal was odd, but Maxson believed that the mechanism opened "a possibility of high powers at low weight and cost with excellent dependability," and he was able to convince the bureau of the efficacy of the concept. In December 1933, BuAer called upon the NAF to begin the development of a screw-type catapult. The factory responded with a design for a launcher with the capacity to accelerate a sixty-five-hundred-pound airplane to sixty-five miles per hour. The power plant was a single-bank radial engine driving a tubular screw mounted on rollers. The XS, Mark I project, however, never advanced beyond a one-eighth-scale working model before being abandoned.[32]

Maxson was the progenitor of another unusual NAF catapult concept. In January 1938, he became project engineer for a centrifugal launching mechanism that would allow aircraft to take off from a restricted area under their own power. The structure was an elevated circular track around which ran a wheeled car. The airplane hung on a cable pendant below the car. The aircraft circled beneath the track until it built up enough speed, at which point the pendant was released. A magnetic or friction brake brought the car to rest at the loading point, where another airplane was hoisted into position. Maxson believed the device offered the advantages of launches in any direction without having to use an external power source. The 325-foot diameter of the track did create space problems, but he thought a deck could be placed on the structure for arrested landings. Further, the resulting enclosed space could be used as a hangar and repair shops. Nothing came of the idea, but it did illustrate some of the novel approaches being taken by NAF personnel to the problem of operating aircraft at sea.[33]

A prewar project on which the NAF expended a great deal of time, effort, and money was a large catapult for launching navy flying boats. Throughout the 1930s, the service had not been happy with the limited range of its patrol aircraft and was constantly searching for ways to improve their performance. Heavily loaded flying boats wasted a great deal of fuel simply getting off the water. In November 1937, BuAer called upon the factory to develop a design for a large-capacity hydraulic catapult that could launch a 60,000-pound four-engine flying boat at a speed of 120 miles per hour. A little more than a month later, the NAF completed preliminary studies of the unit, which the bureau designated the Type XH, Mark III catapult. Weighing approximately 180 tons, the catapult cost an estimated $600,000 to develop, manufacture, and test. The NAF proposed, also, that two of the units be placed parallel to each other with a launch car riding on both catapult tracks to thrust a 120,000-pound flying boat into the air.[34]

In March 1938, Rear Admiral Cook, the chief of BuAer, suggested that the Bureau of Construction and Repair consider building a lighter or a tender on which the large catapult could be mounted. Cook thought it possible that the catapult would double the range of a 60,000-pound flying boat carrying a two-ton bomb load. Cook added that his bureau "has become convinced that for naval purposes the catapult provides the most practicable solution [to the range limitations of patrol planes], and is proceeding with preliminary consideration of an appropriate unit." BuAer determined that the catapult would weigh close to two hundred tons, have a length of about 250 feet (nearly the length of a football field), and be able to accelerate a thirty-ton aircraft to 120 miles per hour. The barge or lighter would permit forward basing of the catapult. Linking two of the giant catapults together would enable the launch of airplanes weighing upward of 120,000 pounds.[35]

Captain Albert C. Read refined the concept of the flying boat catapult. Pointing to the Germans' use of catapult ships on their South American air routes and the British Short-Mayo scheme of piggybacking a small airplane on a larger one, Read saw the catapult as an opportunity for the navy to accomplish major gains in the range of operational aircraft. Even though no money had been specifically appropriated for the large catapult project, BuAer and the Bureau of Construction and Repair had been going ahead with preliminary development work on the catapult and lighter and had plans under way to modify a Martin PBM-1 Mariner flying boat for catapult launch.[36]

Read was not above exaggeration in stating the bureau's case for the large catapult. In the comparative data he presented to emphasize the potential of the large catapult, he used performance and range figures that the bureau hoped could be achieved by a larger and more advanced flying boat than the PBM-1. Normally, he said, such an aircraft could achieve a range of 4,350 statute miles with a one-thousand-pound bomb load; using the catapult, its range was nearly doubled to 7,650 statute miles. With a seven-thousand-pound bomb load, the flying boat's range went down to a little more than 3,000 miles. The catapult allowed the same airplane with an identical payload to fly 6,380 miles. In 1938 there was no aircraft in the navy's inventory that could even come close to the 4,300-mile range; the PBM-1 had a maximum range of about 2,100 statute miles, which if doubled using a catapult launch would still make the PBM's maximum range less than what Read estimated it to be under normal launch conditions. Realistically, the PBM maximum takeoff weight (MTOW) using the catapult could be increased 31 percent from 37,310 pounds to 54,000 pounds. Read was, however, correct that the lighter planned for the catapult would be large enough to carry fuel for the patrol aircraft, would have its own hauling-out capability, and would in general serve as a mobile, self-contained floating base for flying boat operations.[37]

On 8 November 1938, the bureau issued two project orders to the Naval Aircraft Factory totaling $225,000 to begin development and construction of the Type XH, Mark III catapult, but it quickly became obvious that because of its size and complexity years would pass before the catapult was complete. This did not sit well with Admiral Cook, who expressed "concern" about how little the NAF had done following the preliminary design study and said that the Germans apparently had solved most of the technical problems with large catapults that continued to perplex NAF engineers. Lieutenant Commander Charles A. Nicholson was more straightforward, condemning the factory for its "complete inability" to handle the Mark III project. "From the rate of progress shown on this project," Nicholson said, "even with special provisions for additional draftsmen, etc., it is evident that the Naval Aircraft Factory cannot be depended upon to any great extent" to supply the navy's catapult requirements. On his and other officers' recommendations, the bureau told the NAF to sound out the Baldwin-Southwark Company, already a supplier of parts for catapults, to determine if it could manufacture large hydraulic units of the Mark III type.[38]

To a great extent Nicholson's criticism was unwarranted. The Germans had by no means solved all the problems of large catapults. Their units operated on compressed air, had extremely slow recycling rates, and with a capacity of launching a thirty-seven-thousand-pound aircraft at ninety miles per hour were considerably less powerful than the Mark III. The big NAF catapult involved much specialized engineering and the procurement of components that were not common to other hydraulic units. Moreover, the factory was not equipped in 1938–39 to machine or assemble the large forgings and castings needed for such a catapult and had to subcontract with the Philadelphia Navy Yard and various private firms for the parts. Even the catapult pier was too small to test the unit before installation on the lighter. The ability of the Baldwin-Southwark Company to do the job was called into question in September 1940, when the bureau classified as "unsatisfactory" some of the castings produced by the firm for the Mark III. The situation was so bad that the bureau warned Baldwin-Southwark that it might contract with another manufacturer for the castings unless "prompt and effective measures to improve the present unsatisfactory situation are not taken."[39] Nicholson's criticism came far too early in the program to be fair and he failed to realize that the Mark III was pushing the state of the art in advanced, high-capacity catapults.

Captain Ernest M. Pace, Jr., who had become manager of the NAF in 1940, provided some idea of the complexity of the Mark III project in January 1941. The principal purpose of the letter was to explain that it would not be possible without "considerable alterations" to modify the Mark III so that two of the catapults could be used to launch a sixty-ton flying boat. Pace went on to say that the development of the Mark III "has been a task of major magnitude. All features of this catapult have been extremely difficult to design and many items incorporated are still experimental in character. The catapult engine itself produces twenty-five times more energy than in any previous hydraulic design."[40]

Ill-founded though it was in most respects, Nicholson's November 1938 critique of the NAF and the Type XH, Mark III catapult project turned out to be prophetic: more than two years passed before the factory completed the job. Not until 16 January 1942 were the catapult and lighter (AVC-1) ready for initial tests with the XPBM-1 (number 1247). By then the catapult had grown to a monster weighing 450 tons. The first dead load launches occurred at the NAF in March, and the first live launching of the XPBM-1 took place on 19 May. The XPBM-1 launch went smoothly, although the test suggested that changes in the means of handling the aircraft on the lighter and modifications to the launching car braking mechanism should be made before moving on to higher velocities and greater loads. By this time, however, exasperation at BuAer with the delays had combined with the realization that JATO, a rocket-assisted takeoff device, could meet the original catapult requirement. BuAer was considerably less enthusiastic by the spring of 1942 about pouring more money and effort into large catapults. The Mark III test program continued at a low priority through the end of the year, at which point the bureau canceled the project. Commander Leslie C. Stevens echoed the sentiments of many in January 1943: "I can see no application for this barge & catapult & therefore no reason for putting effort forth on further tests."[41]

The Type XH, Mark III was not the only large-capacity catapult project to engage the Naval Aircraft Factory's engineers. Once it became apparent that the NAF would not be able to adapt the Mark III to launch a 120,000-pound aircraft, BuAer held an informal conference in March 1941 to discuss what should be done to procure a catapult of that capacity. The bureau had plans for the acquisition of ninety examples of a fifty-ton Boeing flying boat, designated XPBB-1, which had a range of nearly 4,300 miles and incorporated provisions for catapult launching in its design. Two days after the conference, BuAer called upon the factory to submit a preliminary proposal for a catapult to launch the XPBB-1.[42]

The factory's proposal, ready by the end of June 1941, called for a catapult, designated the Type XH, Mark VII, that could launch the XPBB-1 at a speed of 130 miles per hour. Like the Mark III, the Mark VII would be mounted on a lighter, and the aircraft would be transferred from the water to the catapult using either hydraulic jacks or an extremely large crane and hoisting slings. The NAF estimated that the entire project, including design data, complete drawings, tests, and manufacture of one Mark VII, would cost approximately $1.2 million. With the proviso that the factory must come up with a practical means of getting the airplane into launch position, BuAer authorized the NAF to go ahead with a more detailed design for the Mark VII. By the summer of 1942, the factory was ready to test the Mark VII launch car, at which point the bureau, finding JATO more practical and cost-effective, canceled further work on the catapult.[43]

Arresting gear was in many respects the analogue to the catapult, and again the NAF played a central role in the development of this important aviation equipment. When Eugene Ely made his historic touchdown on the temporary deck erected aft on the armored cruiser *Pennsylvania* in 1911, a crude system of cables strung athwartship and anchored to sandbags retarded his forward momentum. Thereafter, the United States and Royal navies experimented with various solutions to the vexatious technical problems associated with stopping an airplane landing aboard a ship while providing the necessary directional stability to prevent the aircraft from accidentally going over the side.[44]

Experiments began at the Naval Air Station, Hampton Roads, in the summer of 1921 using a revolving circular platform one hundred feet in diameter fitted with a wire arresting gear system modeled along the lines of those being tested by the British. Lieutenant A. M. Pride was in charge of the work at Hampton Roads, and Godfrey deC. Chevalier, now a lieutenant commander, supervised the NAF's development of arresting gear equipment. The major undertaking at Philadelphia in mid-1921 involved the conversion of fifteen Aeromarine 39-B floatplanes to wheeled undercarriages and fitting them with axle and tail hooks. Several different sets of hooks were manufactured for test purposes. The Hampton Roads platform incorporated fore-and-aft wires that engaged the axle hooks, thereby trapping the airplane and minimizing its yaw on landing. At the same time, the tail hooks on the airplane caught the transverse wires, which, acting through sheaves connected to weights ascending in two 30-foot towers, halted the aircraft's forward momentum.[45]

Arresting gear experiments at Hampton Roads became more urgent as the conversion of the navy's first carrier, *Langley*, approached completion in 1922. A crew from the *Langley* conducted experiments at Hampton Roads that improved some of the details of the arresting gear. The *Langley* itself used an arresting gear system similar to the experimental unit at Hampton Roads. It consisted of longitudinal wires for directional control and transverse wires connected through sheaves to weights below decks. Chevalier made the first arrested landing on the *Langley* on 26 October 1922. But research continued on improved methods of absorbing the energy of an arrested landing. Carl L. Norden, with Warren Noble and others, devised a system of brakes actuated by air pressure. This mechanism replaced the weight system aboard the *Langley* and, in its Mark II version, went into the carriers *Lexington* and *Saratoga*.[46]

Two major advances occurred in the evolution of arresting gear in the late 1920s and early 1930s. One was the elimination of the longitudinal or fore-and-aft wires. These wires, which were considered essential in controlling the airplane on landing, often crossed each other if the aircraft bounced after the axle hooks had engaged the wires. This created an enormous amount of drag on the axle and usually caused the airplane to nose over, damaging the propeller and parts of the aircraft structure. In 1929, Leslie Stevens explained that the fore-and-aft wires were unnecessary. Nearly one thousand landings had been made on the test platform at Hampton Roads and on the *Langley* and the *Saratoga* using only the transverse wires. "No condition of roll, pitch, or bad weather," he wrote, "can be foreseen that will introduce additional hazard into carrier operations by the elimination of longitudinal wires. On the contrary, it is firmly believed that the hazard of landing will be appreciably reduced under adverse conditions." Stevens concluded with a recommendation to cancel all requisitions for hooks and other equipment associated with the use of fore-and-aft wires. By 1930 the longitudinal wires were no longer used in American carriers or in the Hampton Roads test installation.[47]

The second major change in arresting gear was the development by the Experimental Division at Hampton Roads starting in 1931 of a self-contained hydraulic system with an oil-filled cylinder and piston. When an airplane engaged one or more in a series of wires stretched across the carrier deck, its forward momentum was transmitted through a set of sheaves to the piston, which, moving rapidly, forced oil out of the cylinder through a control valve into a storage tank or accumulator. Opening the valve released the oil, pushing the piston back down the cylinder and returning the arresting wires to their original positions. The first units of this type of arresting gear could stop a four-ton airplane landing at speeds of up to sixty miles per hour.[48]

The NAF did not take part in arresting gear research and development during these years; the work was split between BuAer in Washington and Hampton Roads, and most of the manufacturing was done at the Norfolk Navy Yard. The factory did, however, supply axle hooks and tail hooks for an assortment of carrier aircraft during the 1920s and in the 1930s held a number of small orders for arresting gear parts and components.[49]

Philadelphia got back into the mainstream of arresting gear development in November 1933, when BuAer called on the NAF to prepare and submit designs for a multiple-wire airplane crash barrier. Existing barriers, used to protect airplanes parked forward on the flight deck from aircraft missing the arresting wires, often were ineffective or caused severe damage to the aircraft and injury or death to the pilot. A fatal accident on the carrier *Saratoga* earlier in the year was the immediate cause of the bureau's concern. The factory proposed a new barrier design and received authority in

February 1934 to manufacture two of the devices. The bureau then requested design studies for an improved barrier to be installed on the new carrier *Ranger*, and the NAF on its own initiative began studies of barriers for the *Lexington* and the *Saratoga*. In 1934 and 1935, the NAF manufactured and tested barriers for the newest carriers, *Yorktown* and *Enterprise*.[50]

As early as March 1934, BuAer considered plans for removing the arresting gear platform from Hampton Roads to the NAF. At the same time, a new hangar, shop space, and office, drafting, and storage facilities would be constructed at Philadelphia. By August, however, the bureau had backed off on the proposal. Three years later, on 29 June 1937, the situation changed radically when BuAer decided to combine all catapult and arresting gear operations under the Ship Experimental Unit (SEU) and locate the unit at the NAF.[51] The SEU was responsible for static and dynamic tests of catapults and arresting gear and their components, parts, and controls. This was an important step in the rationalization of catapult and arresting gear work, resulting in virtually the complete centralization of this important research and development activity at Philadelphia.

Not long after the establishment of the SEU, BuAer directed the factory to design and provide specifications for a new arresting gear unit. Designated the Mark IV, Mod 3A, the gear was similar to earlier versions of the Mark IV developed at Hampton Roads and had the capacity of arresting the landing of a sixteen-thousand-pound airplane from eighty-five miles per hour. Following this was the Mod 5, which was lighter than the Mod 3A but had the same capacity. The first ten World War II *Essex*-class carriers and most light carriers and escort carriers were equipped with Mod 5s manufactured at the Norfolk Navy Yard and by the Bethlehem Foundry and Machine Company.[52]

Its development of catapult and arresting gear placed the Naval Aircraft Factory in the forefront of this vital activity before and during the early years of World War II. Although Moffett's vision of giving every ship in the fleet the capability for operating aircraft was never realized, by World War II important progress had occurred that helped make aviation an indispensable part of naval planning and operations. Launching and recovering aircraft from carriers, battleships, and cruisers became routine largely as a consequence of the technical advances at the NAF during the 1920s and 1930s. These long-term and often expensive development projects were not attractive to private industry, and naval officers did not want them too far removed from their own immediate purview. The organization and engineering experience of the Naval Aircraft Factory made it an ideal venue for such work, which as time went on came to supplant aircraft and engine production as its major reason for being.

9

Pilotless Aircraft

Catapults and arresting gear were part of the highly specialized experimental functions of the Naval Aircraft Factory in the 1930s; so, too, was the NAF's development of pilotless aircraft and guided weapons. These projects involved years of intensive research, flight testing, and limited production. The results of the effort were mixed: the target drones developed by the factory were an unqualified success, but the guided weapons brought only marginal dividends after the expenditure of much time and money. Nevertheless, the NAF's research helped build a foundation upon which the navy based its post–World War II rocket and missile programs.

Who should be credited with the invention of pilotless aircraft is a matter of some conjecture, but the British seem to enjoy priority. In 1916, A. M. Low began experiments with radio-controlled aerial torpedoes for the Royal Flying Corps, which were meant to ram and destroy Zeppelin bombers. After trials with "home-built" aircraft, Low turned to the Royal Aircraft Factory at Farnborough, which, along with private manufacturers, provided small airplanes for subsequent tests. Following World War I, the Royal Aircraft Establishment (the successor to the Royal Aircraft Factory and roughly comparable to the American NACA) continued work with pilotless aircraft. By 1925, the British had achieved some breakthroughs; one airplane flew for nearly forty minutes, carrying out radio-directed maneuvers before landing safely.[1]

There was parallel interest in pilotless aircraft in the United States, where Elmer A. Sperry had shown the effectiveness of gyroscopic stabilization in ships and his son Lawrence had experimented with gyroscopes and automatic pilots in airplanes. As early as 1916, Elmer Sperry patented an aerial torpedo or flying bomb with preset or automatic control systems. It did not have active radio control. Little urgency was given to the proposed weapon until April 1917, when the Naval Consulting Board approved the project and the Sperry Gyroscope Company received the contract for its prosecution. Curtiss Aeroplane and Motor produced a small biplane according to Sperry's specifications. The results of flight tests in 1918 were disappointing. Seemingly endless problems with the launching mechanism, the airframe, and the automatic controls plagued the project until its cancellation in January 1919.[2]

Sperry's navy program drew the army into research on pilotless aircraft during the war. Charles F. Kettering, the brilliant automotive engineer, headed a flying bomb program established by the army in December 1917. He was particularly impressed by Sperry's work for the navy and appointed Sperry as a consultant on control systems for the army project. By late October 1918, the army missile had been successfully test flown, with additional flights following in 1919. Lawrence Sperry continued work on the weapon for the army in the early 1920s. Some aircraft achieved hits on targets at ranges of up to ninety miles during trials in 1922.[3]

One of the reasons cited for the lack of success of the Sperry flying bomb was the automatic control system, which, because it did not accept commands after launch, could not direct the weapon toward alternative or moving targets. During the 1920s, the navy's Bureau of Ordnance sought to solve this problem by directing aircraft by radio-control systems. A Curtiss N-9 floatplane was used for the tests, which began in 1923 using a safety pilot to take off and land the airplane and to correct any in-flight control deficiencies. In September 1924, an N-9 completed a forty-minute flight without a pilot, although the airplane sustained some damage in landing. Later experiments involved a higher-performance, float-equipped Vought VE-7H, but when this aircraft crashed on takeoff in December 1925, the navy abandoned the project.[4]

British developments in pilotless aircraft eclipsed American ones in the late 1920s and early 1930s. While American experiments lay dormant, the British forged ahead with Larynx, a three-hundred-mile-range catapult-launched weapon for use against naval and land targets. Successful flights took place in 1927–29. The British air staff determined in 1930 to proceed with a target aircraft to provide more realistic gunnery training. This decision led to the conversion of a Fairey biplane with advanced radio-guidance equipment. As the Fairey Queen, this airplane participated in exercises at Gibraltar in 1933 that graphically demonstrated the deficiencies in British anti-aircraft fire. The Royal Aircraft Establishment, seeking a less complex and expensive aerial target, designed the Queen Bee after the Gibraltar tests. By the end of 1933, the Queen Bee had completed its first test flights, and in later years it was instrumental in providing realistic antiaircraft training.[5]

More than anything else, it was the British Queen Bee that stung the Americans into reviving their own experiments with robot airplanes in the 1930s. On 19 August 1935, the Plans Division of the Office of the Chief of Naval Operations recommended to Admiral King that the Bureau of Aeronautics undertake the development of pilotless aircraft "in view of supplying target planes for fire to destruction from anti-aircraft guns." But it was not until Admiral William H. Standley, the chief of naval operations, returned from the 1936 London Naval Conference that these ideas coalesced. While he was in England, Standley had been present at Queen Bee demonstrations and, suitably impressed by the proficiency of the British in the pilotless aircraft field, he determined that a similar program would be established in the United States.[6]

BuAer received authorization from the chief of naval operations on 1 May 1936 to begin the target aircraft project. An AEDO, Lieutenant Commander Delmar S. Fahrney, learned on 20 July that he was to be the officer in charge of the program. A native Oklahoman, he was in the class of 1920 at the Naval Academy, graduating a year early because of the wartime speedup and demand for officers. He served tours of duty on battleships and destroyers before learning to fly at Pensacola in 1923–24. As did so many other promising officers in the Construction Corps, Fahrney pilgrimaged to MIT, where he earned his master's degree in aeronautical engineering in 1930. In later years, he served in the carrier *Lexington*, where he found time to develop aircraft and components designs that his commanding officer, Captain Arthur B. Cook, passed on to

BuAer. Fahrney's technical aptitude impressed Cook, and when he moved to Washington as BuAer chief in June 1936 he was instrumental in securing important jobs for his protégé. Fahrney was chief inspector at the NAF when the bureau assigned the pilotless aircraft project to him.[7]

Fahrney's first task was to come up with a proposal for the pilotless aircraft program. In a twelve-page memorandum dated 6 August 1936, he set out in detail the objectives he planned to achieve and how he expected to carry them out. He determined that the NAF was "the natural base for the accomplishment of the early stages of the development and test program." Situating the project in Philadelphia made sense because the factory had the capability to manufacture the necessary mechanical control systems and to modify test aircraft. Mustin Field was adequate for early flight testing, and Lakehurst was convenient for later, more hazardous trials that required more space. Another advantage of the NAF was that it was relatively close to the Naval Research Laboratory at Anacostia, which was to supply the radio equipment according to the specifications drawn up by the project engineers. As for the airplanes themselves, Fahrney recommended buying four JH-1 Stearman-Hammond-Y pusher-propeller aircraft for modification as radio-control targets. The JH-1 was unusual. It had been designed as a low-cost "airplane for everyman," but like so many other aircraft in the 1930s it proved too expensive to attract a mass market. It did, however, have many of the attributes Fahrney wanted for the radio-control program—relatively economical operation, a high degree of aerodynamic stability, and a tricycle undercarriage to simplify takeoffs and landings. Fahrney also asked for a Great Lakes TG-2 scout-torpedo bomber for use as the control airplane. The total project cost was estimated at $77,500.[8]

The 6 August memo was really a manifesto allowing Fahrney to advance his view of the long-term navy involvement in pilotless aircraft. He averred, among other things, that robot airplanes could be used as "aerial torpedoes" to make low-level or diving attacks on sea and ground targets. These missiles, he thought, could employ television as part of their guidance apparatus. Radio control and a television monitoring system might also reduce the risks inherent in evaluating new aircraft. Dive tests were especially dangerous, often ending in the deaths of skilled test pilots and the destruction of valuable equipment. Fahrney's broad vision also encompassed significant advances in high-frequency radio technology and the use of radio-control airplanes for carrying mail from one ship to another at sea.[9]

Standley approved only the first part of Fahrney's proposal—the radio-controlled target aircraft—on 9 September. He assigned Fahrney as officer in charge of the project at the NAF and to the newly created special designs desk at BuAer in Washington. The same day he received notification of the CNO's approval of the project, Fahrney told Captain Webster that the Naval Aircraft Factory would in the "near future" be called upon to design, develop, and manufacture the parts needed for the radio-control actuating mechanisms. Working from solenoids through a modified Sperry Gyro Pilot hydraulic system, these links provided rudder/aileron, elevator, throttle, flap, and ground-steering control. The factory was also responsible for designing and building the equipment to be used by the control pilot when remotely flying the airplanes.[10]

In spite of the high priority BuAer accorded the pilotless aircraft program, Fahrney and the nineteen people working under him encountered a myriad of problems demanding imaginative solutions. Delays in the delivery of the JH-1 Stearman-Hammonds forced the purchase of a New Standard NT trainer. As modified by the NAF, the airplane's wings included 4 percent more dihedral for enhanced in-flight stability. Less vexing was choosing a code name. Following discussions with Naval Research Laboratory people in November, all agreed that the navy radio-control aircraft should be referred to as drones, thus maintaining the connection with the British Queen Bee. Thereafter, the word *drone* became a generic term for all American remotely piloted target aircraft. After the first test of the NT drone at Anacostia in March 1937 revealed serious control deficiencies, the NAF supplied a directional gyroscope to keep the airplane on a constant heading and reduce the active input from the operator. When Sperry could not supply servomotors and hydraulic valves in time, the NAF's instrument shop, under Lieutenant (j.g.) Robert F. Jones, came up with a servo that replaced the cluster of three in the Sperry-supplied system.[11]

On the ground in a mobile field cart, or in an airborne control aircraft, the "pilot" of the drone at first flew the aircraft using a yoke and wheel linked to hydraulic gear, the movements of which opened and closed electrical circuits. A frequency-modulated (FM) radio set developed by the Naval Research Laboratory transmitted the signals to the receiving equipment on the drone. After a short time, the Fahrney group discovered that the bulky yoke and wheel could be dispensed with, and they substituted instead a small stick with push-button and toggle switches manipulated by the thumb and forefinger. The miniature control stick came to be known as the "beep control" because of the small movements needed to activate it and the short-duration signals (or beeps) emitted by the radio transmitter.[12]

Further extemporizing was needed when it became apparent that Stearman-Hammond was not going to be able to have the JH-1s available any time soon. The NT had provided valuable experience with the radio-control systems, but because it was a "tail dragger," the control pilot had to land it. With the JH-1s still unavailable in the summer of 1937, Fahrney decided that, rather than incur further delays, four Curtiss N2C-2 Fledgling trainers should be bought, along with another TG-2 control airplane. BuAer concurred, and by early August the NAF had the first of the Curtiss biplanes in hand for modifications. Besides fitting the aircraft with the radio-control apparatus, the NAF modified them with tricycle gear, considered essential for safe remotely piloted takeoffs and landings.[13]

The Fahrney group got results with the N2C-2s in the fall of 1937. On 7 October, the first of the airplanes took off and landed under radio control but with a safety pilot aboard in case there were any problems. Fahrney was encouraged also that the tricycle gear showed no evidence of nosewheel shimmy during taxiing—a common fault of similar landing gear configurations. As the experiments progressed, Fahrney decided that it was time to move away from Philadelphia. Lakehurst seemed the logical venue for further tests, but after some deliberation Fahrney chose the air station at Cape May, an excellent field in a sparsely populated area where there was little air traffic at that time of the year. By the middle of November all was ready for the first tests of the N2C-2 without a safety pilot. At this point, Commander Ralph Barnaby of the NAF had one of his usual inspirations; because an aviator's first solo marked a milestone in his or her flight training, the inaugural radio-control flight without a safety pilot should also be accorded recognition. He suggested it be called a "nolo," and everyone agreed that the word

A Curtiss N2C-2 trainer modified with tricycle landing gear for radio-control experiments at the NAF in the fall of 1937. (80-G-416332, National Archives)

had just the right descriptive ring. On the afternoon of 15 November, an N2C-2 took off without a safety pilot, flew for ten minutes, and landed. The only blemish on an otherwise flawless experiment was the collapse of the drone's undercarriage, which caused minor damage to the fuselage.[14]

Two JH-1s finally arrived at the Naval Aircraft Factory early in September, and work began almost immediately to outfit them for radio-control experiments. The Stearman-Hammonds did not need extensive modifications to the airframe or ancillary equipment. NAF engineers chose a more compact and lighter-weight radio-control installation for the JH-1s, involving considerably more design effort than had gone into the NT or the N2C-2 drones. By mid-October, Fahrney reported that the modifications were "progressing rapidly," but it was not until December that the first of the airplanes was ready for tests at Cape May. After four takeoffs and landings with a safety pilot, the JH-1 made its first nolo flight on 23 December.[15]

The radio-control group at the NAF had a busy off season in the winter and early spring of 1938. Four airplanes—two N2C-2s and two JH-1s (the NT had been retired from service in November)—had to be prepared for the resumption of test flights. Factory personnel perfected a device that automatically kept the drones' wings level, allowing the operator to land the drone using only the elevator and throttle controls. Responding to a request from Cook, the NAF also produced specifications for an expendable target drone. The design, which went to BuAer on 25 February 1938, met the bureau's criterion of low cost through such features as simplified fuselage construction with square-section structural members, compartmented plywood wings for flotation, "off-the-shelf" engines, and the use of plastic materials when possible. With quantity production, the unit cost of the drones could be as low as $4,000.[16]

Because the pilotless aircraft program at the NAF was highly confidential, a phone call in March 1938 from a reporter on the *New York Herald Tribune* requesting more information about the project raised some eyebrows at BuAer. The duty officer in Washington told the reporter that Cook, the bureau chief, "did not wish any publicity in this respect and would much prefer that the story be entirely squashed, in the interests of national defense." But the story ran on 11 March in both the *Herald Tribune* and the *Philadelphia Inquirer*. Webster explained the breach of security to the chief of naval operations, Admiral William D. Leahy, as soon as he could. Lewin B. Barringer, the editor of *Soaring* magazine and an officer with the 103d Observation Squadron of the Pennsylvania National Guard, had been using Mustin Field for two years. He thus had the opportunity to observe some of the experiments by the Fahrney group, and he related what he knew to the *Herald Tribune* reporter. Three days later, Barringer found himself in the office of Admiral W. T. Cluverius, the commandant of the Philadelphia Navy Yard. He apologized for committing a "gross error of judgment," and Cluverius warned him that the National Guard's use of Mustin Field was a privilege that would be withdrawn if similar incidents occurred in the future. The records show no further security violations in connection with the project, which was remarkable considering that much of the activity took place within one of the nation's largest metropolitan areas.[17]

To assure the confidentiality of the program as well as obtain more airspace and year-round flying weather, Fahrney moved flight testing from the East Coast to the West Coast in the summer of 1938. After a series of tests at Cape May for the benefit of top-level officers, Fahrney oversaw the transferral of personnel and equipment to a new site at Otay Mesa south of San Diego. Reconstituted as Project DOG, the program supplied target drones for fleet antiaircraft gunnery practice from August 1938 through the end of 1939. The trials dramatically demonstrated the utility of the drones and the deficiencies of previous antiaircraft training. Orders went out for more drones and radio-control equipment.[18]

From that point on, the role of the NAF in the target drone program had less to do with testing than with the design, development, and installation of radio-control equipment. In 1938, NAF technicians started work on a compact and reliable radio-control unit that could be easily fitted into the cockpit of most operational aircraft without any structural alterations. By the summer of 1939 the units were ready for installation in four N2C-2 airplanes. The N2C-2s were the last of a batch of twelve that had been ordered by BuAer in October 1938. Getting them ready in time for exercises with the fleet involved a crash effort by the NAF. Fahrney reported in December 1938 that the first drone had been completed, and he praised the NAF's people for their "highly commendable work in carrying out a complicated and exacting program in a short period of time." By September 1939, all twelve drones had been completed and delivered. The fleet expressed general satisfaction with the N2C-2 drones, but those with the compact radio-control equipment drew some criticism. The commanding officer of the fleet utility wing at the Naval Air Station, San Diego, complained in January 1940 that the drones showed assembly defects and their radio-control units quickly became contaminated with dirt, dust, and other foreign matter.[19]

The N2C-2s were not the only radio-control conversion project taken on by the NAF in the fall of 1938. In October, Webster submitted a request to BuAer for a Vought O3U-6 Corsair observation airplane to be fitted with the new compact radio-control unit. Because the aircraft had conventional rather than tricycle gear, Fahrney and others thought it ideal for demonstrating the feasibility of modifying large numbers of aircraft as drones. As it resulted, two airplanes went to Philadelphia for conversion—an O2U-3 Vought Corsair and an O3U-6—and the O2U-3 was ready for flight tests in May 1939. The tests went fairly well, although the airplane at first had a nasty tendency to ground loop. The experience gained with the

Lieutenant Commander Delmar S. Fahrney (center, standing) and the
group he assembled at the Naval Aircraft Factory in 1936–37 to develop a
radio-controlled target aircraft. In the background is a Curtiss N2C-2 target drone. (72-AF-215296, National Archives)

O2U-3 was valuable when work began on the O3U-6, which
required some modifications to the ailerons and tail surfaces before
it proved the practicability of the drone conversion. Before the end
of 1939, fourteen O3U-6s had arrived at the NAF for modification as
drones, and in 1940 the factory shipped twenty radio-control units
to San Diego for the field conversion of O3U-6s. Some of these
airplanes received tricycle landing gear because that was still shown
to be best for radio-control landings. From 1941 on, the NAF
modified and tested prototype aircraft with the radio-control equipment and furnished drone operating groups with the now-standard-
ized radio-control units. Space and manpower at the factory were
thus freed for higher-priority tasks.[20]

Every so often a technology proves to be a nexus, stimulating a
series of related innovations. This occurred with the target drone
program at the NAF, which was a catalyst for subsequent pilotless

aircraft projects. In his 6 August 1936 proposal, Fahrney had theorized that remote-control systems might be applicable to test flying, particularly the highly dangerous vertical dives and pullouts that could and did overstress aircraft structures. But how could performance information be relayed to the engineers on the ground in the absence of a test pilot? Fahrney had the answer in "repeat-back" instruments (what is now referred to as telemetering equipment or, more commonly, telemetry) that recorded vital flight data and transmitted them to a receiver. Cook said he was interested in the concept and in October 1937 asked for more details on the equipment and how it could be integrated into the structural testing of aircraft.[21]

Fahrney and Webster responded to Cook's request in January 1938. Fahrney reported that the Naval Research Laboratory had already begun experiments with radio data links for recording airspeed and engine revolutions per minute. Webster followed with a plan to use remote-control devices for flight testing of aircraft beyond their structural limits—in other words, until they crashed. It was critical to provide enough information to allow the control pilot to take the airplane through the complicated flight regime called for while also recording and transmitting engine performance, altitude, airspeed, attitude, and acceleration data up to the point of actual structural failure. Webster predicted close cooperation between the NAF and private industry. Bell Telephone Laboratories, for example, had developed remote sensing instruments that radioed data picked up from stress points in the aircraft. These data were recorded on the ground using either a sound-track film system supplied by RCA or an oscilloscope arrangement that had been developed by the Naval Research Laboratory.

For the long term the most significant aspect of Webster's proposal was his suggestion that a television camera be mounted in the cockpit of the airplane undergoing tests. Focused on the aircraft's instrument panel, the camera would immediately communicate to the control pilot all the information he needed to fly the airplane as well as transmit and record data critical for the interpretation of the structural readings obtained from the other equipment. Expecting his proposition would be brushed aside as science fiction, Webster emphasized: "Although reference to television may be considered to be fanciful, it is understood that the R.C.A. Manufacturing Corporation has produced and sold such equipment."[22]

Under the dynamic leadership of David Sarnoff, RCA had made dramatic progress with electronic television by 1938. RCA's success with the new technology was largely attributable to Vladimir K. Zworykin, a Russian émigré, who, while working for Westinghouse, had developed the iconoscope, the precursor to the black-and-white television camera. Sarnoff hired Zworykin and provided him with money and research facilities at the Victor Talking Machine Company plant in Camden, New Jersey. RCA had acquired the phonograph concern and had reorganized it as the RCA Victor Company in 1929. In 1932, Zworykin installed an iconoscope on the roof of the Camden factory and transmitted still pictures to a cathode-ray tube receiver a few miles distant. RCA began two-way television transmissions between New York and Philadelphia in 1936 and the next year introduced a mobile unit with two cameras and a relay transmitter for remote pickups. Of equal import and perhaps the inspiration for Webster's suggestion that television be used in flight testing was the first successful demonstration of airborne television in 1937. As part of a contract with the Soviet Union to develop a television system for air reconnaissance, RCA technicians equipped a Ford Trimotor with a camera and transmitter. During tests at Camden, a mobile unit received clearly discernible pictures of the ground as the airplane passed overhead.[23]

Though by no means fully perfected, television could not be dismissed as pure whimsy in 1938, and Webster's proposal therefore struck just the right chord with knowledgeable officers in BuAer. Lieutenant Commander Leslie C. Stevens of the bureau's research and development section went to Philadelphia in March to discuss television as a means of transmitting aircraft performance data. Two days later, Lieutenant Commander Raymond D. MacCart of the NAF and three representatives from RCA, including Zworykin, met to talk about the role of television in the pilotless aircraft project. They reached a consensus that television could be important and agreed to carry out preliminary studies. At that time, however, there was no money available to buy or test television equipment.[24]

More than a year passed before the NAF received the bureau's approval to begin the flight testing project. Responding to an order from the acting chief of BuAer, Captain Marc A. Mitscher, Webster asserted in September 1939 that much of the technology developed in connection with the target drone program could be applied to in-flight structural testing. He emphasized, moreover, that "the application of television to the problem of flight tests by radio control for structural purposes is in need of immediate development if the desired objectives are to be obtained within a reasonable time." Funds should be made available to buy television equipment, install it in an airplane, and start flight tests as soon as possible. Mitscher concurred, and on 14 October 1939 the bureau earmarked $48,000 of its structural testing funds for the project.[25]

The decision to experiment with television in connection with flight testing was pivotal. It forecast on one hand a program at the NAF that during the war years underscored the value of remotely piloted, instrumented aircraft for certain experimental flight activities. On the other hand, and in a more immediate sense, BuAer's interest in television gave Fahrney the opportunity to explore the use of pilotless aircraft as weapons. As early as 1934, Zworykin had informally proposed using television in an airborne missile. In November 1935, he submitted a design for an "aerial torpedo with an electric eye" to the Bureau of Ordnance, which rejected the idea largely because the weapon was too small to carry a warhead of sufficient penetrating power to sink a large warship. But Zworykin had planted a viable seed. In February 1937, a joint Bureau of Ordnance–Bureau of Engineering–Bureau of Aeronautics committee issued a generally favorable report on incorporating television into an aerial torpedo. At the same March 1938 conference at which MacCart, other NAF representatives, and people from RCA had discussed television as part of a telemetry system, the question arose of applying the technology to "transmit . . . pictures of the terrain beneath a plane which is controlled by radio or other means in order that the position of the airplane could be checked." Fahrney strongly advocated the establishment of an experimental program and found crucial support in BuAer from both Lieutenant Commander Stevens and Admiral Towers, who agreed to the project, code-named FOX. Fahrney became officer in charge.[26]

BuAer subsequently authorized the Naval Aircraft Factory to buy television equipment and begin tests to determine if it could be made to work in a remotely piloted weapon. Experiments started early in 1940, first with ground tests to determine picture quality and range parameters. By June, Fahrney's team had installed the equipment in a Lockheed XJO-3 twin-engine airplane with tricycle landing gear and had begun the airborne phase of the experiments.[27]

In the meantime, Admiral Harold R. Stark, the chief of naval operations, in February 1940 ordered BuAer to start work on an aircraft capable of delivering thousand-pound bombs against practice targets. Stark wanted one of the NAF's TG-2 control airplanes modified so that it could be used for such tests. The concern within the Office of the Chief of Naval Operations was that because of fusing problems, live bombs released from low altitudes during tests presented a hazard for manned airplanes, but that apprehension gave Fahrney the opening he wanted. It did not take an intellectual leap to shift the focus from a radio-controlled bomb-carrying test airplane to a weapon that could release bombs or torpedoes in combat. Fahrney presented a convincing case, and on 22 March 1940, the chief of BuAer, with the blessing of the CNO, ordered the assault drone project to start under the aegis of Project FOX at the NAF.[28]

While preparations began at the NAF to modify a TG-2 for the assault drone experiments, Lieutenant Jones, who was responsible for Project DOG target drone operations with the fleet, was pursuing an independent course. As early as September 1938, Jones had conducted dive tests with target drones on the West Coast. Although these and other trials resulted in the loss of two aircraft, Jones thought they pointed to the possibility of using drones to attack naval targets. He wrote the chief of BuAer in the fall of 1939 that the remotely piloted aircraft could function "as a unit in a 'mechanized suicide squadron' " that "would be foolproof and nerve proof." Jones continued experiments on his own at Cape May with drones as aerial rams, some with a crude photocell homing system, until Fahrney protested that this was unnecessary duplication of the Project FOX effort at Philadelphia. Eventually, with Jones's reluctant consent, Fahrney integrated the aerial ram work into FOX, then canceled it when tests failed to demonstrate its effectiveness.[29]

The nascent assault drone project remained in a state of flux throughout 1940, and it was some time before it crystallized into a coherent form. There was little agreement initially about how the aircraft should attack the target. Should it release conventional bombs or torpedoes? Or should it strike the target directly with a warhead? Some officers raised the question of guiding the drone to a target outside the visual range of the control pilot. Admiral James O. Richardson, the commander in chief of the United States Fleet, considered drones practical for offensive purposes and urged "energetic action" in their development. But he did not think the drones could be effective beyond the sight of the operator, thus greatly limiting their tactical efficiency.[30]

Television presented the solution to this problem, but with Project FOX moving at a snail's pace in the fall of 1940, Fahrney could not immediately take advantage of its possibilities. Mitscher stressed that the assault drone program should quickly resolve the problems of guidance and control to assure effective operation out of the sight of the operator. Fahrney added that the NAF had shown "little progress" with the TG-2 as a torpedo and bomb-dropping assault drone because of personnel shortages at Philadelphia. He urged that BuAer issue a "strong directive" to stimulate rapid development of the weapon.[31]

A dearth of personnel and lack of direction from higher up in the naval bureaucracy were important contributing factors to delays in the NAF's assault drone program. Another obstacle was the scarcity of control aircraft. Conversion of a TG-2 had to be held in abeyance until the NAF received a replacement control airplane. In March, the factory had evaluated and reported favorably on a twin-engine Beech 18S as a potential control aircraft. It was commodious enough for two complete radio-control units and associated personnel. Based on the recommendations of Project FOX, Beech took an 18S and faired in an extension above the cockpit to provide better visibility for crew members during radio-control maneuvers. The first of the airplanes, designated JRB-1, did not arrive in Philadelphia until October, and only then could modifications of a TG-2 begin.[32]

Fahrney made every effort in late 1940 to get the assault drone program off dead center, beginning with a tour of three Army Air Corps bases to study the progress being made by that service with guided weapons. The army was at that time committed to a low-cost flying bomb invented by Kettering at General Motors. Uncertain in late 1940 how the Kettering flying bomb would be directed to its target, the army was investigating both radio control and a preset mechanism. There was also the possibility, according to Fahrney, that the weapon could follow some sort of "localizer beam" transmitted by radio sets. Despite considerable effort on the part of the air corps, Fahrney was sure the navy was well ahead in the development of guided weapons. He ended a long memorandum to the engineering section of BuAer by urging the navy to assign higher priority to the assault drone program, thus guaranteeing its continued predominance in the field. "As far as can be determined," he wrote, "the Navy has outstripped all [other services] in the development of radio control for aircraft and it now appears logical that the Navy should develop the first radio controlled aerial torpedo. Its tactical applications are many and studies and experiments are warranted."[33]

Fahrney's prodding led Rear Admiral Towers to issue an order in January 1941 establishing the NAF assault drone program on a level that promised quicker results. Towers specified that the NAF concentrate on a torpedo-carrying drone and that tests be so structured as to determine the effective range of the weapon. Furthermore, he ordered, "The bureau is particularly desirous that the technique of operating offensive torpedo-carrying radio-controlled aircraft in quantity be pushed to a conclusion, and that sufficient flight tests of aircraft television be carried out to permit recommendations of useful application for naval work together with the next steps which appear desirable along this line." Although Towers perceived that the NAF might encounter difficulties obtaining enough experienced personnel, he urged the "vigorous prosecution" of the program.[34]

At last Fahrney had from BuAer the mandate he needed to get the NAF assault drone project on track. It was clear that the bureau wanted the weapon to be a torpedo carrier, and from Towers's order television was the preferred method of guidance. These decisions greatly simplified Fahrney's task and provided much-needed direction to the program, which at times seemed to have a scattershot character that did nothing to increase its appeal among skeptics. The decision to give the project higher priority meant that Fahrney was also in a better position to secure the officers and men needed to demonstrate the practicality of the assault drone. After a year that brought meager results, the assault drone project finally began to live up to its promise in 1941.

Television remained the technical cornerstone of the assault drone program. By the spring of 1941, the XJO-3 television installation, after some initial problems, began functioning well. Project FOX people used the airplane to make simulated torpedo runs on ships in the Delaware River. They found the transmissions of such clarity as to allow the operator "to define targets . . . regardless of lighting conditions." The Lockheed did not, however, have any radio-control gear on board. To mimic torpedo attacks, the ground operator radioed instructions to the pilot, who then flew the aircraft as directed. Transmission distances of up to sixty miles were possible, and clear images of vessels were acquired from eight miles away. And this was with a heavy, bulky RCA commercial camera and transmitter; improved units promised to work even better.[35]

More conclusive results came from tests with the TG-2, which was finally ready to fly by the summer of 1941. NAF technicians fitted a nacelle containing the television camera and associated transmitting apparatus to the left bomb rack of the stubby biplane. The unit, developed by RCA and known as the Jeepette, was much smaller and lighter than that flown in the XJO-3. For two weeks in July and August, the Project FOX team flew fifty simulated torpedo attacks with the airplane under full radio control although with a backup pilot aboard. All but three of the tests were successful. The ground receiving set at Mustin Field clearly showed an image of the target when the airplane was six miles distant, despite a great deal of smoke and haze and some interference from the adjacent radio-control transmitter. Further trials at Cape May included the release of torpedoes as well as bombs. Although the TG-2 crashed because of an electrical failure during the drop tests, the results overall were encouraging to the advocates of the assault drone concept.[36]

The Project FOX assault drone experiments in 1941 were positive in other respects. It was found early in the year that a control pilot could manipulate a drone while flying his own aircraft. This virtually assured that drones could be directed from single-seat fighter airplanes and helped answer a question that many in BuAer had about controlling multiple flights of pilotless weapons. Tests also confirmed the practicality of a radio reflecting altimeter. Conventional barometric altimeters were ineffective at the extremely low altitudes the torpedo-carrying drone would have to fly as it bore in on the target. An RCA engineer, R. C. Sanders, perfected the new device, which was ready by early 1941 and performed well during the TG-2 simulated torpedo attacks that summer.[37]

As the flight-testing phase of the assault drone project picked up momentum, Fahrney added several talented people with radio-control experience to the Philadelphia group. One of these was Lieutenant (j.g.) Eugene R. Dare. Fahrney had met Dare at Guantánamo in 1939 during fleet exercises with target drones. Dare subsequently joined Project DOG and worked with Jones's target drone squadron before coming to Philadelphia in March 1941. A second person was Lieutenant (j.g.) Molton ("Molt") B. Taylor. Fahrney's acquaintance with Taylor had also begun as a result of the 1939 Guantánamo exercises. In 1941, Taylor joined the elite squad of radio-control experts at Philadelphia and soon demonstrated, in Fahrney's estimation, "a remarkable grasp" of the operational complexities of the assault drone program.[38]

Project FOX flight testing began to tax the facilities at Mustin Field and Cape May. Captain Ernest M. Pace, Jr., who had taken over as manager of the NAF in June 1940, explained to BuAer that "the intensity of radio controlled work will more than double" before the end of the year. He said that an auxiliary facility was badly needed and suggested that the navy consider leasing Andelot Field near Chestertown on Maryland's Eastern Shore to ease the burden imposed by the increased tempo of activities at Philadelphia and Cape May. Mitscher said he would do what he could to see that the flight test facilities at Cape May were upgraded. But Fahrney was certain that Project FOX would need a new flying field in the near future.[39]

On the whole, the assault drone program was in good shape in the fall of 1941. BuAer assigned two additional TG-2s to the NAF in September, which somewhat eased the equipment shortages that had burdened Project FOX earlier in the year. Pace reported to BuAer that the flight tests with television guidance showed that "effective attacks on targets can be launched and driven home" with a high degree of success. He also foresaw that radar, which had been under development for some time by the navy, might augment television in the assault drone and make possible attacks in low-visibility conditions. Pace cautioned, though, that the navy should make no commitments to a large-scale operational assault drone program until the completion of additional flight testing.[40]

Pearl Harbor was then only weeks away, and a crisis atmosphere pervaded Washington that autumn. On 24 October 1941, Fahrney and Lieutenant Commander Stevens met with officers from the Bureau of Ordnance to map out the future of guided weapons in the navy. They decided that one hundred obsolete TBD Douglas Devastator torpedo bombers should be made available as soon as possible for conversion to assault drones. Furthermore, they concluded, the navy should acquire a low-cost aircraft designed expressly for the assault drone mission. Within days, the project took on a new sense of urgency when the CNO insisted that "progress on the assault drone program is a matter of great interest . . . to the service at large" and looked ahead to combat applications of the new weapon.[41]

On the eve of war, the Naval Aircraft Factory had in place a major research and development program standing poised to vault to operational status. The assault drone project, having evolved from the highly successful target drone effort, showed considerable promise in 1941. It had drawn the attention of the chief of naval operations and had received a commitment from his office that assured its permanence at least for the foreseeable future. Whether the assault drone program would achieve everything its advocates promised was still open to question. But that proof would have to come in the crucible of war. For the time being, the NAF had secured its position as a major part of the navy's growing research and development establishment and was affirmed as a leader in new technologies and advanced weapons.

10

War and Reorganization

Forged in the heat of World War I, the Naval Aircraft Factory had struggled through the vicissitudes of peace for more than twenty years, showing a remarkable resiliency and ability to adapt to changing political and military circumstances. After 1938, the NAF faced the uncertainties of another world war, which, if the past held any lessons for the future, were to present enormous challenges to the nation's technical and procurement agencies. Those strains pulled the factory in a multitude of directions and precipitated major changes in its organization. Increasingly, the NAF became a factory in name only, as its activities centered on advanced technical projects, special weapons, testing, and research and development. At the conclusion of the war, the Philadelphia complex was hardly recognizable to the old hands who had lived through the awkward interim between the great world conflicts.

Events abroad dictated the direction of naval preparedness in the late 1930s, making coordinated military and naval planning difficult. Successive crises—Munich in late September 1938, followed by the occupation of all of Czechoslovakia in March and the cynical Soviet-German pact in August 1939—culminated in the German invasion of Poland and war in September 1939. Hitler's blitzkrieg against the West in the spring of 1940 climaxed in the total collapse of France, the isolation of Britain, and an emergency in the United States. The United States responded with presidential and congressional initiatives to augment the material and personnel of the armed forces. One of these reactions was the dramatic appeal by President Roosevelt on 16 May 1940 for fifty thousand aircraft to bolster the nation's defenses. This unheard-of number of airplanes, more than had been produced by the entire American industry in the previous twenty years, presented a dilemma for planners used to thinking in terms of a few hundred aircraft annually, and turmoil ensued as the military air arms shuffled priorities and set up organizations to coordinate aircraft procurement.[1]

Arbitrarily, the navy was assigned 13,500 of the aircraft targeted by the chief executive. Representatives of the Bureau of Aeronautics served on key planning bodies organized in the aftermath of the request for 50,000 airplanes while simultaneously revising strategies for the procurement of aircraft and the recruitment of personnel. Of most concern to the service was the passage in June 1940 of the National Defense Expediting Act. Known also as the Vinson Act, this measure delegated broad authority to the secretary of the navy to negotiate contracts for ships, aircraft, and other equipment. For the duration of the emergency, the secretary had discretionary power to modify, renegotiate, or otherwise alter any existing contracts for aircraft or ship production. Gone was the fear of profiteering and the merchants of death. Suspension of the Vinson-Trammell Act in July 1940 discontinued profit limitations and the requirement that 10 percent of the navy's aircraft and engines be produced in government plants.[2]

Staffing was one of the biggest problems facing the Naval Aircraft Factory during the national emergency. Throughout the 1920s, the NAF had had to compete with private industry in recruiting engineering talent, and the budgetary restrictions of the early Depression years had precluded any expansion of personnel. Then, after 1935, the aircraft industry, benefiting from the growth of commercial air transport and a succession of military expansion programs, absorbed most of the engineers and technicians graduating from the country's institutions of higher learning. At the same time, the NAF and other government agencies such as the NACA offered important opportunities for young engineering graduates to hone their skills and prepare for other jobs in the design and production of aircraft—postgraduate work of a sort. The obverse of this situation was that there was a high level of turnover in the engineering department at the factory.[3]

The Naval Aircraft Factory as it looked in August 1939 just before the outbreak of war in Europe. Note Mustin Field in the background. The circle on the field is the platform used for tests of carrier arresting gear. (72-AF-216990, National Archives)

During the 1930s, the NAF provided valuable experience for engineers fresh out of college by giving them hands-on training. The experiences of J. Hartley Bowen and William J. Cox are cases in point. Bowen graduated from Drexel Institute of Technology with a degree in chemical engineering in 1938 and, finding few jobs in the Philadelphia area, took and passed the civil service examination. After one year at what he considered a dead-end job in industry, Bowen had a successful interview at the NAF and went to work in July 1939 as a junior engineer working on army/navy specifications. Later he moved up to a supervisory position, responsible for paint testing and the development of aircraft cleaning and preservation compounds. As William J. Cox neared completion of his aeronautical engineering degree at the University of Pittsburgh, the head of his department encouraged him to seek a job at the NAF, believing that the factory would provide a broader range of practical experience for an entry-level employee than would a similar position in private industry. Cox arrived at the NAF in August 1939 and almost immediately went to work as a draftsman. His earliest jobs were drawings for the N3N-3 and SBN projects at the NAF.[4]

With the crisis of 1940–41 and the expected rapid expansion of the aircraft industry, the NAF had to explore means of bolstering its already shaky personnel situation. In May 1940, Admiral A. E. Watson, commandant of the Philadelphia Navy Yard, reported on the adequacy of the NAF to face the national emergency. The factory, Watson said, had an almost overwhelming number of projects, among them the production of twenty aircraft and eleven engines monthly, airplane and engine overhauls, and the manufacture of instruments, catapult launch cars, test stands, and arresting gear. Monthly expenditures were about $1 million. But the plant faced an imminent problem in obtaining and retaining aeronautical engineers and technical personnel, who were being attracted by higher-paying jobs in the private sector. Watson said that the NAF's working hours and leave policy "make for ineffectiveness" and that civil service employment could not compete with jobs outside government. William H. Miller, following temporary assignment to the factory in the spring of 1941, believed aircraft design and manufacturing were crucial to the recruitment and retention of personnel. He said the NAF had to develop original airplane designs if it were to keep a nucleus of educated and highly motivated personnel: "The Naval Aircraft Factory has long been an important source of supply of aeronautical engineers for the industry and the Bureau. It can only continue to be such if the Bureau permits it to engage in the design and manufacture of aircraft under conditions which are most favorable to the successful performance of that function."[5]

Personnel increases brought their own pressures in the pre–Pearl Harbor years. In February 1939, 1,853 employees worked at the NAF; by January 1940, this figure had gone up to 2,591. At the beginning of the national emergency in the spring of 1940, there were 3,000 workers at the factory, and the number continued to climb through the remainder of the year and into 1941. By May 1940, the factory was on a two-shift, six-day-a-week schedule. Recreational facilities were strained as the number of employees increased. Officers had access to the navy yard's officers' club. Enlisted personnel and civilians used Building 489 at the yard, but it was obvious that more attention would have to be paid in the future to employees' recreation needs.[6]

Concerns over security at the Naval Aircraft Factory in 1940 directly and indirectly affected personnel. Radio control and catapult and arresting gear projects were among the most important activities at Philadelphia classified as confidential. For a four-week period in February and March 1940, the Federal Bureau of Investigation conducted an intensive survey of the factory. The result was a detailed review of the NAF, its workers, their activities, and deficiencies in the factory's security arrangements. The report revealed continuing worries about espionage activities; the factory manager admitted that it "was easy, under the existing system, for espionage or sabotage agents to obtain employment" at the NAF. A screening system was in place whereby all civil service employees were fingerprinted and their records forwarded to the FBI, but there were many workers who had come to the factory before these procedures had been instituted.

For want of better criteria to identify potential enemy agents and saboteurs, the FBI focused on aliens, foreign-born workers, and those with pro-Nazi or communist sympathies. The factory did hire aliens, despite rules against doing so. During its survey, the FBI found one of these people, a Swedish cafeteria worker, but did not recommend his dismissal. A total of 280 foreign-born employees worked at the NAF, most of whom were of Italian origin, not surprising given the large Italian population of South Philadelphia. Others were of English, Russian, and Polish extraction. Many worked in skilled jobs as machinists, sheet metal workers, and mechanics. Again, the FBI made no recommendations about their disposition or revising the guidelines for NAF employment.

The FBI relied entirely on informants to pick out potentially threatening employees with Nazi or communist leanings. One German-born machinist was alleged to be a member of the German-American Bund, a group of pro-Nazi extremists. The informant testified that he had entertained Germans in his home and had returned to Germany on at least one occasion since 1939. FBI investigators duly filed this information, but a check of NAF employment records revealed only one person with the same last name as the alleged Bund member, and that person had an entirely satisfactory record. Informants registered complaints against at least eight other workers with supposed Nazi ties, but none of the accusations could be verified. The FBI could identify only one NAF worker who had been a member of the Communist party, and a field investigation of another worker suspected of communist proclivities revealed nothing that would warrant dismissal as a security liability.

In the climate of 1940, the FBI survey could have sparked a witch-hunt with long-lasting detrimental effects on the morale of workers and the efficiency of the factory's operations. To its credit, the FBI dismissed accusations stemming from personal dislikes or grievances and followed up informants' testimony with apparently impartial inquiries. No purge of workers ensued. The bureau did recommend more thorough security checks of all employees and offered advice on how potential security risks could be eliminated. Many of the bureau's suggestions, however, were either too costly to implement or were impractical, and so far as is known they were never put into effect. On the whole, the FBI's survey and report on the NAF were remarkably balanced, if not particularly instructive, in coping with personnel security problems.[7]

After Pearl Harbor, the security issue became more or less submerged in the sheer numbers of employees who joined the burgeoning work force at the NAF. From about three thousand workers in 1940, the factory's employment figures tapered off and then bottomed out early in 1941, reflecting a gradual reduction in manufacturing as the N3N-3 and other programs wound down. By the end of the year, however, the upward trend had resumed, and the number of workers at the factory reached 5,300. The greatest increase came in 1942 and 1943. In December 1942, the factory employed 12,000 people; 13,400 worked at the factory in June 1943, the high-water mark during the war years. Before the end of the year, employment dropped off to 10,200, and that figure declined to 9,800 in May 1944 before rebounding to 11,800 in December.[8] Policy changes and administrative reorganization accounted for much of the fluctuation in personnel in 1943 and 1944, which in turn complicated recruitment, training, and placement programs.

Training civilian and military personnel to undertake the multiplicity of jobs at the NAF during the war proved especially critical.

For years, each department at the factory had been responsible for its own training programs. The war, however, created a need for centralized administration of the various training activities. As a follow-up to a May 1942 directive from the Navy Department, the NAF created the training division within the personnel relations department to coordinate the factory's responsibilities in this vital area.[9]

Civilian indoctrination took place in schools that specialized in apprentice training, inspection, and shop, engineering, and clerical instruction. Apprentice instruction had been conducted in the schools at the navy yard since 1930, but in April 1943 the NAF began its own apprentice program. Among the trades covered were aircraft engine mechanic, aircraft instrument maker, aircraft metalsmith, carpenter, and electrician. Inspection received considerable attention during the war. On 22 October 1940, the navy, responding to a severe shortage of qualified aircraft inspectors, authorized the establishment of the Aeronautical Inspection School at the NAF. The school operated until recruitment of trainees slacked off in 1943, which prompted BuAer to discontinue the activity in September 1943. Shortly after Pearl Harbor, the NAF faced a similar predicament in the area of radio and radar inspectors, leading to the creation of the Radio and Radar Inspection School in July 1942. The school offered both basic and advanced courses in avionics before it was closed at the end of 1943. Some of the training division's more specialized course offerings were stenography, typing, applied mechanics, electrodynamics, welding, crane operation, blueprint reading, and production management. The training division also maintained an extensive library of films and professional journals for employee use. By the end of the war, nearly sixty-three hundred people had completed one or more courses offered by the division.[10]

Officers and enlisted men took courses at the NAF to sharpen their professional knowledge and skills. Since the mid-1920s the factory had operated the Aviation Instrument School, instructing enlisted personnel in the operation, installation, and maintenance of these vital pieces of equipment. The school expanded in the fall of 1940, but by August 1942 it had outgrown the facilities at the NAF and was moved to the Naval Training School in Chicago. Another specialized training program centered on the Catapult and Arresting Gear School established at the NAF on 26 January 1942. A logical

The expansion of the NAF during World War II led to the creation of training schools. Here two women work on equipment at the factory's Radio and Radar Inspection School in September 1943. (80-G-77462, National Archives)

extension of the factory's research and development program in catapults and arresting gear, the school stressed classroom work as well as practical experience using the test installations at Mustin Field. The NAF had offered postgraduate classes for officers since 1927. These included courses in flight familiarization, advanced airplane design, the theory of flight, and the installation of various types of aviation ordnance.[11]

Labor unions presented their own challenges during the war years. Employees at the NAF were partially organized; most shop workers by 1940 belonged to locals linked to the American Federation of Labor (AFL). The AFL was traditionally oriented toward craft workers rather than unskilled industrial laborers, who most often gravitated to the Congress of Industrial Organizations, or CIO. Two locals at the NAF had affiliation with the CIO: the Industrial Union of Marine and Shipbuilding Workers of America organized one of the shops; and the United Federal Workers of America (UFWA) represented employees in the inspection shop. White-collar workers, including drafting, engineering, and supply personnel, did not belong to labor organizations.[12]

Despite an instance in the fall of 1942 when UFWA workers complained of inadequate sick leave and violations of civil service regulations whereby people worked in jobs for which they were not classified, the NAF was able to avoid major labor trouble. Perhaps a flexible personnel system had evolved that was capable of adjusting to and meeting any dissatisfaction among the factory's workers. On 20 March 1942, the factory authorized the establishment of the personnel division, headed by Commander V. F. Grant, which was responsible for labor relations, employee compensation, and employee services. Under personnel were special war production committees that provided liaison with shop committees. The committees met periodically with shop masters and department heads, as well as on a monthly basis with the factory manager and his staff. In instances when grievances could not be resolved, the officer in charge of the personnel division had the authority to intervene to settle matters on his own. "Excellent cooperative relationships are experienced in these dealings," according to an official history of the facility prepared in 1944. Former employees thought that was the case, as well. William J. Cox said there was an esprit at the factory during the war; everyone seemed willing to forge common bonds and pull together "for the Fleet."[13]

As they had during World War I, women began to make up a larger proportion of the NAF work force. And as was the case during the previous conflict, there was no fundamental reversal of women's roles in the industrial economy. Women came to the NAF and to industry in general out of a patriotic desire to assist in the war effort and to augment the family income. They did not go to work with the idea of permanently displacing men in traditionally male-dominated jobs, nor did they regard their new positions as permanent feminist beachheads in the workplace. Women who came to the NAF during the war usually took jobs long considered socially acceptable outside the home: clerical positions, for example, or as librarians. They considered less traditional jobs acceptable "for the duration." Women worked as quality inspectors, drivers, and in jobs associated with photographic reproduction and printing. More than 40 percent of the workers in the production shops were women by the end of 1943. This statistic is misleading, however. Only a few women held higher-paid jobs as riveters and machine-tool operators; most worked as seamstresses in the fabric shop where parachutes were manufactured.[14]

A handful of women invaded such traditional male strongholds as engineering, drafting, and laboratory work. The factory employed one woman, Mary French, as an aeronautical engineer. She was the only civilian female aeronautical engineer in the entire Bureau of Aeronautics. French taught woodworking to women apprentices during World War I before moving into drafting and then engineering, specializing in standards. There she helped establish performance data and testing procedures for aircraft and engine parts. Heading the drafting division of the engineering department was Karl White, who had come to the factory in May 1932 with a bachelor of science degree from the University of Kansas. Under White were a number of sections and groups, many of them containing significant numbers of women. The reproduction section, which had been entirely male before the war, had three men and thirty women by June 1945. Yet none of the women was in a position of major responsibility. Ship installation design, which handled catapult and arresting gear and was the biggest and most important section in the drafting division, remained a male bastion throughout the war. Some laboratories, notably materials and chemistry, employed women. Hartley Bowen insisted that a well-trained woman chemist was equal or superior to her male counterpart, but by 1943, he thought the quality and training of the women coming to work in the labs had fallen off.[15]

More than a hundred women at the NAF were WAVES (Women Accepted for Volunteer Emergency Service). Officially, WAVES were members of the Women's Reserve of the United States Naval Reserve. WAVE officers interviewed incoming employees, taught training courses, and worked as clerks, receptionists, air traffic officers, aides, and administrative assistants. One WAVE, Ensign Priscilla Wrenn, had specialized in aeronautical engineering at the University of Minnesota and was an assistant project engineer at the NAF in 1944. Most of the enlisted WAVES held office positions, but a few worked in the tower at Mustin Field and some were aerographers and radio personnel. Anna Barbour, a radiowoman, flew more than four hours per month in a variety of aircraft as part of her job.[16]

Blacks also came to the NAF in large numbers during the war, but, like women, they made few inroads into positions in the labor force usually reserved for white males. Most blacks worked as janitors or in food service; others were painters, maintenance workers, or laborers. In some areas, blacks exhibited considerable occupational mobility during the war, taking and holding jobs traditionally held by whites, but that does not seem to have been the case at the NAF. Those blacks who received special recognition for their wartime service at the NAF were all in menial jobs considered socially acceptable for members of their race. George Edwards, for example, came out of retirement in 1942 to work as a janitor, mopping miles of dirty floors and emptying thousands of waste baskets to win the war against the Axis. Anna V. Tines had been a matron at the NAF since 1917; her contribution was a device to prevent the clogging of drains at the factory. Blacks belonged to the Naval Aircraft Factory Victory Association, an organization that the UFWA regarded as a company union that reinforced racial segregation and discrimination.[17]

Whereas in World War I blacks and women had only limited means of airing grievances, in World War II they could turn to the Fair Employment Practices Committee (FEPC). Created in mid-1941, the FEPC was handcuffed by loopholes in civil service regulations that gave wide latitude to personnel officers to reject employment applications without having to show cause. But the FEPC did help convey a sense that the federal government was seriously interested in redressing some of the worst abuses brought on by racial and sexual discrimination. Some forty cases relating to alleged discrimination at the Naval Aircraft Factory came before the Philadelphia regional office of the FEPC between Pearl Harbor and the middle of 1944. Most concerned people who were passed over for whites in the hiring process or were not promoted because of their race.[18]

Rear Admiral Milo F. Draemel, commandant of the Philadelphia Navy Yard, insisted that there was "no basis for charges of discrimination against [workers] on account of race, color or any other reason." He further assured the regional director of the FEPC that at the NAF there were "many employees of the colored race who are performing very valuable service and their assigned work is thoroughly satisfactory." Despite the admiral's assurances, the NAF's record was at best spotty in appointing blacks to higher-paid jobs or in moving them up to more skilled positions. In the fabric shop, under Austin Joy, there were several cases in late 1943 of black women who were allegedly not advanced or were dismissed because of their race. More striking was an incident in early 1942 involving a black man with a degree in electrical engineering from New York University who was unable to get a job in the factory's engineering department. That discrimination was the reason he was not hired has to be given credence considering the crying need at the NAF for skilled personnel immediately after Pearl Harbor. Almost every case brought to the attention of the FEPC ended with a satisfactory adjustment—usually a promotion or the hiring of the person by some other government agency—and after mid-1944, the records show no cases.[19]

Whether the NAF was more or less racially biased in its employment policies than other aircraft plants or government installations is impossible to determine. Nevertheless, workers' morale during the war was generally satisfactory. The rate of absenteeism, a good indicator of workers' temperament, was relatively low at the NAF, averaging about 5 to 7 percent per month by the end of 1944. One of the ways NAF officers and managers boosted morale was by sponsoring recreational programs for war workers. In the winter months, the NAF fielded a basketball team, and in the summer men's and women's softball teams competed against one another. Golfers played in a tournament in September 1944. The most popular sport was bowling; the NAF sponsored leagues that included teams representing most of the factory's shops and divisions. Sports events and league standings received coverage in an employees' publication, *Air Scoop*. Appearing monthly starting in December 1943, *Air Scoop* was a breezily written, well-illustrated magazine that included features on major production programs, outstanding individuals, the history of the factory, short pieces covering news from the shop floor, and information on friends and former employees in the military services. Safety attracted a great deal of attention in *Air Scoop*; the entire September 1944 issue was devoted to the problem, and virtually every number highlighted shops that set records for consecutive days without an accident.[20]

A contributor to *Air Scoop* was twenty-four-year-old Isaac Asimov, who had just begun to establish a reputation as a writer of popular science and science fiction. Articles by Asimov on the testing and development of sea marker dyes at the Aeronautical Materials Laboratory appeared in the November 1944 and January 1945 issues of the magazine. Asimov arrived in Philadelphia in May 1942, joining another writer at the NAF, Robert A. Heinlein. Heinlein, a 1929 Naval Academy graduate who had retired from the service in 1934 for health reasons, was recognized as perhaps the best science fiction writer in the country. He came to the NAF through a friend at the Philadephia Navy Yard and was instrumental in bringing Asimov to the factory. His intervention was also responsible for attracting another talented writer, L. Sprague de Camp, a naval reserve lieutenant and author of works in popular science and patent law.[21]

Asimov had bachelor's and master's degrees in chemistry from Columbia University and was just starting his Ph.D. program at New York University when the war caught up with him. He worked in the chemical laboratory in the Aeronautical Materials Laboratory under Bernard Zitin and J. Hartley Bowen. Asimov wrote about his experiences at the Naval Aircraft Factory in the first volume of his autobiography, *In Memory Yet Green*, published in 1979. The work in the chemical lab was routine, "not very demanding to the intellect, but it meant the kind of meticulous record-keeping I liked, and it kept me absorbed." In 1944, Asimov was given responsibility to investigate various aircraft seam-sealing compounds and prepare a general specification for such materials. After the seam-sealing project, he headed a program to determine what chemical marker dyes could be seen best from the air and to develop test procedures for those dyes. The only problem with this was that the dyes had to be checked for visibility from the air, and Asimov had never been in an airplane before. Hartley Bowen remembered Asimov as someone who "was afraid of airplanes. He could write science fiction about space travel but he wouldn't get in an airplane." The marker dye project left Asimov with no options, and he made several flights in March 1945, which did not leave him "the least bit keen on airflight." Bowen recalled that Asimov "was quite upset" about the experience. Asimov's career at Philadelphia ended when he was drafted into the army in November 1945.[22]

Changes in the top leadership of the NAF accompanied the remarkable expansion of personnel at Philadelphia during the war years. Captain W. W. Webster had taken over as manager of the NAF from Captain Samuel J. Zeigler in July 1936. Webster was possibly the best-remembered and most respected top man at the factory since Fred Coburn. Ralph Barnaby recalled that he was "a very fine man; a great manager of the factory." "Outstanding" was the word Hartley Bowen used. As manager, Webster had supported such research and development projects as pilotless aircraft, catapults, and arresting gear, and he had seen the NAF through the difficult SON and SBN projects, as well as the early stages of the N3N-3 program.[23]

Webster left the factory on 10 June 1940 to become general inspector of naval aircraft in New York, responsible for the work of the Brewster company's plant in Long Island City. Webster was replaced a week later by Captain Ernest M. Pace, Jr. This was Pace's third posting to the NAF. He had served at the factory from 1919 to 1923 and again in 1932. Pace was a Naval Academy graduate (class of 1912) and, like many in BuAer, had completed a postgraduate course at MIT. Forty-nine years old in 1940, the bespectacled Texas native saw the NAF through a period of expansion to meet the needs of the war emergency, administered the N3N-3 production effort at its apogee, and initiated two other major aircraft manufacturing projects at the factory.[24]

Pace, however, left little impression on factory old-timers, possibly because his assignment to Philadelphia was sandwiched between the two tours of the charismatic W. W. Webster, who returned as factory manager on 26 December 1941. Pace, meanwhile, went back to BuAer, achieving flag rank in 1943. BuAer took the extraordinary step of sending Captain Webster back to Philadelphia (he was the first officer to hold the position twice) as a direct result of the disaster at Pearl Harbor and the realization that energetic leadership was needed to carry the factory through the crisis. Certainly Webster's appointment was the right decision given his experience and the admiration he commanded among the personnel at Philadelphia, but it ended in one of the great tragedies in the history of the factory.

On 16 March 1943, Webster took off from Mustin Field in a twin-engine Beech SNB piloted by Lieutenant J. B. Bennett to fly to Washington for one of his periodic meetings at BuAer. The weather was less than optimal; a fog blanketed much of the Delaware Valley, and it was unseasonably warm. Ralph Barnaby remembered that he

Captain W. W. Webster returned to the Naval Aircraft Factory as manager in December 1941 after serving previously as manager in 1936–40. Capable and well liked, Webster died in an airplane accident on 16 March 1943. (72-AF-212552, National Archives)

and Webster's secretary tried to dissuade him from flying that day, but Webster thought conditions were improving. Shortly after the two officers left, the field lost radio contact with their airplane, and then an hour or so later, word came to the factory that there had been an accident near Marcus Hook. Both occupants of the aircraft had been killed. Barnaby, Fahrney, and others at the factory correctly assumed that it was Webster's aircraft, but some hours passed before there was official confirmation of his death. Investigations uncovered no probable cause for the accident, although fog and high humidity may have contributed. It was a day of disaster for the Naval Aircraft Factory because only hours after Webster's accident, another NAF airplane crashed near Newtown Square, killing an officer and an enlisted man.[25]

Following memorial services at Philadelphia on 19 March, Webster's body was interred at Arlington National Cemetery. On Memorial Day 1945, the navy remembered Webster with the dedication of a bronze plaque at the NAF. The eulogy held that "Captain W. W. Webster was loved for his unfailing kindness and his understanding of human problems. He was respected for his mastery of aeronautics and his able administrative qualities. . . . Naval aviation lost a capable and far-seeing man and the employees of the Naval Aircraft Factory lost a true friend." Subsequently the street separating the main buildings at the NAF from Mustin Field was named Webster Road, and on 1 June 1943, a flight test field at Priest Point, Maryland, near the Naval Air Station, Patuxent River, received his name. Few were more deserving of these posthumous honors than Walter Wynne Webster.[26]

Captain J. Ross Allen, chief engineer at the NAF, served as acting manager until 15 May, when Samuel Zeigler arrived to take over the position left void by Webster's sudden and unexpected death. This was Captain Zeigler's second turn in the top spot at the NAF; he had served as manager in 1934–36.[27] Then he had been largely responsible for the reinstitution of aircraft production under the Vinson-Trammell Act; on this tour he faced difficult administrative decisions as the factory underwent a fundamental reorganization in the summer of 1943.

For some time there had been an awareness that the existing administrative structure of the NAF was inadequate to meet the varied responsibilities that had been assigned to the factory. In response to this and well before Zeigler returned to Philadelphia, the NAF's supply operation had been split off and established as a separate command. In the early 1920s, the NAF supply department had become the main source of parts and equipment for the navy's air arm. This was an increasingly burdensome function as naval aviation expanded in the 1930s and the factory's work load increased. To streamline parts flows, BuAer in late 1933 established a separate stock control section in its Material Division, and in 1934 the NAF set up a reporting system relying on semiannual inventories at operating bases. Further improvements came in February 1940, when BuAer, acting on the recommendation of Captain Webster, authorized the establishment of field inventory and field requisition sections in the NAF supply department. These gave the factory a better idea of fleet needs and allowed it to adjust its inventories more efficiently to meet those requirements.[28]

The centralization of aviation supply at Philadelphia made sense, but it also meant that the supply department of the NAF was hard-pressed to meet all of the navy's aviation supply needs while simultaneously filling the demands of the factory, which was undergoing a major expansion. The solution was the establishment, on 26 April 1941, of the Aviation Supply Office as a "separate and distinct activity" from the supply department of the NAF. Even though it was located at the NAF, the ASO was entirely autonomous, responsible for procurement and distribution of all parts in addition to the operation of aviation supply annexes at the Naval Air Station, Norfolk, and the Naval Supply Depot in Oakland, California. The plan also set up supply depots at Clearfield, Utah, and Mechanicsburg, Pennsylvania.[29]

Following its formal establishment on 1 October 1941, the Aviation Supply Office underwent rapid expansion under its first commanding officer, Captain Oscar W. Leidel. Occupying the entire second floor of Building 76, the ASO had to cope with a flood of parts orders and accompanying paperwork. Manual record-keeping systems gave way to mechanical ones, and a daily teletype arrangement provided for the immediate dispatching of essential spare parts. Farther down the priority list were semicritical items and routine supplies. Requisitions for these arrived in Philadelphia on a monthly basis to be filled through normal channels. One of the biggest difficulties was confusion over the allocation of parts for maintenance and those sent out under routine replenishment procedures. Under some circumstances, one part would be shipped for immediate maintenance requirements and for storage to meet future needs. Obviously, a single part could not accomplish both ends. This muddled situation ended in early 1943 when the ASO took over responsibility for the distribution of all maintenance parts in addition to its responsibility for the usual stock items.[30]

A concomitant to these changes was the rapid increase in expenditures, which in turn opened the ASO to charges of inefficiency and conflict of interest. From January to April 1941, the supply department of the NAF spent approximately $5 million; during a comparable period in 1943, the ASO disbursed $113 million. At one point in March 1942, a longtime NAF and ASO employee complained to the assistant supply officer about what he thought was a potentially embarrassing link between an ASO employee and the Breeze Corporation, a supplier of solvents. The allegations reached the secretary of the navy, but he considered the charges too general to warrant a full investigation. Still, the incident served as a warning that ASO purchasing officers must, according to one commentator, "be above any suspicion or breath of suspicion" in their relations with vendors.[31]

The enormous quantities of supplies funneled through Philadelphia and the resultant personnel increases seriously strained the already limited facilities at the NAF. From about 250 people in late 1941, the ASO grew to more than 500 by the first months of 1942 and to about 1,750 by the summer of 1943. The office took over additional space at the NAF, but it soon became imperative to find more room. In response to the overcrowding problem, Secretary of the Navy Frank Knox authorized the detachment of the ASO from the NAF in February 1943 to a new command, the Naval Aviation Supply Depot (NASD). Commissioned on 17 July 1943 at Oxford Avenue and Martin's Mill Road in North Philadelphia, the NASD was designed expressly to meet the immediate and future needs of naval aviation supply.[32]

The separation of the Aviation Supply Office from the NAF was partial acknowledgment that the factory's activities had become so diverse that administrative reorganization was essential. As early as August 1942, the Office of the Commander in Chief of the United States Fleet (COMINCH) considered the advantages of establishing the factory as a flag command, with its activities reconstituted as subordinate entities. Captain Pace, now assistant chief for material at BuAer, addressed the question in a memorandum to the bureau's director of planning. "The whole matter of setting up the NAF as a flag command should be approached with caution," he wrote. "In many respects [the] NAF is so closely linked with the Navy Yard that it functions as a division of the Navy Yard. . . . There is a theoretical dividing line between the NAF and the rest of the Yard, but in the past this has been a variable line that has been adjusted to meeting changing conditions."[33]

Pace questioned how this cooperative arrangement would be affected if there were two admirals at League Island: "It is possible, of course, that this same coordination could be worked out between the Commandant and the flag command, but there would be certain confusion at first, and it is doubtful that the Commandant could ever be as sympathetic to the problems of the NAF as a co-equal that he feels toward the NAF as an element of his own organization." Pace concluded that the NAF organization should remain as is, although he did admit that "maintenance of the status quo . . . does not, however, preclude the possibility of assigning an officer of flag rank as Manager of the Factory. . . . provided he were junior to the Commandant."[34]

The relationship of the NAF to the navy yard at Philadelphia had always been ambiguous. The NAF was not, as Pace stated, "an element" of the navy yard organization. It was an entirely separate administrative entity even though it was physically part of the League Island complex. He was correct about the variability of the lines of responsibility between the yard commandant and the factory manager and the high degree of cooperation that had been attained over the years. Yet he failed to stress the occasional jurisdictional disputes that had arisen since at least 1926, when Moffett had successfully defended the NAF's separate accounting, supply, and transportation functions in the face of strong opposition from the yard commandant. Rather than exacerbate such problems, a higher-ranking NAF manager would be in a stronger position to maintain the traditional demarcation between the yard and the factory and to preserve BuAer's special interests. Nor did Pace's memorandum take into account the massive wartime expansion of the NAF. By the summer of 1942, the factory had more than ten thousand people engaged in a wide range of research and development, testing, modification, and manufacturing activities. Reorganization along more functional lines and the assignment of a flag officer may well have been long overdue.

Planning for such reorganization proceeded through the remainder of 1942 and into the spring of 1943. COMINCH completed a draft memorandum for BuAer in September 1942 that embodied most of the changes thought necessary to rationalize the establishment at Philadelphia. The memorandum called for the creation of the Naval Air Material Center, under which would be the Naval Aircraft Factory, the aeronautical laboratories, the Ship Experimental Unit, and the Aviation Supply Office. Heading the new organization would be a superintendent of "suitable rank." There was no commitment at this point to the assignment of a rear admiral to command the new center, nor was there any statement about how Mustin Field fit into the new scheme.[35]

The COMINCH memorandum, with revisions, became the instrument for reorganization of the NAF. But it was not until after Captain Zeigler took command that the actual changes occurred.

Zeigler issued three bulletins in June and early July 1943 that implemented a more definite separation of the test and development and overhaul and conversion activities at the NAF. The bulletins also limited the number of personnel who reported directly to the manager. General Order 198, issued by the secretary of the navy on 20 July 1943, formalized the sweeping changes already accomplished by Zeigler. This document established the Naval Air Material Center (NAMC) at Philadelphia. Individual commands within the NAMC were the Naval Aircraft Factory, the Naval Aircraft Modification Unit (NAMU), the Naval Air Experimental Station, and the Naval Auxiliary Air Station at Mustin Field. The Aviation Supply Office remained outside the NAMC command structure.[36]

The NAMC units had clearly delineated responsibilities reflecting the desired functional changes. The Naval Aircraft Factory, under the manager, was to carry out manufacturing and production. Overhaul and conversion work, which had assumed major proportions since the 1930s and had been carried out by the modification branch of the NAF, fell under the Naval Aircraft Modification Unit, headed by its commanding officer. The Naval Air Experimental Station, administered by a director, was to include all former NAF laboratories and was responsible for research and development, testing, and the ship installation activities of the SEU. Finally, the Naval Auxiliary Air Station made up the airfield, hangars, offices, shops, and flight-test facilities at Mustin Field, in addition to administering other navy flying fields within the Fourth Naval District. Supply and plant functions nominally remained as departments of the newly constituted NAF, although they served all four NAMC commands.[37]

Predictably, there was negative reaction to the reorganization plan. Rear Admiral Draemel wrote to the vice-chief of naval operations that "certain problems of administration make it desirable that the Center be under the Commandant of the Navy Yard . . . rather than an independent entity." He argued that services, housing facilities, and personnel recruitment and training were so interwoven between the NAMC and the yard that separation would lead to duplication and inefficiency. But the changes stood; the vice-chief replied that the NAMC "shall remain an independent entity . . . as directed by ComInCh and CNO."[38]

Under the revised administrative organization at Philadelphia, naval personnel, some of whom had long association with the NAF, assumed new positions and responsibilities. From 12 August 1943, Captain Zeigler wore two hats—as commanding officer of the NAMC and as manager of the NAF—until 5 February 1944, when Captain Lloyd Harrison took over the top NAF job. On 27 September 1944, Zeigler concluded his tour as the NAMC commanding officer, and Captain Donald Royce arrived at the NAMC, hoisting his flag as rear admiral.

Royce graduated seventh in the Naval Academy class of 1914 and then received an advanced degree in marine engineering and naval architecture from MIT in 1920, won his wings at Pensacola in 1922, and served five years in BuAer's design section. He served at the NAF from 1927 to 1931 as assistant chief engineer, chief engineer, and production superintendent. At the time of his return to Philadelphia, Royce was director of BuAer's Production Division. Another familiar face at the NAMC was Captain Lisle J. Maxson, who had long experience with the development of catapults and became the first director of the Naval Air Experimental Station. Command of the Naval Auxiliary Air Station, Mustin Field, fell to Commander George L. Heap.[39]

One of the most important new jobs was that of commanding officer of the Naval Aircraft Modification Unit. Because a major responsibility of the NAMU was the development of pilotless aircraft, it was reasonable that Captain Fahrney, the officer in charge of special projects at BuAer and the NAF, should become the first head of the new unit. When Fahrney took over the top job at the NAMU on 12 August 1943 he found to his displeasure that his unit faced a severe shortage of space. Fahrney had previously completed a study of alternative sites in the Philadelphia area where the NAF's advanced weapons projects could be carried out and had recommended the Philadelphia Municipal Airport. Later, Fahrney submitted a formal proposal to locate the NAMU at the airport, and it received the approval of the bureau and the chief of naval operations. By July 1943, $510,000 had been tentatively allocated for the lease of land at the airport, the construction of a hangar, the erection of security fencing, and paving of runways. The National Defense Research Committee planned to build an administration and laboratory building on the property. Yet within a little more than a month, the army, concerned about safety in connection with mu-

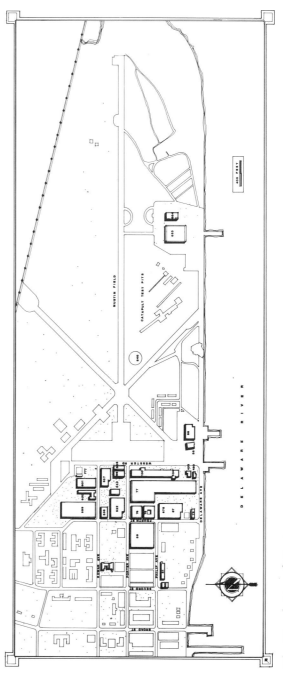

The Naval Aircraft Factory

Building 58	Hangar (1918)	Building 489	Welfare Building (Navy Yard)
Building 59	Plant No. 1 Assembly (1918)	Building 532	Machine shop (1936)
Building 60	Lumber kiln (1918)	Building 533	Engine test house (1936)
Building 61	Storehouse (lumber) (1918)	Building 534	Final assembly (1936)
Building 75	Office/administration (1918)	Building 536	Flight administration (1938)
Building 76	Storehouse (1918)	Building 537	Hangar/catapult housing (1938)
Building 77	Plant No. 2 Assembly (1918)	Building 540	Arresting gear test platform (1938)
Building 86	Storehouse/hangar (1920)	Building 599	Aeronautical Engine Laboratory (1941)
Building 87	Structural assembly (1919)	Building 600	Aeronautical Materials Laboratory (1941)
Building 96	Hangar (1931)	Building 601	Aeronautical Materials Laboratory (1941)
Building 133	Hangar (1920)	Building 653	Hangar (1943)
Building 435	Engine test house (1935)	Building 654	Forge shop (1943)
Building 480	Dispensary (1944)	Building 678	Cafeteria (1943)

Note: Detail of map follows on succeeding pages.

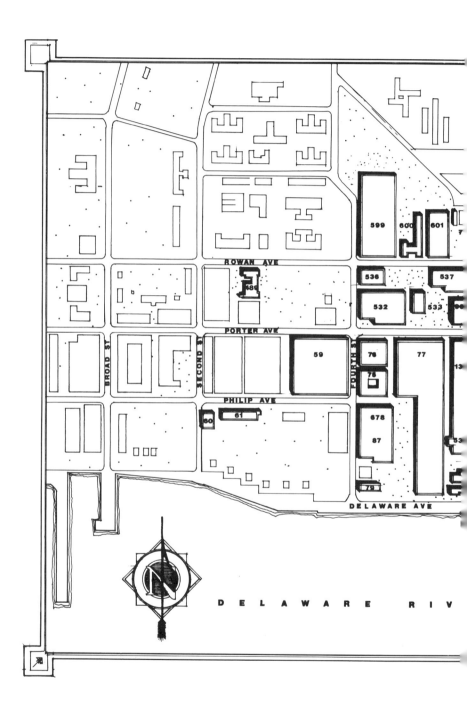

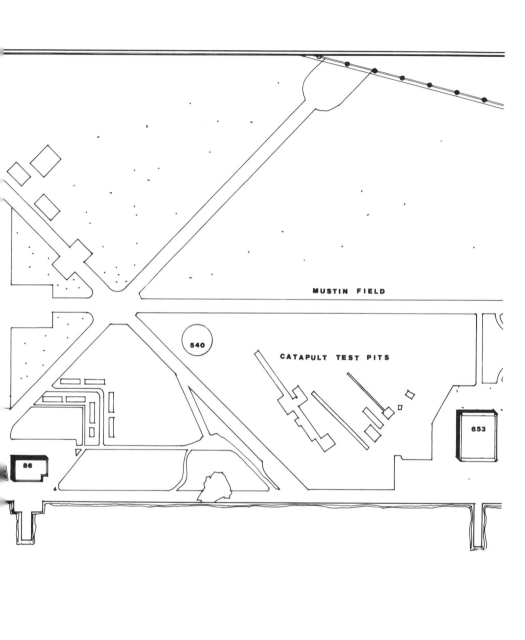

MUSTIN FIELD

540

CATAPULT TEST PITS

653

86

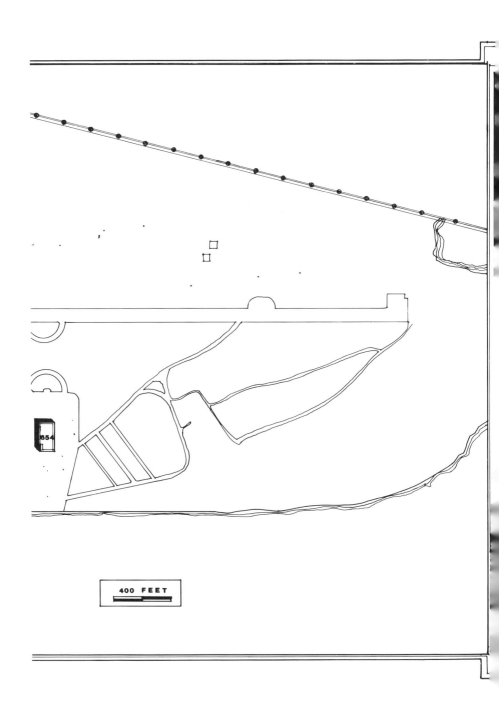

400 FEET

nitions stored at nearby Fort Mifflin, vetoed these ambitious plans, and the Civil Aeronautics Board on 23 December 1943 ordered the airport shut down to commercial traffic and to all but essential military flights. Fahrney's second choice was the Naval Air Station, Willow Grove, about fifteen miles north of center city Philadelphia, but the air reserve unit stationed there objected to sharing the base with the NAMU.[40]

It took an unusual combination of circumstances involving the troubled Brewster Aeronautical Corporation to resolve the critical space problems of the NAMU. The paths of Brewster and the NAF had crossed unhappily on the SBN project in 1938–42. In February 1941, an agreement was reached under which the Defense Plant Corporation would build and Brewster would lease a new assembly plant on 370 acres of farmland near Johnsville, a few miles east of the Naval Air Station, Willow Grove. Brewster occupied the facility upon its completion in December 1941 and in February 1942 began production of SB2A Buccaneer dive bombers. Delay followed delay until the navy became so frustrated with Brewster's management that the service determined that only drastic measures could resolve the problem. Consequently, in April 1942, President Roosevelt authorized the navy to take over Brewster and its production facilities. George Westervelt came out of retirement to oversee Brewster's aircraft production while the company underwent a thorough reorganization. Under new management, Brewster completed the SB2As and made considerable headway on an order for the manufacture of fifteen hundred Vought Corsairs at Johnsville, but festering labor problems and parts shortages gnawed at the firm and disillusioned many about its long-term prospects as a navy contractor. In May 1944, the navy abruptly canceled the Corsair contract; about half the airplanes were still undelivered.[41]

Brewster's distress proved to be salvation for the NAMU, delivering it from the space crunch it had faced since its inception. The Brewster factory at Johnsville was a modern plant with a million square feet of space—exactly what the NAMU needed for its modification and conversion work. Captain Zeigler was one of the first to recognize the potential of the Brewster plant. In January 1944, he wrote that the NAMU's "current performance under all circumstances" was "creditable," despite administrative obstacles, a heavy work load, and problems recruiting civilian workers. But largely because of space restrictions, the NAMU was "not now in a position to take on large projects." Zeigler suggested: "The Brewster Johnsville plant has been surveyed, and is well suited with very little change, to make an excellent modification unit to handle large projects. . . . This station would be very glad to undertake the organization and management of a Unit at Johnsville, for modifications and conversions in quantity;—but cannot do it successfully here at League Island."[42]

On 1 July 1944, the navy reached an agreement with the Defense Plant Corporation to take over Brewster's lease. The cost to the navy by April 1945 was a little more than $3.3 million exclusive of equipment. Captain Ralph Barnaby, assigned as commanding officer of the NAMU, effected a smooth transition while simultaneously supervising a major expansion of the unit's work force and activities. By the end of the year, nearly fifteen hundred former Brewster employees had been hired by the navy and the total number of workers at Johnsville reached about three thousand. Their jobs included the development of guided missiles and pilotless aircraft, airborne radar installations, and the modification, conversion, and repair of service aircraft.[43]

The removal of the Naval Aircraft Modification Unit from Philadelphia to Johnsville relieved some of the space problems at League Island, yet there never seemed to be enough room to accommodate the expanded activities and the numbers of new employees in 1942–43. In June 1942, BuAer approved appropriations totaling $2 million for expansion of the physical plant at the NAF. This included money for the construction of a new hangar (Building 653), ramp, seaplane parking area, forge shop (Building 654), and a new heating plant and cafeteria (Building 678). Two months later, contracts went out for more than $300,000 in improvements to Mustin Field, among which were runway extensions, new lighting, and grading and fill work.[44]

The administrative and physical changes at Philadelphia were convincing evidence of the effect of wartime mobilization on the Naval Aircraft Factory. Augmented procurement, personnel increases, and, most important, the restructuring of the NAF's organization transformed the old factory into what at the time was possibly the navy's largest single aviation complex. Still, despite all the changes of the war years, the factory continued in its traditional

Expansion of the NAF during World War II included construction of a new hangar for flying boats (Building 653). Here it is shown partially completed in early 1943. (80-G-13923, National Archives)

role as a manufacturer of limited numbers of aircraft. That function, so controversial in the past, elicited ongoing debate about how best the NAF and its successor organizations could meet the demands of naval aviation.

11

Kingfishers and Nomads

Rear Admiral John H. Towers, the chief of the Bureau of Aeronautics, found himself defending the Naval Aircraft Factory. On 9 January 1941, he was testifying before the House Naval Affairs Committee on the status of the naval defense program and was facing hard questions about the status of the NAF and its continued design and production of airplanes. Melvin Maas, a Republican from Minnesota, wanted to know if it was true that airplanes obtained from the NAF were more expensive than those acquired from private sources. Towers replied that it was difficult to get an exact cost comparison between the NAF and private contractors "because of reasons which I think you understand, of the salaries of officers and the question of overhead and charges for management, and so forth."

Maas did not find this answer convincing and pressed Towers: "I am not opposed to the Naval Aircraft Factory at Philadelphia, but I do not think it is performing its maximum functions for the Government. . . . It seems to me the Naval Aircraft Factory could perform its most useful function if it were used to translate pure research into development for actual production." The national emergency, Towers countered, left the navy no choice. The sudden need for thousands of training airplanes meant that all production facilities, civilian and government alike, had to be used to the fullest. "We had to get them quickly," Towers said of the N3N-3s and other trainers ordered in recent years. Maas had the final say on the issue. "I hope when you finish up these training planes," he told Towers, "that you will find more valuable and useful employment for the Naval Aircraft Factory than producing copied airplanes."[1]

Advocates of the continued design and production of airplanes at the Naval Aircraft Factory had traditionally stressed three reasons to justify their position: the navy had to maintain an independent cadre of experienced aeronautical engineers and designers to develop advanced aircraft and to communicate its requirements to private contractors; the navy needed to manufacture a certain number of its own aircraft to monitor costs (the yardstick) and to ensure a competitive environment for the procurement of the airplanes needed by the service; finally, it was necessary occasionally to bypass the usual contractual channels to obtain highly specialized aircraft for short-term emergency purposes. Early on, World War II brought more design and production projects to the NAF, but these victories had a Pyrrhic quality to them, for they eventually led the navy to revise its policy regarding the design and manufacture of service aircraft.

Congressman Maas had wanted the NAF to move away from the production of aircraft into what he considered more fruitful ventures, yet even as he spoke the navy was in the process of assigning another major order to the factory. When it became obvious that the N3N-3 and SBN production runs would conclude by the end of 1941, BuAer cast about for an airplane that the factory could produce in sufficient numbers to keep intact its engineering, drafting, and shop-floor work forces. Toward the end of 1940, Commander William Nelson of the NAF suggested that the factory begin manufacturing F4U Corsair fighters, but BuAer's Plans Division overruled this, recommending instead that production of between 200 and 578 Curtiss SO3C Seamew floatplanes "will keep the Naval Aircraft Factory profitably employed."[2]

Evidently the bureau rejected this proposal, deciding instead to assign to the factory an order for the production of a similar floatplane designed and built by Vought-Sikorsky—the OS2U Kingfisher. Far superior to the SO3C, the OS2U was the aircraft that had won the design competition against the NAF's XOSN-1 in 1937. Vought went on to deliver more than two hundred examples of the OS2U-1 and OS2U-2 before the end of 1941, and it had undertaken production of an improved version, the OS2U-3. But Vought's plant capacity in Stratford, Connecticut, had reached its limits, and the navy wanted to free up space so that the company could accelerate the delivery rate of F4U Corsair fighters. BuAer therefore determined to shift the manufacture of three hundred Kingfishers to the Naval Aircraft Factory.[3]

The project order authorizing production of the airplanes arrived in Philadelphia on 30 January 1941. It called for an airplane, designated OS2N-1, identical to the Vought OS2U-3, the first example of which was to be delivered in December of that year. Twenty more of the craft were to follow in January 1942, with the remainder delivered at a rate of forty per month until the completion of the $8.2 million project. Captain Marc Mitscher, the acting bureau chief, stressed that the airplanes were "urgently needed to meet the needs of the Naval service under the national defense program."[4]

To expedite the program, it was understood that the NAF would take possession of materials and parts that Vought already had on hand for Kingfisher production and that the factory would honor all of Vought's commitments to subcontractors. Vought was to provide a complete set of drawings, a list of the changes made to the airplane, and as much other assistance as possible to start production at Philadelphia. Captain Ernest Pace, who had succeeded Webster as manager of the NAF, emphasized the urgency of the program to all of the factory's department heads: "The National Emergency makes it important that every effort be made to get this work accomplished without delay." Because other projects were pending, Pace stressed, "the Factory workload makes it doubly important that no time be lost in obtaining the necessary data and materials with which to put men to work in the shops . . . at the earliest possible moment."[5]

Vought and the NAF developed a schedule for transferring production from Stratford to Philadelphia. NAF representatives met with their opposite numbers at Vought to discuss procedures for delivering aluminum directly to Philadelphia rather than routing it through Stratford. In May, a problem arose with the Briggs Manufacturing Company in Detroit. A subcontractor for OS2N-1 wing panels, Briggs found that its monthly output fell short of what the NAF needed to meet its originally planned delivery dates. Vought did its best to get Briggs to increase production, and by August the problem was on the way to resolution. The company also cut back Kingfisher production to free up materials for dispatch to Philadelphia. Nevertheless, the NAF encountered bottlenecks in receiving important parts and components, and by the end of 1941 some of its shops were jammed with partially completed aircraft and components. To keep things moving, the NAF contracted with firms in the Philadelphia area for some of the parts, but Pace admitted that many key items could be obtained only through Vought.[6]

Problems in delivery of OS2N-1 materials and components led to BuAer's intervention late in 1941. A conference at Stratford between NAF and Vought personnel ended with Vought holding that it could make "no commitments" for parts deliveries beyond those that would allow the NAF to complete ten airplanes per month. This was far below the originally planned Kingfisher production rate and created what Admiral Towers called a "very serious situation." Towers eventually secured assurances from Vought that the company would supply the NAF with parts for twenty airplanes in February, March, and April 1942. In May, the figure would rise to thirty and then go up to fifty through the end of the OS2N-1 production run.[7]

Vought upheld its part of the agreement, and the NAF was able to sustain the planned rate of production. The factory delivered its first Kingfisher (number 01216) to Anacostia for tests before the end of January 1942. With a maximum takeoff weight of 5,265 pounds in its landplane version and 5,600 pounds with floats, the OS2N-1 was actually about 400 pounds lighter than the Vought OS2U-3. Otherwise the two airplanes were identical, with wing areas of 262 square feet and spans of 35 feet, 11 inches. OS2N-1 trials went smoothly, although there were reports that the airplane had to be pushed into a dive before it could be looped. As this was not a commonplace floatplane maneuver, the deficiency did not delay acceptance of the aircraft. Quantity production was well under way by March, with twenty-one airplanes delivered that month. Production reached fifty aircraft per month in July, although it dropped to forty in September and October.[8]

During deliveries of OS2N-1s to the Naval Air Station, New York (formerly Floyd Bennett Field), ferry pilots lost some of the airplanes. Subsequent investigation determined that the pilots had picked up the wrong aircraft in Philadelphia, and when the serial

An NAF-built OS2N-1. The factory produced three hundred of these airplanes in 1942. (80-G-217057, National Archives)

numbers did not match, the New York unit reported the airplanes
missing. The mixup had comic opera overtones, with everyone
scrambling to find where the airplanes had gone, but no one in
BuAer was laughing. Captain L. A. Pope summed up the feelings
within the bureau in September 1942. He said the navy had put a
great deal of work into expediting the production of urgently needed
aircraft, "and it is expected that those activities concerned with the
delivery of those aircraft will function in such a manner as to aid and
not impede the efforts of this bureau and the over-all war effort."
Thereafter, the NAF and operating units paid more attention to ferry
pilot instructions and to aircraft serial numbers.[9]

Other problems arose in 1942. Five Kingfishers from the NAF
went to the Naval Air Station, New York, preparatory to a flight to
San Juan, Puerto Rico. During the journey, several airplanes experienced difficulties with leaking floats and electrical system failures.
Ordinarily these could have been corrected had the airplanes been
flown for a day or so at Philadelphia, but on the flight to San Juan

repair facilities were not available. In another instance, there were complaints that an OS2N-1 shipped from the NAF to a unit at Coco Solo had a chronically overheating engine, which had contributed to a fatal accident with the airplane. Subsequent investigation revealed, however, that the airplane and others had been operated at nearly seven hundred pounds over their recommended gross weight and that pilots had routinely exceeded the maximum takeoff horsepower. Finding no basic flaws in the NAF-built airplane, BuAer cautioned that operating units had to accept the responsibility for ensuring safe flight performance.[10]

Despite these problems, the OS2N-1 program ranks with the N3N-3 project as one of the most successful at the NAF. The last Kingfisher left the factory before the end of November 1942, only two months later than estimated in the original delivery schedule.[11] There was generally close liaison with the Vought company that smoothed over some of the rough spots early in the program. And, most encouraging, the OS2N-1s were good aircraft that put in yeoman service with the fleet. It bode well for the factory as BuAer began seriously to consider placing another large production order at Philadelphia.

For years, navy patrol forces had depended on long-range flying boats for scouting and antisubmarine operations. The NAF, with its PN series of flying boats, had played a vital role in the design of the navy's flying boats into the 1930s. Private firms further advanced the concept of the large, twin-engine flying boat during the decade; one of the most successful and celebrated of the type was the Consolidated PBY. Making its first flight in 1935, the PBY established itself as the navy's principal patrol aircraft, going through several models by 1940. The PBY-5, with a range of nearly two thousand miles, was ideal for patrol duties in the far reaches of the central Pacific and for protecting shipping in the Caribbean and the Atlantic during the years before Pearl Harbor. Consolidated also produced an amphibian variant, the PBY-5A, with tricycle landing gear, that further enhanced the flexibility of this magnificent airplane.[12]

Consolidated won major production contracts for PBY-5s and PBY-5As in 1939 and 1940. Under Lend-Lease, quantities of these airplanes went to the British, who assigned them the name Catalina in October 1940; a year later, the United States also adopted the name. The large orders limited Consolidated's capacity to engineer further improvements to the aircraft. Specifically, BuAer wanted to upgrade the takeoff characteristics of the PBY, extend its range, increase its payload, and augment its armament. Because of the difficulties Consolidated would have effecting such modifications without disrupting production, the bureau directed the NAF to design and manufacture an improved version of the Catalina, which was designated PBN-1 in 1940. Production of PBNs, the bureau argued, would not conflict with the NAF's current OS2N-1 order and would retain the factory's engineering and production staff intact through at least 1944.[13]

It should have been no surprise to veterans of aircraft production programs at the NAF when there were problems getting the PBN project going. In April 1941, the bureau told the factory to prepare cost estimates and a proposed delivery schedule for 156 PBN-1s. The prospect of another large production order, coming close on the heels of the OS2N-1 contract, delighted Captain Pace, but he could not guarantee accurate cost estimates until BuAer determined the extent of the modifications to the aircraft. Consequently, Pace estimated that the entire order, plus 16 percent spares, would cost $20 million and the first airplane could be delivered in July 1942, provided the design was identical to that of the PBY-5 and all data and drawings arrived from Consolidated by September.[14]

Because the primary objective of the PBN project was to carry out extensive modifications to the Catalina, Pace's estimates were a starting point only and could not be adhered to closely. Admiral Towers informed Pace that the factory would receive a $20 million project order for the airplanes as soon as supplementary appropriations came through and that the NAF could requisition material and shop equipment in anticipation of production. It was not yet clear what the changes would be when the formal project order went out from BuAer on 16 July 1941.[15]

While BuAer wrestled with the proposed changes to the PBN-1, the NAF established an administrative framework for the program and a liaison with Consolidated. John F. Horrisberger became project engineer for the PBN-1, and William J. Cox was named assistant project engineer. Both had prior experience with the SBN program. In the third week of June a representative from the NAF—probably Horrisberger—made a preliminary visit to the Consolidated factory in San Diego. A delegation from the NAF then traveled to the West Coast to familiarize themselves with the PBY and its production. Despite these personal contacts, the NAF had a great deal of trouble wresting updated drawings and specifications from Consolidated, which had not revised the data as changes had been made to the airplanes on the production line. To speed up the process, Pace asked for and received a recently completed PBY-5 so that NAF engineers and draftsmen could take dimensions and make templates of critical parts. Not until December, however, did all the necessary information arrive in Philadelphia.[16]

By that month, too, the NAF had a clearer picture of the changes BuAer wanted. There were major alterations to the fuselage. The NAF airplane had a hull 64 feet, 8 inches long, compared with the 63-foot, 10-inch hull of the PBY-5. The extra length came from a finer "clipper" bow, which also had a "clamshell"-type hatch and a power turret with a 0.50-caliber gun. The changes to the bow were to improve water handling and takeoff properties, as were the employment of a twenty-degree diagonal step located slightly farther aft, the five-foot extension of the rear planing surface or afterbody, and the addition of a small breaker step forward of the tail surfaces. There was also a complete redesign of the wing-tip floats.

Though less noticeable than the modifications to the hull, other changes to the PBN-1 involved a considerable amount of redesign. Engineers reworked and strengthened the outer portions of the 104-foot, 3-inch wing to incorporate auxiliary fuel tanks, which, when combined with two tanks in the hull, increased the total fuel capacity of the airplane from 8,850 pounds to 12,510 pounds, and brought the range of the already long-legged aircraft up from 1,965 miles to 2,590 miles. Additional modifications incorporated in the airplane were the provision of space for more advanced radar, an updated electrical system, augmented armor protection, a new Sperry autopilot, strengthened aileron surfaces, and an oil dilution system for better cold weather starting. The engines themselves were 1,200-horsepower "dash 92" versions of the Pratt and Whitney R-1830. The maximum takeoff weight of the PBN-1 was 36,353 pounds, compared to 26,200 pounds for the PBY-5, a 27 percent increase; the top speed was 9 miles per hour slower than the PBY-5's 195 miles per hour. Finally, the navy gave the name Nomad to the new flying boat, although most preferred to call it simply PBN-1.[17]

The PBN-1 design remained in a state of flux through the end of 1941, complicating the NAF's job in getting the production line going. Further muddying the waters was uncertainty at BuAer about how many flying boats should be built and what the rate of production should be. Just as the navy desperately needed trainers in 1939–40, in late 1941 it needed all the patrol planes it could get. Captain Dewitt C. Ramsey, the assistant chief of BuAer, asked Pace how many PBN-1s the NAF could produce per month without having to increase the existing facilities at Philadelphia. Pace said the factory theoretically could turn out twenty-five of the aircraft per month but that doing so would preclude all overhauls and modifications to other navy airplanes. He also said that the design changes to the PBN-1 would set back delivery of the first airplane to November 1942.[18]

Pace's response raised questions in the bureau's Plans Division about the PBN-1 program and the revised delivery schedule. One officer commented that the NAF had better "get going like the rest of the industry." Captain W. W. Webster, however, defended the NAF. He reminded Towers that the July 1942 completion date for the first airplane had been set in April and that it had been made clear at the time that the estimate was predicated on no change orders coming through for the aircraft. The November 1942 date, Webster said, "is the best which can be met." He doubted that the factory could attain a PBN-1 delivery rate of twenty-five per month without rearranging shop space, disrupting the OS2N-1 program, or eliminating the reserve capacity of the plant, which already had little left in the event the bureau decided to assign a high-priority emergency project to the NAF. Webster concluded that the bureau should expect no more than thirteen airplanes per month from the NAF.[19]

Webster's assessment of the situation made a great deal of sense. Production of twenty-five PBN-1s per month would overtax the NAF's resources; Consolidated, with a more up-to-date plant layout, had a capacity of only thirty airplanes monthly. Furthermore, hiring the nearly one thousand additional employees for the program would be difficult in the prevailing labor climate of late 1941. To meet the ambitious schedule suggested by BuAer, the NAF would have to subcontract major components from outside suppliers, many of which were already at or near capacity. The NAF did, in fact, reach an agreement with Brewster Aeronautical in June 1942 to supply 164 PBN-1 outer wing panels, despite the problems with the SBN and other difficulties the troubled firm was having with its navy contracts.[20]

Not until close to the end of the year did BuAer and the Naval Aircraft Factory work out a schedule of deliveries for the PBN-1s. On the day of the Japanese attack on Pearl Harbor, Towers approved a production rate of sixteen airplanes per month, which was more than Webster thought practicable but significantly fewer than the twenty-five previously suggested. Ten days later, on the seventeenth, the bureau issued a tentative schedule, calling for completion of the first PBN-1 in November 1942, another in December 1942, and then working up to ten airplanes in April 1943, thirteen in May, and finally sixteen in June. This rate was to be maintained through the end of 1943, with the remaining four airplanes in the 156-airplane order to be delivered in January 1944. This schedule was revised on 18 November 1942 when the NAF received an order for an additional 124 aircraft, bringing the total to 280, worth an estimated $38 million and stretching out deliveries another year.[21]

Construction of the first PBN-1 began in the spring and proceeded without major difficulties through the summer of 1942. The first airplane off the line was actually the third in the order (number 02793), but the NAF used number 02791, completed five days later, for preliminary trials at Philadelphia. These tests started in the middle of October, although some weeks passed before the airplane was fully fitted out with the power turret and other gear. Flight tests continued into November 1942, by which time some vexing problems appeared. Shifting the step to the rear caused the aircraft to plane with its bow lower in the water than that of a PBY. On takeoff, this resulted in more spray than was acceptable. The addition of temporary wooden strips to the bow of the airplane suppressed the spray, and the NAF began immediately to design antispray fairings for airplanes already in production.[22]

Of far more concern than the spray was the PBN-1's behavior in the air. Since its first test flight in 1935, the PBY had exhibited poor rudder response; Ralph Barnaby said that, despite its generally admirable handling qualities, the airplane was laterally unstable. Over the years Consolidated had made minor changes to the rudder but had not solved the problem. There was expectation in BuAer that the PBN-1 would be significantly better and finally lay to rest some of the pilots' complaints about the PBY's aerodynamics.[23]

Flight tests of the PBN-1 at Philadelphia in November revealed, however, that the airplane was not an improvement over the PBY and in fact handled worse in some ways. It suffered from lack of stability, and the control forces were heavier than anticipated. Lieutenant Commander R. W. Mackert of the NAF flight test department reported: "As compared to recent tests of PBY type airplanes it appears that the subject plane exhibits a closely comparable lack of lateral stability, slightly better directional stability, and slightly less longitudinal stability." He was disappointed, for he had envisioned the PBN-1 as "an excellent opportunity for elimination of the unsatisfactory items reported in trials of the PBY series." In BuAer, one officer commented: "The PBN-1 is off to a bad start hydrodynamically and is no better aerodynamically than the PBY-5."[24]

Captain Webster, who had taken over as manager of the NAF in December 1941, was confident in December 1942 that the problems with the PBN-1 could be overcome and that even though delivery of the next two airplanes would be delayed the targeted production schedule could be met. He told Rear Admiral John S. McCain, the new BuAer chief, that the airplane would go to Anacostia in February 1943 for acceptance trials. There was no hint that he expected problems with the aircraft once it left Philadelphia.[25]

Whatever confidence Webster had in the PBN-1 evaporated over the next few months, for aircraft number 02791 did not perform well in the acceptance tests. The airplane arrived at Anacostia in February 1943 and almost immediately went through a rigorous evaluation. The results underscored the preliminary findings about the poor aerodynamics of the big flying boat: its stability was substandard. Lieutenant R. H. Crossfield of the inspection and survey team at Anacostia phoned Captain J. Ross Allen at the NAF to give him the bad news, hinting that there was a possibility the PBN-1 contract would be canceled. At BuAer G. W. Anderson was incensed by the weak showing of the PBN-1. He wrote, "This is the straw that breaks the camel's back." The Martin PBM flying boat had not performed as well as expected, the big four-engine Consolidated PB2Y had experienced directional stability problems during tests in 1938, and now, Anderson said, "the Aircraft Factory *copy* of the

PBY. I am at a loss to understand what our material talent (?) has been doing on our boats in the past two years. With millions of dollars and our whole VPB [patrol bomber] program hanging on the ropes it is recommended that this whole subject be thoroughly investigated." BuAer decided to hold a conference in Washington to determine what to do next.[26]

A great deal was at stake on 19 March 1943 when seventeen people involved with the PBN-1 project met at the Bureau of Aeronautics. Captain Allen and Commander Barnaby headed the NAF delegation, their moods rendered even more somber by Webster's death only three days earlier. Opening the meeting with a statement that the stability of the PBN-1 was "somewhat worse" than previous versions of the PBY, Lieutenant Commander Mackert summarized the PBN-1's woes and offered two suggestions: one, which had already been tested and found effective, was a new vertical stabilizer and rudder; the other, which would be less expensive, was the addition of small vertical surfaces to the tips of the horizontal stabilizer. Following wind tunnel testing, NAF engineers found that wake turbulence from the wings disrupted the airflow around the vertical stabilizer and determined that the best course was to add height to the fin and rudder to get a critical area above the turbulence. They also thought that PBN-1s already on the assembly line could receive the new surfaces without seriously disrupting the production schedule. The conference ended with the understanding that the PBN-1 would get a vertical stabilizer nearly two feet taller than that of the PBY-5 and a balanced rudder. Everyone hoped these would end the directional stability problems once and for all.[27]

The redesign of the vertical tail surfaces solved the PBN-1's aerodynamic problems. In April, the airplane made three flights with the taller fin and the balanced rudder, and the directional stability was found to be excellent. The results of the trials led to a decision later in the month to fit the modified surfaces to all PBN-1s in production and to have the NAF manufacture surfaces for retrofit to PBN-1s that had already been completed.[28]

Though the changes solved the aerodynamic shortcomings of the airplane, they generated other problems. In an oral history interview, Vice-Admiral Herbert Riley said that the NAF had "exceeded their authority" in redesigning the PBN-1 without informing BuAer.

The new tail and rudder, Riley admitted, significantly improved the airplane, but they also resulted in a "bastard" that had little parts interchangeability with other aircraft in the PBY series. Nothing indicates that the NAF in any way exceeded its authority, and it is apparent from the 19 March meeting that BuAer was well aware of the problem and the proposed NAF solution. Furthermore, Consolidated later adopted the vertical fin and rudder design for its PBY-6A amphibian, which appeared in 1945, without, apparently, any complaints about "bastardization." The feeling remained, and Riley made it clear, that the PBN-1 was an airplane "that we couldn't use any place."[29]

Questions about workmanship and quality control also cast a shadow over the PBN-1. Complaints circulated in May 1943 that some of the PBN-1s delivered to the Atlantic Fleet had faulty riveting. Captain Allen insisted that the problem did not affect the safety of operations and stressed that the airplanes should be flown under service conditions to uncover any additional defects. The NAF dispatched a team of civilian workers to Norfolk to drill out and replace the defective rivets and to rectify any other deficiencies in the airplanes.[30]

In airplanes as in personal relationships, first impressions carry an inordinate weight, and that was the case with the PBN-1. Recognizing that the flying boat faced an uphill struggle to gain acceptance and understanding that its approval by the navy's operating forces could help to determine whether the NAF received additional production orders, the factory went out of its way to show that its product met the navy's requirements. The NAF sent a PBN-1 to Pensacola for evaluation. Captain Lloyd Harrison of the NAF reported that aviators at Pensacola "expressed informally satisfaction with the PBN in comparison with the PBY-5 *for fleet use*; in certain cases this extended to a marked preference for the PBN." Harrison also noted that the material condition of the PBN-1 was not in any way inferior to that of PBY-5s newly delivered from Consolidated. Another PBN-1 went to the navy's new flight test facility at Patuxent River, Maryland, for extended tests, which also ended favorably.[31]

NAF people also dispatched a PBN-1 to the West Coast in July 1943. Senior pilots at the Naval Air Station, Alameda, and at San Diego flew the airplane, finding that it had superior takeoff and better water-handling characteristics than the PBY-5. They also liked the extra fuel capacity and range, although they preferred having an additional 0.50-caliber gun in the bow turret and more armor protection. Unfortunately, the riveting nemesis returned to haunt the PBN-1; fifty-four hull rivets had to be replaced in San Diego during the testing session. Nevertheless the overwhelming reaction to the airplane was positive, and one test pilot said that the "situation here is very good" in regard to fleet acceptance of the PBN-1.[32]

The situation was not so good at Philadelphia, where PBN-1 production had slipped badly because of having to solve the stability problems, materials shortages, securing components from subcontractors, and the efforts expended in trying to sell the airplane as a supplement to the PBY. Production in August 1943 was four aircraft, compared to the sixteen originally called for. By September 1943, the NAF had completed only sixteen airplanes since deliveries had begun earlier in the year. Deliveries were so far behind that BuAer decided in October 1943 to cancel the additional 124 airplanes that had been ordered on 18 November 1942. Most of the subcontracts remained intact, however, and the components were diverted from the PBN program to PBY-6As constructed in a new Consolidated plant at New Orleans.[33]

Captain Samuel Zeigler, who was both manager of the NAF and commanding officer of the Naval Air Material Center in the fall of 1943, pushed to get the PBN-1 program on schedule. To do so, it was first necessary to clear up deficiencies in the assembly process. At least some of the defects in the PBN-1s were the result of inexperienced workers and inadequate supervision. Other problems were traced to errors in the drawings and specifications and to inadequate jigs and assembly fixtures. Zeigler oversaw the correction of these shortcomings, and the PBN program turned the corner in 1944. By May, deliveries were up to eleven airplanes a month, and although production slipped to only three in September, it jumped back to eleven in November and twelve in December. Unfortunately, costs went up, too—63.5 percent, according to estimates in September 1943. This overrun brought the total expenditures for the PBN program to $62.6 million.[34]

The improvement in production rates came too late for the PBN-1. By 1944, persistent problems with the aircraft and the

The Naval Aircraft Factory's biggest World War II production job was 156 PBN-1 flying boats. Similar to the PBY-5, the NAF airplane had greater range and payload capacity. Deliveries began in October 1942, with the last airplane leaving the factory in March 1945. (80-G-403281, National Archives)

repeated setbacks in the delivery schedule had thoroughly disillusioned the navy's operating forces, which in any case had virtually all the flying-boat types they needed and were in the process of switching over to such land-based aircraft as the PB4Y. Even though the PBN-1 had been formally accepted by the navy, there was no optimism in BuAer that a use could be found for it. The remaining option was to send the PBN-1s to the country's allies. After deals with the British and the Australians collapsed, the Russians requested additional flying boats to augment the license-built PBYs that they had been using since before the war. Because no PBYs were available and it was obvious that there were no other customers for the PBN-1, Commander Herbert Riley suggested that the airplanes be allocated to the Soviet Union. Following meetings with the BuAer chief, Admiral McCain, the navy agreed to send the PBN-1s to Russia.[35]

Riley worked out the details of getting the PBN-1s to the Soviet Union. The Russians insisted on air delivery by Soviet crews, which involved bringing their personnel to the United States and indoctrinating them in the operation of the PBN-1. This could not be done at the NAF. Its facilities were already stretched taut, and it was a daunting prospect to have Russians in unfamiliar airplanes taking off and landing on the congested Delaware River. Moreover, McCain did not want "a couple hundred Russians on a snooping job at the Aircraft Factory," with its confidential research and development projects. The solution was to have the PBN-1s ferried to the navy seaplane base at Elizabeth City, North Carolina, where the airplanes would be picked up.[36]

Project ZEBRA, the transfer of PBN-1s to the Soviet Union, began in May 1944. From Elizabeth City, the Russians flew 48 of the airplanes to Murmansk via Newfoundland and Iceland. A British "safety crew" accompanied the Russians as far as Reykjavik. The British picked up another 90 airplanes at Elizabeth City and flew them by a circuitous route to Baghdad, where they were accepted by the Russians, who ferried them to Baku. The Russians received 137 of the PBN-1s by March 1945 (a fire destroyed one of the airplanes before delivery). It is not clear what they did with the airplanes, although they may have been used by patrol forces in the Pacific. Some complaints were received from the Soviet Purchasing Commission in August 1944 about defects in the PBN-1s, chiefly the "mass failure" of manifold pressure gauges, minor fuel leaks, cracks in the supporting brackets for the exhaust stacks, and problems with the engine cowling flaps. The NAF recommended servicing and maintenance procedures to correct some of the problems and took measures in the assembly process to deal with the others.[37]

When the last PBN-1 (number 02946) left the NAF on 19 March 1945, the factory faced the hard reality of not having a major aircraft production order for the first time since 1935. Rear Admiral Donald Royce, who had succeeded Zeigler as NAMC commanding officer, marked the completion of the PBN-1 project with a letter to BuAer. Citing the many changes in the PBN-1 design, conflicts with higher-priority jobs at the NAF, and how thin the factory had spread its engineering expertise to cover all the activities at Philadelphia, he defended the factory's record with the flying boats. "Altogether," Royce said, "I consider the PBN program no mean accomplishment." He thought that BuAer had not fully recognized the effort put into the project and urged "a pat on the back for NAF" from the bureau.[38]

BuAer's "pat on the back" came three days later from Admiral Ramsey, the bureau chief: "I congratulate each one of you upon the successful completion of the PBN-1 program. NAF Philadelphia has always had a greater variety of work than any other aircraft manufacturer and the necessity of distributing engineering and production talent over many projects has at times created difficulties which you have always surmounted." Ramsey emphasized that "all hands" at the NAF deserved credit for seeing the PBN project through to completion and concluded with "a hearty 'Well Done!' "[39]

Such praise was well deserved, for the Naval Aircraft Factory had taken on a formidable task with the PBN-1. In the first place, the factory set out to improve on a design for a flying boat that already met most of the navy's requirements for a long-range patrol plane. Then BuAer added to the specification of the PBN-1, with changes to fuel capacity, navigation equipment, armament, and armor increasing the weight of the airplane. On top of the modifications came the difficulties obtaining drawings from Consolidated in San Diego, placing the NAF in the awkward position of trying to get the most accurate and up-to-date design data at the same time BuAer was pushing through orders that inevitably brought changes to those data. Finally, and perhaps most ironically, BuAer pressed the factory to increase production of an airplane about which operating squadrons were increasingly dubious and forced the NAF into the unenviable role of trying to convince the bureau of the worth of an aircraft the design of which had been largely dictated by BuAer itself. That the people at the NAF accomplished it at all was no mean achievement.

While applauding the Naval Aircraft Factory, both Royce and Ramsey had stressed the NAF's limitations in accomplishing long-term research and development projects along with advanced aircraft design programs. This reality, which had first manifested itself in conjunction with the XN5N-1 project, led to the decision by BuAer to end aircraft design at the NAF. Many at the NAF or close to it had thought for some years that a design capability was necessary for the retention and motivation of a corps of experienced engineers and draftsmen and for the navy to have access to their expertise. In June 1940, Captain Ernest Pace said he had "little misgiving" that the bureau could obtain all the prototype designs it needed from private industry. But he saw the factory's design section as an "ace in the hole in case there is difficulty in getting industry to undertake all the experimental and development work" needed by the navy. It was therefore incumbent on the bureau to keep at least a small design team at Philadelphia. Pace said: "Once the design section is broken up I anticipate that under present conditions it will be extremely difficult to reconstitute it, should a future need arise." To retain a "nucleus" of the NAF's staff, BuAer allocated $30,000 for the general "design, investigation and study of airplanes and aeronautical material." The bureau later assigned designs for a fighter and a scout bomber to the NAF.[40]

The question of retention of the NAF aircraft design team came up again in the summer of 1941, when the factory found itself once more without a major project. Arguing that a big aircraft design project was needed to keep the factory's design section intact, Pace told BuAer that he thought the factory needed to work on a new patrol bomber to replace the venerable PBY. He said: "To enable the Factory to favorably continue its mission of airplane development and, more specifically, to enable the engineering force to maintain its standing in the art of airplane design, the assignment of a complete airplane design and experimental manufacturing project would be apropos."[41]

This suggestion struck a resonant chord in BuAer, which called upon the NAF on 7 August to develop a design for a twin-engine patrol bomber of about forty thousand pounds with a range of at least nineteen hundred miles. To correct what was considered the "greatest defect" of the PBY and PBN, namely inadequate defensive armament, the bureau asked the factory to work into its design of the patrol aircraft three power turrets, each with twin 0.50-caliber guns. Recognizing that the bureau was asking the NAF to meet a tough requirement, Captain Dewitt C. Ramsey cautioned, "It is hoped that an attractive solution can be obtained, but it is believed that it will require much ingenuity to produce a design which will warrant the expense and time of prototype construction."[42]

Apparently there was plenty of ingenuity in Philadelphia, for by the beginning of 1942 the NAF had submitted four alternative designs. One of these incorporated X-configuration engines buried in the wings and driving the propellers through drive shafts and gear sets. Another featured a single X-type engine in the fuselage driving contrarotating propellers; the wings of this airplane would also function as floats when the craft was on the water. The remaining two designs, for airplanes in the twenty-seven- to thirty-eight-thousand-pound range, were less imaginative.[43]

The unconventional nature of some of these ideas tended to reinforce thinking in the bureau that the NAF was a "dream factory" and that it was incapable of devising a truly competitive patrol plane design. The PBN-1 experience did little to dispel that prejudicial attitude. But the truth was that the NAF's mission was not to develop designs in competition with those of private industry. All too often people forgot that NAF designs were to augment those of private contractors, the factory's staff probing unusual design concepts and giving BuAer an in-house design capability. That did not mean, however, that BuAer could sidestep decisions about the Naval Aircraft Factory's traditional roles of airplane design and production. Even though he had upheld the production function of the NAF before Congress in January 1941, Admiral Towers realized shortly after Pearl Harbor that the factory would be hard-pressed to meet the demands imposed by war. Towers said, "There is reason to believe that we will be confronted with an increasing amount of high priority experimental work. . . . The total capacity of the Naval Aircraft Factory to build production aircraft is small compared to that of the industry, whereas the capacity for miscellaneous experimental work is high." He reasoned: "It is consequently considered that efforts should be directed towards stabilizing the production work load of the Naval Aircraft Factory rather than towards increasing the load, so as to minimize possible conflicts between experimental and production priorities."[44]

Captain W. W. Webster brought matters to a head in February 1942. Like Nelson and Pace, he wanted BuAer to assign a major airplane design project to the NAF to keep the factory's engineering and drafting staff intact. Webster precipitated a detailed examination of the Naval Aircraft Factory and its functions with the view toward determining whether the installation should continue to design and produce airplanes. BuAer was divided into two camps. Sydney Kraus advocated giving the NAF a patrol plane design project. The factory's engineering people were highly competent, he argued, and such a job complemented the work they were doing on the PBN-1. But his was a minority opinion; the majority was considerably less sanguine about the wisdom of preserving the NAF's design capability.[45]

Commander Leslie C. Stevens and Captain J. E. Ostrander, Jr., provided the most cogent arguments for the opposition. Admitting that he "would like very much to see an experimental design put with the NAF," Stevens scrutinized the NAF's options and dismissed a high-altitude fighter, an advanced torpedo bomber, or an observation airplane as possible design studies to place at the factory. As for a patrol bomber, which others had emphasized as the most logical choice, Stevens said simply that it "was not attractive." "The alternative," Stevens said, "is to tell NAF to wait until we have a job for them. . . . Meanwhile, we are getting more exper. work out of NAF (other than prototypes) than ever before. There is plenty for them to do." Ostrander's comments were similar. In his opinion, the NAF had more than enough work to preserve its engineering staff, and he could "see no necessity for 'made work.' "[46]

Towers sided with Stevens and Ostrander: "Tell N.A.F. 'no original design project for some time.'" The factory officially learned of the decision on 7 May 1942, when Towers wrote to Webster that BuAer had made "a careful survey to determine if a complete airplane design project can be advantageously allocated to the Naval Aircraft Factory at this time. . . . The bureau regrets to inform you that its present program for such prototype aircraft as appear suitable for the factory is believed to be adequately in hand." Towers did provide some consolation: "It is believed . . . that the urgency and importance of special projects which only the factory can best accomplish will continue to increase."[47]

This was a bitter pill to swallow for the NAF, which since the beginning had been almost continually involved in aircraft design and development programs. Some at Philadelphia were not willing to accept Towers's decision as final. In January 1943, Webster made another plea to BuAer, asking whether the bureau might consider assigning to the NAF a small-scale or specialized project that was not likely to attract private industry. In a later appeal to the bureau, Webster pointed out that there were inconsistencies in the bureau's policy. He cited Towers's 1941 letter concerning the importance of experimental work at the NAF and the need to cut back on production, contrasting this with directives in 1942 to expedite PBN-1 production as much as possible and the high priority given to the manufacture of spare parts and components for other aircraft: "You can readily see from the foregoing that there is some conflict of policy relative to the Factory's primary mission, or at any rate the policy is subject to frequent reversals without clear enunciation as to what is expected of us." There was some sympathy for Webster's position. In February BuAer set priorities for special projects at the NAF but did not alter the 7 May 1942 decision.[48]

As commanding officer of the NAMC, Samuel Zeigler took perhaps a broader and more realistic view of the situation than did Webster, who may have been too close to the factory and its people to be truly objective. A planning document from J. H. Stevenson in November 1943 summarized Zeigler's suggested policy: "to utilize the sources of NAF primarily on the urgent special projects authorized by the Bureau, and to use as a fill-in job, any quantity manufacture that may be successfully accomplished without interference, in any way, with the higher priority work."[49]

Zeigler's so-called fill-in jobs helped use the manufacturing personnel brought together at Philadelphia for the PBN-1 program. One project was the reconditioning of service aircraft. Earlier in the war, BuAer had assigned to the factory the overhaul and modification of fifty PBY-5s; further PBY-5 reconditioning jobs came in the fall of 1944, until the NAF was overhauling ten airplanes per month. Another was an order for the assembly of one hundred PBY wing center sections that the factory received from Consolidated's New Orleans plant in late 1944.[50] These programs kept the NAF's assembly shop people busy through the end of the war, but they were a far cry from the complete airplane design and manufacturing work that everyone had been accustomed to before Pearl Harbor.

Planning for the postwar era took into account the decisions reached in 1942 regarding the mission of the Naval Aircraft Factory. In November 1944, Captain Charles M. Huntington, manager of the NAF, called upon BuAer to consider some $3 million in expenditures to modernize the factory's equipment and physical plant to meet the navy's expected requirements after the end of the war. Huntington's request raised the issue, as Lieutenant Commander George H. Chapman of the bureau's air stations branch suggested in

January 1945, of "the wisdom of spending large sums of money on a facility which, by modern standards, is judged obsolescent." To Chapman the question encompassed "whether the NAF can be made an up-to-date factory capable of great flexibility for all types of overhaul and production tasks and suitable for the possible needs of the Navy, for many years to come, or whether this is the proper time to start all over again at some new location, possibly taking advantage of surplus plant facilities which may become available."[51]

Chapman thus called into question not just the NAF's role in the design and production of aircraft but the factory's very existence. He went on say that BuAer should consider the "saturation" of buildings at the Naval Air Material Center, the inadequacy of Mustin Field to handle larger aircraft, and the general lack of space at League Island for experimental activities. Rather than expending any great sums on upgrading existing facilities, which might not meet anticipated requirements, Chapman urged the bureau to investigate an entirely new installation somewhere in the Philadelphia area, which might cost no more than $6 or $7 million.[52]

Not everyone agreed with Chapman's assessment of the future of the NAF-NAMC. One who most assuredly did not was Rear Admiral Donald Royce, commanding officer of the NAMC. He wrote to the chief of BuAer urging that another aircraft production order be placed at Philadelphia, striking a familiar refrain: "To avoid the deterioration and possible loss of the skill and efficiency of the design and manufacturing organization, it is recommended that BuAer give early consideration to the subject of additional complete aircraft manufacture at NAF." Royce also saw real advantages in the production of aircraft at the NAF in the postwar years. These included the development of more precise plans and specifications for contractual purposes, carrying out changes to aircraft without incurring additional costs from private manufacturers, having a facility to do some of the less desirable production work that would not ordinarily interest private companies in peacetime, retaining the yardstick as a check on costs, and being able to use navy engineering people to conduct highly specialized development projects. "I recommend," he concluded, "that BuAer plan to continue aircraft production at NAF for the reasons outlined. . . . To this end, a small production program of 10 medium sized airplanes per month should be assigned in order that the ability to design and build aircraft at

NAF will not be lost or deteriorate to such a point that considerable cost, delay, confusion and disappointment will attend any attempt to revive it." Royce was certain that such a project would "not interfere with the testing and experimental programs" at the NAF but would "serve to supplement and strengthen them."[53]

Royce's plea strongly underscored the emerging dichotomy over the future of the NAF and the place of aircraft design and construction in the factory's mission. It was obvious from Towers's 1942 statement and subsequent events that BuAer's consensus did not favor the design of complete aircraft and major production runs of service airplanes at the NAMC or the NAF—at least until the war was over. It was also apparent by 1945 that many thought the navy should turn to the NAF henceforth only for the manufacture of components and that its workers would no longer enjoy whatever existential pleasure there was in the design and assembly of complete airplanes. Aeronautical engineers had to recognize that Philadelphia was no longer the place to learn their trade or gain a "postgraduate" education in aircraft design. And Chapman's appraisal presented the threat of dissolution of the factory altogether once the war work was finished. Royce, however, represented an old and dedicated camp within the naval establishment that wanted the Philadelphia aviation complex to continue in its traditional roles. In any case, the NAMC and the aircraft factory stood at a crossroads in 1945, with some paths made impassable by circumstances and policies and others rendered more difficult by the technological demands of war.

It is interesting to compare the situation in 1945 with that of 1921–22, when Admiral Moffett determined that the NAF would restrict its design function and not engage in the series production of aircraft. Then the concern had been primarily political and how to reconcile the needs of a depressed aircraft industry with the institutional and procurement demands of the navy. Moffett understood that the airplane remained a largely unknown quantity in the early 1920s and was unwilling to leave its development entirely outside the immediate purview of the service. By World War II, the situation was much different. Then the airplane was a substantially mature technology, and the deciding factors were not so much political and technological as they were estimates of the material and administrative capacity of the factory to carry out the plethora of high-priority experimental programs dictated by war. The eclipse of these elements of the factory's conventional mission could be mourned, but few at Philadelphia had time to do so, for there were too many other things to do that seemed just as important to winning the war. One of these was research and development into guided weapons, which promised during World War II to revolutionize the nature of modern warfare.

12

Assault Drones,
Glombs, and Guided Missiles

Pearl Harbor was only weeks away when Admiral Harold R. Stark, the chief of naval operations, wrote to Rear Admiral Towers about the importance of the NAF's assault drone project and its potential for combat use. Stark's 28 October 1941 missive was the navy's charter for the development of a series of guided weapons. Most of these originated in Commander Delmar S. Fahrney's Project FOX group, which had been organized in 1938 to explore television guidance systems for aerial torpedoes. If the work seemed to go off in many directions at once, the lack of a clear focus was largely owing to the radically new concepts and technology involved with guided weapons and the changing nature of the war itself. And if the various projects encountered what appeared to be shortsighted opposition from within the Bureau of Aeronautics, it was because of the problems associated with coordinating the development and procurement effort and defining the tactical roles for such unconventional weapons. The picture was not complete by the end of the war, but its dimensions were sufficiently well known to lay the groundwork for integrating the new technology into the navy during the 1950s and 1960s. As was the case with other advanced research and development projects, the Naval Aircraft Factory and its successors played an important part in transforming often vague ideas into reality.

The requirements for the assault drone were challenging, to say the least. In November 1941, BuAer issued general specifications for the missile. After a two-and-a-half-hour overwater flight, the weapon had to be able to take evasive action using television guidance before releasing a one-ton Mark XIII torpedo within five hundred to seven hundred yards of the target. A one-hundred-pound charge would detonate when the air vehicle struck the target, which could be either stationary or moving. The bureau called upon the NAF to design a minimal-cost, expendable airplane powered by two three-hundred-horsepower engines. The aircraft would have to withstand the forces of catapult launches and would use jettisonable landing gear. BuAer further suggested that the NAF consider using molded plywood or other plastic materials in the construction of the aircraft and that its design provide for a maximum of subcontracting. Finally, the bureau advised: "This project is considered of great potential importance, and both its early completion and its extremely confidential nature should be given special consideration."[1]

Captain W. W. Webster, manager of the Naval Aircraft Factory and a firm supporter of Fahrney's pilotless aircraft projects, lost little time putting together a design package. Working closely with Fahrney's team, NAF engineers drew up a proposal and presented it to BuAer in January 1942. At a cost of $354,000, the factory would supply complete drawings and design data, one airplane for static tests, and four prototypes to be used for flight tests. The twin-engine monoplane would be fabricated from molded plywood. Tests with a television-equipped TG-2 drone would be continued to refine the assault drone guidance system. Because of the need to move quickly with the project before the factory got heavily involved with the PBN program, flight tests were to begin in early July.[2]

Following a review of the NAF proposal, BuAer informed the factory on 14 February 1942 that it should "proceed at once" with the design and manufacture of the prototype aircraft, to which the bureau assigned the designation XTDN-1. The bureau made minor changes to the factory's specification, including the substitution of 220-horsepower Lycoming O-435 engines for the Franklins originally called for. This was because of the "quicker availability" of the Lycoming, and the change would not require major design alterations.[3]

Events moved even more swiftly the following month, when the Office of the CNO pressed for the speedy development, production, and employment of the assault drone. On 11 March, only one day before he handed over the job of chief of naval operations to Ernest J. King, Admiral Stark said, "It is desired to proceed immediately with the steps necessary to adapt the 'drone' for warfare." On 23 March authorization came from the bureau for the procurement by 1 November of one hundred of the aircraft, which were by now designated TDN-1s. The bureau encouraged the factory to subcontract portions of the production order, but to preserve the confidentiality of the program, final assembly and testing would be done in Philadelphia. The assignment of A-1-a priority to the $1 million production order indicated the significance accorded the assault drone program.[4]

A major reason for Washington's eagerness to move ahead with the assault drone project was the presence in the Office of the CNO of Captain Oscar Smith. Shortly after Pearl Harbor, Smith, who commanded the Atlantic Fleet Base at Norfolk, described the assault drone as a "suicide pilot who will not falter." In early February, he wrote to Admiral Stark about the potential of aerial torpedoes and asked to head such a project. Within a week, Smith became director of the Plans Division in the Office of CNO and began a survey of existing radio-control projects, concentrating on BuAer's DOG and FOX efforts.[5]

Neither BuAer nor those who had been with the pilotless aircraft projects from the beginning welcomed such interest from so high up in the naval establishment. Primarily, they feared the injection of another layer of responsibility. But they also worried that pressure from the CNO would place an additional burden on the productive capacity of the Naval Aircraft Factory, disrupting the assault drone program at a crucial juncture in its early development and raising unrealistic expectations about the production timetable and the weapon's performance in combat.

People at the Naval Aircraft Factory seemed to have a clearer understanding than Captain Smith of the complexity of the assault drone project and the obstacles standing in the path of its orderly development. In January 1942, Lieutenant Molt Taylor summarized some of the problems. The drones first had to be maneuvered into proximity to the target and then directed to impact using a television camera with an extremely limited field of vision. Azimuth and range had to be accurately calculated to assure a hit. Captain

Webster also knew of the pitfalls that lay ahead. Presently, television had an optimal visual range of four miles, and signals could be received at up to thirty miles, but work would have to be "prosecuted intensely" to attain a higher level of performance. Webster also saw the need to develop an effective radio altimeter, improved and more compact radio-control equipment, and possibly a lightweight radar system for terminal guidance under less than ideal visual conditions.[6]

The Project FOX assault drone test program that had begun in the summer of 1941 reinforced prevailing attitudes at Philadelphia about the complexity of the undertaking. On 4 March 1942, using one of the television-equipped TG-2s acquired in September 1941, Fahrney's group at the NAF carried out simulated torpedo attacks, low-altitude bomb runs, and mock collisions with targets. The exercise also included radio-control takeoffs and landings, approach runs to targets on the Delaware, and evasive maneuvers. The results, however, were inconclusive. Only 32 percent of the torpedo runs and 12 percent of the low-altitude bombing attacks were successful, although 80 percent of the collision attacks were driven home. The television guidance system functioned well, with optical ranges up to six miles.[7]

Did these results justify making a major commitment to the production and employment of the new weapon? Some in BuAer thought not. Captain J. E. Ostrander, Jr., considered the assault drone impractical as an operational weapon and viewed the existing television guidance system as an interim step toward the development of a fully radar-directed drone. Leslie C. Stevens, now a captain and assistant director of the bureau's Engineering Division, amplified Ostrander's misgivings: "I am not sold on this being a weapon of operational value until its major limitations can be removed by the application of radar. . . . These drones would be cold meat for enemy aircraft & in the absence of aircraft I believe that the normal weapons now in use would be as effective due to the greater ease of their mobilization & employment."[8]

Additional tests, however, belied such pessimism and pointed to the viability of the assault drone as a weapon. At Quonset Point, Rhode Island, in April 1942, the Project FOX crew conducted ten torpedo drops using a TG-2 fitted out with a radio altimeter and television guidance. On some runs, the Mark XIII torpedo failed to

function satisfactorily—not surprising considering the problems the
navy had in 1942 getting its torpedoes to work at all. During other
tests the drone did not perform the necessary evasive maneuvers.
Overshadowing these deficiencies, however, were spectacular results on 9 April. Flying nolo—without a safety pilot—the TG-2
attacked the destroyer *Aaron Ward* while the ship was cruising at
fifteen knots. From the control airplane eight miles distant, Lieutenant Taylor picked up the target on television at an optical range
of four miles, directed the drone to within three hundred yards of the
ship, and released the torpedo, which passed directly beneath the
vessel. "This was . . . historic," Fahrney later wrote, being "the first
surface-to-surface guided missile attack ever conducted." From a
field at Lively, Virginia, on 19 April 1942 Lieutenant Taylor directed
a television-equipped Great Lakes BG-1 drone to an impact with a
target raft towed at eight knots in Chesapeake Bay. The television
equipment obtained a visual image of the target at a distance of five
miles, allowing Taylor, in a Beechcraft JRB control airplane, to steer
the drone to a collision with the raft.[9]

The success of these tests led to the establishment on 22 May
1942 of Project OPTION. With Captain Smith as officer in charge,
OPTION was responsible for the development of a service weapon
and the preparation of plans for its employment in combat within
the shortest possible period of time. Fahrney's Project FOX group
remained in charge of guided weapon research and development, and
BuAer retained authority over the missiles' design and production. It
was a curious and contentious division of responsibility that,
although it reflected the prevailing balance of interests in Washington, did nothing to expedite current guided weapons programs.[10]

In the meantime, the TDN-1 program gathered momentum at the
Naval Aircraft Factory. Early in May, Webster provided revised cost
estimates and a suggested production schedule for the initial batch
of one hundred airplanes. The completion date of 1 November,
Webster said, "while very difficult of accomplishment, is believed
possible by resorting to every conceivable means at the Factory's
disposal and considering cost to be of minor importance." One
hundred TDN-1s plus 10 percent spares would cost $2,750,000, and
444 radio-control units would cost $1,320,000 more. But, Webster
warned, this schedule "will set back the PBN-1 [flying boat] program
by approximately two months." Deliveries were to begin in August

with six examples and then work up to an output of ten weekly through the end of October. Most of the large molded plywood assemblies would be subcontracted, with final assembly and testing in Philadelphia. Largely because of his experience with wooden aircraft structures, John S. Kean became the TDN-1 project engineer.[11]

The NAF's TDN-1 cost estimates and the prospect of further delays in the PBN-1 program prompted Towers to ask Webster for clarification. "It was understood when the XTDN program was set up," Towers wrote, "that no interference with construction of combatant aircraft would be imposed. The order of 100 TDN-1 airplanes must not impose any delays on the PBN-1 program, therefore, it is requested that the drone production set-up be reexamined and interference eliminated." In addition, Towers insisted that the factory make every effort to reduce the unit costs of TDN-1s. Put on the defensive, Webster replied that the size of the TDN-1 project, the need for research and development, and the strict deadline for completion of the aircraft meant that "some interference with a program as large and all inclusive as the PBN-1 project, appeared unavoidable." Yet Webster was certain that whatever delays did occur in the PBN-1 program would not extend beyond the first "two or three" flying boats. Webster thought TDN-1 unit costs could eventually be pared to $21,000 per airplane.[12]

Not only cost but the scale of the assault drone production program elicited debate. On 3 April 1942, the CNO authorized an additional one hundred missiles. Recognizing that heavy burdens on regular aircraft manufacturers precluded their large-scale production of drones, the navy awarded the new contract to the Interstate Aircraft and Engineering Company, with plants at El Segundo, California, and DeKalb, Illinois. The Interstate aircraft, designated TDR-1, was virtually identical to the NAF's TDN. From two hundred airplanes, the program went up to one thousand on 22 May with the creation of Project OPTION. The logic behind the rapid increase in production was that it would be a mistake to introduce the new weapon into combat piecemeal, thereby giving the enemy time to devise effective countermeasures. When officers in BuAer suggested that this level of production would be difficult to sustain, Admiral Frederick J. Horne, the vice-chief of naval operations and a strong supporter of the guided missile concept, said that the "need for this weapon is so urgent" that every effort should be made to meet the production goals. Towers was incensed by the "damn the torpedoes" approach to the assault drone program and the Office of the CNO's pronouncement of a fivefold increase in production. He estimated that the anticipated program would require ten thousand people, including thirteen hundred naval aviators, and would cost $235 million, seriously straining existing resources.[13]

In early June, Fahrney, Pace, Jones, and others met to discuss the production program in light of Towers's reservations. They agreed that Interstate could manufacture thirty airframes per month in its present plants and that it could increase output to three hundred to five hundred per month with extensive subcontracting. RCA was expanding its production facilities to supply television equipment for the assault drones. The first television apparatus to be supplied in large quantities was in the one-hundred-megacycle frequency range and was code-named BLOCK I; following this was higher-frequency equipment known as BLOCK III. Despite this encouraging progress, the conferees concluded that at this early date—before either the NAF or Interstate had delivered prototypes—it was impossible to make reasonable estimates of productive capacity. Towers subsequently recommended, and the Office of the Chief of Naval Operations agreed in August, to cutting back the program to an initial production order of five hundred.[14]

In Philadelphia, meanwhile, much of the effort concentrated on completing the first XTDN-1. In March, Fahrney delivered a model of the XTDN-1 to the Washington Navy Yard for wind tunnel tests. These helped to confirm the basic soundness of the design, which was highly conservative because of the problems of making precise calculations of aerodynamic stresses on wooden structures. To reduce costs as much as possible, the NAF had at first proposed using engines that rotated in the same direction. But when subsequent investigations revealed that this could lead to directional control problems, the factory added counterrotating engines to the TDN-1 specification. On 1 June, a mockup board with Fahrney and fourteen others convened in Philadelphia to inspect the general layout of the aircraft and the placement of instruments and guidance equipment. The board reported a month later that the mockup was generally satisfactory but recommended relocation of the gyrostabilizers and inspection hatches and minor changes to the cockpit for the safety pilot. Also on the board's list for alterations were improvements to the jettisonable landing gear and provisions for moving the airplane around and storing it on shipboard. There was no provision for folding wings in the TDN-1 specification; these were thought an unnecessary complication and expense.[15]

For a time, there were difficulties defining engine and propeller requirements for the XTDN-1. BuAer had at first thought Lycoming O-435s would be best, assuming that they would be ready before the Franklins, but Lycoming was unable to supply engines until November. The NAF then was forced to revert to noncounterrotating Franklin X0-300 power plants for the first aircraft and to consider the use of Lycoming R-680 radials in later versions. For the TDN-1s' fixed-pitch wooden propellers the NAF turned to Sensenich Brothers in Lititz, Pennsylvania. NAF engineers wanted to test the propellers on the first XTDN-1 before letting a production order to Sensenich, but Webster thought this would set back delivery dates and said that the factory would have to "take the chances involved" in starting production before all tests were completed.[16]

The first XTDN-1 (number 27873) made three test flights at Philadelphia on 15 November 1942. A high-wing monoplane, the XTDN-1 had a wing span of forty-eight feet and was thirty-seven feet long. It had a maximum takeoff weight of 7,000 pounds, including a 1,000-pound dummy torpedo and a 100-pound general-purpose bomb in the cockpit area. The top speed was 145 miles per hour. Later production versions carried 2,000-pound torpedoes. A comparison of the NAF missile and the better-known German Fieseler Fi.103 (or V-1) is both interesting and informative. The German weapon had a maximum takeoff weight of 4,806 pounds, including a warhead weighing 1,870 pounds, and, powered by a pulsejet engine, had a top speed in excess of 400 miles per hour. With a compass mechanism, preset before launch, the Fi.103 could attack only large-area targets about 150 miles distant, whereas the assault drone had a far more sophisticated guidance system and was intended to destroy ships at ranges of up to 600 miles. Fahrney (by now promoted to captain) said that the first XTDN-1 tests went well: "Ground handling is excellent and limited air work indicates that the plane will perform according to plan." Captain Oscar Smith was also pleased with the results of the tests, which indicated to him that the XTDN-1 "will be satisfactory for its purpose."[17]

BuAer's Board of Inspection and Survey received the first XTDN-1 in December, tested it until March 1943, and reported on the results of its evaluation of the aircraft at the end of the month. Flown at Mustin Field and at Philadelphia Municipal Airport, the aircraft was found "to be in all respects satisfactory." In the last test, at Patuxent River, Maryland, the hundred-pound bomb in the missile was detonated, destroying the drone in flight. This aircraft, however, was not equipped with complete radio-control and television guidance systems. The second airplane (number 27874), tested by Fahrney's group early in 1943, had all the necessary control and guidance equipment, as did the remaining two prototypes.[18]

Even though the original 1 November 1942 completion date for the TDN-1s came and went, the Naval Aircraft Factory did well in meeting less ambitious production goals. Captain Lloyd Harrison, Webster's assistant, handled most of the detail work in connection with the program. By taking extraordinary measures, including manufacturing many parts in-house and using up virtually all the materials available in Philadelphia, the factory completed the first twelve TDN-1s before the end of 1942. Later aircraft involved considerable subcontracting, with the Singer Manufacturing Company in South Bend, Indiana, and the Brunswick-Balke-Collender Company in Muskegon, Michigan, providing mechanical and structural components. When TDN-1 deliveries resumed in the middle of March, they averaged between four and five aircraft daily through May. Brunswick-Balke-Collender, however, assembled the last thirty TDN-1s, the first of which arrived at the NAF early in August for final inspection and flight testing.[19]

The Naval Aircraft Factory continued its involvement in the assault drone program in 1943. NAF representatives helped Interstate with the design and development of the TDR-1, particularly with the installation and testing of the guidance equipment. The factory also tested the XTDR-1, the first Interstate drone. Most TDN-1s went to Utility Squadron 6, a training unit based at Cape May, New Jersey, close enough for NAF people to stay on top of the evaluation process and to deal directly with problems as they arose. One of these was with the jettisonable tricycle landing gear. Designed and constructed to break cleanly away from the aircraft, the

The TDN-1 was the prototype assault drone developed by the Naval Aircraft Factory. One hundred were manufactured in 1942–43. The photo shows the airplane with a safety pilot aboard. (J. Hartley Bowen, Jr.)

gear could not hang up on the fuselage, wings, or control surfaces. At the same time, the equipment had to be robust enough to handle the anticipated bomb and torpedo loads and the acceleration forces of catapult launches from aircraft carriers. The inadequacy of ordinary release mechanisms such as those used for torpedoes and bombs led the factory in June 1943 to undertake the development and production of a hydraulically actuated release device.[20]

Assault drones saw only limited use in combat in the western Pacific in 1944. The navy established two operational assault drone units, known as Special Tactical Air Groups, or STAG. STAG-1 launched TDR-1s against Japanese targets at Bougainville and Rabaul in September and October, expending forty-eight assault drones, of which thirty-seven reached the vicinity of their targets and twenty-four actually struck them. For all the effort that went into the assault drone program, this was a meager payoff that, when coupled with Interstate's production problems, caused most high-ranking officers to dismiss the assault drone effort as a failure.[21]

Not everyone concurred with this assessment of the assault drone project, pointing to mitigating factors in its development and operational use that had contributed to the disappointing results in the Pacific theater. Well before this, though, the guided weapons program had moved on to what everyone hoped was more fertile ground. One of the fields tilled by Fahrney's group was the application of radio-control and other guidance systems to gliders. Experiments with glide bombs dated back to World War I. Starting in 1916, the Germans developed a biplane glider that was released from an airship and directed to its target using a wire guidance system. In August 1918, the airship *L-35* successfully directed such a missile to a target nearly five miles distant. One of Germany's principal aeronautical research laboratories had experimented by 1940 with radio-controlled free-fall bombs. This work eventually led to the Fritz-X, a controlled-trajectory bomb that was successfully used against British and Italian warships in 1943. It does not appear, however, that the German research directly inspired the Americans, who were initially attracted not by the potential accuracy of the weapon but by the glider's capacity to carry large combat payloads.[22]

Fahrney conceived of the idea of a radio-control combat glider in December 1940, following this brainstorm with a more detailed proposal in which he argued that a small fighter could tow a pilotless glider with a bomb load equal to or greater than that of a large, multiengine airplane. Once near the target, the fighter could release the glider and direct it by radio control and television to impact, while staying out of range of antiaircraft fire or fighter defenses. As a bonus, the glider could be used as a tanker aircraft. Fahrney's concept took more definite form in BuAer's Plans Division, which in March 1941 concluded that "such a bomb would provide a powerful offensive weapon that could be readily used by either carrier or shore-based airplanes."[23]

It was natural that the development of the glider as a weapon would become the responsibility of the Naval Aircraft Factory. On 19 April 1941, the bureau issued a small project order to the NAF to begin work. The effort was to proceed in stages, starting with a small, two-seat glider and progressive experiments with radio-control equipment, stabilizing devices, towing techniques, and television guidance. After successful tests, the project would advance to the construction of a fifteen-thousand-pound glider that could deliver a large load of explosives against particularly "hard" targets. Possibly the most experienced glider man in the navy, Commander Ralph S. Barnaby, who at the time was the assistant chief engineer at the NAF, took major responsibility for the project. From his typically fertile mind sprang an appropriate name for the weapon—"Glomb," a contraction of "Glider bomb."[24]

The glider program, code-named Project GEORGE and including Glomb development, encountered difficult technical obstacles not long after it got under way at the NAF. Upon receipt of the project order, the factory acquired two Schweizer LNS-1 sailplanes to begin tests of radio-control equipment. Because the Schweizers, designed for sport soaring, did not have the performance characteristics desired of the Glomb, the NAF augmented these experiments in June with a Taylorcraft lightplane converted to a glider. Designated XLNT-1, this aircraft demonstrated that a radio-control glider could be successfully guided to its target, but it soon became apparent that a great deal of work lay ahead before the Glomb could be considered a viable weapon. A major obstacle was devising an effective means of towing the pilotless gliders. Experiments with a Great Lakes BG-1 assault drone towed by a Douglas TBD-1 Devastator torpedo bomber in the spring and summer of 1942 revealed control deficiencies in the glider. Nearly a year slipped by while the Glomb team worked to perfect "autotow," a device that transmitted the vertical and horizontal deviations of the glider tow line to instruments connected to the glider's autopilot. Part of the delay was also caused by the need to concentrate most of the factory's resources on the TDN-1 program in 1942–43.[25]

The Glomb program finally began to show results in 1943. Early in the year, BuAer assigned Lieutenant Taylor to work full time on glider projects at the NAF. On 4 April, the factory successfully tested autotow with an LNT-1 minus safety pilot and followed this later in the month with flights of an autotow-equipped Waco LRW-1 glider. Next came evaluations of a variety of gliders to determine their suitability for conversion to Glombs. The aircraft tested included big British-built Hotspurs and Horsas, American Wacos, and small Taylorcraft, Piper, and Aeronca lightplanes converted to gliders.[26]

The little Taylorcraft won. Manufactured in Alliance, Ohio, for the army, the TG-6 was a high-wing, three-seat monoplane with the performance characteristics necessary for training personnel in

Glomb operations and testing radio-control and television guidance systems. In September 1942, the NAF had acquired three Taylorcrafts for conversion to XLNT-1s. Once the decision was made to use the TG-6 for Glomb development, the factory received thirty-one more Taylorcrafts in 1943 for modification as LNT-1s and LNT-2s. Two XLNT-1s went to Patuxent River, Maryland, in September 1943 for tests against surface targets. Although neither test was a complete success, the navy saw enough potential in the Glomb project to award a production order to Taylorcraft late in the year.[27]

Beginning in April 1944, the Naval Aircraft Factory carried out acceptance tests of the first production Glombs, which were designated LBT-1 and were similar in appearance and performance to the LNTs. Fortunately, the logbooks of Al Barber, a test pilot for Taylorcraft, have been preserved and portions of them have been published. They are revealing about the unusual characteristics of the Glombs and some of the routine hazards of testing them. The LBT-1 typically had a maximum takeoff weight of five thousand pounds, could be towed at more than 240 miles per hour, had a sink rate of twenty-two-hundred feet per minute, and landed at about 120 miles per hour. An F4F Wildcat fighter usually served as both the towplane and the control plane for the Glomb tests, although Lockheed PV-1 Venturas were also used. With Barber as the safety pilot, the LBT-1 went through a rigorous evaluation, including top-speed tow tests, dives at up to 260 miles per hour, and five-G pullouts. On a flight from Mustin Field in May 1944, Barber reported the following incident: "Take-off was started on Runway 14 being towed by a Wildcat, tow plane was noticed to lead to the left due to a direct cross wind from the right. Tow plane got into the air but not enough to clear a cart of radio equipment by side of runway. After tow plane hit cart, visibility was zero from cloud of dust and dirt. Glomb was cut and pulled up over dust and dirt cloud . . . full spoilers were then applied and a series of yawing maneuvers were used to slow the plane for landing. A full stall landing was made." Barber added, "This type of landing not recommended."[28]

Fahrney had originally thought of the Glomb as an aircraft that could deliver a large explosive payload against heavily protected and defended targets. This concept coincided in 1941 with the navy's plans for large gliders to carry marines into combat or to deliver spare engines to flying boats at advanced bases. In pursuance of that mission, the Naval Aircraft Factory submitted a design in July 1941 for a large, wooden, twin-hull amphibian glider capable of carrying twenty-four fully equipped troops, artillery, or other cargo. The factory followed this with four different designs for a smaller glider that could carry twelve troops or an equivalent combat load. Of the four designs, the one that appeared to offer the most promise was an amphibian with a low wing that provided stability in the water and eliminated the need for floats. The navy let contracts to the AGA Aviation Corporation of Willow Grove, Pennsylvania, to construct the twenty-four-place glider and to the Allied Aviation Corporation and the Bristol Aeronautical Corporation to build versions of the float-wing glider. Subsequently the navy canceled the AGA order, but Allied delivered two XLRA-1s and Bristol completed a pair of XLRQ-1s.[29]

The navy's interest in large combat gliders continued into 1942, and the NAF remained involved in the design and development of these aircraft. On 29 June 1942, the chief of naval operations ordered the factory to construct a large glider following one of two designs suggested by BuAer: the first for a high-wing monoplane capable of carrying six tons of fuel to a forward battle position or delivering ten thousand pounds of explosives against a land or naval target; and the second for a similar craft with a capacity of nine tons of fuel or an identical weight of explosives. The NAF opted for the larger of the two designs. Accordingly, the bureau issued a project order for the construction of three gliders, designated XLRN-1, the first of which would be used for static tests and the other two for flight tests.[30]

As work on the XLRN-1 slowly progressed into 1943, the navy's requirements for the aircraft changed dramatically. The NAF's mockup of the glider, including space for the installation of radio-control and television guidance systems, was ready by 1 October 1943. A team of inspectors headed by Lieutenant Commander Grayson Merrill completed its evaluation and issued a report on 25 October. The report was critical of the NAF's design and questioned the anticipated mission of the glider in light of the shifting fortunes of the naval war. In the first place, the design and construction of the wooden glider did not lend themselves to quantity production, and the size of the craft limited its use in most operational zones. The glider's originally intended use as a tanker had to be ruled out when it was found that fuel could not be safely transferred from the craft while it was under radio control. In addition to these shortcomings, there were few airplanes in the navy inventory that could tow the big glider; the PBY-5A was satisfactory for hauling it when lightly loaded, but only the R5D-1, the navy version of the four-engine Douglas DC-4, could tow the glider at its full gross weight.[31]

Although there was some sentiment for canceling the XLRN-1 project, BuAer elected to continue it for the potentially valuable engineering information it could provide. Captain Barnaby recalled being impressed with the sheer size of the XLRN-1 as it took shape at the NAF in early 1944: "I used to get into the shop and watch progress on it and as it got near completion, each time I'd look at it, I'd go home and eat more Wheaties. It was a monster." When completed, the XLRN-1 had a maximum takeoff weight of 37,764 pounds (nearly 10,000 pounds more than a fully loaded DC-3), and a wing span of 110 feet, and it could be towed at speeds up to 180 miles per hour. Flight tests took place at Patuxent River, beginning in October 1944. Using a PBY-5A as a towplane, the XLRN-1 (number 36431) exhibited undesirable handling characteristics—notably a lack of longitudinal stability—which Barnaby thought were severe enough to require virtually a complete redesign of the tail surfaces. Facing the prospect of such extensive modifications to the XLRN-1 at Patuxent River and to the second aircraft, which was nearly complete at Philadelphia, Barnaby recommended that the project be ended. BuAer concurred, and the two aircraft were scrapped.[32]

Begun with great enthusiasm, the NAF Glomb and glider programs ended with little to show for the considerable time and money expended on them. Consistently the advocate, Fahrney thought the Glomb was "logical" and that it could have been an economical and effective weapon. Nevertheless, tests in 1944 and 1945 revealed nagging problems with the autotow system and were complicated by logistical and equipment difficulties. An accident with a Taylorcraft Glomb at Traverse City, Michigan, in July 1945, combined with the rapidly evolving strategic situation in the Pacific, led to cancellation of the project.[33]

The large glider had become an aircraft without a mission by 1944, and it also suffered from technical deficiencies that promised no easy solution. Admitting that he was "not particularly enthusiastic about the glider as a military weapon," Barnaby said the XLRN-1 program and other projects "proved to be a pretty costly experiment." He also maintained that the NAF's experience with the XLRN-1 showed conclusively that wooden gliders "of this size are not feasible." Nevertheless, the Glomb and glider programs had some residual benefits. They extended the NAF's involvement with guided weapons and enhanced the factory's leadership position in the new technology. Even though glider development did not have the operational success that had been hoped for, it led, among other things, to methods of recovering disabled aircraft. The NAF's "towing service," as Barnaby called it, became a common practice during the war and was an efficient way to return aircraft to repair bases.[34]

Together with its assault drone, Glomb, and glider projects, the NAF participated in the wartime development of rocket and turbo-jet-powered missiles. Early in the pilotless aircraft project at the NAF, Fahrney had suggested a high-performance weapon that could be carried by aircraft and used against surface and air targets. The idea was still in the back of his mind in 1939 when he learned of the work being done on rocket propulsion by Frank J. Malina at the Guggenheim Aeronautical Laboratory of the California Institute of Technology (GALCIT). In combination with radio control and television guidance, rocket power promised major performance gains for missiles, but the press of other business prevented Fahrney from pursuing the concept actively until the spring of 1943.[35]

In May 1943, Fahrney and Ivan H. Driggs, a civilian scientist working at BuAer, submitted a plan for the development of a guided weapon that could be used against either aircraft or small ships. It was to be powered not by a rocket but by a small turbojet, the 9.5A, which Westinghouse was already working on under a navy contract. BuAer approved the proposal on 19 July 1943 and established the project at the NAF, which the next day became part of the new Naval Air Material Center. The project and the missile received the name Gorgon, for the winged dragonlike creature of Greek mythology whose terrible aspect—a head covered with snakes—turned men instantly to stone. In August 1943, Driggs completed the specifications and general arrangement drawings for the Gorgon. It was to weigh about 760 pounds, with the 9.5A turbojet could attain an estimated top speed of between 475 and 510 miles per hour, and could deliver a fifty-to-one-hundred-pound warhead. There was little that was unorthodox about the design or the configuration except that Driggs called for a cast magnesium airframe.[36]

The Gorgon program went ahead at a relatively low priority at the NAMC until 19 October 1943. At that time, BuAer raised the priority classification of the project and called upon the center to submit estimates for the manufacture of fifty Gorgons. In addition, largely because of delays in the development of the 9.5A turbojet by Westinghouse, the bureau directed the NAMC to prepare designs for a Gorgon powered by a liquid-fuel rocket then under development by Lieutenant Robert C. Truax of the Naval Engineering Experiment Station at Annapolis. Of the fifty Gorgons, the bureau wanted half to be turbojet-powered and half rocket-powered.[37]

In October 1943, NAMC and BuAer representatives met in Washington to review the status of the Gorgon project and to plan its future course. At the conference there was agreement that the NAMC would go ahead with the simultaneous development of two Gorgon airframe designs: one of conventional configuration, and the other of the canard type, with control surfaces located in front of, rather than behind, the wing. Each type would be fitted with RCA BLOCK I television equipment and would be powered by either a Westinghouse turbojet or the rocket under development at Annapolis. By November, the NAMC had completed a mockup of the Gorgon with the conventional layout and had two mockups of the canard type under construction. At about this time, Lieutenant Taylor became the Gorgon project engineer, largely because of his extensive experience with other guided weapons programs.[38]

As the Gorgon program got under way in Philadelphia, BuAer made important decisions regarding the construction of the missile. It had been determined that the Gorgon should be as simple as possible, even if that simplicity incurred weight penalties. It had also been decided that the fuselages would be fabricated of molded plywood, similar to the material used in the NAF's assault drones. But following up on Driggs's original suggestion about the use of magnesium, officers in the bureau's structures branch thought that "marked production advantages" might accrue if the Gorgons were built with monocoque fuselages made of the lightweight metal. The NAMC and the NAF had experience with magnesium alloy in aircraft structures and established a liaison in February 1944 with

Dow to investigate the potential of magnesium in the Gorgon program.[39]

The Gorgon program made encouraging progress early in 1944. The NAMC completed a mockup of the canard-configured missile by the end of February, and on 17 March a board arrived in Philadelphia to inspect the results. The mockup board found the Gorgon design basically sound, although it did make suggestions for changes. The board's most important reservation about the Gorgon design was the weight of the missile's warhead. As originally planned, the Gorgon was to carry one hundred pounds of Torpex, an explosive roughly twice as powerful as TNT, but the mockup board thought the weapon's structure should be strengthened to accommodate a heavier payload. Captain Barnaby said that the NAMC would investigate improvements to the Gorgon's capacity but cautioned that the missile was "a highly experimental article" and that armament studies were better left until the aerodynamic, guidance, and propulsion questions were resolved. Based on the mockup board's recommendations, BuAer subsequently directed the NAMC to proceed with the construction of vehicles for flight and structural tests.[40]

Despite these developments, the press of time and events dictated changes in the Gorgon and the test program at the NAMC. It proved impossible to incorporate magnesium into the Gorgon airframe, which ended up with a monocoque fuselage of molded plywood. Only the missile's control surfaces were metal, and it was cast aluminum not magnesium. There were also problems with the turbojet engine planned for some of the early Gorgons. Westinghouse became bogged down with the 9.5A turbojet, causing the Gorgon program to shift its orientation toward the Annapolis rocket motor and other power plants, including pulsejets. Because the NAMC lacked equipment for aerodynamic tests of the Gorgon at Philadelphia, it turned to the NACA's Langley laboratory. In June, Langley tested the missile in the canard configuration with the rocket motor and the Westinghouse turbojet. The results indicated some longitudinal stability problems with the aircraft but no inherent design defects or insurmountable aerodynamic deficiencies.[41]

By this time, the Gorgon program had settled into a pattern that continued through the end of the war. Principal responsibility for the design, engineering, and construction of the missiles rested with the Naval Aircraft Factory. The Naval Aircraft Modification Unit, first at Philadelphia and after early July 1944 at the former Brewster plant at Johnsville, handled the testing and subsequent development work on the Gorgon. Both the NAF and the NAMU were subordinate commands within the NAMC. To determine the best airframe–power plant combination, four missile designs were to be tested: the Gorgon II-A, which was of the canard configuration with rocket propulsion; the Gorgon II-B, of identical configuration but with the Westinghouse 9.5A turbojet; the Gorgon III-A, which had a conventional wing and tail configuration and a rocket motor; and the Gorgon III-B, with the conventional layout and the Westinghouse 9.5A turbojet. The NAF began deliveries of Gorgon IIs to the NAMU on 1 September 1944 and completed eighteen of the missiles before the first week of December. By the spring of 1944, the factory was well along with the design phase of the Gorgon III, and engineers anticipated deliveries of the first five of the missiles in October. As it had with the assault drones, the NAF subcontracted many of the Gorgon components. The Singer Manufacturing Company in South Bend, Indiana, became the major supplier to the NAF of wooden structures for the missiles.[42]

In early 1945, the NAMU was ready for flight tests of the Gorgon, using the venerable PBY-5A that had been previously employed in towing tests of gliders and Glombs. The initial test was with a II-A fitted with radio-control gear but minus the Annapolis rocket motor. On 17 January, the PBY-5A released the missile at an altitude of ten thousand feet over Warren Grove, New Jersey, with an FM-2 Wildcat fighter trailing as the chase plane. In a matter of seconds, the Gorgon began a series of rolls that the control operator was unable to stabilize and that led eventually to a spiraling dive into the ground and destruction of the missile. Before the second test flight on 3 February, modifications were made to the radio-control unit to prevent the roll and stabilization problems and a parachute was provided for emergency recovery of the aircraft. Shortly after the Gorgon dropped away from the mother ship, its parachute deployed, streaming back over the missile's tail. Nevertheless, the Gorgon behaved in an otherwise exemplary manner and was safely glided to a landing.[43]

For the powered flights of the rocket-propelled Gorgon II-A, the

The Gorgon II-A. Built by the Naval Aircraft Factory, its testing in the spring of 1945 was the responsibility of the Naval Aircraft Modification Unit in Johnsville, north of Philadelphia. The missile was powered by a rocket motor developed by the Naval Engineering Experiment Station in Annapolis. Note the Gorgon's canard configuration. (80-G-189142, National Archives)

NAMU shifted from Warren Grove to the ocean off Cape May because of worries about the toxicity of the acid aniline oxidizer and fuel combination in the Annapolis unit. The first test took place on 8 March. The PBY-5A carried the missile, with an FM-2 serving as the control plane, a Martin JM-1 (the navy version of the B-26 twin-engine medium bomber) as the chase plane, and two SB2Cs following to make a photographic record of the test. Molt Taylor reported that the rocket fired as planned ten seconds after the Gorgon dropped away from the PBY, and the missile "accelerated at a surprisingly rapid rate." By the time it had exhausted its fuel, the Gorgon was more than five miles ahead of the JM-1 and was flying at an estimated 550 miles per hour. Later in the month, the NAMU group completed a second flight test of the Gorgon II-A. This time, the missile had a television camera on board to record airspeed readings. After noting a speed of 400 miles per hour on the television screen in the control aircraft, an observer saw the pointer on the airspeed indicator "going around the dial at an alarming rate." The test ended when the missile "for some unexplained reason," completed a right-hand turn and then dove vertically into the sea.[44]

Molt Taylor fretted about the Gorgon's speed, control difficulties, and the chase planes staying within sight of the missile as it zoomed ahead of them. He wondered about the limits to human direction of a missile capable of such velocities: "The entire operation is of such speed that the human mind is not capable of keeping up with the flight." He thought that the turbojet-powered Gorgon would be more easily controlled. Nevertheless, he considered the rocket-powered Gorgon tests valuable for resolving some of the questions about stability, control, and launching techniques and was enthusiastic about the results of the program thus far.[45]

Some thought the Gorgon would make a good high-speed test vehicle for the NACA, but through the early stages of the navy program, the committee had shown virtually no interest. The Gorgon II-A flight tests and the velocities attained by the missile, however, caught the NACA's attention. In March 1945, two engineers from NACA's Langley laboratory talked with NAMU people about the Gorgon, and less than a month later, on 2 April, Rear Admiral Lawrence B. Richardson, BuAer's assistant chief, directed the NAMU to begin work on a new Gorgon variant. Designated the III-C, the missile used the same airframe as the III-A but had a more powerful rocket motor. Twenty of these were to be manufactured at the NAF for the NACA and delivered to NACA's new flight test station at Wallops Island, Virginia.[46]

Gorgon production for the NACA in the spring of 1945 came at the same time that early deliveries of Westinghouse turbojets for the II-B and III-B Gorgons seemed more doubtful than ever. Westinghouse got two 9.5A units to the NAF before the middle of January, but the engines' performance at high altitudes was inferior. The company was hard at work on an improved model, the 9.5B, but it could not promise deliveries before July. The NAF, in the interval, had taken on the development of a modified Gorgon III-B, designated the TD2N, to be used as a high-speed target drone. It was critical that Westinghouse straighten things out as quickly as possible, for

The rocket-powered Gorgon III-C was derived from the Gorgon III-A specifically for use by the NACA in high-speed flight tests. The NAF built twenty of these missiles in 1945–46. (80-G-703496, National Archives)

all indications were that the requirements for its turbojets were on an upward curve.[47]

As a result of the expansion of the missile program, problems with turbojet deliveries, and changing weapon requirements, Rear Admiral Ramsey, the chief of BuAer, surveyed the Gorgon program in April 1945. Currently at the NAMC were orders for 130 of the missiles, broken down into 21 II-As, 4 II-Bs, 34 III-As, 16 III-Bs, 20 III-Cs, and 35 TD2Ns. Ramsey wanted "to review and modify the original concept of this missile and to revise the overall policy for guidance of the project." Instead of developing a completely operational air-to-surface or air-to-air weapon, the Gorgon program would henceforth be "visualized mainly as an experimental engineering project to be utilized to develop and test power units, control systems, and intelligence systems for high speed missiles." More specifically, the NAMC should concentrate on experimentation with television guidance equipment, homing devices, and advanced propulsion systems for the Gorgon series. The center would also complete various test programs related to the Gorgon and finish the TD2N target drones.[48]

Ramsey's letter forecast a badly needed rationalization of the Gorgon program and related projects, but within days, events conspired to disrupt this orderly approach. Although Germany surrendered on 8 May 1945, Japan stubbornly held on, giving every indication that the guns would not fall silent in the Pacific until some time in 1946. Before victory could be achieved, it seemed the navy would have to bear most of the burden of shore bombardment, putting its ships and men at high risk as the American forces closed in on the Japanese home islands. Anything that could be done to reduce the expected American losses would be welcome.

Captain Barnaby and Lieutenant Commander Taylor in April 1945 discussed over the telephone the current state of affairs and how it affected the NAMC's Gorgon program. Continued delays in deliveries of Westinghouse turbojets, they agreed, precluded any quick adaptation of II-B or III-B Gorgons as long-range shore bombardment missiles, but they saw hope in a new Gorgon model, designated the II-C. The missile, powered by a fourteen-inch pulse-jet under development by the Naval Engineering Experiment Station and nicknamed the Junior Buzz Bomb, could be catapult-launched from escort carriers or other ships and directed to its target using radio control and television. Barnaby and Taylor thought it could become operational within a relatively brief period of time. Even though Ramsey had only recently directed that the NAMC regard the Gorgon program as a research and development project, BuAer concurred with Barnaby and Taylor and outlined a production program for the II-C that envisioned delivery of two hundred of the missiles by 1 December.[49]

But the Gorgon's stony gaze did not transfix Rear Admiral Donald Royce, the commanding officer of the NAMC. Royce was not optimistic about a major weapons production program at Philadelphia and Johnsville that would tie up much of the resources of his center and divert it from research and development. He warned that there could be problems and delays in the development of the pulsejet engine and the catapult launch method and that the Gorgon would probably have to be redesigned to incorporate a metal rather

Developed by the NAF in 1945–46, the Gorgon II-C was a pulsejet-powered, canard-configuration missile to be used in round-the-clock bombardment of the Japanese home islands. The atomic bomb precluded its use. (80-G-651025, National Archives)

than a molded plywood airframe. Barnaby, Taylor, Fahrney, and others were undeterred by the potential technical obstacles, which they thought could be overcome with a minimum of difficulty, and they foresaw the Gorgon II-C as a powerful new weapon that would be capable of delivering a thousand-pound warhead with great accuracy at ranges of up to 130 miles.[50]

Royce was correct that the Gorgon II-C would occupy much of the NAMC's time and assets. BuAer began the program by directing the center to manufacture thirty-six Gorgon II-Cs and in August ordered the procurement of sixty-four more. The bureau expected the NAMC to deliver two hundred before the end of the year and then increase production to two hundred per month. By April 1946, output was to go up to five hundred monthly. In the third week of June 1945, the effects of the Gorgon II-C program were obvious;

Gorgon II-A, II-B, and III-C projects were at a virtual standstill while the center concentrated its efforts on engineering studies of the pulsejet-powered II-C. Yet just as the II-C program began to increase in tempo, the Pacific war suddenly came to an end, bringing cancellation of the major production orders and a significant reduction in the scope of the project. The first Gorgon II-C (redesignated KGN-1 in October 1945) did not fly until September 1946.[51]

Other than the II-C, the only Gorgon project that went ahead with any conviction in 1945 was the TD2N, a high-speed target drone similar to the Westinghouse turbojet-powered Gorgon III-B. In June 1945, the NAMU conducted a drop test of a TD2N without its engine. Released from the PBY-5A at six thousand feet over Cape May, the TD2N glided down to about five hundred feet under radio control before its parachute deployed and the drone was recovered intact. The first powered TD2N test flight on 27 June was not a success. Although the turbojet engine operated throughout the flight, the radio-control system did not, and the drone crashed into the sea off Cape May. Another test on 17 August went much better. The drone, with its engine already running, dropped away from the PBY, flying for twenty-one minutes at a speed of about 190 knots and performing various maneuvers under radio control. Unfortunately, the craft was not recovered intact. At about one hundred feet over the runway at Cape May, the parachute deployed, but the inflatable bag intended to cushion the impact of landing caused the drone to bounce over on its back, badly damaging the fuselage and causing minor damage to the wings and tail surfaces. Still, this was the first successful test of the Gorgon with the Westinghouse turbojet and was an encouraging step forward in this long-delayed program.[52]

Test flights of the TD2N continued through the end of the year. The NAMU delivered nine of the drones to XVJ-25, a squadron established to work with high-performance target aircraft. During a familiarization exercise with one of the TD2Ns before XVJ-25 personnel at the Naval Air Station, Wildwood, New Jersey, in November, the drone stalled before the parachute deployed, crashed onto the runway, and was demolished. A demonstration for the press at the Naval Air Station, Atlantic City, the next month went much better. This time the TD2N, under radio control, made several high-speed passes over the reporters and completed a series

Gorgon II-Cs at the NAMU in Johnsville in 1946. One hundred of the missiles were ordered, but not that many were delivered. (80-G-703500, National Archives)

of maneuvers before being brought down to a successful parachute landing. The Atlantic City flight showed the capability of the TD2N, but continued difficulties with the Westinghouse engine and the generally high cost of the program led to its cancellation on 12 March 1946.[53]

The course of the Pacific war had dictated the NAMC's development of the Gorgon II-C as a long-range surface-to-surface guided weapon. The war in its latter stages also brought about the NAMC's development of a short-range surface-to-air missile intended to counter Japanese suicide or kamikaze attacks. BuAer already had under study since the fall of 1944 Lark, a high-performance liquid-fueled rocket that followed a radar beam to its target. In February 1945, the bureau gave high priority to Lark and late the following month directed the NAMC to submit a proposal for the design, development, and manufacture of fifteen missiles. As the center began work on Lark, however, it became apparent that the missile would not soon be operational, and in the meantime the specter of the kamikaze loomed large. Rear Admiral Ramsey phoned Captain Barnaby at the NAMU to discuss the problem and potential means of getting an antiaircraft missile to the fleet as expeditiously as possible.[54]

Molt Taylor was among those at the NAMU who began thinking about alternatives to Lark. Another was Clair Bennett, who suggested that a "quick and dirty" solution to the problem was an interim missile using a standard JATO solid-fuel rocket unit for propulsion. On 10 May 1945, when the NAMU submitted a design proposal for Lark, it stated that it was going ahead with preliminary investigations of a stopgap weapon, code-named Little Joe. In reply, BuAer said that it preferred Lark but added that Little Joe suggested an immediate solution to the problem presented by the kamikaze and authorized continuation of the project. Subsequently, the NAMU dropped out of the Lark project to concentrate its efforts on Little Joe.[55]

Little Joe was one of the few "crash" projects taken on by the NAMC and its subordinate commands during the war. There was nothing fancy in the missile's design and construction; the NAMC made use of readily available materials and as many existing components as possible. The missile was eight and a half feet long, was fabricated of mild steel sheet, and had simple cruciform wings and control surfaces. A flare in the tail of the missile facilitated visual sighting as the weapon closed on the target under radio control. Small booster rockets lifted Little Joe from a twenty-foot-long launching rail fixed to a modified forty-millimeter antiaircraft gun mount, while the one-thousand-pound-thrust JATO unit propelled the missile to an estimated altitude of ten thousand feet. Little Joe carried a one-hundred-pound warhead that was detonated by a standard proximity fuse. The first of fifteen missiles authorized by BuAer was ready on 21 June, and initial flights began at a test range used by the Applied Physics Laboratory of Johns Hopkins University at Island Beach, south of Seaside Park, New Jersey.[56]

The Little Joe test program started off well but then encountered a series of frustrating setbacks. Two launches took place at Island Beach on 20 July 1945. Both were completely successful, and, according to Fahrney, constituted the first successful flights in the United States of a surface-to-air missile "in combat configuration." Commander S. W. Brown of BuAer praised the Little Joe project as "a fine example of really excellent experimental and development work of which NAMC is capable." Nevertheless, two subsequent tests of Little Joe failed: one when the launching rockets malfunctioned and another—at Patuxent River in August—when the JATO unit did not ignite. Not until 25 October did the missile complete another successful test flight, nearly two months after the formal surrender of Japan.[57]

The NAMU continued the Little Joe program into 1946, although most of the launches took place from the navy's test range at the Marine Corps Air Station, Mojave, California. Yet with the end of the war, there was no requirement for the continuation of such emergency projects. Consequently, BuAer concentrated on the development of Lark, which offered a great deal more potential as a surface-to-air weapon than Little Joe. On 12 March 1946, the bureau directed that Little Joe be terminated.[58]

Molt Taylor answered a questionnaire circulated by Delmar Fahrney as Fahrney was preparing a manuscript history of the navy's pilotless aircraft and guided missile program in the early 1950s. Taylor wrote on the questionnaire that the navy's guided weapon program would have accomplished more had Fahrney and others been left alone to do their jobs. He said that the intraservice conflicts over the various projects "were difficult to understand."[59]

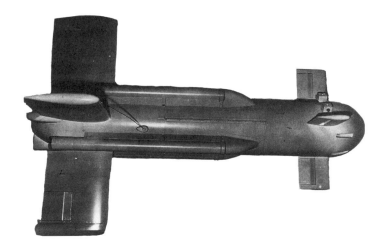

Little Joe was a "quick and dirty" effort in 1945 to develop a missile to counter the Japanese kamikazes. Power came from a thousand-pound-thrust solid rocket JATO unit. (80-G-703462, National Archives)

From Taylor's perspective that was probably true, but the development of every weapon system involves conflict and compromise in the decision-making process. The more complex and expensive the weapon system the more involved and difficult decision making becomes. The navy's assault drone and guided missile programs promised to revolutionize warfare. They did not; in fact, they had absolutely no influence on the outcome of the conflict. Some argued that the paucity of results was owing to a decision in the Office of the Chief of Naval Operations to move ahead too quickly with the assault drone, a weapon that had severe operational limitations, when more advanced weapons waited in the "pipeline." Others, pointing to the failure of the navy's guided weapon program as evidence of misplaced priorities, wanted the service to devote all its energies to conventional, combat-proven weapons.

If they did nothing else, the guided weapons projects at the NAF-NAMC showed how intricate such advanced weapons programs were and how difficult it was to balance the planning, funding, and execution of the research and development effort that went into them. It is highly unlikely that the navy could have achieved nearly the results it did within a relatively brief period of time had these projects been contracted to private firms. The Philadelphia-area aviation complex was ideally suited to take and sustain the initiative for such weapons as the assault drone, Glomb, and Gorgon, and perhaps more than any organization it placed the navy in an excellent position to exploit the potential of these and other guided weapons in the postwar era. At the same time, these programs highlighted the growing concentration of research and development at the Naval Air Material Center and its subordinate commands.

13

To Support the Naval Air Effort

Strong currents pulled the Naval Aircraft Factory and the Naval Air Material Center away from aircraft production during World War II. No official policy decisions had been made on the subject, yet it was clear to nearly everyone that the NAMC's major roles were in research and development, the procurement of specialized equipment and weapons, aircraft conversion and modification, and the testing of materials, structures, instruments, electronics, and aircraft engines. As Rear Admiral Lawrence B. Richardson wrote in 1944: "The NAMC is the only naval activity qualified to undertake the greatly diversified projects necessary to properly support the naval air effort of this war."[1]

So extensive and sundry were the projects undertaken by the NAF-NAMC that a comprehensive examination would itself constitute a book. Instead, this study will cover only those projects that were particularly unusual, congruent with other research and development programs, or had a bearing on the eventual peacetime activities of the installation. The picture one gets from this overview is of almost bewildering complexity yet with a common thread—to do whatever was necessary to provide the navy with the material to fight and win the war.

One of the most significant programs at Philadelphia was the development, manufacture, and installation of catapults and arresting gear. The NAF engineering department had responsibility for the design and manufacture of this equipment, while the testing and shipboard installation had been assigned since June 1937 to the factory's Ship Experimental Unit. After the United States became an active belligerent in World War II, the NAF stepped up its efforts to keep pace with the increasing requirements for this specialized equipment.

One extraordinary NAF catapult project stemmed from the realization early in World War II that fighter and patrol aircraft lacked the range to protect convoys from German U-boats or aircraft in the North Atlantic and that there would not soon be enough aircraft carriers available for convoy escort duties. The British introduced a desperate stopgap measure whereby "war-weary" Hawker Hurricane fighters were launched from naval and merchant ships equipped with rocket-propelled catapults. The aircraft could not be recovered aboard the vessels, leaving the pilots with the unattractive options of either bailing out or trying to ditch next to the ship.[2]

Officers in the Bureau of Aeronautics followed these British developments with considerable interest in 1941, eventually concluding that a rocket catapult to launch airplanes from merchant ships offered distinct advantages, not the least of which was, as Captain Dewitt C. Ramsey said, "a very short fabrication time as compared with current service types." In August 1941, the NAF began preliminary design studies of the catapult, working with the Naval Engineering Experiment Station (NEES) in Annapolis on the development of a rocket motor. Designated the Type XJ, Mark I, the catapult, though weighing only seventy-one hundred pounds, had the capacity to launch a seventy-five-hundred-pound aircraft at a speed of eighty-three miles per hour. By January 1942, the factory had completed a tentative design for the shuttle of the catapult, but it was not ready to submit complete manufacturing plans until the NEES finished work on the solid-rocket motor. Because of delays in the development of an effective braking system for the launching car, the XJ, Mark I was not ready for tests until October 1943. By that time enough escort carriers had joined the fleet to obviate the need for launching aircraft from merchant ships.[3]

Experience with the XJ, Mark I was valuable for a related catapult project—the Type J, Mark II. BuAer was interested in a catapult to launch small observation aircraft from landing ships, particularly the LST, in support of amphibious operations. On 27 March 1944, the bureau authorized the Naval Air Material Center to begin work on a rocket catapult using a standard one-thousand-pound-thrust JATO unit to launch a twenty-one-hundred-pound airplane at a speed of about forty-five miles per hour. The NAMC quickly advanced from the submission of its proposal in May to the beginning of tests in Philadelphia on 19 June. Following these, the catapult was sent to San Diego for installation on an LST and an additional series of tests during the first week of October. These, too, were successful, but BuAer did not authorize further evaluation of the catapult or call on the NAF for a production program.[4]

Engineers continued to look for alternatives to the hydraulic-pneumatic catapults, which were heavy and had complicated cable-and-sheave systems requiring careful adjustment and constant maintenance. Two wartime designs were particularly noteworthy: one was an electric catapult, promising high velocities and rapid recycling for multiple launches; the other was a slotted-cylinder catapult, which eventually proved important to the development of the steam catapult. In 1942, BuAer issued a $280,000 project order to the NAF for the design, development, and testing of an electric catapult. Manufactured by Westinghouse and designated the XEE, the catapult used a linear alternating-current electric motor to launch a twenty-thousand-pound aircraft at speeds up to 90 miles per hour. It underwent evaluation at the NAMC in June 1944. The results of the tests led to a contract on 1 September 1944 with Westinghouse for the development of the XE-2, a much larger-capacity unit for launching a five-thousand-pound aircraft at 200 miles per hour or a fifty-thousand-pound aircraft at 115 miles per hour.[5]

Though early prospects for the electric catapult were bright, the mechanism was not the answer to the navy's need for higher speeds and greater capacities. That came after the war with the steam catapult, based on the principle of the slotted cylinder. This relatively simple concept, which the Germans had experimented with in connection with their guided weapons program, was a tube with a slot running its entire length. Passing through the slot and attached to a piston in the cylinder was a fitting to which the launching shuttle was connected; a flexible metal seal prevented the escape of the propellant gas—in this case, compressed air. On 21 December 1944, BuAer directed the NAMC to begin work on the catapult, designated the Type XAT, Mark I. Intended to launch small target drones at speeds up to seventy miles per hour, the catapult was not outstanding in its size or capacity, but it provided important engineering experience with the slotted cylinder that the NAMC drew upon when it turned to larger catapults incorporating the same principle.[6]

Because of the NAF's considerable background in the development of catapult equipment, it was natural for the factory to modify army air forces fighters for catapult launchings. The immediate need was in conjunction with Operation TORCH, the Allied landings in North Africa in November 1942. As the outline for the amphibious operation took shape in the summer of 1942, planners identified the need for additional air support provided by army fighters catapulted from aircraft carriers. In June, the NAF began working with a Lockheed P-38, a Bell P-39, and a Republic P-47 to determine what modifications, parts, and equipment were needed. But it was the Curtiss P-40, which was the major component of the army fighter force dispatched to North Africa, that received the most attention. On 3 August, BuAer authorized the factory to manufacture three hundred sets of catapult bridle attachments and hold-down links for P-40s bound for Operation TORCH. Army fighter pilots also familiarized themselves with catapult procedures and made test shots from Mustin Field before participating in the North African landings.[7]

The catapult conversion of the army P-40s for the North African invasion proved highly successful, leading to the production at the NAF of similar catapult kits for other army fighter aircraft. The Bell P-39 with its tricycle landing gear presented a challenge, but in the process of solving the problems, the NAF accumulated a fund of information about tricycle landing gear that was directly applicable to postwar navy aircraft. The factory completed catapult launch tests of a P-47 in December 1943 and shortly thereafter received project orders for fifteen hundred catapult kits for P-47s and P-51s. TORCH was not the only major operation that saw the catapult launch of army air forces fighters. Lacking offloading facilities ashore after the invasion of Tarawa in November 1943, the navy catapulted P-39s; in June 1944, escort carriers catapulted P-47s during the invasion of Saipan.[8]

Along with catapults, the Naval Aircraft Factory continued its work with arresting gear. Throughout most of the war, the NAF concentrated on improvements to and production of the Mark IV unit, which had first gone to sea in 1942. But as the size and weight of carrier aircraft increased, BuAer turned to the factory in February 1942 for development of a new type with the capacity to arrest the landing of a thirty-thousand-pound aircraft from speeds up to ninety miles per hour. Basically, the factory adhered to the bureau's dictum that the new gear retain as much commonality with the Mark IV as possible, but by the time the NAF submitted its preliminary proposal in December 1942, there were some significant changes. The Mark V, as it was designated, differed from its predecessor chiefly in that it was mounted on the gallery deck rather than being hung from underneath the flight deck. This was done in part because of the greater size and weight of the Mark V components. There were also changes in the control valves, sheaves, and deck pendant supports. The first Mark V went aboard the *Essex*-class carrier *Bennington* in 1944, which completed more than one thousand landings with the gear by November. Production orders for 299 of the Mark Vs went to the Norfolk Navy Yard.[9]

Part of the NAF's task in connection with catapults and arresting gear during World War II was the testing and calibration of the equipment by the Ship Experimental Unit before installation at the shipyard. This work was typically done at Philadelphia before the units were sent to the builders, but by early 1942 the magnitude of the carrier program, combined with the addition of shipyards inexperienced with the specialized equipment of aircraft carriers, dictated a change. BuAer determined that tests should be done at the NAF only on the first production catapult or arresting gear unit; subsequent examples would be delivered from the manufacturer to the shipyard, where personnel from the NAF oversaw installation and field testing.[10]

Captain W. W. Webster, manager of the NAF, agreed that the bureau's decision was "a sound procedure if installations aboard are adequately inspected and tested." He added that frequent inspections of catapults and arresting gear were necessary throughout the construction process and as the ship was fitting out at the yard because of the shipyard's general unfamiliarity with the equipment and an apparent inability to wade through and comprehend the accompanying engineering data. Under the new arrangement, Webster estimated that the NAF required twenty-three additional enlisted men to carry out the field testing at yards scattered around the country. BuAer concurred, stating that "every possible aid in the form of additional personnel should be given to the Naval Aircraft Factory for this important work." Captain Ramsey, then the bureau's assistant chief, recommended in February 1942 that four catapult inspection crews and four arresting gear inspection crews be organized at Philadelphia to conduct the fieldwork.[11]

The need for new procedures soon became evident. In June 1941, the NAF received a major order to provide the arresting gear for escort carriers being converted from merchant ships for the British in American yards. Following accepted practice, the factory inspected the arresting gear, made adjustments, and sent the equipment on to the yard with instructions for installation. When a team from the NAF arrived at the New York Navy Yard in March 1942, however, they found that the arresting gear installed in the carrier *Avenger* was still in an "incomplete condition." When the NAF group was finally able to carry out dynamic tests of the equipment, some parts malfunctioned. Finding no inspection records and concluding that the failure of the arresting gear had been caused by poor workmanship and negligence in following installation instructions, the NAF recommended that all escort carrier conversion yards send key personnel to Philadelphia for an indoctrination program and that the NAF thoroughly check arresting gear installations before static and dynamic testing.[12]

Following this pattern, catapult and arresting gear installations, under close scrutiny by NAF teams at the shipyards, went smoothly. One difficulty reported by the Norfolk Navy Yard was "severe damage" to arresting gear units from metal shavings and chips that fell into the sheaves during the construction and outfitting phases. Because the foreign matter was virtually impossible to remove, the arresting units usually had to be disassembled, repaired, and reinstalled. Another problem resulted from the navy's obsession with paint. It was not uncommon for crews to paint arresting gear components in the mistaken belief that this protected them and enhanced their appearance. But the practice eventually built up layers of paint on operating parts, causing subpar performance and breakdowns. Noting that the gear was adequately protected with zinc chromate when it was installed, the NAF recommended that no further painting be done.[13]

Not only did the first years of the war bring about a shift in the NAF's responsibilities for the installation and testing of catapults and arresting gear, but it also led to an awkward division of responsibilities for this important aviation equipment. General Order 198 of 20 July 1943 had created the Naval Air Material Center and its subordinate commands, including the Naval Air Experimental Station. Within the NAES was the Ship Installations Division, which came to share with the NAF some of the burden for catapults and arresting gear. To correct this anomalous situation, an order of 20 September 1943 transferred the Ship Installations Division to the NAF's engineering department, once more centralizing most catapult and arresting gear activities. Only the responsibility for disbursing spare parts remained outside the purview of the NAF, residing with the Aviation Supply Office. Concerned about reports that the ASO's inexperience with catapults and arresting gear had caused understocking of critical spares, BuAer established a "little ASO" at the NAF on 8 January 1944 specifically to handle the procurement and distribution of this material.[14]

With most of the responsibility for catapults and arresting gear once more centralized at the NAF, Rear Admiral Ramsey, who had become chief of BuAer in August 1943, wanted to establish current requirements and plan for future needs. Ramsey declared: "Experience gained in the present war has established the fact that catapults installed on carriers are important to proper operation of all types including CVE's, CVL's, and CV's. Under certain conditions of wind, fleet dispositions, aircraft loadings or for logistic reasons, catapult operations are mandatory. The need for reliable catapult machinery, therefore, cannot be over emphasized. The vital function of arresting gear needs no comment." Ramsey went on to say, "In order that the development of catapults and arresting gear will keep pace with airplane development and the needs of the fleet, it is considered essential that an engineering development group be established at the NAMC for exhaustive development and research work in connection with this equipment." In conclusion, Ramsey ordered Captain Samuel Zeigler, the NAMC commanding officer, to study and report on problems with the development of catapults and arresting gear at Philadelphia.[15]

Within a month, Zeigler complied with the directive, sending Ramsey a summary of the catapult and arresting gear activities at the NAMC and the center's requirements for additional permanent test installations and personnel. He said he was "in complete agreement with the ideas presented [by Ramsey] regarding the need for a development and research program for catapults and arresting gear." He did not, however, consider it necessary to create a separate engineering and development group. Instead, he pointed out, the present engineering and test staff should be augmented and more intimate ties established with technical officers in BuAer and project engineers at the NAF. Specifically, he recommended a $300,000 increment for catapults and arresting gear and the instrumentation needed for testing them. He called for fifteen officers, twenty civilian engineers and draftsmen, and sixty-four enlisted men and civilians to handle the additional work load.[16]

BuAer approved Zeigler's request, which Rear Admiral Richardson said "is considered an excellent plan."[17] This, coupled with the organizational changes of late 1943 and early 1944, formed the operating blueprint for the NAMC's catapult and arresting gear work through the end of the war and secured the center's position of leadership in the design, development, and testing of this and other highly specialized aviation equipment.

Similarly, the NAF-NAMC pursued other projects that underscored BuAer's commitment to the Philadelphia installation for research and development. Radar was one of them. The navy's involvement with this technology stemmed from experiments by Commander A. Holt Taylor and a civilian, Leo C. Young, at the Naval Aircraft Radio Laboratory at Anacostia in September 1922 that demonstrated the disruption of high-frequency radio signals by passing vessels. In 1934, Taylor and Young, having transferred to the Naval Research Laboratory (NRL), began investigating means of pulsing high frequency radio waves, a technique that eventually led to the first operational radar sets on navy ships in October 1941. By the end of 1940, the Radiation Laboratory at MIT, concentrating on airborne microwave radar systems, had begun its own research program.[18]

Since 1936, Commander Delmar Fahrney, officer in charge of the navy's pilotless aircraft project, had been closely monitoring the development of radar, which he thought would eventually be superior to television and radio control as a guidance system for assault drones. Two avenues of development looked promising: one was a compact microwave unit that fit in the missile itself, the emissions allowing the weapon to home in on its target; the other was an airborne search unit in the control aircraft that illuminated the target, providing an electronic path or beam for the missile to follow. At a meeting with MIT researchers in May 1941, Fahrney learned that such a "beam rider" was possible with further development of existing equipment. In August of that year an agreement was made to have MIT begin work on a radar system in connection with the assault drone project, then just beginning to take shape under Fahrney at the NAF. The NRL was to undertake research into repeat-back or telemetry equipment for the assault drone.[19]

In the meantime, on 23 April 1941, BuAer established Project ROGER at the Naval Aircraft Factory. The multifold mission of ROGER was to assist MIT and the NRL in their radar research, to study radar as a homing device for assault drones and other guided weapons, to participate in the design and flight testing of airborne radar installations, and to investigate radar as a means of directing bombing through overcast. Much of the electronic equipment was developed and tested in the NAF's Aeronautical Radio Laboratory.[20]

Airborne radar was an attractive means of extending the eyes of the navy's patrol aircraft, and as early as October 1941 the NAF participated in the procurement of search radars and the modification of aircraft to carry and operate them. But Fahrney and others involved with the assault drone program naturally viewed airborne radar as a means of guiding a weapon to its target and were therefore interested in the conversion of aircraft under Project ROGER to carry radar sets and in the development of compact units for the missiles themselves. One of the first airplanes to be fitted with radar—in early 1942—was a Project FOX Beech JRB drone control aircraft, but the unit was so bulky that installation in all but the largest aircraft was impractical. For Project OPTION, the assault drone program, the NAF converted a Grumman TBF-1 torpedo bomber to a control aircraft in early 1943. Included among the extensive modifications were the removal of the dorsal turret and gun and the addition of a retractable radar housing in the bomb bay. During a brief test flight of the TBF in February 1943, the airplane vibrated and exhibited control problems when the radar housing was extended below the fuselage. Wind tunnel tests at the Washington Navy Yard helped resolve the situation, and in October 1943 the

NAF began conversion of twelve TBFs as assault drone control aircraft.[21]

One of the most extensive projects to involve the ROGER group at the NAF was the testing of the Pelican glide bomb and the conversion of aircraft to carry and provide guidance for the weapon. In June 1942, the National Defense Research Committee, through the navy's Bureau of Ordnance, began the development of Pelican, an unpowered air-to-surface missile that homed in on its target using a combination of an on-board radar receiver and a beam emanating from a search-type radar in the control aircraft. The NAF conducted the first drop tests of a Pelican in the summer of 1942 using an old Northrop BT-1 dive bomber to carry and drop the missiles and an R4D to haul the radar gear. The first Pelican equipped with the radar receiver underwent a successful trial using a ground radar set at Warren Grove, New Jersey, on 12 November 1942.[22]

Pelican, in the meantime, had been given high priority as an antisubmarine weapon, and the NAF came under enormous pressure to determine which aircraft were most suitable for conversion as Pelican carriers. After several types of airplanes passed through the NAF in 1943–44, the choice narrowed to the Lockheed PV-1 Ventura, modified to carry a one-thousand-pound Pelican Mark II under each wing, a fifteen-hundred-pound Pelican Mark III beneath the fuselage, and the necessary radar guidance equipment. On 1 January 1944, the NAMC received orders to convert a single PV-1 as a Pelican carrier (or "parent," as it was known), followed by a directive to modify thirty-one more aircraft using the first PV-1 conversion as a prototype.[23]

The NAMC's Pelican parent conversion program encountered problems almost from the start. Although tests of the prototype went smoothly, Captain Zeigler determined that the anticipated delivery schedule of converted PV-1 Pelican carriers could not be met. The main reasons he cited were delays in materials deliveries, problems completing the necessary engineering work, and late changes in the conversion specifications. Rear Admiral Towers, however, thought that the Pelican conversions took precedence over all other NAMC projects and authorized Zeigler to pull people away from PBN-1 production to speed up the Pelican delivery schedule.

As a result of the delays, BuAer cut the program back to sixteen airplanes, the last of which left Philadelphia in late July.[24]

The Project ROGER test group, relocated to the new NAMU facility at Johnsville, conducted a series of trials of the missile using the hulk *James Longstreet* as a target. The first of these failed, but on 31 July 1944 two Pelicans struck the ship. Ironically, just as the Pelican program began to show results, questions about the range of the PV-1, coupled with a decree from the Office of the CNO that henceforth all guided weapons had to be designed for launch from carrier aircraft, led Admiral King in September to cancel the project. Pelican tests continued into the fall of 1944, however, using production examples of the missile to gather data for a follow-on air-to-surface glide bomb code-named Bat.[25]

As it had with Pelican, the NAMC played an important role in both the testing and the conversion of operational aircraft in the Bat program. Bat was another Bureau of Ordnance project, similar in many respects to Pelican but carrying a thousand-pound warhead and having an active radar transmitter instead of merely a receiver as was the case with the earlier weapon. Because it did not have to rely on a large, search-type radar for guidance, Bat could be launched from carrier aircraft and thus had a great deal more operational flexibility than Pelican. By February 1945, the Naval Air Material Center had completed successful catapult launch tests of an SB2C-1 with a Bat missile and had begun the conversion of forty-five Consolidated PB4Y-2 Privateers as Bat carriers. Bat saw limited combat use in the Pacific in 1945, primarily against Japanese merchant and naval vessels but also against such highly radar-reflective land targets as bridges.[26]

Other conversions took place at the NAF-NAMC during the war. The factory fitted thirty-two F4U-2 Corsair night fighters with radar units and autopilots in 1942. In March 1940, the NAF received an $80,000 project order for the modification of twenty obsolete F4B biplane fighters to target drones. Because of this and similar projects, Captain W. W. Webster, manager of the NAF, recommended to BuAer that the factory be designated for the conversion of all the navy's target drones. Although the naval air stations at San Diego and Quonset Point, Rhode Island, also carried out target drone conversions, the bureau directed the lion's share of the work to Philadelphia. The NAF, for example, converted 47 Vought SUs and

30 Vought SBUs to radio control in 1942–43, followed in 1944 by the conversion of 150 SO3Cs and SO3C-2s, Curtiss observation aircraft that had been withdrawn from service as a result of operational problems.[27]

Of higher priority at the NAMC was the development and testing of guidance and control systems for four-engine bombers as part of Project ANVIL. Since at least 1943, the navy had considered the possibility of using worn-out or "war-weary" heavy bombers as assault drones to deliver large explosive payloads against well-protected targets, but there was little enthusiasm for the idea until early 1944. Then, on 21 March, Captain Harry B. Temple, director of the Special Weapons Section in the Office of the Deputy Chief of Naval Operations for Air, called upon BuAer to investigate the feasibility of such conversions, using a Consolidated PB4Y-1 assigned to the NAMC for preliminary engineering studies. The PB4Y-1 was the navy's version of the B-24 Liberator four-engine bomber, used for long-range patrol and antisubmarine duties since the summer of 1942.[28]

As the NAMC began the PB4Y-1 drone-conversion engineering study, high-level discussions took place in Washington among naval and army air forces officers and representatives of the National Defense Research Committee about the possible uses of B-24 drones against targets in Europe and the western Pacific. The feeling was that the navy's radio-control systems were good enough to do the job and that the drones could be effective. Yet Captain Temple considered a large-scale program beyond the navy's purview, and on his recommendation, Admiral King issued orders canceling the NAMC preliminary study on 27 May.[29]

Work at Philadelphia was held up less than a month. In the army air forces, mounting concern about the threat to British population centers from German missile sites across the Channel led to the establishment on 23 June 1944 of Project APHRODITE. The object of this high-priority and top-secret program was to pack old B-17s with explosives and direct them against the targets by radio control. Because the army radio-control system, known as AZON (for *azimuth only*), had been developed for free-fall bombs, there was less than complete assurance that it would work with a large four-engine bomber. Therefore, planners expanded APHRODITE to include the navy, whose assault drone guidance system was more advanced than AZON. On 24 June, BuAer revitalized the PB4Y drone conversion project at the NAMC, expanding it to include data for the modification of aircraft on a production basis.[30]

Commander Victor H. Soucek was the project officer at Philadelphia. Working round-the-clock, NAMC technicians installed the guidance equipment in the PB4Y (number 32271). The modifications included an autopilot, television transmitter, radio-control receiving unit, servos, relays, and an ordnance control system to arm and fire the ten-ton load of Torpex. Two PV-1s were to function as control aircraft. Soucek recommended that the aircraft not be taken off nolo; rather it should be flown by a volunteer pilot, who, once the airplane was safely off the ground, would check out the guidance and fusing mechanisms before parachuting to the ground. This was the procedure that had been followed by the army with its AZON-controlled aircraft and it provided a measure of comfort for those who were naturally worried about robot aircraft filled with twenty thousand pounds of high explosives circling above English towns and cities.[31]

Part of the NAMC's responsibilities for the project, which shortly received the code name ANVIL, included familiarizing operational personnel with the electronic gear and testing equipment and procedures. Commander James A. Smith headed Special Attack Unit 1 (SAU 1) formed on 1 July to carry out the mission. He and the officers and men under him had already had some assault drone training at the Naval Air Station, Traverse City, Michigan, when they arrived at the NAMC in early July for three days of intensive indoctrination. During this brief period, Soucek's group conducted ground and flight tests. Everything functioned normally, except that during one flight, the arming circuit on the ordnance control board was accidentally energized, possibly as a result of FM radio signals emanating from a transmitter somewhere in the Philadelphia area. There was no time, however, to determine what had caused the actuation of the circuit before the SAU shipped to England.[32]

It is not within the scope of this study to go into detail about the brief and tragic operational history of SAU 1. The general outline of the story is known to most who are familiar with the history of the air war in Europe, and the deaths of Lieutenants Joseph P. Kennedy, Jr., and Wilford J. Willy on the first ANVIL mission, 12 August 1944, as a result of the premature detonation of the PB4Y's explosive payload have been the subject of considerable interest. Attention focused more sharply on the incident with the publication in 1970 of Jack Olsen's *Aphrodite: Desperate Mission*, a popular account largely based on interviews with the principals involved in the project. This book is explicit that Lieutenant (j.g.) Earl Olsen and Ensign James Simpson, both assigned to the SAU, knew that there was faulty wiring in the arming circuit of the ordnance control board in Kennedy and Willy's PB4Y. Yet, because of bureaucratic inertia and indifference at the higher levels of command, they were powerless to correct the problem and possibly prevent the accident.[33]

The ordnance control board was part of the Naval Air Material Center's PB4Y drone conversion package. According to Olsen's book, Ensign Simpson said, "There's a twelve-year-old girl at the pub down the road that could have done a better job of designing this system." Lieutenant Olsen agreed, adding, "It's the worst piece of junk I've ever seen." Among the several investigations of the accident, one, headed by Lieutenant Hugh P. Lyon, surveyed thirteen probable causes, ruling out all but two: "jamming" of the arming circuit either deliberately by the Germans or inadvertently by stray FM signals and instability of the Torpex explosive. There was no mention in the board's report of indifferent workmanship by the NAMC in the PB4Y conversion, even though Lieutenant Olsen was a member of the investigatory body and presumably would have made his voice heard.[34]

In accordance with the Lyon committee's recommendations and similar findings in a report of 14 August by Commander Smith, the next ANVIL mission, flown on 3 September, used a mechanical fusing system and TNT as the explosive. The pilot safely parachuted from the PB4Y, which continued on to its objective, the German submarine pens on the island of Helgoland in the North Sea. Although the drone veered off course at the last moment and missed the target, in all other respects the flight was a success and a vindication for advocates of television guidance and radio control systems for these weapons. Nevertheless, the navy canceled Project ANVIL and broke up the operational unit.[35]

There can be no doubt that a serious malfunction occurred to cause the failure of the first ANVIL mission. Yet can the finger of culpability be pointed only at the NAMC, as Olsen's book would have us believe? Certainly the haste of the PB4Y conversion and the crash nature of the project have to be considered. It is possible that the people at Philadelphia could have wired the circuits of the ordnance control board wrong or made incorrect adjustments to the radio receiver that armed the explosive payload of the PB4Y. It is equally possible that in the rush to get the job done, normally meticulous inspectors could have overlooked obvious faults in the electronic gear. The fact remains, however, that the NAMC, and the NAF before it, had considerable experience with this equipment through the assault drone program, and there had never been even a hint that the arming systems of these weapons or their assembly and testing were in any way deficient.

More balanced and more revealing about what actually led to the 12 August disaster is Hank Searls's *The Lost Prince: Young Joe, the Forgotten Kennedy*, published a year before Olsen's book. The Searls volume is also a popular account, but it shows evidence that the author closely examined the various investigations and reports that followed the first ANVIL mission. Nowhere is there mention of deficiencies at the NAMC. Rather, the cause, as cited in a report by Lieutenant Clayton W. Bailey of 19 September 1944, most likely was the insertion of a safety pin in the arming unit by the operating personnel in England. When an FM signal, inadvertent or otherwise, reached the arming mechanism, the pin prevented a solenoid switch from opening, and that, in turn, overheated and detonated the fuse. Bailey did imply that the radio receiver used in the arming device was overly sensitive and that it probably should not have been open simultaneously to frequencies on two channels. It is clear from his report, however, that field modifications were the most probable cause of the premature explosion.[36]

Earlier than ANVIL and less urgent was another secret program known as Project MIKE. An airborne electronic minesweeping system, MIKE emerged in the spring of 1941 in response to air-dropped German magnetic mines, which at the time threatened serious disruption of American and British shipping. In April 1941, the CNO ordered BuAer to look into clearing mines using airplanes equipped with lightweight yet powerful electromagnets. In turn, the bureau directed the Naval Aircraft Factory to undertake a feasibility study, using the XPBY-1 flying boat then assigned to the NAF as a test bed for the electronic installations. The British experience with a similar device installed in Wellington bombers and already showing results in neutralizing magnetic mines was expected to be useful. Some at BuAer urged the prosecution of the project because they saw possible applications for the aerial detection of submerged submarines in addition to minesweeping.[37]

Project MIKE gestated in the NAF's instrument development section through the summer, finally taking definite form in early September. The electronic wizards at the NAF envisaged an enormous coil or loop, 48 feet in diameter, consisting of nearly 23,000 feet of aluminum strips wound concentrically in layers. The most serious immediate problem was that alumimum could not be obtained in strips more than 150 feet long. The strips thus had to be welded together, which could result in unacceptable cumulative electrical resistance caused by the thousands of joints. Around the coil was an aerodynamic shell pierced by at least four scoops to admit cooling air. Because no one was sure how much heat would be generated by a coil of this size, the engineers recommended fabrication of a smaller loop to obtain data on resistances and heating. A gasoline-powered generator was to provide current. On the ground magnetometers would be used to measure the strength of the magnetic field as the airplane passed overhead.[38]

Captain Ernest M. Pace, Jr., manager of the NAF, sent additional details of the project to BuAer in September. Installation of the coil and related equipment in the old prototype Catalina demanded extensive modifications to the airplane. These included fitting more powerful R-1830–66 engines and alterations to the interior of the aircraft to accommodate the generator and other equipment. Even with more robust engines, the airplane would have to use between 85 and 90 percent of its power to maintain an airspeed of 120 knots; at that speed, range went down to about 440 miles. Pace estimated the cost of the project to be $75,000, exclusive of any follow-on experiments that would likely be carried out with actual magnetic mines. If assigned high priority, the project could be completed within six months.[39]

The technical challenges presented by the project did not deter BuAer from authorizing the NAF on 19 September 1941 to go ahead with the design and installation of the coil and associated equipment. But first, wind tunnel tests were needed to determine the aerodynamic characteristics of the coil. The bureau also assigned a PBY-5 to the factory for the project because the XPBY-1 already there was slated for important instrument, autopilot, and sound-proofing tests. There were not many spare Catalinas in the late summer of 1941 so the bureau warned that it might be some time before the NAF could begin modifications.[40]

Facing the prospect of delays, the NAF and BuAer decided to use the extra time to expand Project MIKE to include more fundamental research. Pace informed the bureau in October that the factory was contracting with the Moore School of Electrical Engineering at the University of Pennsylvania to study the optimal size and shape of the coil and the strength and distribution of magnetic fields. Up to this point, the assumption had been that the Americans would follow in the footsteps of the British, but Pace argued that, under the immediate pressure of war, the British might not have had the opportunity or the resources to perfect their system. BuAer agreed with Pace and authorized a small development contract with the Moore School in November. At about the same time, contacts were made with the National Defense Research Committee to begin a study of the cooling problem.[41]

For various reasons, Project MIKE never reached its full potential. The NAF encountered no major problems with the structural modifications to the PBY-5, but it did run into other difficulties during tests in 1942. One was in the fabrication of the coil itself. As the strips of aluminum were wound into the coil, the insulation around the strips cracked, causing short circuits. This problem became more acute with the buildup of moisture in the coil following a series of takeoffs and landings. Field repairs of the unit were, as Captain W. W. Webster told the bureau in July 1942, "difficult under the most favorable conditions." The aerodynamics of the loop and its shell were not entirely satisfactory, either, seriously degrading the performance of the aircraft.[42]

Alternative schemes, among them using three aircraft with the coil looped among them and a more compact coil located within the airplane itself, did not receive serious consideration by BuAer. In September 1942, Commander Leslie Stevens said that "Project Mike has served its purpose—to have *a* method of electrical sweeping engineered & available. The problem does not warrant further development to get *better* results." Moreover, by that time, the threat from the German magnetic mines had eased, and fewer numbers of the mines were being found. At the end of October 1942, the bureau canceled the project.[43]

Project MIKE illustrated one of the shortcomings of American weapons procurement during World War II. In contrast to the British, who were constrained by limited resources yet nevertheless developed weapons good enough to get the job done, the Americans almost always strove for something better. In the quest for an optimal system, the Americans often wound up with nothing, usually after the expenditure of considerable sums of money and the occupation of a great deal of precious engineering talent. It was fortunate that the Germans did not use their submarines to lay magnetic mines in American coastal waters, for it is unlikely that MIKE or any similar project would have been able to counter such a threat until at least 1943.

MIKE, however, was only one of hundreds of research and development projects undertaken by the NAF-NAMC laboratories during World War II. Under the reorganization scheme of 20 July 1943, the instrument development section became the core of the new Aeronautical Instruments Laboratory (AIL) within the Naval Air Experimental Station. Under civilian head engineer Martin W. Trawick was a staff of about one hundred, who completed a wide sweep of development projects during the war. A few of these were a proportional bank adapter for automatic pilots; a rudder control unit for the Norden bombsight; a true airspeed computer; a remote oil pressure gauge; a vector plotting machine; a remote-indicating gyro-stabilized compass; sextant bubble cells; altimeters; fuel gauges; and new methods of celestial navigation. In addition to these projects, the AIL continued the testing of devices supplied by the army, other government agencies, and private instrument companies.[44]

The Aeronautical Materials Laboratory, which had been formed in 1935, tackled an equally varied smorgasbord of projects during the war. The lab's approximately two hundred people studied aircraft coatings and finishes, elastomeric materials, plastics, and adhesives. AML technicians worked closely with engineers on the TDN and Gorgon projects. Those aircraft made extensive use of molded plywood and other plastic materials, and therefore close attention had to be given to structural adhesives in their design and construction. With greater quantities of intricate and expensive equipment being produced and shipped overseas, it was necessary to assure that those materials arrived without damage and in a generally undeteriorated condition. The lab concentrated on preservation and packaging materials. Research in these areas yielded pliofilm, a plastic wrapping material, and desiccant agents to achieve low-humidity environments for sensitive electronic gear. For aircraft soundproofing the AML studied and developed specifications for fiberglass and a material known as Stonefelt. Important criteria were flame and moisture resistance and the ability of the materials to withstand rapid temperature changes and severe vibration.[45]

One job that involved J. Hartley Bowen and the materials laboratory was in connection with the big Type XH, Mark III catapult and the XPBM-1 flying boat. In 1941, still seeking as much range as possible from the aircraft, BuAer wanted to equip the airplane with six-hundred-gallon fuel tanks integral with the wings. An anticipated problem was that the extra weight of the fuel might tear the wings off if the airplane had to make an emergency landing with full tanks. To facilitate rapid jettisoning of the fuel load, the AML developed a CO_2 system that forced all the gasoline out of the tanks in four minutes. This system, however, raised questions about leaks and the dangerous accumulation of gasoline vapors in the hull as the fuel streamed out near the sides of the aircraft. Bowen's job was to produce a dye and an odoriferous organic compound that could be mixed with water to permit the quick and accurate identification of leaks. On a test flight with the XPBM-1, Bowen and Lieutenant Commander John T. Hayward went through the fuel-jettisoning drill, and a horribly sickening smell permeated the airplane. After landing, Hayward rushed over to Bowen wanting to know "what the hell I'd put in the tanks because he thought he was going to throw up in the cockpit." Bowen replied, "Well, you wanted something to smell, and I figured I'd make it smell. He agreed that it smelled."[46]

Structures research at the AML during the war followed the usual lines of static and dynamic investigations but also included the flight testing of aircraft under radio control to obtain structural data without endangering a pilot. In early 1938, Captain Webster had suggested that television could be used as a repeat-back or telemetering device for data transmission during the flight testing of radio-controlled aircraft beyond their structural limits. A year later, BuAer set aside a modest sum for the program. Webster reported on

The Aeronautical Materials Laboratory in Building 601 included among its many responsibilities the static and dynamic testing of aircraft components. Here a wing undergoes static tests in the spring of 1945. (80-G-483580, National Archives)

the status of NAF flight testing in February 1942. The factory had fitted a Vought O3U-6 Corsair with a target-drone radio-control unit and equipment to record flutter and oscillations of the airplane's control surfaces during vertical dives and high-speed pullouts. Television monitored instrument readings during the tests.[47]

Throughout 1942, the NAF evaluated various telemetering systems in connection with the material lab's structural flight-testing program. In November 1942, representatives of the NAF, BuAer, and the NACA attended a conference at Philadelphia to discuss telemetering apparatus. The AML reported that it had evaluated equipment supplied by the Wurlitzer Company that used five channels to transmit data on airspeed, acceleration, engine manifold pressure, and engine speed. With modifications, structural strength data could also be sent and recorded using the Wurlitzer gear. But the AML was confident that it had a better system using three channels to transmit airspeed, acceleration, and data from four strain gauges on the airplane. The laboratory had also tested television and found that it could transmit significantly more data on a single channel than multiple pickups could on several frequencies.[48]

Based on these findings and tests with such high-performance aircraft as the Grumman F6F Hellcat, BuAer established the structural flight-testing program at the NAF on 4 August 1943 under the code name Project WOLF. With an initial appropriation of $100,000 and substantial increments in 1944 and 1945, WOLF conducted high-speed dive tests of F6F and F4U fighters, the Curtiss SB2C dive bomber, and the TBM torpedo bomber. In some of these trials, the airplanes attained speeds of up to 550 miles per hour, which approached the structural limits of the aircraft and would have placed a human pilot at extreme risk.[49]

By early 1943, the AML routinely used a large altitude chamber for testing materials, component parts, and human physiology at various pressures and temperatures. The chamber, simulating altitudes up to sixty-three thousand feet, showed some of the deficiencies in training and instructions for navy pilots flying at high altitudes. In April 1943, nine fighter pilots from a carrier training group at nearby Willow Grove used the chamber. During the test, they "went up" to eighteen thousand feet without oxygen, staying there ten minutes before some of them showed signs of anoxyia. With oxygen masks on, the subjects were taken to thirty-five thousand feet, where within minutes two of the pilots lost consciousness. Observers quickly revived them, and they suffered no ill effects. The demonstration confirmed that the operating instructions for this oxygen equipment were inadequate and could have led to death or injury of personnel. In a subsequent report, the AML recommended improvements in the equipment, its operation, and navy high-altitude training procedures.[50]

During the war about 125 people worked at the Aeronautical Engine Laboratory, where Kermit J. Leach was the civilian head engineer. There were no major departures in the research and testing activities of the AEL, although the lab enjoyed infusions of money and underwent considerable expansion during the war. Project orders for new equipment and its installation totaled nearly $1.1 million from 1940 through early 1942. By the late winter of 1943, the laboratory faced a severe space and equipment crunch. Captain Webster wrote to BuAer about the AEL's work load and its immediate requirements. Much of the lab's space and equipment had been taken over in recent years by the factory's production division in support of the engine manufacturing program. Webster argued that the lab needed new facilities for testing superchargers and turbochargers, new electrical and refrigeration equipment, two new dynamometer rooms, an engine and propeller test stand for power plants up to six thousand horsepower, and three new engine test cells. He estimated the cost of expansion to be at least $2 million. BuAer acted quickly on Webster's plea, approving an allotment of $2.5 million for the expansion of Building 599 and the acquisition of new equipment for the AEL in June 1943.[51]

In keeping with wartime power plant trends, much of the AEL's research centered on the performance of aircraft engines at high altitudes and low temperatures. In cooperation with the NACA, the AEL in 1943–44 studied methods of increasing the efficiency of engine superchargers, concentrating its attention on airflows through the impeller at high Mach speeds and low temperatures. Calibration of the engine with the supercharger or turbocharger was also important, as was type testing of the equipment supplied by private firms.[52]

One of the big concerns facing the laboratory and the aeronautical industry toward the end of the war was the turbojet engine. The turbojet promised major performance gains over conventional reciprocating engines but raised questions about fuel consumption and the materials needed to withstand the stresses imposed by high combustion temperatures and operation at tens of thousands of revolutions per minute. Turbocharger research at the AEL helped lay the groundwork for studies of turbojets, but it was clear by early 1945 that there simply was not enough room to expand the lab to include the testing and development of the new power plants. Consequently, in early 1945, BuAer, with the help of the AEL, began exploring alternative sites for the establishment of an aeronautical gas turbine laboratory. Eventually the place selected was a large area near Mercer Airport in Trenton, New Jersey.[53]

Smaller labs rounded out the research and testing facilities at the NAMC. One of these was the Aero Medical Department within the Naval Air Experimental Station. Created in December 1943 and numbering only about a dozen officers and enlisted men and women by 1945, the department undertook a remarkable variety of projects in the latter stages of the war. A great deal of the research centered on improvements to the design and operation of oxygen equipment and protective flight clothing. For this work, the Aero Medical Department made extensive use of the AML's altitude chamber. The department also studied the effects of explosive decompression on human subjects, providing the first reliable data on this potential danger to high-altitude, pressurized flight. Lieutenant Commander Donald Gressley, a Medical Corps officer, was first to undergo explosive decompression, surviving the ordeal unscathed.[54]

To a thoughtful observer of events in 1945, the increased emphasis on the procurement of specialized equipment, together with structures, materials, power plant, aeromedical, and other research, provided a glimpse of the future for the NAF-NAMC. Less obvious, as events moved inexorably to the dramatic and portentous climax of the war, was how these activities affected aircraft production and where the Philadelphia-area complex fit into peacetime aviation procurement. External factors, including new technologies, political change, and procurement policy, combined with internal decision making and a series of reorganizations at Philadelphia to push the NAF-NAMC away from more traditional and familiar missions into challenging fields associated with research and development in the postwar era.

Epilogue

Research and Reality

As it entered the perplexing and turbulent postwar years, the Naval Air Material Center was a much different place than the Naval Aircraft Factory had been before the war. At the time of the Japanese attack on Pearl Harbor, the factory had employed about fifty-three hundred people; by September 1945, twice that number of naval personnel and civilians worked at the NAMC. More significant than the doubling of the work force at Philadelphia was the transmutation of the factory into a center with component facilities engaged in research, development, testing, and evaluation (RDT&E). The seeds of change had been planted with the wartime expansion of operations research and an awareness of the depth of analysis needed to direct complex organizations in the development and employment of advanced weapons.[1] Compounding this shift was the creation in 1943 of the Naval Air Material Center and the decision by the Bureau of Aeronautics to end aircraft design and production at Philadelphia.

Despite indications that the NAF would no longer undertake aircraft design and production, the factory continued many of the projects it had on hand at the end of the war. The most important was the PBY overhaul program, which had been taken on as a fill-in following the completion of the factory's PBN-1 job. Upon completing the wartime PBY-5 overhauls in the fall of 1945, the NAF began a new overhaul program, delivering six PBYs in January 1946 and maintaining that pace through the middle of the year. Between the first of July and the end of December 1946, the NAF overhauled another sixty-two PBYs.[2]

The Naval Air Experimental Station and its laboratories continued power plant, structures, materials, and aeromedical research and testing during the early postwar era. In 1946, the Aeronautical Engine Laboratory supervised flights of a Grumman F7F fighter fitted as a test bed for a ramjet engine and completed qualification trials of the forty-five-hundred-pound-thrust Rolls-Royce Nene engine. Pilot safety was another area that occupied the attention of the NAES. The Aeronautical Materials Laboratory installed an ejection seat manufactured by Britain's Martin-Baker Aircraft Company in a twin-engine Douglas JD-1 bomber—the first time a navy aircraft received such equipment. After ground tests, Lieutenant (j.g.) A. J. Furtek successfully ejected from the JD-1 at Lakehurst, New Jersey, on 30 October 1946.[3]

Changes at the NAES came first in the organizations engaged in materials and structures research. These had been functions of the Aeronautical Materials Laboratory (AML) since 1935, but materials and structures work was so different that having both together was more for administrative convenience than for functional efficiency. The expansion of materials and structures research and the growth of the AML during the war led to the division of the lab along functional lines on 16 December 1946. The new Aeronautical Structures Laboratory (ASL) under head engineer John S. Kean took over the structures research and testing previously concentrated in the Aeronautical Materials Laboratory. In the reorganization, John F. Hardecker became the AML's head engineer. Both labs remained under the administration of the NAES.[4]

That organization assumed new form as the navy's research and development requirements became more urgent in the late 1940s. In 1944, planning had begun for the construction of a centrifuge for the testing of human subjects under acceleration and other stresses, and in May 1946 the navy awarded contracts totaling more than $2.3 million for the facility. Because space remained at a premium in Philadelphia, the decision was made to locate the large centrifuge at the NAMU in Johnsville, with groundbreaking on 19 June 1947.[5]

As construction of the human centrifuge went ahead, the navy effected a reorganization of the NAMC. In accordance with a directive dated 13 August 1947, the NAMU was removed from the

NAMC and reconstituted as the Naval Air Development Station (NADS). Under the scheme, the Aeronautical Radio and Radar Laboratory and the Aeronautical Instruments Laboratory immediately transferred to the NADS, with other labs following in later years. One of the new labs established at Johnsville on 24 May 1949 was the Aviation Medical Acceleration Laboratory (AMAL), responsible for research using the big centrifuge. Not surprising considering the complexity of the equipment, delays postponed the operational date of the centrifuge to 2 November 1951, when Captain J. R. Poppin, director of the AMAL, became the first human to "ride" it.[6]

Because of the more distinct orientation of the NADS toward research and development, the station's manufacturing and overhaul activities drifted back to the NAF in Philadelphia. The factory specialized, as it had for some time, in jobs that did not ordinarily attract private industry or that needed to be completed quickly to meet an unusual requirement. One such task was the design and construction of a stabilized launch apparatus for Project SANDY, an experiment to fire a captured V-2 rocket from an aircraft carrier. The NAF began work on the project in June 1947 and shipped the launch apparatus to the Norfolk Navy Yard within six weeks. NAF people were present on 6 September 1947 for the launch from the heavy carrier *Midway*.[7]

Still to be resolved amid the postwar realignment of the NAMC, NAMU, and the various laboratories was aircraft production and the requirements explicit in the Vinson-Trammell legislation. Huge aircraft and engine procurement programs before and during World War II provided more than enough work, but in the inevitable contraction of the postwar years, private industry once again confronted the specter of economic uncertainty. From 1944 to 1947, manufacturers saw orders fall by 90 percent. At the same time, Congress and the executive branch strove for a national aviation policy that would reconcile differences among the competing interests while guaranteeing a sound aeronautical industry as part of the country's defense.[8]

Sentiment in Congress to repeal the two clauses of the Vinson-Trammell legislation considered most obnoxious to industry reflected that concern. One of the clauses was the 10 percent profit limitation that had been imposed on private manufacturers; the other was the provision requiring that at least 10 percent of the navy's aircraft be produced in government factories. Congressman Carl Vinson took the first steps to eliminate the restrictive provisions of his own legislation. Agreeing with critics that the act had served its purpose, he introduced a measure in the House in January 1946 to repeal the offending portions of the Vinson-Trammell Act. In 1947, the House and the Senate agreed to consolidate Vinson's bill with two nearly identical measures into H.R. 3051.[9]

A subcommittee of the House Armed Services Committee held hearings on the bill in the late spring and early summer of 1947. Rear Admiral Alfred M. Pride, the BuAer chief, urged elimination of Vinson-Trammell's 10 percent production requirement. He argued that it worked "to the definite hardship and disadvantage of the Government" and if strictly enforced "would result in Government competition with a private industry which is believed to need all available peacetime military business if it is to maintain itself ready for another emergency in the future." Pride agreed with wording in the bill that authorized rather than required the president or the secretary of the navy to procure 10 percent of the service's aircraft from government factories. In the event of excessive costs or collusion to restrict competition, the navy could, if it wanted, turn to government factories for the necessary procurement. But the service should not be required to do so, as it had been under the original Vinson-Trammell Act.[10]

Members of the committee queried Pride about the activities at Philadelphia and Johnsville and how they fit in with the provisions of the Vinson-Trammell legislation. Pride said that at present neither the NAMC nor the NAMU was manufacturing airplanes but that it was clear the law could compel them to do so. Pride thought that was "extremely undesirable," adding that it was "extravagant" for the navy to manufacture airplanes. "The purpose of the act was to provide a yardstick to check on the costs of manufacture by private contractors. It never served as a yardstick because the methods of estimating costs were different." Instead of producing aircraft, it was much better to use the NAMC and the NAMU for small contracts that were not attractive to private manufacturers, for research and development, and for repair and maintenance. "Such services," Pride said, "would be rendered impossible if it became necessary to use these establishments for the manufacture of 10 percent of the Navy's aircraft and engines."[11]

Although the House and Senate Armed Services committees quickly recommended passage of H.R. 3051, no vote took place before the end of the session. Finally, in March 1948, during the next legislative session, the bill came up for consideration. Senator John C. Gurney, a Republican from South Dakota, urged its swift approval because "we all know that the Government is not now and never has been able to produce 10 percent of airplanes and aircraft engines." But then the measure bogged down. A. Willis Robertson, a Democrat from Virginia, said that the bill, far from being simply a statement of economic reality in the aircraft industry, jeopardized every government installation in the nation. He feared that "the ultimate effect of this legislation will be to take business away from Government yards which they would otherwise secure under the existing law." Francis John Myers, a Democrat from Pennsylvania, wanted the record to show "that I am definitely and absolutely opposed to the bill." In the bitter partisan atmosphere of 1948, it was rare for Republicans and Democrats to agree on any issue, but in this case there was a consensus that the Vinson-Trammell Act should not be altered. Owen Brewster, a Republican from Maine, urged tabling the bill as a "very wise" move under the circumstances. The Senate voted accordingly, and the Vinson-Trammell Act repealer made its way to legislative limbo, never to reemerge.[12]

Nevertheless, the congressional debate had made it clear that naval officers and many highly placed public figures did not favor the production of aircraft and engines by the navy. Further confirmation of this opinion came as a result of the deliberations of the President's Air Policy Commission. Created by President Harry S. Truman on 18 July 1947 and chaired by Thomas K. Finletter, a highly regarded State Department attorney, the commission had a membership list heavily weighted toward private enterprise. Hearings began in mid-September. As had been the case with the Lampert Committee and the Morrow Board in the 1920s, aircraft manufacturers used the commission to plead their case for a national policy to alleviate short-term dislocations and to ensure the long-term health of their industry. They did not seem to be overly concerned about aircraft production in government plants, which during the war had been only a small fraction of the total output, but they were characteristically insistent about proprietary design rights. J. Carlton Ward, Jr., president of the Fairchild Engine and

Aircraft Corporation, made the point that private industry had been more efficient in promulgating aircraft designs: "Under Government auspices, the time it took to generate a new type was longer than it took the private industry to generate a new type, so for the most part that facility was furnished to industry and was turned into a laboratory and did manufacture industry designs under license from industry, rather than its own creative designs."[13]

Naval aviation officers generally agreed that government procurement policies should be adjusted to conform to the realities facing the aircraft industry in the postwar years and resisted continuation of the restrictive provisions of the Vinson-Trammell Act. Captain Lloyd Harrison, director of BuAer's Procurement Division and formerly manager of the Naval Aircraft Factory, presented the bureau's position. Harrison repeated the bureau's opposition to the clause in the Vinson-Trammell legislation requiring the construction of 10 percent of naval aircraft and engines in government plants: "This requirement is presently virtually unworkable. The attempt to comply with it by withdrawing some of the war plants from post-war private use would be a major undertaking in terms of management and personnel, and would result in Government competition with a private industry which is believed to meet all available peacetime military business if it is to maintain itself ready for another emergency in the future."[14]

The importance of research and development to postwar naval aviation was apparent in the statement prepared in October 1947 by Rear Admiral Pride for the Finletter Commission. Pride viewed research and development as "essential to keep pace with progress for the very specific objective of technical superiority in the air." Government agencies, including the NACA and the armed services, had been for some time developing coordinated programs for research and development in such areas as rocket and turbojet propulsion, supersonic aircraft, guided weapons, advanced materials, and electronics. Yet Pride saw a critical lack of government facilities to meet the navy's and other services' research and development needs, and he called on the commission to back congressional legislation to establish coordinating bodies and to fund long-term research and development programs.[15]

The Finletter Commission's report, provocatively titled *Survival in the Air Age*, appeared on 1 January 1948. The commission

Looking west across Mustin Field toward the Naval Aircraft Factory in late December 1948. To the right on the snow-covered field are over-hauled PBYs awaiting delivery. At the lower left are consolidated PBY4Y-2s, the navy's version of the Liberator bomber. (80-G-442988, National Archives)

recognized that the aircraft manufacturing industry was vital to the nation's defense and was heavily dependent on the government for its well-being. The panel called for the modification of procurement policies to stimulate the industry, including retention by private companies of the design rights to advanced aircraft and "in as far as possible" production by the firm that had developed the aircraft. Another issue addressed by the Finletter Commission was government competition with private industry in the manufacture of aircraft. The commission supported the repeal of the 10 percent provision of the Vinson-Trammell Act, which, "should it become fully operative . . . would work to the disadvantage of the Government." At the same time, the commission agreed that there should be safeguards, providing the secretary of the navy with the authority to manufacture airplanes and engines in government plants should it seem that private firms were in collusion to restrict competition, if the prices charged were too high, or if "such use of Government factories appears to be in the public interest."[16]

Although the Finletter Commission report and the failure of the Vinson-Trammell Act repealer did not close the door to aircraft and engine production at the NAF-NAMC, a realistic appraisal was that the installations would continue to stress RDT&E. At the Naval Air Material Center most of the research and development in the early 1950s concentrated on catapults. By the late 1940s existing hydraulic catapults had reached the limits of their capacity, and the new jets, with their relatively poor low-speed lift and engines that did not rapidly "spool up" to maximum thrust, required advanced catapults for carrier launches.

The NAF had under development since December 1944 the slotted-cylinder catapult, lighter and potentially more powerful than hydraulic units. The first of these was the Type XAT, Mark I, the success of which encouraged BuAer to authorize the NAMC in September 1945 to begin the design and development of the slotted-cylinder Type XC, Mark I. Powered by gunpowder charges as was the Mark I, the XC, Mark II followed in the progressive development of the slotted-cylinder principle. The XC, Mark II underwent successful tests in April 1951. Two additional slotted-cylinder catapults designed and developed at Philadelphia were the XC, Mark VIII and the XC, Mark IX, both intended to launch jet-powered target drones. Basically identical, the XC, Mark IX at ninety-nine feet was three times longer than the XC, Mark VIII, accelerating target aircraft to speeds of 192 miles per hour. Authorized in March 1949, the explosive-powered catapults underwent tests in late 1951.[17]

Experience with the slotted-cylinder principle placed the NAF in an advantageous position to follow the British lead in the development of the steam catapult. In 1949, the Royal Navy installed a prototype steam catapult in the light carrier *Perseus*. The device underwent a rigorous testing program that culminated in July 1951 with the first launching of a piloted aircraft from the carrier. In early 1952, the *Perseus* arrived at Philadelphia, where the NAF participated in a series of test shots. Impressed by the performance of the steam catapult, BuAer determined in April 1952 that the NAF should proceed with its development under a cooperative arrangement with the British. The Type C, Mark XI, based on the British BXS-1 but using higher steam pressures, was the result. In a December 1953 test, the Type C, Mark XI propelled a 23,670-pound dead load to a velocity of 156 miles per hour. The *Hancock*, an *Essex*-class carrier, received the first Type C, Mark XI catapults in May 1954.[18]

Concurrently with the development of the steam catapult, NAF technicians worked on a new means of attaching airplanes with tricycle landing gear to the catapult launching shuttle. Normally a bridle connected the shuttle with the main gear, but the bridle went overboard with every launch. On some carriers, a net beneath the forward part of the flight deck caught the bridle, allowing its reuse, but it was still far from a satisfactory arrangement. Another problem, evident during the intense carrier operations during the Korean War, was bridle breakage. Based on an idea of Commander Thomas D. Davies, chief engineer at the NAF, the factory went ahead with the design and development of a nose-gear attachment to the catapult shuttle. Featuring an automatic hook-on, the device promised significant improvements in the efficiency of catapult launching procedures, but it was some time before a majority of the navy's carrier aircraft dispensed with the launching bridles.[19]

Jets and heavy-attack aircraft also presented special problems in the landing phase of carrier operations, mainly because of the airplanes' greater weights and higher speeds compared to their World War II counterparts. The Mark V arresting gear developed during the war proved for a time to be adequate to the task of recovering the first jets, but within a few years larger aircraft seriously compromised the retarding capacity of the Mark V units. BuAer directed the NAF in November 1950 to develop an arresting gear engine with four times the energy-absorption power of the Mark V. The factory manufactured and tested the prototype of the new gear, designated Mark VII, which could bring a sixty-seven-thousand-pound airplane to a stop from speeds of up to 121 miles per hour. The McKiernan-Terry Corporation manufactured forty Mark VII, Mod 1s, similar to the prototype but lighter and capable of arresting the landing of seventy-three-thousand-pound jets. Newer *Essex*-class ships and all *Forrestal*-class carriers were equipped with Mark VII, Mod 1s.[20]

Many of the aircraft used by the navy in the immediate postwar period had tricycle landing gear. Tricycle gear created a potential hazard if the aircraft missed the arresting wires and came into contact with conventional athwartship barriers used to protect airplanes parked forward on the flight deck. In May 1944, the NAF conducted a series of tests with the twin-engine Grumman F7F Tigercat fighter and a standard wire barrier. The results showed that the nose wheel of the airplane tended to draw the cable into a loop that often wrapped around one or both of the propeller hubs. Parts of the wire could be cut and thrown at great velocity through the aircraft fuselage. Worse yet, if the crippled aircraft were a jet, the barrier's main cable could pass up and over the nose of the airplane, tearing off the windshield and canopy and killing or seriously injuring the pilot. Consequently, the factory undertook the development of a new barrier consisting of nylon fabric webbing suspended across the flight deck. The system had three components: a horizontal strap fixed at a height that allowed the cockpit of the airplane to pass under it; another horizontal strap at deck level; and a series of vertical nylon ribbons strung between the two horizontal straps. The aircraft fuselage passed between the vertical ribbons, which wrapped around the wings, decelerating the airplane and bringing it to rest with a minimum of damage.[21]

As the NAF concentrated on catapults, arresting gear, and aircraft barriers, the laboratories of the Naval Air Experimental Station continued their power plant, materials, structures, and aeromedical work. Although much of the emphasis remained on piston engines, the Aeronautical Engine Laboratory placed increasing stress in the late 1940s and early 1950s on testing turbojets under a variety of simulated operational conditions. For icing tests of turbojet engines, the AEL established a facility on the summit of New Hampshire's Mount Washington, which experiences some of the most severe winter weather conditions in North America. Experiments begun in the winter of 1947–48 with a McDonnell FH-1 fighter revealed that axial-flow turbojets were prone to icing, which restricted the flow of air and caused overheating and failure. The AEL's research led the way to improved anti-icing materials and operating procedures.[22]

The work of the Aeronautical Materials Laboratory likewise reflected technological trends in the late 1940s and early 1950s. The 1946 atomic bomb tests at Bikini Atoll aroused concern about the effects of radiation exposure on materials and people. The AML established the Radiological Defense Section in 1947 to undertake projects—most highly classified—in these areas. The lab carried out an extended evaluation of a contaminated airplane from the Bikini tests, concentrating particularly on how radioactivity affected metals, fabrics, and rubber compounds. In August 1951, the lab completed and reported on a study of a radiation protective suit developed by the NAES. The AML found that the garment, consisting of two layers of a material known as Vapotex sandwiched between layers of nylon, provided protection against certain kinds of radiation but did not resist the penetration of gamma rays so that lead flakes had to be woven into the fabric. Related to such studies in 1951 was the lab's work with filters for removing radioactive particles from aircraft ventilators, analyses of cleaning and decontaminating compounds, and studies of portable radiation detection devices.[23]

More in keeping with the traditional mission of the lab was materials testing. The AML evaluated a foam aircraft engine cleaner and a two-part paint remover suitable for varied climatic conditions. Starting in 1946, the lab extensively investigated alloys of titanium, a lightweight, heat-resistant metal that had many of the strength, corrosion-resistance, and tensile properties of stainless steel and was particularly attractive for use in turbojet engines. A promising area of research was plastics. By 1952, the lab had set up the High Polymer Division to conduct research and development in synthetic rubber, plastics, and textiles. Together with continued testing of plastics for aircraft canopies and windows, the division studied materials and fabrics for clothing, parachutes, webbing, and cords.[24]

At the Aeronautical Structures Laboratory the emphasis continued to be on research and development and laboratory and flight testing of aircraft structures and their components. Better to accomplish those missions, the ASL installed a large testing machine in 1948. With a capacity of 5 million pounds, the hydraulically actuated device could test aluminum and magnesium alloy specimens up to thirty feet long and ten feet wide. It enabled the structures lab for the first time to conduct rigidity and compression tests and tests to destruction of full-size aircraft wing panels. Drop tests, a spectacular part of the lab's work, involved lifting structures with a seventy-thousand-pound-capacity crane and releasing them to simulate the dynamic forces of an aircraft landing.[25]

One of the newest labs at the NAES was the Aeronautical Medical Equipment Laboratory (AMEL), created on 1 December 1948 from the Aero Medical Department and responsible for investigations in aviation medicine and the effects of extreme conditions of altitude, temperature, vibration, and acceleration on human beings. The AMEL played an active role in the development of ejection seats for high-performance jets and trained aviators in the operation of the seats using a test tower erected for that purpose. The lab also participated in the development and testing of new crash helmets, improved parachute harnesses, cockpit lighting, and exposure suits. One project with important implications not only for high-altitude flight but also for manned space flight in the next decade was the lab's testing of full-pressure suits in cooperation with the B. F. Goodrich Company and other firms. Input from the AMEL was useful to the development of the full-pressure suit used during Project Mercury, the nation's first manned space effort.[26]

Two other labs were components of the NAES in the late 1940s and early 1950s—the Aeronautical Instruments Laboratory and the Aeronautical Photographic Experimental Laboratory. In addition to development and testing of the usual array of aircraft instruments, the AIL was responsible for the world's first successful helicopter autopilot. Airplane autopilots had been around for decades, but such a device for helicopters presented daunting technical challenges, particularly as a result of the inherent aerodynamic instability of rotary-wing aircraft and the high stick forces involved with their controls. Under L. S. Guarino, the AIL's helicopter autopilot project climaxed with the successful test of a navy Sikorsky HO3S-1 at Mustin Field on 1 September 1950. By the end of 1951 the Aeronautical Photographic Experimental Laboratory had pioneered a device that attached to the standard aircraft gun camera, keeping it focused on ground targets even after the attacking airplane had veered off and permitting more accurate assessment of damage. Both labs transferred to Johnsville at the end of 1953.[27]

For the most part, the NAMC kept pace with rapid changes in the areas of turbojet propulsion, nuclear energy, new materials, and data processing. The tasks were time-consuming, tedious, and required sophisticated and expensive equipment, and the increasing work loads strained the money and staff resources of the facility by the end of the decade. Thus, following successive periods of adjustment and relative stability in the early 1950s, the NAMC and its components underwent further administrative changes as the navy attempted to enhance and coordinate its RDT&E programs in the late 1950s and early 1960s.

Starting in the mid-1950s, the Naval Air Material Center and its subordinate commands went through a proliferation of administrative changes so bewildering that the aviation facilities emerging from those reorganizations seemed to bear little resemblance to the old NAF-NAMC. Yet a continuity remained. For one, the organizational descendants of the NAF-NAMC remained within a fifty-mile radius of Philadelphia; for another, many of the veteran workers from the Naval Aircraft Factory stayed on, some not to retire until the 1970s. Finally, the basic missions—principally RDT&E and ship installations—continued long after the NAF passed out of existence at League Island. This functional link, coupled with geographical proximity to Philadelphia, served as a constant reminder of the factory's remarkable institutional persistence.

Administratively, the alternate addition and deletion of layers of command pulled the NAF-NAMC complex in two directions simultaneously. The requirement for coordination of the diverse activities in the Philadelphia area led to the establishment on 20 June 1954 of the Naval Air Development and Material Center. With headquarters at Johnsville, the new command held administrative responsibility for the Naval Air Development Center at Johnsville, the Naval Air Material Center at Philadelphia, the Naval Air Turbine Test Center at Trenton, New Jersey, and the Naval Air Test Facility (Ship Installations) at the Naval Air Station, Lakehurst, New Jersey. The Johnsville office then became headquarters for the Naval Air Research and Development Activities Command, which superseded the Naval Air Development and Material Center on 27 January 1959. As this new administrative level took shape in the 1950s, the individual laboratories—at Philadelphia and Johnsville, especially—exercised more autonomy than ever before. Often the result was confusion, lack of direction, duplication of effort, and paradoxically a decline in the navy's confidence in its own research and development activities as it increasingly turned to private contractors for such work.[28]

The most significant administrative change affecting the Naval Aircraft Factory occurred in 1956. In the fall of 1955, BuAer, recognizing that ship installations (chiefly catapults and arresting gear) occupied a significantly greater share of the NAF's activities, had considered phasing out the factory's manufacturing, overhaul, and repair functions. On 9 May 1956, following a series of conferences, the bureau redesignated the NAF as the Naval Air Engineering Facility (Ship Installations) (NAEF [SI]). Much more than a name change was involved. Starting at the top, the manager's title became commanding officer, more in keeping with standard naval practice and symbolic of the shift away from the installation's manufacturing functions. The assistant to the manager became the executive officer, again consistent with usual naval assignments. BuAer charged the NAEF(SI) with research, engineering, design, development, prototyping, and maintenance of aircraft and guided missile launching and recovery equipment.[29]

On the heels of these organizational shifts came changes affecting the status of the laboratories at Philadelphia. In early February 1957, the Navy Department dissolved the Naval Air Experimental Station, which had been one of the original subordinate commands established within the NAMC in 1943. Under the new scheme, the Aeronautical Engine Laboratory, the Aeronautical Structures Laboratory, the Aeronautical Materials Laboratory, and the Air Crew Equipment Laboratory (ACEL), all formerly components of the NAES, became independent departments within the NAMC. Not only did the reshuffling elevate the labs' status and reflect the increasing importance of RDT&E, but it streamlined the administrative apparatus by eliminating the intermediate NAES command structure.[30]

Projects undertaken by the labs at Philadelphia underscored the navy's interest in nuclear energy and missile and space technology. The Aeronautical Materials Laboratory, for example, carried out tests in 1958 on materials for a nuclear-powered flying boat planned as a long-range antisubmarine and airborne early warning aircraft. The atomic-powered airplane presented difficult technical problems, not the least of which was the development of dense, lightweight materials for shielding against intense radioactivity. AML technicians used a testing apparatus that bombarded materials with the radioactive isotope cobalt 60. The nuclear-powered airplane proved to be a chimera, but the research and development that went into it provided the navy with a valuable fund of technical information on the effects of radiation and lightweight shielding materials.[31]

The labs played suppporting roles in the early stages of the navy's Polaris ballistic missile development program. Thinking that the relative independence of the labs and their bureaucratic preoccupation with their own projects would hinder the ballistic missile program, the Polaris management people bypassed much of the usual navy research and development apparatus. The NAEF(SI), despite its extensive background in guided weapons launch and recovery and ship installations, was involved only tangentially in the Polaris program, designing and developing the system of solid-propellant gas generators and associated equipment for the missile launching system and Fishhook, a net that arrested full-scale test vehicles in midair before they fell back into the sea.[32]

Nevertheless, the Philadelphia labs did support aspects of the navy's missile and space programs. During the 1950s, the Aeronautical Structures Laboratory was involved in studies of aerodynamic heating. In cooperation with the National Bureau of Standards and the Armour Research Foundation, the lab developed strain gauges that operated at temperatures above 350 degrees Fahrenheit. In December 1957, the ASL sponsored a symposium on the topic. Much of the concentration of the Air Crew Equipment Laboratory was on the development of a practical full-pressure (or "space") suit. This work culminated in the Mark IV suit, which in 1959 was possibly the best available "off-the-shelf" garment. Early that year, the National Aeronautics and Space Administration, the successor to the NACA, called upon the ACEL to evaluate various suits. By July 1959, the lab had completed the evaluation of the Mark IV suit, and NASA determined to use it as a prototype for the equipment developed for the Mercury program.[33]

The Naval Air Development Center at Johnsville received the most publicity during these years in the exciting and challenging arena of space. In connection with the X-15, a manned hypersonic rocket airplane project, the NACA's Langley laboratory developed a complex simulator for pilot training that integrated a mockup of the aircraft's cockpit with the Aviation Medical Acceleration Laboratory's human centrifuge and the NADC's Typhoon digital-analog computer. The result was the capacity by 1958 to simulate operational conditions at all altitudes, speeds, and temperatures to which the X-15 and its pilots would be subjected. During early simulations, researchers found that there had to be a major rearrangement of the cockpit and instrument layout. Under certain conditions, the standard aircraft control stick could not be used; a special console was substituted on which the pilot rested his right arm and flew the X-15 with hand movements alone. The tests confirmed what pilots knew all along but many scientists at the time doubted—that advanced high-speed air- and spacecraft could be flown and that future astronauts would not be mere passengers but active components of the control "loop."[34]

Johnsville's experience with the X-15 program led to cooperation with NASA in the nation's early manned space programs. Acceleration tests with the big centrifuge in July 1958 confirmed the design of the contour couch used in the Project Mercury spacecraft. During August 1959, each of the original seven Mercury astronauts spent about two weeks at Johnsville "flying" simulated liftoff and reentry profiles in the centrifuge; all told, each astronaut spent about ten hours in the centrifuge. The following year, astronauts flew simulations at Johnsville in full-pressure suits and Mercury cockpit mockups in preparation for the suborbital and orbital flights that came in 1961 and 1962. Project Gemini, a program bridging the gap between Mercury and Project Apollo, the manned lunar-landing project, also involved the NADC. During July and August 1963, the NADC tested Gemini spacecraft instrument displays and controls in the centrifuge. In November and December 1964, four Gemini astronauts rode the centrifuge in full-pressure suits through simulated flight profiles. Like the Mercury personnel, each Gemini astronaut accumulated about ten hours in the Johnsville centrifuge before flights in 1965 and 1966.[35]

The Naval Air Turbine Test Center (NATTC) at Trenton, New Jersey, had none of the glamorous connections with the manned space program, but it did emerge as the navy's most important power plant test installation, largely overshadowing the Aeronautical Engine Laboratory at Philadelphia during the 1950s. The NATTC began as the Naval Air Turbine Test Station in July 1951 and moved to a site six miles west of Trenton in November 1955. Activities at the NATTC involved static testing and calibration of turbojet engines and accessories, tests of engines under various acceleration and deceleration loads, and the evaluation of engines under extreme altitude, temperature, and humidity conditions. The center did not have final authority on the acceptance or rejection of a power plant, but its reports and recommendations usually carried considerable weight in determining whether the navy used a new engine or what modifications had to be carried out before the engine went into operation. In one instance, the NATTC found that a power plant required an improved ignition system; in another case, the center recommended fitting an upgraded lubrication system to prevent turbine bearing failures.[36]

There was another administrative change in late 1962 that reinforced the autonomy of the Philadelphia labs and mirrored some of the shifts in the mission of the NAMC. On 14 December 1962, the navy renamed the Naval Air Material Center the Naval Air Engineering Center (NAEC), and the NAEF(SI) became the Naval Air Engineering Laboratory (Ship Installations) (NAEL[SI]), with coequal status with the four previously established semi-independent labs.[37]

The new name did not fundamentally alter the mission of the Philadelphia complex, which remained RDT&E, but the war in Vietnam did generate special problems with which the NAEC had to grapple. By 1966, the war had brought a 40 percent increase in the NAEC's contracts and an expansion in the number of civilian personnel at Philadelphia to cope with the greater work load. One long-term project related to the war was the testing of improved survival equipment for downed aviators. Seemingly trivial but with important operational implications was the NAEC's development of improved bomb-handling equipment for aircraft carriers, permitting the rapid ditching overboard of bombs threatened by fire or nearby bomb explosions.[38]

When the NAEC marked the fiftieth anniversary of the Naval Aircraft Factory in 1967, about three thousand employees worked at the center and its five laboratories. Their activities were as varied and complex as naval aviation itself. The NAEL(SI) continued its work with aircraft launching and recovery apparatus. The Type C, Mark XIII steam catapult, developed by the NAEL(SI), became the standard launcher for the *Forrestal*-class and later carriers. With a length of 250 feet, the catapult could propel a fifty-thousand-pound aircraft to 200 miles per hour or a hundred-thousand-pound aircraft to 144 miles per hour. To land the navy's bigger and faster airplanes, the laboratory was responsible for the Mark VII, Mod 3 arresting gear, capable of bringing a fifty-thousand-pound aircraft to a stop from speeds of 121 miles per hour. This remained the standard arresting gear for the navy's carriers into the 1980s. Development testing of the NAEL(SI)'s catapults and arresting gear moved from Philadelphia to the Naval Air Test Facility (Ship Installations) at Lakehurst. Mustin Field, the naval auxiliary air station adjacent to the NAF and previously the locus of NAF-NAMC catapult and arresting gear evaluation, became too cramped in the 1960s to handle the navy's bigger and faster aircraft. Consequently, the navy ordered the field to inactive status on 18 January 1963.[39]

In the late 1970s and early 1980s, the NAEL(SI) participated in the development of the RAST (recovery, assist, secure, and traverse) mechanism for the navy's LAMPS (Light Airborne Multi-Purpose System). In January 1981, the first RAST system underwent successful shipboard tests. RAST consisted of a cable picked up by a "messenger" hoist in the LAMPS Sikorsky SH-60B helicopter. Placed in tension by a winch on the ship, the cable guided the helicopter down to the rapid securing device, which then mechanically secured a probe on the bottom of the aircraft. Once locked in place, the helicopter could be traversed across the flight deck to one of two hangars.[40]

Another NAEC project was ARAPAHO, begun in early 1972 as a scheme to provide supplemental air defense at minimum cost by equipping merchant ships with flight decks, hangars, and fuel, lighting, and damage-control systems for the operation of helicopters and V/STOL aircraft. A key element of ARAPAHO was modularization of the components to allow conversion within a matter of hours using conventional dockside facilities and civilian workers. Extensive tests at sea took place in 1982, during which four different types of navy helicopters made daytime and nighttime landings and takeoffs. Although the British employed aspects of ARAPAHO in the conversion of merchant ships for the Falklands war in 1982 and other NATO nations have had a continuing interest, Congress failed to provide appropriations for the continuation of the program in 1983.[41]

The Aeronautical Engine Laboratory had considerable difficulty defining its mission in the 1960s. The presence of the NATTC at Trenton and the general decline in the significance of aircraft piston engines threatened to take the AEL out of the mainstream of aviation power plant research and development. Yet the lab was able to preserve its basic expertise in the areas of fuels and lubricants while carving out new fields of research in gas turbine engine controls, combustors, starting systems, and auxiliary power units. Perhaps most important, the AEL took over the testing and evaluation of turboprop airplane and turboshaft helicopter engines, thus precluding any overlap with the NATTC, which continued to specialize in turbojets. By 1966, 95 percent of the lab's work was with turboprop and turboshaft engines. In a reorganization made inevitable by propinquity and the navy's decision to consolidate as many laboratories as possible, the AEL and NATTC merged, effective 1 July 1967, into the Naval Air Propulsion Test Center (later the Naval Air Propulsion Center), with headquarters at Trenton. The former AEL, renamed the Aeronautical Engine Department, however, remained at Philadelphia until 1975, when it relocated to Trenton.[42]

Among the functions of the NAEC's Aeronautical Structures Laboratory in the 1960s were structures and environmental and weapons systems research and testing. The lab studied the strength and fatigue-resistance properties of such new materials as fiberglass and bonded honeycomb, subjecting them to a variety of loading and temperature conditions, and it conducted fatigue tests on the components of the new human centrifuge installed at NASA's Manned Spaceflight Center in Houston, Texas. In its environmental research, the ASL continued long-term studies of aircraft operating with the fleet. Two teams from Philadelphia were sent to attack carriers operating off the coast of Vietnam to gain flight loading and stress data on aircraft involved with strike missions. Increasingly, ASL weapons system specialists collaborated with engineers in the early stages of aircraft design projects to ensure the optimal placement of weapons and internal and external ordnance loads.[43]

As it kept pace with changes in the 1960s and 1970s, the NAEC's Aeronautical Materials Laboratory stressed RDT&E in structural materials, elastomers, plastics, and chemicals. Some of the many projects at the AML were studies of the corrosion and stress properties of alloys, the cold welding of metals in a hard vacuum, and the development of test procedures for reinforced plastics, laminates, and composites. In its evaluation of high-temperature materials, the AML concentrated on exotic alloys of aluminum, titanium, and steel. Nonstructural materials receiving attention at the lab were new elastomers capable of withstanding higher temperatures, corrosive chemicals, and underwater use, fire- and melt-resistant fabrics for flight clothing, coatings for supersonic aircraft, and sealing materials for electrical connectors and electronic equipment. Chemicals included dry-film lubricants that were effective in temperatures up to twelve hundred degrees Fahrenheit, self-lubricating structural materials, and nonpolluting bulk cleaning compounds. AML personnel were active in many professional associations, obtained a large number of patents, and were frequent contributors to technical publications.[44]

Much of the work of the Aerospace Crew Equipment Laboratory in the 1960s and 1970s followed lines established in previous decades—life support equipment, escape systems, and continuing analysis of personnel equipment in use with the fleet. More specifically, the lab studied portable life support systems, regenerative oxygen and CO_2 "scrubbing" systems, improved life rafts and exposure suits, and the ergonomics of cockpit and control layouts. In 1966, the ACEL completed evaluation of a "zero-zero" Martin-Baker rocket-powered ejection seat that permitted pilots to escape from a crippled aircraft at any altitude and speed. The lab used a jet-propelled sled for a spectacular series of tests of the new seat, which subsequently equipped F-4, F-8, and A-6 aircraft.[45]

In keeping with the navy's decision in the 1960s to combine its laboratory facilities, the Aeronautical Structures Laboratory, the Aeronautical Materials Laboratory, and the Aerospace Crew Equipment Laboratory transferred in July 1967 from the Naval Air Engineering Center to the Naval Air Development Center at Johnsville. The laboratories became departments in the NADC, although some years passed before the actual move from Philadelphia to Johnsville was accomplished. The ASL and the AML were the first to leave League Island, and the ACEL followed in 1971. Upon relocating at the NADC, the Aerospace Crew Equipment Department joined with the Aerospace Medical Research Department to form the Crew Systems Department, and the Aero Structures and the Aero Materials departments (along with the Aero Mechanics Department already at Johnsville) consolidated in 1972 into the Air Vehicle Technology Department. The Crew Systems and Air Vehicle Technology departments merged into the Aircraft and Crew Systems Technology Directorate in October 1977. There was also an address change at the NADC. When the Johnsville post office closed in the late 1960s, the center began using the municipality of Warminster as its location and mailing address. All the consolidations, mergers, and name changes marked the reversal of the immediate postwar trend toward functional decentralization of laboratories and a return to an administrative consolidation not unlike the one that resulted in the formation of the Aeronautical Materials Laboratory at the NAF in 1935.[46]

By the early 1970s, the aviation complex at Philadelphia was much reduced in size and mission, consisting only of the Naval Air Engineering Center, which itself had lost three major labs to the NADC at Warminster and which had been moving some of its ship installations activities to the Naval Air Test Facility at Lakehurst. On 20 December 1973, as part of the Shore Establishment Realignment program, an initiative taken to curb government spending by deactivating and consolidating various naval bases, the navy announced the transfer of the NAEC from Philadelphia to Lakehurst, with the NAEC taking over control of the Naval Air Station, Lakehurst. The relocation occurred in phases through 1974 and ended with the termination of naval aviation activities at League Island.[47]

Thus ended a connection between Philadelphia and naval aviation that went back to the 1911 glider of Holden C. Richardson and Henry C. Mustin, two of the navy's pioneer aviators. Though no longer in Philadelphia, the laboratories under new names and in places such as Johnsville, Trenton, and Lakehurst carried forth the legacy of the Naval Aircraft Factory. That legacy was a persistent belief, first expressed by Captain Mark L. Bristol in December 1914, that private industry alone could not provide all the experimental and engineering expertise needed by the navy to support such a complex activity as aviation. As long as there is naval aviation it seems certain that there will be institutions with some links, however remote in time and space, with the Naval Aircraft Factory.

Appendixes

Appendix 1

Aircraft Manufactured by the Naval Aircraft Factory

Type	BuNos.	Years	No. manu-factured	Engines	Maximum takeoff weight (lbs.)	Wing area (sq. ft.)	Perform-ance (mph.)	Remarks
H-16	A-1049-A-1098, A-3459-A-3558	1918	150	2 400 hp. V-1649 Liberties	10,900	1,164	95	First aircraft flew at NAF, 27/3/18
F-5-L	A-3559-A-4038	1918–19	138	2 400 hp. V-1649 Liberties	13,600	1,397	90	Most aircraft canceled
F-6-L	A-4036-A-4037	1919	2	2 400 hp. V-1649 Liberties			90	Improved F-5-L; redesignated PN-6
N-1	A-2282-A-2283, A-4341-A-4342	1918	4	1 360 hp. Liberty	5,900	694	94	First aircraft designed, built at NAF
MF	A-5483-A-5562	1919	80	1 100 hp. Curtiss OXX	2,488	402	72	Curtiss flying boat
VE-7G, VE-7GF	A-5681-A-5700	1919–21	20	1 180 hp. Wright-Hispano E-2	2,100	284.5	117	Vought trainer
VE-7, VE-7SF	A-5942-A-5971	1921	30	1 180 hp. Wright-Hispano E-2	2,100	284.5	117	VE-7SF had flotation gear
VE-7SF	A-6011-A-6030	1921	20	1 180 hp. Wright-Hispano E-2	2,100	284.5	117	Vought built A-6021-6030
VE-7H, VE-7SF	A-6436-A-6444	1922	9	1 180 hp. Wright-Hispano E-2	2,100	284.5	117	From parts for VE-7SF
M-81	A-5701-A-5710, A-5761-A-5786	1920–21	36	1 300 hp. V-1127 Hispano-Suiza	2,068	229	145	Loening monoplane
PT-1	A-6034-A-6048	1921–22	15	1 330 hp. Liberty	7,075	652	96	Patrol-torpedo aircraft
PT-2	A-6326-A-6343	1922	18	1 330 hp. Liberty	7,075	803	100	Patrol-torpedo aircraft
NC	A-5632-A-5635 A-5885-A-5886	1920–21	6	4 400 hp. V-1649 Liberties	27,386	2,380	85	Navy-Curtiss flying boat
TF	A-5576-A-5579	1920–22	4	2 300 hp. V-1127 Liberties or Packards	8,846	930	107	Tandem fighter
SA-1	A-5570-A-5571	1919	2	1 55 hp. Lawrance L-1	695		65	Ship's airplane
SA-2	A-5572-A-5573	1919	2	1 55 hp. Lawrance L-1	810		70	Ship's airplane
HS-3	A-5590-A-5591	1920	2	1 360 hp. Liberty	6,432	803	89	Pusher biplane
GB	A-6059	1922	1	9 400 hp. V-1649 Liberties	70,000	5,894	102	Giant Boat
DT-2	A-6423-A-6428	1922	6	1 400 hp. V-1649 Liberty	7,293	707	104	Douglas torpedo plane
TS-1	A-6300-A-6304	1922	5	1 200 hp. R-787 Lawrance J-1	2,133	228	131	Convertible (landplane) fighter
TS-2	A-6446-A-6447	1922	2	1 240 hp. U-873 Aeromarine		228	131	Convertible fighter
TS-3	A-6448-A-6449	1922	2	1 180 hp. Wright-Hispano E-2			110	Convertible fighter
TR-3	A-6449	1922	1	1 180 hp. Wright-Hispano E-2			122	Racer; from TS-3
TR-3A	A-6448	1923	1	1 300 hp. Wright			—	Racer; from TS-3
Balloon	A-6445	1922	1			80,000 cu. ft.	—	Racing balloon
Rigid Airship	ZR-1	1923	1	6 300 hp. Packards		2.1 mil. cu. ft.	60	Erected at Lakehurst

Aircraft Manufactured by the Naval Aircraft Factory (*continued*)

Type	BuNos.	Years	No. manu-factured	Engines	Maximum takeoff weight (lbs.)	Wing area (sq. ft.)	Perform-ance (mph.)	Remarks
HS-2-L	A-6507-A-6513	—	7	1 350 hp. Liberty	6,432	803	82	Curtiss flying boat (assembled at NAF)
N2N-1	A-6693-A-6695	1923	3	1 200 hp. R-787 Lawrance J-1	2,640		106	Trainer
TG	A-6344-A-6348	1924	5	1 200 hp. Liberty, Aeromarine, or Wright	2,800		98	Gunnery trainer
NO-1	A-6431-A-6433	1924	3	1 350 hp. Curtiss	4,378 (whls) 4,842 (flts)	462	104	Observation plane
NM-1	A-6450	1924	1	1 325 hp. Packard	4,190 (whls) 4,440 (flts)		108	All-metal expeditionary airplane
PN-7	A-6616-A-6617	1923–24	2	2 525 hp. Wright T-2s	14,203	1,217	113	Improved patrol aircraft
PN-8	A-6799	1925	1	2 525 hp. Wright T-3s	13,925	1,217	106	Improved patrol aircraft (later converted to PN-9)
PN-9	A-6878	1925	1	2 525 hp. V-1500 Packard 1A	19,600	1,217	115	1925 Hawaii flight
PN-10	A-7028-A-7029, A-7383-A-7384	1926–27	4	2 525 hp. V-1500 Packard 2A 1500s (later, P&W, Wright)	18,069	1,217	114	All-metal patrol aircraft (redesignated PN-12)
PN-11	A-7527	1928	1	2 525 hp. P&W R-1690s	16,870	1,154	128	All-metal patrol aircraft
XPN-11	A-8006	1929	1	2 575 hp. Wright R-1820-64s	17,900	1,154	128	All-metal patrol aircraft (redesignated XP4N-1)
XP4N-2	A-8483-A-8484	1931	2	2 575 hp. Wright R-1820-64s	17,595	1,154	128	All-metal patrol aircraft
XTN-1	A-7027	1927	1	2 525 hp. Wright R-1750s	9,760 (whls) 10,535 (flts)	886	123	Torpedo bomber
Mercury Racer		1929	1	1 1,200 hp. Packard	5,000		—	Schneider Cup aircraft
XT2N-1	A-8052	1930	1	1 525 hp. Wright	5,282	416	144	Experimental dive bomber
XN3N-1	9991	1935	1	1 220 hp. Wright R-790-8	2,636 (whls) 2,770 (flts)	305	116	All-metal trainer
N3N-1	0017-0019, 0021-0101, 0644-0723, 0952-0966	1936–38	179	1 220 hp. Wright R-790-8 (later, 240 hp. NAF R-760-2)	2,636 (whls) 2,770 (flts)	305	116	All-metal trainer
XN3N-2	0265	1936	1	1 240 hp. Wright R-760-98		305	—	Trainer
XOSN-1	0385	1937	1	1 550 hp. P&W R-1340	5,167 (whls) 5,412 (flts)	378	162	Observation-scout
XN3N-3	0020	1940	1	1 240 hp. Wright R-760-2	2,792 (whls)	305	126	Prototype trainer

Aircraft Manufactured by the Naval Aircraft Factory (*continued*)

Type	BuNos.	Years	No. manu- factured	Engines	Maximum takeoff weight (lbs.)	Wing area (sq. ft.)	Perform- ance (mph.)	Remarks
N3N-3	1759-1808, 1908-2007, 2573-3072, 4352-4517	1940–42	816	1 240 hp. NAF R-760-2	2,802 (whls) 2,940 (flts)	305	126	Yellow Peril
XN5N-1	1521	1941	1	1 240 hp. Wright R-760-6	3,370		135	Prototype monoplane trainer
SON-1	1147-1190	1938–39	44	1 550 hp. P&W R-1340	5,100 (whls) 5,287 (flts)	342	165	Scout-observation aircraft
SBN-1	1522-1551	1940–42	30	1 950 hp. Wright R-1830-38	6,759	259	254	Scout bomber
OS2N-1	01216-01515	1942	300	1 450 hp. Wright R-985-An	5,265 (whls) 5,600 (flts)	262	165	Scout-observation aircraft
PBN-1	02791-02946	1942–45	156	2 1,200 hp. P&W R-1830-92s	36,353	1,400	186	Patrol flying boat
XTDN-1	27873-27876	1942–43	4	2 200 hp. Franklin XO-300s	7,000		145	Prototype assault drone
TDN-1	17292-17391	1942–43	100	2 220 hp. Lycoming O-435s	7,000		145	Assault drone
XLRN-1	36431-36432	1944	2	—	37,764		180	Assault glider
Gorgon II-A	GM nos.	1944–45	21	1 Annapolis rocket	760		550	Canard configuration
Gorgon II-B	GM nos.	1945	4	1 Westinghouse 9.5A turbojet	760		450	Canard configuration
Gorgon II-C	GM nos.	1946	100 ordered	1 14-in. pulsejet	1,688		450	Canard configuration ship-to-shore missile
Gorgon III-A	GM nos.	1944–45	34	1 Annapolis rocket	1,277		525	Conventional configuration
Gorgon III-B	GM nos.	1945	16	1 Westinghouse 9.5A turbojet			450	Conventional configuration
Gorgon III-C	GM nos.	1945	20	1 rocket (more powerful)			550+	Conventional configuration; for NACA
TD2N-1	GM nos.	1945–46	19	1 Westinghouse 9.5B turbojet			450	High-speed target drone
Little Joe	GM nos.	1945–46	15	1 JATO unit	650		475	Antiaircraft missile

Source: This table has been compiled from a number of sources: Swanborough and Bowers, *United States Navy Aircraft since 1911; NAF Cavalcade of Aircraft;* U.S. Department of Commerce, Civil Aeronautics Administration, *U.S. Military Aircraft Acceptances, 1940–1945;* Andrade, *U.S. Military Aircraft Designations and Serials since 1909;* and Wagner, *American Combat Planes.*

Appendix 2

Catapults and Arresting Gear Developed by the Naval Aircraft Factory

Catapults

Type	Years	No. manu-factured	Length (ft.)	Capacity (lbs./mph.)	Weight (lbs.)	Remarks
A, Mark I	1921	3	60	3,500/48	28,000	Compressed air, turntable
A, Mark II	1922–25	27	79	6,000/60		Compressed air, turntable
A, Mark IV	1931–33	35	49.5	6,300/61		Compressed air, turntable
P, Mark V	1927	1	55.5	6,500/65	50,000	Powder, turntable
P, Mark V-1	1927–28	4	55.5	6,500/65	48,000	Powder, turntable
P, Mark VI	1929–38	165	55.5	7,000/65	44,000	Powder, turntable
XA, Mark V	1934	1	49.5	6,300/60		Compressed air, flush-deck (not completed)
XS, Mark I	1933			6,500/65		Screw-type (design only)
XH, Mark I	1934–35	1	34	5,500/45	25,000	Experimental hydro-pneumatic, flush-deck
XH, Mark II	1936	1	55	5,500/65	50,000	Experimental hydro-pneumatic, flush-deck
XHE, Mark I	1936	1	31	10,200/73	12,750	Expeditionary catapult
H, Mark II	1936–37	32	55	7,000/70	50,000	Hydropneumatic, flush-deck
H, Mark II, Mod 1	1942–45	134	73	11,000/70	65,000	Hydropneumatic, flush-deck
XH, Mark III	1942	1	248	60,000/120	900,000	Hydropneumatic, for heavy patrol aircraft
H, Mark IVA	1942–45	117 (total for all Mk. IV)	72.5	16,000/85	223,000	Hydropneumatic, flush-deck (for hangar deck)
H, Mark IVB	1942–45		96.6	18,000/90	233,000	Hydropneumatic, flush-deck (for flight deck)
H, Mark IVC	1942–45		72.5	16,000/85	223,000	Hydropneumatic, flush-deck (for CVEs)
XH, Mark VII	1941–42	1		120,000/130		Hydropneumatic (canceled)
XJ, Mark I	1943	1	86	7,500/83	7,100	Rocket, for merchant ships
XJ, Mark II	1944	1	80	2,100/45	—	Rocket, for LSTs
XEE	1944	1		20,000/90	—	Electric; manufactured by Westinghouse
XAT, Mark I	1945	1	—	—/70	—	Slotted cylinder, for target drones
XAT, Mark II	1945	1	33	300/70	5,855	Slotted cylinder, for target drones
XC, Mark I	1951	1	33	30,000/69	—	Experimental slotted cylinder, gunpowder
XC, Mark II	1951	1	33	—	—	Experimental slotted cylinder, gunpowder
XC, Mark VIII	1951	1	33	350/96.5	40,000	Experimental slotted cylinder, gunpowder
XC, Mark IX	1951	1	99	2,000/192	70,000	Experimental slotted cylinder, gunpowder
C, Mark XI	1954	—	200	39,000/156	—	First U.S. steam catapult
C, Mark XIII			250	50,000/200		Steam catapult for *Forrestal*-class

Catapults and Arresting Gear Developed by the Naval Aircraft Factory (*continued*)

Arresting Gear

Type	Years	No. manu-factured	Length (ft.)	Capacity (lbs./mph.)	Weight (lbs.)	Remarks
Mark IV Mod 3A	1938	1,000 (total for all Mk. IV)	150 (runout)	16,000/85	4,600	First NAF arresting gear
Mark IV Mod 5	1941–42		150	16,000/85		Improved Mark IV
Mark V	1944	300 (299 at Norfolk)	150	25,000/90	16,000	Used in later *Essex*es
Mark VII	1951	1		50,000/121		Mod 1, Mod 3 used in *Forrestal*-class and successors

Source: This table has been compiled from *NAF Cavalcade of Aircraft;* U.S. Navy, BuAer, *Ten Year History.*

Appendix 3

Managers of the Naval Aircraft Factory

Commander Frederick G. Coburn	27 August 1917–15 October 1919
Captain George C. Westervelt	28 October 1919–14 April 1927
Commander Ralph D. Weyerbacher (acting)	14 April 1927–27 September 1927
Commander Ralph D. Weyerbacher	27 September 1927–7 January 1931
Commander Sydney M. Kraus	5 February 1931–8 June 1934
Commander Samuel J. Zeigler, Jr.	8 June 1934–7 July 1936
Captain W. W. Webster	7 July 1936–10 June 1940
Captain Ernest M. Pace, Jr.	17 June 1940–26 December 1941
Captain W. W. Webster	26 December 1941–16 March 1943
Captain Samuel J. Zeigler, Jr.	15 May 1943–27 January 1944
Captain Lloyd Harrison	5 February 1944–24 June 1944
Captain Charles M. Huntington	23 August 1944–April 1946
Captain Alden R. Sanborn	April 1946–July 1949
Captain Joseph N. Murphy	July 1949–July 1950
Captain George F. Beardsley	July 1950–August 1951
Captain Darwin M. Wisehaupt	September 1951–23 April 1953
Captain Harold W. Keopka	23 April 1953–24 May 1956

Appendix 4

**Naval Aircraft Factory Organization Chart
4 October 1917**

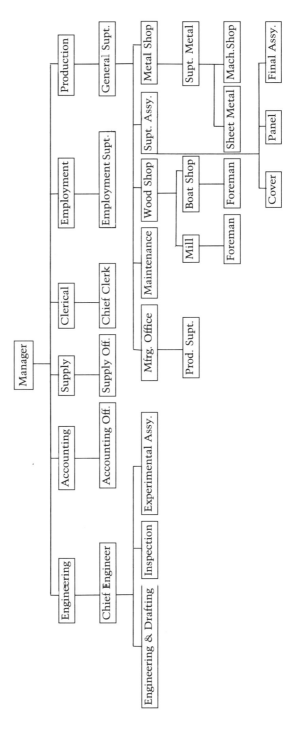

Appendix 5

Naval Aircraft Factory Organization Chart
3 September 1918

Manager

Assistant to Manager

Chief Clerk

Manufacturing — Gen. Supt.

- Mfrg. Office — Asst. to Gen. Supt.
- Plant No. 1 — Supt.
- Plant No. 2 — Supt.
- Factory Night Force — Night Gen. Supt.
- Maintenance — Design
- Tech. Asst. — Hangar

Engineering — Chief Engineer

- Asst. Chief Engineer — Design
- Asst. Chief Engineer — Specs.

Contract Mfrg. — Consulting Engineer

- Exec. Asst.
- Field Work

Supply — Office Manager

- Purchasing
- Material

Accounting — Accounting Officer

Employment — Employment Supt.

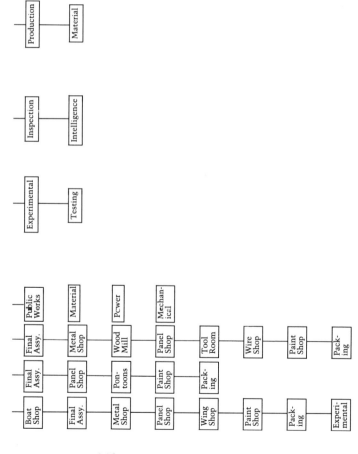

343

Appendix 6

NAVAL AIRCRAFT FACTORY ORGANIZATION CHART
21 April 1943

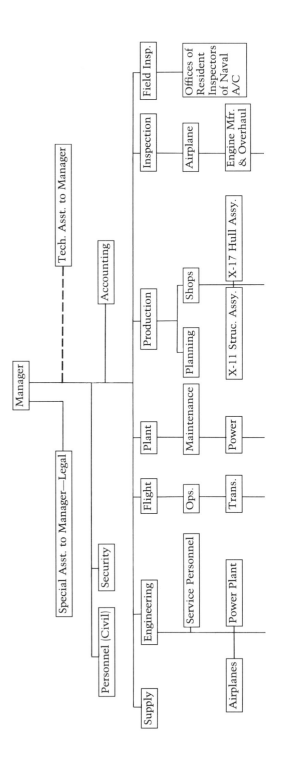

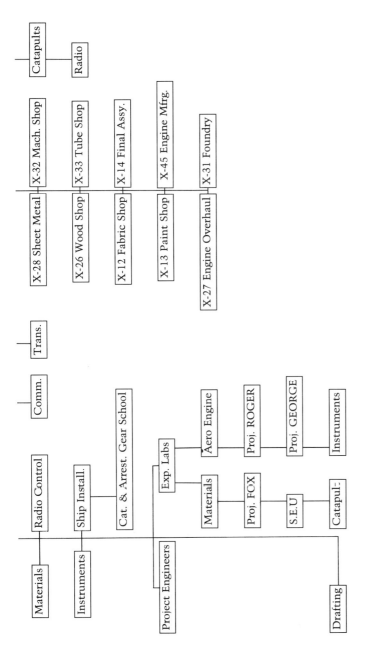

345

Appendix 7

Naval Air Material Center Organization Chart
1 September 1945

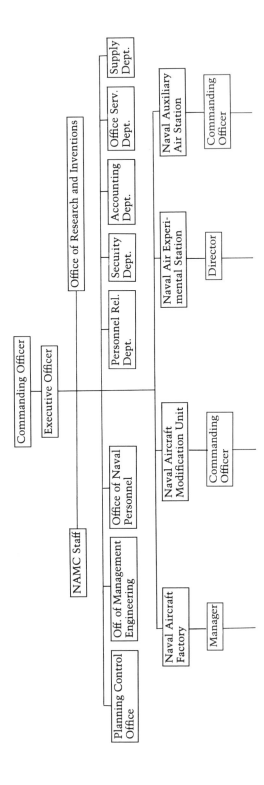

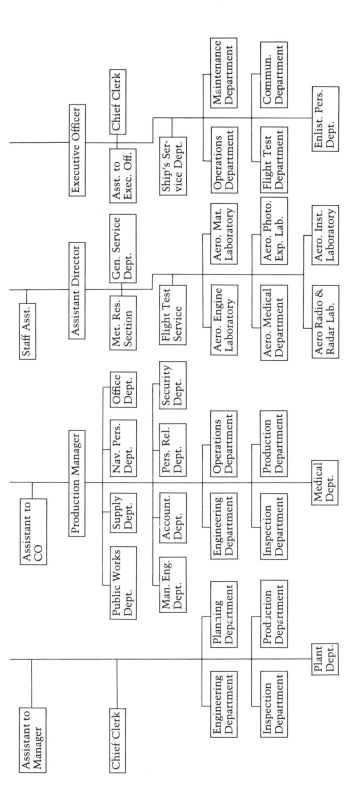

Notes

ABBREVIATIONS

BuAer   Bureau of Aeronautics
BuC&R   Bureau of Construction and Repair
BuY&D   Bureau of Yards and Docks
CNO   Chief of Naval Operations
CO   Commanding Officer
LCMD   Library of Congress Manuscript Division
NA   National Archives
NDL   Navy Department Library
NAS   Naval Air Station
OANHC   Operational Archives, Naval Historical Center
RG   Record Group
SecNav   Secretary of the Navy
USNIP   *United States Naval Institute Proceedings*

INTRODUCTION

1. *Air Scoop* 5 (18 May 1956): 1, 3.
2. McCraw, *TVA and the Power Fight*, 30.
3. For definitions of the military-industrial complex, see Cooling, ed., *War, Business, and American Society*, 4–5.

CHAPTER 1

1. Shrader, *Fifty Years of Flight*, 14–16; Turnbull and Lord, *History of United States Naval Aviation*, 29.
2. Gerber, *Limits of Liberalism*, 81–82, 93–95, 118–19; Daniels, *Wilson Era*, 122.
3. Davis, *Navy Second to None*, 22; Cooling, *Gray Steel and Blue Water Navy*, 165–66, 170–74.

4. Davis, *Navy Second to None*, 45–47; Morrison, *Josephus Daniels*, 59; Cooling, *Gray Steel and Blue Water Navy*, 188–91.

5. U.S., Cong., House, *Hearings before the Committee on Naval Affairs . . . 1915*, 16–17, 278–79.

6. Ibid., 700, 710.

7. Coletta, *Admiral Bradley A. Fiske*, viii–ix; Turnbull and Lord, *History of United States Naval Aviation*, 47; U.S., Cong., House, *Hearings before the Committee on Naval Affairs . . . 1915*, 277–78.

8. Memo, R. M. Watt and R. S. Griffin to Department of the Navy, 14 Dec. 1914, 26983-357 1/2, box 1385, Secretary of the Navy, General Correspondence, 1897–1915, General Records of the Navy Department, Record Group 80, National Archives (hereafter cited as SecNav, Gen. Corresp., RG 80, NA).

9. Ibid.

10. Memo for Daniels [by Fiske?], 19 Jan. 1914, box 500, Aviation 1913–15, Navy file, Josephus Daniels Papers, Library of Congress, Manuscript Division (hereafter cited as LCMD); press release, Navy Department, 27 Oct. 1915, box 71, Naval Aeronautics, 1914–17 file, Mark L. Bristol Papers, LCMD.

11. Armstrong, "Dick Richardson," 32–33; Featherston, "AEDO," 34–35, 40.

12. Smith, *First Across!* 15–18.

13. Press release, 27 Oct. 1915, box 71, Naval Aeronautics, 1914–17 file, Bristol Papers, LCMD; U.S., Cong., House, *Hearings before the Committee on Naval Affairs . . . 1916*, 1:3141, 3594–96.

14. U.S., Cong., House, *Hearings before the Committee on Naval Affairs . . . 1915*, 713; U.S., Cong., House, *Hearings before the Committee on Naval Affairs . . . 1916*, 1:3596.

15. Davis, *Navy Second to None*, 227–31; Jenkins, "Josephus Daniels and the Navy Department," 95–104.

16. Cooling, *Gray Steel and Blue Water Navy*, 203–4, 210–11. See also Freeman, "Armor-Plate and Gun-Forging Plant," 983–1032.

17. Holley, *Ideas and Weapons*, 40–42, 45.

18. Ibid., 45–46, 67, 71–72; Bowman, "Philadelphia Naval Aircraft Factory," 14–15, 17.

19. Bowman, "Philadelphia Naval Aircraft Factory," 13, 25; Coburn, "Problems of the Naval Aircraft Factory during the War," 305.

20. Memo, Joint Report to Chief, BuC&R by Naval Constructors Henry and Coburn, "Proposed Naval Air Craft Factory," 5 July 1917, box 2833, file 28815-1, SecNav, Gen. Corresp., 1916–26, RG 80, NA.

21. Ibid. The estimated cost of the plant in 1988 dollars would be $6.8 million.

22. Paullin, "Early Naval Administration," 1005–7, 1026–27; Weigley, ed., *Philadelphia*, 398, 432.

23. *Pittsburgh Dispatch*, 19 Nov. 1910; *Philadelphia Inquirer*, 21 May 1911.

24. *Philadelphia Inquirer*, 6 Apr. 1912; *Aero Club of America Bulletin* 1 (May 1912): 37; Johnson, *Marine Corps Aviation*, 1–10.

25. Taylor to Daniels, 10 July 1917, 16825-A1, box 2833, file 28815-1, SecNav, Gen. Corresp., 1916–26, RG 80, NA.

26. Daniels, *Wilson Era*, 234, 237–38; Bowman, "Philadelphia Naval Aircraft Factory," 14–15. For an excellent study of the WIB, see Cuff, *War Industries Board*.

27. "Aircraft Factory" (undated), box 289, file 404-Z-3, Bureau of Aeronautics, General Correspondence Initiated in the Bureau of Construction and Repair, 1917–25, Record Group 72, National Archives (hereafter cited as BuAer, Gen. Corresp.

Initiated in BuC&R, RG 72, NA); 10 Aug. 1917 entry, Naval Aircraft Factory Log, Historian's Office, Naval Air Systems Command Headquarters, Washington, D.C.

28. Daniels to Commandant, Philadelphia Navy Yard, 20 Aug. 1917, 28914-736-8, box 2833, file 28815-1, SecNav, Gen. Corresp., 1916–26, RG 80, NA.

29. *NAF Cavalcade of Aircraft*, 4.

30. "How the Navy Builds Flying Boats Ahead of Schedule," press release, 8 Dec. 1918, box 289, file 404-Z-3, BuAer, Gen. Corresp. Initiated in BuC&R, 1917–1925, RG 72, NA; interview with Capt. Ralph S. Barnaby (Ret.), Philadelphia, 12 Oct. 1983; Coburn, "Modern Management Applied to Navy Yards," 955–57, 970.

31. "History of the Naval Air Material Center," 5–6, Aviation History File, Air/Ground Establishments, Philadelphia—Naval Air Material Center, Operational Archives Division, Naval Historical Center, Washington, D.C. (hereafter cited as OANHC).

32. Ibid., 5; *New York Times*, 2 Nov. 1937.

33. Lt. Cdr. E. M. Stark to Lt. C. C. Lohmann, 2 Dec. 1918, box 289, file 404-Z-3, BuAer, Gen. Corresp. Initiated in BuC&R, 1917–25, RG 72, NA; Appendix 7, "Organization NAF, 4 Oct. 1917," "History of the Naval Air Material Center," OANHC.

34. Holley, *Ideas and Weapons*, 55–56; Turnbull and Lord, *History of United States Naval Aviation*, 112–15.

35. Swanborough and Bowers, *United States Navy Aircraft since 1911*, 106–8; Turnbull and Lord, *History of United States Naval Aviation*, 115; memo, "Progress of Naval Aircraft Factory" (undated), box 289, file 404-Z-3, BuAer, Gen. Corresp. Initiated in BuC&R, 1917–25, RG 72, NA.

36. Memo, "Progress of Naval Aircraft Factory," 13 May 1918, 26517, box 289, file 404-Z-2, BuAer, Gen. Corresp. Initiated in BuC&R, 1917–25, RG 72, NA; Hunsaker, "Progress in Naval Aircraft," 250; 22 Nov., 28 Dec. 1917 entries, NAF Log. NAF building numbers relate to all other buildings at the navy yard; number 59 was not the fifty-ninth structure at the NAF.

CHAPTER 2

1. Morison, *Admiral Sims*, 341–42; Turnbull and Lord, *History of United States Naval Aviation*, 115–17, 119–23; "Memorandum of the History of the Naval Aircraft Factory" (undated), box 289, file 404-Z-3, BuAer, Gen. Corresp. Initiated in BuC&R, 1917–25, RG 72, NA.

2. U.S., Cong., House, *Subcommittee of the Committee on Naval Affairs for Investigation of Naval Affairs*, 38; Taylor to Sims, 22 Dec. 1917, box 87, special correspondence file, 1915–18, William S. Sims Papers, LCMD, "Memorandum of the History of the Naval Aircraft Factory" (undated), box 289, file 404-Z-3, BuAer, Gen. Corresp. Initiated in BuC&R, 1917–25, RG 72, NA.

3. "Memorandum of the History of the Naval Aircraft Factory" (undated), box 289, file 404-Z-3, BuAer, Gen. Corresp. Initiated in BuC&R, 1917–25, RG 72, NA.

4. SecNav to bureaus, 25 Jan. 1918, box 289, file 404-Z-2, ibid.; SecNav to Chief, BuC&R, 28 Feb. 1918, Op Air 073–10, box 289, file 404-Z-2, ibid.

5. Smith, *First Across!* 25; Feeley, "Some Aspects of Airplane Inspection," 444–47; Coburn, "Problems of the Naval Aircraft Factory during the War," 316–22.

6. Memo, "Progress of Naval Aircraft Factory," 13 May 1918, 26517, box 289, file 404-Z-2, BuAer, Gen. Corresp. Initiated in BuC&R, 1917–25, RG 72, NA.

7. "The Standardized Flying Boat Arrives—with the Help of Subcontractors," press release, 18 Dec. 1918, box 289, file 404-Z-3, ibid.

8. Coburn to Chief, BuC&R, 11 Mar. 1918, box 289, file 404-Z-2, ibid.; "Memorandum of Progress of the Naval Aircraft Factory" (undated), box 289, file 404-Z-3, ibid.; Daniels to Bureau of Supplies and Accounts, 20 Mar. 1918, 0133-28, file 404-Z-2, ibid.; Coburn to BuC&R, 15 June 1918, 33836, ibid.

9. Memo, Coburn to Hunsaker, 26 Feb. 1918, box 289, file 404-Z-2, ibid., "Memorandum of Progress of the Naval Aircraft Factory" (undated), file 404-Z-3, ibid.; Coburn to BuC&R, 6 June 1918, file 404-Z-2, ibid.

10. U.S., Cong., House, *Hearings before the Committee on Naval Affairs . . . 1920,* 2:2484–86; "Memorandum of Progress of the Naval Aircraft Factory" (undated), box 289, file 404-Z-3, BuAer, Gen. Corresp. Initiated in BuC&R, 1917–25, RG 72, NA; Coburn, "Problems of the Naval Aircraft Factory during the War," 306–8.

11. U.S., Cong., House, *Hearings before the Committee on Naval Affairs . . . 1919,* 1056; Coburn, "Problems of the Naval Aircraft Factory during the War," 306.

12. "Memorandum of Progress of the Naval Aircraft Factory" (undated), box 289, file 404-Z-3, BuAer, Gen. Corresp. initiated in BuC&R, 1917–25, RG 72, NA; Thetford, *British Naval Aircraft since 1912,* 86–89, 197–204; Swanborough and Bowers, *United States Navy Aircraft since 1911,* 114–16.

13. *NAF Cavalcade of Aircraft,* 17; Coburn, "Problems of the Naval Aircraft Factory during the War," 316–17; "Memorandum of Progress of the Naval Aircraft Factory" (undated), box 289, file 404-Z-3, BuAer, Gen. Corresp. Initiated in BuC&R, 1917–25, RG 72, NA; Hunsaker, "Progress in Naval Aircraft," 237–38; Coburn to BuC&R, 15 July 1918, 38470, box 394, vol. 1, file O-ZF-9, BuAer, Gen. Corresp. Initiated in BuC&R, 1917–25; "The Naval Aircraft Factory," 30.

14. Taylor to SecNav, 30 Apr. 1918, box 289, file 404-Z-2, BuAer, Gen. Corresp. Initiated in BuC&R, 1917–25, RG 72, NA.

15. "Memorandum of Progress of the Naval Aircraft Factory" (undated), box 289, file 404-Z-3, ibid.; Coburn to BuC&R, 15 June 1918, 33836, file 404-Z-2, ibid.; Bureau of Supplies and Accounts to BuC&R, 20 June 1918, 74104, ibid.

16. Lt. William J. Lee to BuC&R, 22 June 1918, 935, box 361, file RNAF-Z-1, ibid.; "Memorandum of Progress of the Naval Aircraft Factory" (undated), box 289, file 404-Z-3, ibid.; "Activities at the Philadelphia Naval Aircraft Factory," 681.

17. Taylor to Daniels, 8 Aug. 1918, box 289, file 404-Z-2, BuAer, Gen. Corresp. Initiated in BuC&R, 1917–25, RG 72, NA; Stark to Lohmann, 8 Oct. 1918, file 404-Z-3, ibid.

18. Hunsaker to CO, Queenstown, Ireland, 2 Aug. 1918, 502-Z-1, box 361, file RNAF-Z-1(A), ibid.

19. Lee to BuC&R, 24 May 1918, 753, box 289, file 404-Z-2, ibid.; confidential memo, Office of Aide for Information, Fourth Naval District, Philadelphia, 13 June 1918, box 361, file RNAF-Z-1, ibid.

20. Lee to BuC&R, 26 June 1918, 960, box 361, file RNAF-Z-1, ibid.; Taylor to CNO (undated, possibly 26 June 1918), ibid.

21. Memo, Coburn to Hunsaker, 13 Aug. 1918, 110-Z-11(A), box 4024, vol. 2, file NP 11, Bureau of Aeronautics, General Correspondence, 1925–42, Record Group 72, National Archives (hereafter cited as BuAer, Gen. Corresp., 1925–42, RG 72, NA); Coburn, "Problems of the Naval Aircraft Factory during the War," 317–22.

22. P. N. L. Bellinger to CNO (Aviation), 25 May 1918, 44-10, box 361, file RNAF-Z-1, BuAer, Gen. Corresp. Initiated in BuC&R, 1917–25, RG 72, NA.

23. Coburn, "Problems of the Naval Aircraft Factory during the War," 323.

24. Ibid., 326–27.

25. U.S., Cong., House, *Subcommittee of the Committee on Naval Affairs for Investigation of Naval Affairs,* 157; "Memorandum of Progress of the Naval Aircraft

Factory" (undated), box 289, file 404-Z-3, BuAer, Gen. Corresp. Initiated in BuC&R, 1917–25, RG 72, NA.

26. Coburn to SecNav, 30 Sept. 1918, box 2833, file 28815-21, SecNav, Gen. Corresp., 1916–26, RG 80, NA; Daniels to Manager, NAF, 17 Sept. 1918, ibid.

27. McClure, *Logbook of the Naval Aircraft Association*, 19; Robb, "Navy Builds an Aircraft Factory," 35; "Girls Build Seaplanes for Navy's Flying Fighters," press release, 8 Dec. 1918, box 289, file 404-Z-3, BuAer, Gen. Corresp. Initiated in BuC&R, 1917–25, RG 72, NA; Coburn to Louis M. Howe, ass't. to Ass't. SecNav, 8 Oct. 1918, 58566, box 2833, file 28815-21 1/2, SecNav, Gen. Corresp., 1916–26, RG 80, NA.

28. "Girls Build Seaplanes for Navy's Flying Fighters," press release, 8 Dec. 1918, box 289, file 404-Z-3, BuAer, Gen. Corresp. Initiated in BuC&R, 1917–25, RG 72, NA; Coburn to Howe, 8 Oct. 1918, 58566, box 2833, file 28815-21 1/2, SecNav, Gen. Corresp., 1916–26, RG 80, NA.

29. Coburn to Howe, 8 Oct. 1918, 58566, box 2833, file 2881-21 1/2, SecNav, Gen. Corresp., 1916–26, RG 80, NA; "Girls Build Seaplanes for Navy's Flying Fighters," press release, 8 Dec. 1918, box 289, file 404-Z-3, BuAer, Gen. Corresp. Initiated in BuC&R, 1917–25, RG 72, NA.

30. U.S., Department of Labor, Women's Bureau, *New Position of Women in American Industry*, 47, 74; Greenwald, *Women, War, and Work*, 13, 21, 32–39.

31. Coburn to Louis M. Howe, 21 Dec. 1917, 4772, box 25, Louis M. Howe Papers, Franklin D. Roosevelt Library, Hyde Park, New York; Garfield Bowles et al. to Coburn, 22 July 1918, ibid.; Coburn to Howe, 6 Aug. 1918, 45628, ibid.

32. Coburn to Howe, 4 Aug. 1918, 45610, ibid.; Coburn to Howe, 6 Aug. 1918, 45628, ibid.; Coburn to Commandant, Phila. Navy Yard, 16 Aug. 1918, 44329, ibid.

33. McClure, *Logbook of the Naval Aircraft Association*, esp. 78–94; Weigley, ed., *Philadelphia*, 561.

34. "Memorandum of Progress of the Naval Aircraft Factory" (undated), box 289, file 404-Z-3, BuAer, Gen. Corresp. Initiated in BuC&R, 1917–25, RG 72, NA.

35. Lt. William J. Lee to BuC&R, 24 May 1918, 753, box 289, file 404-Z-2, ibid.; 27 July 1918 entry, NAF Log.

36. Coletta, *Admiral Bradley A. Fiske*, 187–93; U.S. Navy Department, *United States Naval Aviation, 1910–1970*, 35.

37. Coburn, "Data for Bureau's Annual Report," 6 July 1918, box 289, file 404-Z-3, BuAer, Gen. Corresp. Initiated in BuC&R, 1917–25, RG 72, NA; Lt. Cdr. E. M. Stark to Lt. Carl A. Lohmann, 8 Oct. 1918, ibid.; U.S., Cong., House, *Hearings before the Committee on Naval Affairs . . . 1920*, 2:1176.

38. 11 Nov. 1918 entry, NAF Log; Coburn to BuC&R, 1 Nov. 1918, 41860, box 289, file 404-Z-2(A), BuAer, Gen. Corresp. Initiated in BuC&R, 1917–25, RG 72, NA; Taylor to Bureau of Supplies and Accounts, 6 Nov. 1918, ibid.; telegram to contractors, 9 Nov. 1918, ibid.

39. Taylor to Manager, NAF, 12 Nov. 1918, box 289, file 404-Z-2(A), BuAer, Gen. Corresp. Initiated in BuC&R, 1917–25, RG 72, NA; Taylor to Bureau of Supplies and Accounts, 6 Nov. 1918, ibid.

40. U.S., Cong., House, *Hearings before the Committee on Naval Affairs . . . 1919*, 1057; "History of the Naval Aircraft Factory," box 500, Aviation 1917 June–Sept., Navy file, Daniels Papers, LCMD; "How the Navy Builds Flying Boats on Schedule," press release, 4 Dec. 1918, box 289, file 404-Z-3, BuAer, Gen. Corresp. Initiated in BuC&R, 1917–25, RG 72, NA.

41. Taylor to Bureau of Supplies and Accounts, 6 Nov. 1918, box 289, file 404-Z-2(A), BuAer, Gen. Corresp. Initiated in BuC&R, 1917–25, RG 72, NA.

CHAPTER 3

1. 12 Nov. 1918 entry, NAF Log; memo, Coburn to Chief, BuC&R, "Status of Twin Engine Flying Boat Program," 30 Nov. 1918, box 289, file 404-Z-2, BuAer, Gen. Corresp. Initiated in BuC&R, 1917–25, RG 72, NA.

2. Taylor to Manager, NAF, 4 Dec. 1918, 374292-736, box 289, file 404-Z-2(A), BuAer, Gen. Corresp. Initiated in BuC&R, 1917–25, RG 72, NA; 27 May, 25 July, 18 Sept. 1919 entries, NAF Log.

3. Taylor to Manager, NAF, 21 Nov. 1918, box 362, file RNAF-Z-8, BuAer, Gen. Corresp. Initiated in BuC&R, 1917–25, RG 72, NA; Coburn to BuC&R, 4 Dec. 1918, 172086, box 289, file 404-Z-2, ibid.; Taylor to CNO (Aviation), 7 Mar. 1919, box 362, file RNAF-Z-8, ibid.; Swanborough and Bowers, *United States Navy Aircraft since 1911*, 112–13; 28 Jan., 17 Mar. 1919 entries, NAF Log.

4. Swanborough and Bowers, *United States Navy Aircraft since 1911*, 382–85; Taylor to Manager, NAF, 27 Sept. 1919, 0-ZA-24(A), box 366, file RNAF-Z-28, BuAer, Gen. Corresp. Initiated in BuC&R, 1917–25, RG 72, NA.

5. Operations, 8 Sept. 1920, Op 38C-S, box 366, file RNAF-Z-28, BuAer, Gen. Corresp. Initiated in BuC&R, 1917–25, RG 72, NA; Taylor to Manager, NAF, 20 Nov. 1920, box 367, file RNAF-Z-43(A), ibid.; Taylor to Manager, NAF, 27 Jan. 1921, 542393-736-8, ibid.; Taylor to Manager, NAF, 8 Apr. 1921, 52379-629, ibid.; R. Adm. William A. Moffett to Manager, NAF, 22 Apr. 1922, Aer M-2-CK-4/9, ibid.

6. R. Stocker to Manager, NAF, 30 Apr. 1919, box 362, file RNAF-Z-8(A)5/8, BuAer, Gen. Corresp. Initiated in BuC&R, 1917–25, RG 72, NA; P. M. Bates to BuAer, 15 Feb. 1923, G-10/70, box 4025, vol. 6, file NP 11, BuAer, Gen. Corresp., 1925–42, ibid.; Capt. George C. Westervelt to Chief, BuAer, 31 Mar. 1923, 39, box 4025, vol. 7, ibid.

7. U.S., Cong., House, *Inquiry into Operations of the United States Air Services*, pt. 2, 1379; Swanborough and Bowers, *United States Navy Aircraft since 1911*, 284–85.

8. Swanborough and Bowers, *United States Navy Aircraft since 1911*, 454; Taylor to Manager, NAF, 17 Mar. 1921, CR715 Bu-18, 404-Z-1 (A) 4/14, box 4025, vol. 5, file NP 11, BuAer, Gen. Corresp., 1925–42, RG 72, NA; memo to Chief Engineer, NAF, 16 Aug. 1919, box 365, file RNAF-Z-21, BuAer, Gen. Corresp. Initiated in BuC&R, 1917–25, ibid.; Moffett to Manager, NAF, 23 Aug. 1922, RNAF-0, Aer-M-11-QL, O-A-26, box 361, ibid.; Daniels to Chief, BuC&R, 14 Jan. 1921, Op 29-DS-1/12, 3146-69, box 368, file RNAF-Z-47, ibid.; Supply Officer, NAF to CNO, 2 Aug. 1922, 9693, box 369, ibid.

9. Smith, *First Across!* 16–17, 23, 29, 163–75.

10. U.S., Cong., House, *Hearings before the Committee on Naval Affairs . . . 1920*, 1:1621, 1624; CNO to Chief, BuC&R, 17 July 1920, 3084-24, box 393, vol. 13, file O-ZF-5, BuAer, Gen. Corresp. initiated in BuC&R, 1917–25, RG 72, NA; Westervelt to Hunsaker, 1 Apr. 1920, 6056, box 419, vol. 1, file O-ZR-4, ibid.; Westervelt to BuC&R, 29 Mar. 1921, 88, box 393, vol. 13, file O-ZF-5, ibid.; Lt. Cdr. P. N. L. Bellinger to Hunsaker, 15 Jan. 1921, ibid.

11. "History of the Naval Aircraft Factory," box 500, Aviation file, 1917 June–Sept., Navy file, Daniels Papers, LCMD; Coburn to Bureau of Steam Engineering, Bureau of Ordnance, Bureau of Navigation, BuC&R, 16 June 1919, 19732-A, box 4024, vol. 2, file NP 11, BuAer, Gen. Corresp., 1925–42, RG 72, NA; 27 Aug. 1919 entry, NAF Log.

12. Data for annual report, BuC&R, 15 July 1919, box 289, file 404-Z-3, BuAer,

Gen. Corresp. Initiated in BuC&R, 1917–25, RG 72, NA; U.S., Cong., House, *Inquiry into Operations of the United States Air Services*, pt. 2, 1369.

13. U.S., Cong., House, *Hearings before the Committee on Naval Affairs . . . 1920*, 1:1641.

14. Westervelt to Ass't. SecNav, 23 Mar. 1920, box 4025, vol. 4, file NP 11, BuAer, Gen. Corresp., 1925–42, RG 72, NA; U.S., Cong., House, *Inquiry into Operations of the United States Air Services*, pt. 2, 1498.

15. Coburn, "Problems of the Naval Aircraft Factory during the War," 314, 331–32.

16. Memo, Westervelt to Hunsaker, 13 June 1919, box 365, file RNAF-Z-17, BuAer, Gen. Corresp. Initiated in BuC&R, 1917–25, RG 72, NA; 12 Feb. 1919 entry, NAF Log.

17. Memo, Hunsaker to Bureau of Steam Engineering, 19 May 1919, box 364, file RNAF-Z-17, BuAer, Gen. Corresp. Initiated in BuC&R, 1917–25, RG 72, NA; NAF to Chief, BuC&R, 19 Oct. 1920, box 365, ibid.

18. U.S., Cong., House, *Hearings before the Committee on Naval Affairs . . . 1920–21*, 348–49; W. D. Clark, memo for files, 1 Jan. 1923, box 365, file RNAF-Z-17, BuAer, Gen. Corresp. Initiated in BuC&R, 1917–25, RG 72, NA; Moffett to NAF, 11 Jan. 1923, RNAF-2-17 Aer-M-15-FAM, ibid.

19. CNO (Aviation) to BuC&R, 2 Dec. 1918, 0146–975, box 363, file RNAF-Z-11, BuAer, Gen. Corresp. Initiated in BuC&R, 1917–25, RG 72, NA; *NAF Cavalcade of Aircraft*, 18–19.

20. Taylor to CNO, 19 Apr. 1921, O-ZG-1, RNAF-Z-51 (A), file 449, 1-Jan-20–30-Jun-20, General Board Records, OANHC; D'Orcy, "Curtiss Marine Flying Trophy Race," 492.

21. *NAF Cavalcade of Aircraft*, 31–32.

22. Taylor to SecNav, 10 Oct. 1919, box 400, file O-ZF-21, BuAer, Gen. Corresp. Initiated in BuC&R, 1917–25, RG 72, NA; memo, Ens. J. M. McCarthy to Hunsaker, 6 June 1919, box 400, file O-ZF-18, ibid.; Thetford, *British Naval Aircraft since 1912*, 406; Gordon, "Naval Aircraft Factory Giant Boat," 12.

23. Memo, Richardson to Hunsaker, 25 Aug. 1919, "General Specifications for Giant Seaplanes," box 400, file O-ZF-18, BuAer, Gen. Corresp. Initiated in BuC&R, 1917–25, RG 72, NA.

24. BuC&R and Bureau of Steam Engineering to SecNav, 23 Apr. 1920, box 400, file O-ZF-21, BuAer, Gen. Corresp. Initiated in BuC&R, 1917–25, RG 72, NA; memo, Taylor to Moffett, 27 July 1921, RNAF-Z-4, ibid.; *Daily Aviation News Bulletin* 1 (8 June 1920):1; U.S., Cong., House, *Inquiry into Operations of the United States Air Services*, pt. 2, 1375. Specifications are from Gordon, "Naval Aircraft Factory Giant Boat," 34.

25. "Gallaudet Multiple Drive Tested," 279; Gordon, "Naval Aircraft Factory Giant Boat," 12–13, 34; U.S., Cong., House, *Inquiry into Operations of the United States Air Services*, pt. 2, 1375.

26. Gordon, "Naval Aircraft Factory Giant Boat," 17–18; memo of telephone conversation, Hunsaker and Richardson, 3 Nov. 1920, 404-Z-1 O-Z-51(A), box 4025, file NP 11, BuAer, Gen. Corresp., 1925–42, RG 72, NA; U.S., Cong., House, *Hearings before the Committee on Naval Affairs . . . 1920*, 1:1620; U.S., Cong., House, *Inquiry into Operations of the United States Air Services*, pt. 2, 1375.

27. Taylor to Moffett, 27 July 1921, RNAF-Z-4, box 400, file O-ZF-21, BuAer, Gen. Corresp. Initiated in BuC&R, 1917–25, RG 72, NA.

28. *Aviation* 12 (30 Jan. 1922): 143; Gordon, "Naval Aircraft Factory Giant Boat," 23.

29. Smith, "Intercontinental Airliner," 428–49.

30. 8 Oct. 1919 entry, NAF Log.

31. 28 Oct. 1919 entry, ibid.; Barnaby interview, 12 Oct. 1983; Bowman, "Philadelphia Naval Aircraft Factory," 45–46. Biographical information on Westervelt is in Leary, *Dragon's Wings,* 39–41.

32. Bowman, "Philadelphia Naval Aircraft Factory," 32–33, 46; Westervelt to [?], 8 Nov. 1919, box 289, file 404-Z-2, BuAer, Gen. Corresp. Initiated in BuC&R, 1917–25, RG 72, NA; *Naval Aircraft Factory, Philadelphia, Manual Prepared by Lt. R. S. Barnaby, 1920–1921.*

33. Robinson and Keller, *Up Ship!,* xi–xii; U.S., Cong., House, *Hearings before the Committee on Naval Affairs . . . 1919,* 1000–1001, 1057–58.

34. Taylor to Manager, NAF, 20 Nov. 1918, box 363, file RNAF-Z-10, BuAer, Gen. Corresp. Initiated in BuC&R, 1917–25, RG 72, NA; memo, C. P. Burgess, BuC&R, 2 May 1919, box 362, ibid.; Taylor to Manager, NAF, 21 May 1920, box 367, file RNAF-Z-35, ibid.

35. Robinson and Keller, *Up Ship!* 50–51, 63; Taylor to Manager, NAF, 23 Aug. 1919, O-ZR-O(A) 601-Z-1, box 419, vol. 1, file O-ZR-4, BuAer, Gen. Corresp. Initiated in BuC&R, 1917–25, RG 72, NA.

36. Westervelt to Chief, BuC&R, 23 July 1920, 11800, box 419, vol. 2, file O-ZR-4, BuAer, Gen. Corresp. Initiated in BuC&R, 1917–25, RG 72, NA; Taylor to Manager, NAF, 22 Mar. 1920, vol. 1, ibid.; memo, Lt. Cdr. Garland Fulton to Chief, BuAer, 9 Aug. 1921, box 420, vol. 4, ibid.; memo for files, Starr Truscott, 3 Jan. 1920, box 419, vol. 1, ibid.

37. Robinson and Keller, *Up Ship!* 59–60; Taylor to Director of Air Service, U.S. Army, 18 Dec. 1919, O-ZR-O(A), box 419, vol. 1, file O-ZR-4, BuAer, Gen. Corresp. Initiated in BuC&R, 1917–25, RG 72, NA; Design Memo No. 3 by Starr Truscott, 17 June 1922, Aer-M-13-MF, box 421, vol. 6, ibid.; *Daily Aviation News Bulletin* 1 (15 Dec. 1919):1; ibid. 1 (3 Sept. 1920):1; Westervelt to Chief, BuC&R, 13 Jan. 1921, 3909, box 420, vol. 3, BuAer, Gen. Corresp. Initiated in BuC&R, 1917–25, RG 72, NA.

38. Robinson and Keller, *Up Ship!* 64, 68–69; memo for files, H. B. Sanford, 25 May 1922, box 421, vol. 6, file O-ZR-4, BuAer, Gen. Corresp. Initiated in BuC&R, 1917–25, RG 72, NA; Weyerbacher to Chief, BuAer, 27 Jan. 1922, 3851, box 420, vol. 5, ibid.; H. B. Sanford to Supply Officer, NAF, 8 Nov. 1922, 18111, box 422, vol. 8, ibid.

CHAPTER 4

1. *Aircraft Year Book, 1920,* 82. Portions of this chapter appeared in the author's "The Naval Aircraft Factory, the American Aviation Industry, and Government Competition, 1919–1928," *Business History Review* 60 (Summer 1986): 175–98. Reprinted with permission.

2. Rae, *Climb to Greatness,* 1–3; memo, Coburn to BuC&R, 25 Nov. 1918, box 289, file 404-Z-2, BuAer, Gen. Corresp. Initiated in BuC&R, 1917–25, RG 72, NA.

3. The best overview of military aircraft procurement policies and problems is Holley, *Buying Aircraft,* 80–87.

4. Mingos, "Birth of an Industry," 46–47; *Aircraft Year Book, 1920,* 120–22.

5. U.S., Cong., House, *Hearings before the Committee on Naval Affairs . . . 1920,* 1:1610.

6. Ibid., 1610–11, 1634.

7. Ibid., 1634, 1637.

8. Mingos, "Birth of an Industry," 54. For McCook Field-built aircraft in 1919–23, see *Aviation* 18 (26 Jan. 1925): 102–3.

9. Freudenthal, *Aviation Business*, 41–42; Holley, *Buying Aircraft*, 83–84.

10. Memo of conference, 4 Jan. 1921, box 4025, vol. 4, file 404-Z-1(A), file NP 11, BuAer, Gen. Corresp., 1925–42, RG 72, NA; U.S., Cong., House, *Hearings before the Committee on Naval Affairs . . . 1921*, 31–32.

11. Turnbull and Lord, *History of United States Naval Aviation*, 158–59, 186–87.

12. Ibid., 176–85.

13. U.S., Cong., House, *Hearings before the Committee on Naval Affairs . . . 1921*, 94–95.

14. *Aviation* 10 (4 Apr. 1921): 432; Turnbull and Lord, *History of United States Naval Aviation*, 189; Starr, ed., *Dictionary of American Biography, Supplement One*, 21:560–61. Arpee, *From Frigates to Flat-Tops*, is neither a critical nor a reliable biography.

15. Memo, Taylor to Ass't. SecNav, 12 July 1921, box 4025, vol. 6, file NP 11, BuAer, Gen. Corresp., 1925–42, RG 72, NA.

16. Memo, Taylor to Moffett, 22 Aug. 1921, file 404-Z-3(A), ibid.

17. Memo, Hunsaker to Moffett, 21 Oct. 1921, ibid.

18. Bowman, "Philadelphia Naval Aircraft Factory," 56–57; memo, Moffett to SecNav, 9 Jan. 1922, Aer-M-BB, box 4026, vol. 7, file NP 11, BuAer, Gen. Corresp., 1925–42, RG 72, NA.

19. Pearson, "Notes on the History of the Naval Aircraft Factory," 4, emphasizes Moffett's political motives in ending aircraft production at Philadelphia.

20. Moffett to SecNav, 20 Dec. 1923, Aer-M-1-QL, 404–1, box 2833, file 28815–83 1/2, SecNav, Gen. Corresp., 1916–26, RG 80, NA.

21. Moffett to SecNav, 30 Dec. 1922, Aer-M-12-AQ, 22–14, 404–1, box 4025, vol. 6, file NP 11, BuAer, Gen. Corresp., 1925–42, RG 72, NA; Bowman, "Philadelphia Naval Aircraft Factory," 58–59.

22. Holley, *Buying Aircraft*, 85–87.

23. U.S., Cong., House, *Inquiry into Operations of the United States Air Services*, pt. 2, 1388; "Publisher's News Letter," *Aviation* 17 (15 Dec. 1924): 1413.

24. U.S., President's Aircraft Board, *Hearings before the President's Aircraft Board*, 4: 1413, 1416; Mingos, "Birth of an Industry," 61–62.

25. Turnbull and Lord, *History of United States Naval Aviation*, 240–43.

26. U.S., Cong., House, *Inquiry into Operations of the United States Air Services*, pt. 2, 918, 931, 937.

27. Ibid., 1002–3.

28. Ibid., 1124.

29. Ibid., 1496–97.

30. Ibid., 1498–99.

31. Land to Robinson, 7 Feb. 1925, Aer-M-BB, 404–1, box 4026, vol. 8, file NP 11, BuAer, Gen. Corresp., 1925–42, RG 72, NA.

32. U.S., Cong., House, *Report of the Select Committee of Inquiry into Operations of the United States Air Services*, 2, 3–4, 8, 15–16.

33. U.S., President's Aircraft Board, *Hearings before the President's Aircraft Board*, 1:205–6, 247.

34. Ibid., 2: 805–7, 4: 1662–64.

35. Ibid., 4: 1412–39.

36. Ibid., 1650–52.

37. U.S., President's Aircraft Board, *Aircraft in National Defense*, 6–10, 26–29.

38. U.S., President's Aircraft Board, *Hearings before the President's Aircraft Board*, 2: 771–72, 778.

39. Bowman, "Philadelphia Naval Aircraft Factory," 83–84; Featherston, "AEDO," 42–43.

40. Robinson and Keller, *Up Ship!* 63.

41. Weyerbacher, "Proposed Functions of the Naval Aircraft Factory," 2428–31.

42. Ibid., 2431–33.

43. Weyerbacher to Commandant, Phila. Navy Yard, 19 June 1928, L9/NAF(7490), box 4026, vol. 9, file NP 11, BuAer, Gen. Corresp., 1925–42, RG 72, NA; Land to Commandant, Phila. Navy Yard, 20 July 1928, Aer-M-152 SP, ibid.

44. Magruder to SecNav, 25 Oct. 1926, NP-11/OH-4/AS-1, box 4026, vol. 9, ibid.

45. Moffett to Ass't. SecNav (Navy Yard Division), 2 Dec. 1926, ibid.; Moffett to Wilbur, 17 Dec. 1926, Aer-GB, ibid.

46. Moffett to Magruder, 9 Sept. 1927, WAM-GB, William Adger Moffett Papers, Nimitz Library, U.S. Naval Academy, Annapolis, Md.; Magruder to Moffett, 10 Sept. 1927, ibid.

47. Rae, *Climb to Greatness*, 22–23; Bowman, "Philadelphia Naval Aircraft Factory," 88.

CHAPTER 5

1. Moffett to Manager, NAF, 9 Feb. 1922, Aer-M-1-QL, box 370, file RNAF-Z-62, BuAer, Gen. Corresp. Initiated in BuC&R, 1917–25, RG 72, NA; *NAF Cavalcade of Aircraft*, 41–42; Swanborough and Bowers, *United States Navy Aircraft since 1911*, 159–60; Smith, *Aircraft Piston Engines*, 105–6.

2. U.S., President's Aircraft Board, *Hearings before the President's Aircraft Board*, 4:1407; Swanborough and Bowers, *United States Navy Aircraft since 1911*, 161; *NAF Cavalcade of Aircraft*, 56.

3. Westervelt to CNO, 17 Nov. 1923, 17915, box 2833, file 28815-77, SecNav, Gen. Corresp., 1916–26, RG 80, NA; *NAF Cavalcade of Aircraft*, 47–52; Swanborough and Bowers, *United States Navy Aircraft since 1911*, 455.

4. Swanborough and Bowers, *United States Navy Aircraft since 1911*, 314; Moffett to Manager, NAF, 19 Dec. 1927, Aer-M-157-MV, box 5488, file VT2N1/F1-1, BuAer, Gen. Corresp., 1925–42, RG 72, NA; memo, H. C. Richardson for Mr. Clark, BuAer, 14 Jan. 1928, HCR/AQ, ibid.; Weyerbacher to Chief, BuAer, 26 July 1928, XT2N1/L9 (7395), ibid.

5. Capt. H. C. Richardson (by direction, Chief, BuAer) to Manager, NAF, 12 Dec. 1928, Aer-D-153-SP, VT2N1/F1-1, box 5488, file VT2N1/F1-1, BuAer, Gen. Corresp., 1925–42, RG 72, NA; Lt. Cdr. J. E. Ostrander, Jr., memo for files, 22 Mar. 1929, Aer-D-158-MDB, ibid.; Weyerbacher to Chief, BuAer, 7 Nov. 1929, VXT2N1/L9/F1-1 (14806), ibid.; Weyerbacher to Chief, BuAer, 2 Apr. 1930, VXT2N1/L9 (5543), ibid.; A. H. Douglas (CO, NAS Anacostia) to Chief, BuAer, 27 Sept. 1930, VT2N-1/NA6, ibid.; Swanborough and Bowers, *United States Navy Aircraft since 1911*, 314.

6. Weyerbacher, "Metal Construction of Aircraft," 489–93; "Large All-Metal Seaplanes," 397.

7. U.S., Cong., House, *Inquiry into Operations of United States Air Services*, pt. 2, 1602–3; Weyerbacher, "Proposed Functions of the Naval Aircraft Factory," 2433; Weyerbacher, "Metal Construction of Aircraft," 489–90.

8. Weyerbacher, "Metal Construction of Aircraft," 493; U.S., Cong., House, *Hearings before the Committee on Naval Affairs . . . 1920–21*, 350–51, 354; Schatzberg, "In Defense of the Wooden Airplane," 21.

9. "Large All-Metal Seaplanes," 396; Miller and Seiler, "Design of Metal Airplanes," 210–14.

10. Daniels, "Duralumin," 751–52.

11. U.S., Cong., House, *Hearings before the Committee on Naval Affairs . . . 1920–21*, 348–51; Taylor to CNO, 10 June 1921, CR 100 Bu-21, box 400, file O-ZF-24, BuAer, Gen. Corresp. Initiated in BuC&R, 1917–25, RG 72, NA; Hunsaker to Manager, NAF, 8 July 1922, Aer-M-15-WZ, ibid.; "Dornier 'Falke' Fighter," 451–52; *New York Times*, 15 Sept. 1929 (Matthew E. Rodina, Jr., brought to my attention the NAF's assembly of the Super Wals).

12. Richardson, "Development in Naval Aeronautics," 662–64.

13. Ibid., 664–66.

14. McCarthy, "Notes on Metal Wing Construction," 10; "Successful Design of Light Weight Metal Wings," 38–41.

15. Miller, "Metal Aircraft," 584–85; H. C. Mustin (by direction, Chief, BuAer) to Manager, NAF, 6 Apr. 1922, Aer-M-1-QL RNAF-44 601-1; Westervelt to Chief, BuAer, 20 Dec. 1924, 14929; Westervelt to Chief, BuAer. 7 Feb. 1925, 2636 (these documents were made available to the author by William J. Armstrong of the Historian's Office, Naval Air Systems Command Headquarters).

16. Richardson, "Development in Naval Aeronautics," 685.

17. Richardson, "Prevention of Corrosion in Duralumin Aircraft Structures," 24–25; Richardson, "Development in Naval Aeronautics," 677–78.

18. Miller, "Metal Aircraft," 584–85; Richardson, "Prevention of Corrosion in Duralumin Aircraft Structures," 25–26; U.S. Navy Department, *United States Naval Aviation, 1910–1980*, 64.

19. Rawdon, "Corrosion Embrittlement of Duralumin"; Miller, "Metal Aircraft," 384; Robinson and Keller, *Up Ship!* 112; U.S., NACA, *Eleventh Annual Report, 1925*, 34–35.

20. Dix, "Alclad"; "Properties and Uses of Light Alloys," 315; Stout, "Duralumin All-Metal Airplane Construction," 434.

21. Memo, BuC&R, 15 Jan. 1919, box 399, file O-ZF-15, BuAer, Gen. Corresp. Initiated in BuC&R, 1917–25, RG 72, NA; Swanborough and Bowers, *United States Navy Aircraft since 1911*, 115–16.

22. Moffett to Manager, NAF, 11 Jan. 1923, Aer-M-23-ML, box 371, file RNAF-Z-73, BuAer, Gen. Corresp. Initiated in BuC&R, 1917–25, RG 72, NA; Cocklin, "Development of Navy Patrol Planes," 242.

23. Moffett to CO, Aircraft Squadrons, Scouting Fleet, 16 Nov. 1923, Aer-M-11-QL-11/22, box 371, file RNAF-Z-73, BuAer, Gen. Corresp. Initiated in BuC&R, 1917–25, RG 72, NA; PN-7 trial board to Moffett, 26 Dec. 1923, ibid.; Westervelt to CNO, 13 Aug. 1924, 11325, ibid.

24. Moffett to Manager, NAF, 16 Aug. 1923, Aer-M-11-QL, box 371, file RNAF-Z-73, ibid.; Westervelt to Chief, BuAer, 19 Feb. 1924, 5220, ibid.; Moffett to Manager, NAF, 27 June 1924, Aer-M-11-AAM, ibid.

25. Moffett to Manager, NAF, 23 Aug. 1924, Aer-M-1-AAM, box 371, file RNAF-Z-73, ibid.; Westervelt to Chief, BuAer, 11 Sept. 1924, 12501, box 372, file RNAF-Z-81, ibid.; Moffett to Manager, NAF, 22 Sept. 1924, Aer-M-1-MMK, ibid.

26. Westervelt to Chief, BuAer, 7 Mar. 1925, 1650, box 372, file RNAF-Z-81, ibid.; Westervelt to Chief, BuAer, 20 Apr. 1925, 3147, ibid; U.S., Cong., House, *Inquiry into*

Operations of the United States Air Services, pt. 2, 1602; Page, *Modern Aviation Engines*, 2:1436–43.

27. Westervelt to Chief, BuAer, 7 Feb. 1925, 721, box 372, file RNAF-Z-81, BuAer, Gen. Corresp. Initiated in BuC&R, 1917–25, RG 72, NA; Westervelt to Chief, BuAer, 20 Apr. 1925, 3147, ibid.

28. Messimer, *No Margin for Error*, 4–8.

29. Cdr. R. W. Cabiniss to Chief, BuAer, 5 May 1925, 5779, box 5307, file VPN9/F1-1, BuAer, Gen. Corresp., 1925–42, RG 72, NA.

30. Land to CO, NAS, San Diego, 5 June 1925, Aer-M-12-AQ, VPN9/F1-1, 804-6, box 5307, file VPN9/A4, ibid.; Richardson to CO, NAS, San Diego, 16 June 1925, Aer-M-12-AQ, file VPN9/F1-1, ibid.

31. Messimer, *No Margin for Error*, 11–132.

32. Land (by direction, Chief, BuAer), to Manager, NAF, 17 June 1925, Aer-M-15-FAM, box 5308, vol. 1, file VPN10/F1-1, BuAer, Gen. Corresp., 1925–42, RG 72, NA.

33. Moffett to Manager, NAF, 16 Apr. 1925, Aer-M-15-FAM, box 372, file RNAF-Z-81, BuAer, Gen. Corresp. Initiated in BuC&R, 1917–25, RG 72, NA; Project Order, Manufacture of 2 PN-10 flying boats, 29 May 1925, Aer-M-2-BA, box 5308, vol. 1, file VPN10/F1-1, BuAer, Gen. Corresp., 1925–42, ibid.; Weyerbacher, "Metal Construction of Aircraft," 490.

34. Westervelt to Land, 6 Feb. 1926, box 5308, vol. 1, file VPN10/F1-1, BuAer, Gen. Corresp., 1925–42, RG 72, NA; John Rodgers (by direction, Chief, BuAer) to Manager, NAF, 29 Jan. 1926, Aer-A-1-NF, ibid.

35. R. F. Zogbaum to Chief, BuAer, 17 Nov. 1932, box 5312, file VPN12/F1-1, ibid.; Cdr. E. E. Wilson to Chief, BuAer, 22 May 1926, Aer-A-4-ERG, file VPN10/F23, box 5310, ibid.; Weyerbacher to Chief, BuAer, 29 Oct. 1926, 15706, box 5308, vol. 1, file VPN10/F1-1, ibid.; Westervelt to Chief, BuAer, 23 Apr. 1927, 1221, box 5312, ibid.

36. Westervelt to Chief, BuAer, 5 June 1926, 7361, box 5308, vol. 1, file VPN10/F1-1, ibid.; memo, H. C. Richardson, 17 June 1926, ibid.; Westervelt to Chief, BuAer, 15 Apr. 1927, 3982, ibid.; W. W. Webster to Chief, BuAer, 7 Dec. 1927, 15817, box 5309, vol. 2, ibid.

37. R. F. Zogbaum to Chief, BuAer, 17 Nov. 1932, box 5312, file VPN12/F1-1, ibid.; Webster, "Navy PN-12 Seaplane," 1366, 1404; Swanborough and Bowers, *United States Navy Aircraft since 1911*, 335–37.

38. Swanborough and Bowers, *United States Navy Aircraft since 1911*, 335.

39. Moffett to Manager, NAF, 19 Apr. 1927, Aer-M-15-SP, box 5311, vol. 1, file VPN11/F1-1, BuAer, Gen. Corresp., 1925–42, RG 72, NA; Swanborough and Bowers, *United States Navy Aircraft since 1911*, 335–36.

40. Weyerbacher to Chief, BuAer, 24 Aug. 1927, 7870, box 5311, vol. 1, file VPN11/F1-1, BuAer, Gen. Corresp., 1925–42, RG 72, NA; Weyerbacher to Commandant, Phila. Navy Yard, 19 Oct. 1928, 12596, vol. 2, ibid.; W. W. Webster (by direction, Manager, NAF) to CO, NAS, Anacostia, 26 Oct. 1928, ibid.

41. Project Order, 63–28, 26 Jan. 1928, box 5311, vol. 1, file VPN11/F1-1, ibid.; W. W. Webster (by direction, Manager, NAF) to Chief, BuAer, 11 Apr. 1929, 6217, ibid.; S. M. Kraus to Chief, BuAer, 6 July 1931, 10513, box 5312, vol. 4, ibid.

42. Swanborough and Bowers, *United States Navy Aircraft since 1911*, 254, 316, 337, 444; R. D. MacCart to Manager, NAF, 13 Apr. 1928, box 5311, vol. 1, file VPN11/F1-1, BuAer, Gen. Corresp., 1925–42, RG 72, NA; R. F. Zogbaum to Chief, BuAer, 17 Nov. 1932, box 5312, file VPN12/F1-1, ibid.

43. Enclosure, S. M. Kraus to BuAer, 10 Feb. 1934, F1-1, box 4027, vol. 11, file NP 11, BuAer, Gen. Corresp., 1925–42, RG 72, NA.

44. Crouch, *Eagle Aloft*, 564–65; Westervelt to Hunsaker, 3 Apr. 1922, 55, box 371, RNAF-Z-69, BuAer, Gen. Corresp. Initiated in BuC&R, 1917–25, RG 72, NA; Westervelt to Chief, BuAer, 7 June 1922, 9431, ibid.

45. D'Orcy, "Curtiss Marine Flying Trophy Race," 490–92; Moffett to Manager, NAF, 31 May 1923, Aer-M-15-FD, RNAF-56, 404–1, box 4026, vol. 7, file NP 11, BuAer, Gen. Corresp., 1925–42, RG 72, NA; *Aviation* 15 (24 Sept. 1923): 365; ibid. 15 (8 Oct. 1923): 436–37; Barker, *Schneider Trophy Races*, 92, 142, 146–49; Swanborough and Bowers, *United States Navy Aircraft since 1911*, 126–27; *New York Times*, 13 Nov. 1926.

46. U.S., Cong., Senate, Subcommittee of the Committee on Naval Affairs, *Lieut. Alford J. Williams*, 5–6, 28.

47. Ibid., 14, 28–29; Kean, "Looking Backward," 3–4; *Air Scoop* 8 (28 Oct. 1960): 1; *New York Times*, 19 Aug. 1929.

48. Kean, "Looking Backward," 11–12; *Aviation* 27 (Aug. 17, 1929): 344; Page, *Modern Aviation Engines*, 2:1491–95.

49. *New York Times*, 9, 11, 19, 22, 26 Aug. 1929; Kean, "Looking Backward," 12; U.S., Cong., Senate, Subcommittee of the Committee on Naval Affairs, *Lieut. Alford J. Williams*, 25–26, 44–47.

50. U.S., Cong., House, *Inquiry into Operations of the United States Air Services*, pt. 2, 1344, 1360; "Chemistry and Naval Aviation," lecture by J. Hartley Bowen, Jr.

51. Moffett to SecNav, 30 Dec. 1922, Aer-M-12-AQ, 22-14, 404-1, box 4025, vol. 6, file NP 11, BuAer, Gen. Corresp., 1925–42, RG 72, NA.

52. SecNav to BuAer, 6 Feb. 1923, SONYD-1-Kr-2/1 5103-1198, vol. 6, file NP 11, ibid.; Moffett to Manager, NAF, 13 Feb. 1923, Aer-M-12-AQ 22-14 404–1, ibid.; *Air Scoop* 7 (1 May 1959): 2; "History of the Naval Air Material Center," 26–27, OANHC.

53. McCord, "Aeronautical Engine Laboratory," 275–87; Robinson and Keller, *Up Ship!* 82–83, 101, 140–41.

54. U.S., Cong., House, *Hearings before the Committee on Naval Affairs . . . 1920*, 1:1175, 1804; Taylor to CNO, 9 June 1920, box 362, file RNAF-Z-8(A), BuAer, Gen. Corresp. Initiated in BuC&R, 1917–25, RG 72, NA.

55. Moffett to SecNav, 4 May 1923, Aer-M-BB 161-0, 404-1, box 2833, file 28815-57, SecNav, Gen. Corresp., 1916–26, RG 80, NA.

56. Moffett to Manager, NAF, 7 Oct. 1924, RNAF-O, Aer-M-2-CK, O-F-4, box 361, BuAer, Gen. Corresp. Initiated in BuC&R, 1917–25, RG 72, NA; U.S., Cong., *Inquiry into Operations of the United States Air Services*, pt. 2; 1353–54.

57. R. Adm. L. M. Nulton to Chief, BuAer, 27 Jan. 1922, 4000-4, box 4025, vol. 6, file NP 11, BuAer, Gen. Corresp., 1925–42, RG 72, NA; "War History of the Fourth Naval District," vol. 5, pt. 8, I-24, copy in Navy Department Library (hereafter cited as NDL); *Aviation* 15 (23 July 1923): 104; SecNav to Commandant, Fourth Naval District, 14 Apr. 1924, box 2833, file 28815-96, SecNav, Gen. Corresp., 1916–26, RG 80, NA; *Aero Digest* 15 (Sept. 1929): 89.

58. SecNav to CNO, Commandant, Phila. Navy Yard, et al., 23 June 1926, Aer-1-HS P11-4(1), file NP 11/N1-9 (260223), box 3313, SecNav, Gen. Corresp., 1926–42, RG 80, NA; Harold Pitcairn to Herbert Hoover, 10 June 1926, file NP 11/N1-9 (260610), ibid.; C. Townsend Ludington to Wilbur, 11 June 1926, file NP 11/N1-9 (260611), ibid.

59. SecNav to CNO, Commandant, Phila. Navy Yard, et al., 23 June 1926, Aer-1-HS P11-4(1), file NP 11/N1-9 (260623), box 3313, ibid. For Mitten's PRT Air Service, see Trimble, *High Frontier*, 130–31.

60. Armstrong, "Henry C. Mustin," 29–33.

61. *Philadelphia Inquirer*, 18 Sept. 1926; Bureau of Aeronautics, *News Letter* 4 (25 Sept. 1926): 5.

CHAPTER 6

1. Weyerbacher to Chief, BuAer, 15 May 1929, 1370, box 4026, vol. 9, file NP 11, BuAer, Gen. Corresp., 1925–42, RG 72, NA.

2. Ingalls to Chief, BuAer, 25 Sept. 1929, NP11/A9-10/290925, box 4027, vol. 10, file NP 11, ibid.

3. Moffett to Ingalls, 6 Nov. 1929, Aer-D-157-EC, ibid.

4. Weyerbacher to Chief, BuAer, 23 Dec. 1929, ibid.; Moffett to Manager, NAF, 7 Jan. 1930, Aer-A-ML-AQ, ibid.

5. *New York Times*, 16 Oct. 1929, 8, 14 Mar. 1930.

6. U.S., Senate, Subcommittee of the Committee on Naval Affairs, *Lieut. Alford J. Williams*, 19–29, 41–50.

7. See correspondence in file NP11/P8, box 3314, SecNav, Gen. Corresp., 1926–42, RG 80, NA; John H. Towers to Manager, NAF, 8 Apr. 1931, Aer-M-1-BA-AQ, box 4027, vol. 10, file NP 11, BuAer, Gen. Corresp., 1925–42, RG 72, NA.

8. *Register of Commissioned and Warrant Officers, 1930*, 26–27; Kraus, "Naval Aircraft Factory," 46.

9. Cook to Manager, NAF, 28 Nov. 1931, Aer-M-2-BA, L9-3, box 4027, vol. 10, file NP 11, BuAer, Gen. Corresp., 1925–42, RG 72, NA; Lt. Cdr. J. Ross Allen, memo for files, 8 June 1932, Aer-D-1-AQ, L5-1(2), ibid.; Capt. A. B. Cook (Acting Chief, BuAer) to Manager, NAF, 31 July 1931, Aer-D-111-MJB-8/11, S83-4, S83-BB, box 1438, vol. 2, file S83-4, Bureau of Aeronautics, Confidential Correspondence, 1922–44, Record Group 72, National Archives (hereafter cited as BuAer, Confid. Corresp., 1922–44, RG 72, NA); Smith, *Airships Akron and Macon*, 47.

10. Moffett to SecNav, 3 May 1932, Aer-M-AQ, box 1206, file NP 11, BuAer, Confid. Corresp., 1922–44, RG 72, NA; memo, Cook to Moffett, 24 Oct. 1932, Aer-1-ML, box 4027, vol. 11, file NP 11, BuAer, Gen. Corresp., 1925–42, ibid.

11. For the loss of the *Akron*, see Smith, *Airships Akron and Macon*, 77–92.

12. Buell, *Master of Sea Power*, 72–96.

13. Turnbull and Lord, *History of United States Naval Aviation*, 284–85; *Aircraft Year Book for 1934*, 4–5, 126; Holley, *Buying Aircraft*, 113–25.

14. *Congressional Record*, House, 73d Cong., 2d sess., vol. 78, pt. 1, 295, 1623; U.S., Cong., House, *Hearings before the Committee on Naval Affairs . . . 1933–1934*, 158–61, 260–63, 274–77, 291–308; Turnbull and Lord, *History of United States Naval Aviation*, 285.

15. U.S., Cong., House, *Hearings before the Committee on Naval Affairs . . . 1933–1934*, 313; U.S., Cong., House, *Hearings before the Subcommittee on Aeronautics*, ibid., 341, 476–78.

16. U.S., Cong., House, *Hearings before the Subcommittee on Aeronautics*, 571–73.

17. Ibid., 943–53.

18. Ibid., 1005–6.

19. Ibid., 1113–14.

20. Richard K. Smith to the author, 17 July 1988.

21. U.S., Cong., House, *Hearings before the Subcommittee on Aeronautics*, 1114–15.

22. *Congressional Record*, Senate, 73d Cong., 2d sess., vol. 78, pts. 3 and 4, 2874–75, 3794, 3801–2; *Congressional Record*, House, 73d Cong., 2d sess., pt. 5, 5026.

23. *Aviation* 33 (Apr. 1934): 118–19.

24. Albion, *Makers of Naval Policy*, 252–53; U.S., Cong., *Statutes at Large*, vol. 48, pt. 1, 503–5.

25. Warner, "Notes on a Great Confusion," 116.

26. Kraus to Chief, BuAer, 24 Feb. 1934, F1-1/A3-1(27), box 4027, vol. 11, file NP 11, BuAer, Gen. Corresp., 1925–42, RG 72, NA; memo, Cook to Chief, BuAer, 9 Mar. 1934, Aer-1-ML, ibid.; Kraus to Chief, BuAer, 21 May 1934, F1-1/A3-1(70), ibid.

27. Adm. William H. Standley to King, 25 Aug. 1934, A1-3/QN (340619), box 4027, vol. 11, file NP 11, BuAer, Gen. Corresp., 1925–42, RG 72, NA; memo, A. D. Bernhard, Plans Division, BuAer, 28 Sept. 1938, Aer-PL-1-EMN, box 4028, ibid.

28. King to SecNav, 20 Sept. 1934, Aer-M-AQ F21, box 4027, vol. 11, ibid.

29. Memo, McCrary to Chief, BuAer, 2 Oct. 1934, Aer-1-ML, box 4028, vol. 14, ibid.

30. Ibid.

31. King to Manager, NAF, 19 Oct. 1934, Aer-ML-NP11, L8-3 LL/NP11, box 4027, vol. 11, ibid.

32. Ibid.

33. "History of the Naval Air Material Center," 2, OANHC; Zeigler, "Naval Aircraft Factory," 92–94.

34. Zeigler to Bureau of Supplies and Accounts, 28 Nov. 1934, L10/L8-3 (12079), box 4027, vol. 12, file NP 11, BuAer, Gen. Corresp., 1925–42, RG 72, NA; Zeigler to Chief, BuAer, 30 Jan. 1935, A3-1/A1-3(18), box 4027, vol. 12, ibid.; King to Manager, NAF, 12 Feb. 1935, Aer-MA-REM L8-3, ibid.

35. *New York Times*, 21 June 1934; King to Chief, Bureau of Yards and Docks, 5 Feb. 1935, Aer-MA-61-BA, N5/NP11, L1-2, vol. 12, file NP11, BuAer, Gen. Corresp., 1925–42, RG 72, NA; Contract NOy-2334, 6 Feb. 1935, ibid.

36. Zeigler to Chief, BuAer, 8 Feb. 1935, A1-3(420), box 4027, vol. 12, file NP 11, BuAer, Gen. Corresp., 1925–42, RG 72, NA; Chief, Bureau of Yards and Docks to Commandant, Phila. Navy Yard, 27 Aug. 1935, P14-Z(1)/NO4, box 4028, vol. 13, ibid.; Commandant, Phila. Navy Yard to Chief, BuAer, 16 Feb. 1937, N10-2/N1-9, ibid.

37. King to Manager, NAF, 29 Oct. 1934, Aer-E-13-EP, box 5026, vol. 1, file VN3N1/F1-1, ibid.

38. Zeigler to Chief, BuAer, 28 Nov. 1934, 16450, box 5026, vol. 1, file VN3N1/F1-1, ibid.; King to Manager, NAF, 24 Dec. 1934, Aer-E-13-EP, ibid.; King to Manager, NAF, 31 Dec. 1934, Aer-E-4-RY, F21, box 4027, vol. 12, file NP 11, ibid.

39. King to Manager, NAF, 9 Feb. 1935, Aer-E-13-EP/BA, box 5026, vol. 1, file VN3N1/F1-1, ibid.; Zeigler to Chief, BuAer, 19 Feb. 1935, 841, ibid.; *Air Scoop* 2 (Sept. 1945): 7.

40. Zeigler to Chief, BuAer, 12 Mar. 1935, 46, box 5026, vol. 1, file VN3N1/F1-1, BuAer, Gen. Corresp., 1925–42, RG 72, NA; mockup inspection checklist, 22 Mar. 1935, ibid.; Souvenir program, *20th Anniversary Naval Aircraft Factory, 1917–1937*, n.p.; Andrews, "Yellow Bird," 24–25; Tillman, "N3N Story," 288–89.

41. Memo of telephone conversation, 23 Aug. 1935, Oster with Ralph Weyerbacher, BuAer, 11049, box 5027, vol. 2, file VN3N1/F1-1, BuAer, Gen. Corresp., 1925–42, RG 72, NA; Oster to Chief, BuAer, 27 Aug. 1935, 15581, ibid.; Zeigler to

Chief, BuAer, 12 Sept. 1935, 18020, box 5027, vol. 2, file VN3N1/F1-1, ibid.;
Zogbaum to Chief, BuAer, 18 Dec. 1935, ibid.

42. Memo of telephone conversation, 12 Dec. 1935, Oster and Cdr. Donald Royce,
BuAer, 22434, vol. 3, ibid.

43. Project Order no. 107-35, 30 Apr. 1935, box 5026, vol. 1, ibid.; Project Order no.
158-35, 29 June 1935, ibid.; "History of the Naval Air Material Center," 16, OANHC;
Richardson, "Progress at the Naval Aircraft Factory," 40.

44. Cook, memo of conference, 23 July 1936, Aer-M1, box 5028, vol. 5, file
VN3N1/F1-1, BuAer, Gen. Corresp., 1925–42, RG 72, NA.

45. "History of the Naval Air Material Center," n.p., OANHC.

46. Zeigler to Chief, BuAer, 4 Oct. 1935, 18068, box 5039, file VN3N2/F1-1,
BuAer, Gen. Corresp., 1925–42, RG 72, NA; report, Webster to Chief, BuAer, 19 Aug.
1936, ibid.; report, Webster to Chief, BuAer, 17 Sept. 1936, ibid. (see also route slip
comments on above documents).

47. Webster to Chief, BuAer, 24 May 1939, 10938, box 5040, vol. 1, file VN3N3/
F1-1, ibid.

48. Project Order no. 58-40, 21 June 1939, box 5040, vol. 1, file VN3N3/F1-1, ibid.;
Webster to Chief, BuAer, 26 July 1939, 15910, ibid.; Lloyd Harrison to CO, NAS,
Pensacola, 4 Apr. 1940, box 5041, vol. 2, ibid.; Swanborough and Bowers, *United
States Navy Aircraft since 1911*, 338–39.

49. Webster to Chief, BuAer, 24 Jan. 1940, VN3N3/F1-1 (1910), box 5041, vol. 2,
file VN3N3/F1-1, BuAer, Gen. Corresp., 1925–42, RG 72, NA; Harrison to CO, NAS,
Pensacola, 4 Apr. 1940, ibid.

50. Lt. Cdr. R. E. Farnsworth (by direction, Chief, BuAer) to Manager, NAF, 5 Feb.
1940, Aer-E-246-FAM, ibid.; William Nelson to Chief, BuAer, 13 Mar. 1940, 1958,
ibid.

51. Capt. S. M. Kraus (by direction, Chief, BuAer), to Manager, NAF, 17 May 1940,
Aer-M-AQ VN3N3/F1-1 F21(R-760), ibid.; Capt. M. A. Mitscher to Manager, NAF, 28
May 1940, Aer-PR-2-EMR, ibid.; R. Adm. J. H. Towers to Manager, NAF, 18 Sept.
1940, Aer-PR-21-FDB F21(R760–8), box 5041, vol. 3, ibid.

52. William Nelson to Chief, BuAer, 3 June 1940, VN3N3/F1-1 (53), box 5041, vol.
2, file VN3N3/F1-1, BuAer, Gen. Corresp., 1925–42, RG 72, NA; Capt. M. A.
Mitscher to Manager, NAF, 12 June 1940, Aer-PR-BA VN3N3/F1-1 F21 (R-760-8),
ibid.; Mitscher to Manager, NAF, 12 Aug. 1940, Aer-PR-13-ELT VN3N/F1-1, box
5041, vol. 3, ibid.

53. Webster to Chief, BuAer, 10 Mar. 1942, VN3N3/F1-1 (2845), box 5041, vol. 5,
ibid.; memo, Capt. Ralph E. Davison for Chief, BuAer, 17 Mar. 1942, ibid.; Towers to
Manager, NAF, 21 Mar. 1942, Aer-M-AQ, VN3N3/F1-1, ibid.

54. Report of Unsatisfactory or Defective Material, submitted by NAS, Corpus
Christi, 19 Dec. 1942, box 4581, vol. 8, file VN3N3/L11-1, BuAer, Gen. Corresp.,
1943–45, ibid. For information on N3Ns in service see vols. 1-9, file VN3N3/L11-1,
ibid. Flying impressions are from Tillman, "N3N Story," 290.

55. Rea and Newton, *Wings of Gold*, 98. Additional information on the N3N-3
appears in Andrews, "Yellow Bird," 24–25.

56. King to Manager, NAF, 9 Oct. 1934, Aer-E-4-AM F21, box 4027, vol. 11, file NP
11, BuAer, Gen. Corresp., 1925–42, RG 72, NA.

57. Memo, Lonnquest to Chief, BuAer, 6 Nov. 1934, Aer-E-4-AM F21, box 4027,
vol. 12, ibid.

58. King to Manager, NAF, 22 Mar. 1935, Aer-E-4-RY, F21, box 4028, vol. 13, ibid.;

King to Manager, NAF, 28 Mar. 1935, ibid.; memo, T. C. Lonnquest, 19 June 1935, Aer-E-4-RY, box 5026, vol. 1, file VN3N1/F1-1, ibid.

59. Richardson, "Progress at the Naval Aircraft Factory," 40–41; Capt. J. H. Hoover to Chief, BuAer, 31 Aug. 1936, L5-1(2), box 4028, vol. 14, file NP 11, BuAer, Gen. Corresp., 1925–42, RG 72, NA; "History of the Naval Air Material Center," 16, OANHC.

60. Mitscher to Manager, NAF, 28 May 1940, Aer-PR-2-EMR, box 5041, vol. 2, file VN3N3/F1-1, BuAer, Gen. Corresp., 1925–42, RG 72, NA; Towers to Manager, NAF, 18 Sept. 1940, Aer-PR-21-FDB, F21 (R-760-8), box 5041. vol. 3, ibid.; Mitscher to Manager, NAF, 12 June 1940, Aer-PR-BA, VN3N3/F1-1, F21 (R-760-8), box 5041, vol. 2, ibid.; E. M. Pace, Jr., to Chief, BuAer, 7 Oct. 1941, A1-3/F21-1 (23914), box 5041, vol. 5, ibid.

61. Smith, *Aircraft Piston Engines*, 177–80; Pearson, "Notes on the History of the Naval Aircraft Factory," 8.

CHAPTER 7

1. Webster to Chief, BuAer, 1 Sept. 1936, VOS F1-1(4745), box 5153, vol. 1, file VOS, BuAer, Gen. Corresp., 1925–42, RG 72, NA; Webster to Chief, BuAer, 2 Oct. 1936, VOS F1-1(19525), ibid.; memo, C. L. Helber to Material, Engineering, Procurement Divisions, BuAer, 3 Nov. 1936, Aer-E-13-EP VOS NP 11, ibid.; *NAF Cavalcade of Aircraft*, 66.

2. *NAF Cavalcade of Aircraft*, 65–66; Swanborough and Bowers, *United States Navy Aircraft since 1911*, 401–2.

3. Cook to Manager, NAF, 15 Apr. 1938, Aer-E-10-EP VN, box 1525, vol. 1, file VN, BuAer, Confid. Corresp., 1922–44, RG 72, NA.

4. Webster to Chief, BuAer, 22 Apr. 1938, VN/F1-1 (8268), ibid.

5. Engineering Desk, BuAer, comments on NAF monoplane trainer (no date), ibid.

6. Webster to Chief, BuAer, 24 June 1938, VN/F1-1 (14628), ibid.; Webster to Cook (personal letter), 24 June 1938, ibid.

7. Memo, Cdr. A. C. Davis to Chief, BuAer, 25 June 1938, ibid.; Webster to Chief, BuAer, 22 July 1938, VN/F1-1 (1871), box 5048, vol. 1, file VN5N1/F1-1, BuAer, Gen. Corresp., 1925–42, ibid.; memo, Cdr. F. W. Pennoyer to Chief, BuAer, 5 Aug. 1938, Aer-E-16, LID, VN, box 1525, vol. 1, file VN, BuAer, Confid. Corresp., 1922–44, ibid.

8. Capt. J. H. Towers (Acting Chief, BuAer) to Manager, NAF, 25 Aug. 1938, Aer-E-16-EP VN, box 5048, vol. 1, file VN5N1/F1-1, BuAer, Gen. Corresp., 1925–42, ibid.; William Nelson (by direction, Manager, NAF) to Chief, BuAer, 21 Nov. 1938, XN5N1/F1-1 (21644), ibid.; Report of Mock-Up Inspection of the XN5N-1 Airplane, 8 May 1939, ibid.

9. Webster to Chief, BuAer, 2 May 1939, VN5N1/F1-1 (38), box 5048, vol. 1, file VN5N1/F1-1, BuAer, Gen. Corresp., 1925–42, RG 72, NA.

10. Webster to Chief, BuAer, 3 Nov. 1939, VN5N1/F1-1 (20413), ibid.

11. William Nelson (Acting Manager, NAF) to Chief, BuAer, 27 Oct. 1939, VN5N1/F1-1 (20303), ibid.; Cdr. H. R. Oster (by direction, Chief, BuAer) to Manager, NAF, 22 Dec. 1939, Aer-E-246-FAM, ibid.; Nelson to Chief, BuAer, 8 Apr. 1941, VN5N1/F1-1 (3475) box 5048, vol. 3, ibid.

12. Capt. A. C. Read to Manager, NAF, 19 May 1941, box 5047, file VN5N1/A4, ibid.

13. Memo, Ralph Barnaby for Manager, NAF, 9 July 1941 (28501), box 5048, vol. 3,

file VN5N1/F1-1, ibid.; Capt. L. M. Grant to BuAer, 14 Jan. 1944, MP-7/m/q, VL/F13-4, box 4581, file VN5N1/F1-1, BuAer, Gen. Corresp., 1943–45, ibid.; Smith quote in Barnaby interview, 12 Oct. 1983.

14. U.S., Cong., House, *Hearings before Subcommittee of Committee on Appropriations . . . 1938*, 532–34.

15. Ibid., 534.

16. Ibid., 534–35.

17. Swanborough and Bowers, *United States Navy Aircraft since 1911*, 143–44; W. W. Webster to Chief, BuAer, 24 June 1937, VSON1/F1-1 (2000), box 5468, vol. 1, file VSON1/F1-1, BuAer, Gen. Corresp., 1925–42, RG 72, NA; Webster to Chief, BuAer, 17 June 1937, VSON1/F1-1 (1993), ibid.

18. Webster to Chief, BuAer, 12 July 1937, VSON1/F1-1 (10351), box 5468, vol. 1, file VSON1/F1-1, BuAer, Gen. Corresp., 1925–42, RG 72, NA; Capt. A. C. Read (Ass't. Chief, BuAer) to Manager, NAF, 26 Oct. 1937, Aer-Pr-2-BA, ibid.

19. Webster to Chief, BuAer, 8 Aug. 1938, VSON1/F1-1 (1867), ibid.

20. Richard K. Smith to the author, 18 July 1988.

21. William Nelson (Acting Manager, NAF) to Chief, BuAer, 3 Oct. 1938, VSON1/F1-1, box 5468, vol. 1, file VSON1/F1-1, BuAer, Gen. Corresp., 1925–42, RG 72, NA; Webster to Chief, BuAer, 1 Nov. 1938, VSON1/F1-1 (21623), ibid.; Webster to Chief, BuAer, 31 Oct. 1938, VSOC3/F1-1 (21619), ibid.

22. Webster to Chief, BuAer, 25 July 1939, VSON1/F1-1 (1640), box 5469, vol. 4, ibid.; memo, C. L. Helber (class Desk "C," BuAer) to Plans Division, BuAer, 10 Apr. 1939, box 5469, vol. 2, ibid.; telegram, NAF to BuAer, 3 June 1939, box 5469, vol. 3, ibid.; Webster to Chief, BuAer, 28 Sept. 1939, VSON1/F1-1 (2227), box 5469, vol. 5, ibid.

23. Webster to Chief, BuAer, 29 Apr. 1938, VSON1/F1-1 (2354), box 5468, vol. 1, ibid.; Webster to Chief, BuAer, 28 Sept. 1939, VSON1/F1-1 (2227), box 5469, vol. 5, ibid.; Mitscher to Manager, NAF, 5 Aug. 1939, Aer-Pr-3-MKH, box 5469, vol. 4, ibid.; Webster to Chief, BuAer, 9 Feb. 1940, VSON1/F1-1 (1204), box 5469, vol. 5, ibid.

24. Webster to Chief, BuAer, 9 Feb. 1940, VSON1/F1-1 (1204), box 5469, vol. 5, ibid.; L. B. Richardson (by direction, Manager, NAF) to Chief, BuAer, 8 Oct. 1937, VSON1/F1-1 (12536), box 5468, vol. 1, ibid.

25. Maas, "Fall from Grace," 118–19; Swanborough and Bowers, *United States Navy Aircraft since 1911*, 417; Cdr. E. M. Pace, Jr. (by direction, Chief, BuAer) to Manager, NAF, 27 June 1938, Aer-PR-BA, box 5397, vol. 1, file VSBN1/F1-1, BuAer, Gen. Corresp., 1925–42, RG 72, NA.

26. Maas, "Fall from Grace," 119–20.

27. Pace (by direction, Chief, BuAer) to Manager, NAF, 27 June 1938, Aer-PR-BA, box 5397, vol. 1, file VSBN1/F1-1, BuAer, Gen. Corresp., 1925–42, RG 72, NA; Design changes contemplated on Model XSBA-1 Airplane, 19 Aug. 1938, ibid.; Webster to Chief, BuAer, 19 Aug. 1938, VSBN1/F1-1 (10984), ibid.; R. Adm. A. B. Cook (Chief, BuAer) to Manager, NAF, 29 Sept. 1938, Aer-Pr-3-EMR, ibid.

28. Webster to Chief, BuAer, 18 Aug. 1939, VSBN1/F1-1 (15934), ibid.; E. M. Pace, Jr. (Manager, NAF) to Chief, BuAer, 19 Sept. 1940, VSBN1/F1-1 (20804), box 5397, vol. 2, ibid.; Pace to Chief, BuAer, 1 Nov. 1940, VSBN1/F1-1 (22121), ibid.

29. Swanborough and Bowers, *United States Navy Aircraft since 1911*, 417; Cdr. E. M. Pace, Jr., to CO, NAS Anacostia, 3 Jan. 1941, VSBN1/F1-1 (1802), box 5397, vol. 2, file VSBN1/F1-1, BuAer, Gen. Corresp., 1925–42; Pace to Chief, BuAer, 6 May 1941, VSBN1/F1-1, ibid.; Cdr. E. W. Clexton (Commander Aircraft, Atlantic Fleet) to Chief, BuAer, 24 Oct. 1941, F1(X602), ibid.

30. "History of the Naval Air Material Center," 16, OANHC; U.S. Department of Commerce, Civil Aeronautics Administration, *U.S. Military Aircraft Acceptances, 1940–1945*, 140, 142.

31. Cdr. E. M. Pace, Jr., to Chief, BuAer, 10 Feb. 1941, A1-3/F21-1 (115), box 4029, vol. 17, file NP 11, BuAer, Gen. Corresp., 1925–42, RG 72, NA; Pace to Capt. W. W. Webster, BuAer, 14 Aug. 1941, ibid.

32. Capt. Lloyd Harrison (by direction, Manager, NAF) to prospective CO, NAMC, 11 Aug. 1943, PP-MIA, L9-3(9) (15537), box 4771, vol. 4, file VPBN1/F1-1, BuAer, Gen. Corresp., 1943–45, ibid.; U.S. Department of Commerce, Civil Aeronautics Administration, *U.S. Military Aircraft Acceptances, 1940–1945*, 142, 144.

33. Bureau of Aeronautics, "Daily Aviation News Bulletin" 1 (3 Jan. 1920); Bureau of Aeronautics, *News Letter* 7 (10 July 1929): 14; Capt. A. B. Cook to Chief, BuAer, 24 Oct. 1932, box 4027, vol. 11, file NP 11, BuAer, Gen. Corresp., 1925–42, RG 72, NA; Project Order, 7 Apr. 1941, Aer-Pr-21-KH, F43-1(2), box 4029, vol. 17, ibid.; Cdr. W. H. Hamilton to Manager, NAF, [Apr. 1942] Aer-Ma-1182-MHC, F43-1(2), box 4029, vol. 18, ibid.

34. Lt. Cdr. T. C. Lonnquest (by direction, Chief, BuAer) to Manager, NAF, 20 Feb. 1935, Aer-E-4-RY, L5-2, box 4030, vol. 1, file NP 12, BuAer, Gen. Corresp., 1925–42, RG 72, NA; Lt. Cdr. T. L. Sprague to Manager, NAF, 21 May 1935, ibid.; memo, 17 July 1935, conference at NAF, Aer-E-47-IE, MS F23, box 4028, vol. 13, file NP 11, ibid.; Capt. W. W. Webster to Chief, BuAer, 24 Mar. 1937, N8-10 (316), box 4031, vol. 2, file NP 12, ibid.

35. Webster to Chief, BuAer, 24 Mar. 1937, N8-10 (316), box 4031, vol. 2, file NP 12, ibid.

36. Memo, Pennoyer to Ass't. Chief, BuAer, 24 Feb. 1938, Aer-E-EP, ibid.

37. Capt. J. H. Towers (Ass't. Chief, BuAer) to Chief, BuY&D, 17 May 1939, Aer-PL-2-AWG, N32-3/NP11, ibid.; Capt. W. W. Webster to Chief, BuAer, 27 Nov. 1939, N19 (88), ibid.; G. W. Lewis, NACA, to Chief, BuAer, 1 Nov. 1940, ibid.; A. E. Watson to Chief, BuAer, 17 Oct. 1941, N(599) (F), ibid.

38. Memo, Drain to Material Branch, BuAer, 24 Aug. 1934, Aer-E-25-EC, L5-1(2), box 4027, vol. 11, file NP 11, ibid.

39. Ibid.; U.S., Cong., Senate, *Hearings before a Special Committee Investigating the National Defense Program*, pt. 24, 10715.

40. Sydney Kraus (by direction, Chief, BuAer) to Manager, NAF, 18 Aug. 1939, Aer-E-251-SG, box 5040, vol. 1, file VN3N3/F1-1, BuAer, Gen. Corresp., 1925–42, RG 72, NA; Webster to Chief, BuAer, 30 Oct. 1939, 19529, ibid.

41. Webster to Chief, BuAer, 30 Oct. 1939, 19529, ibid.

42. "Chemistry and Naval Aviation," lecture by J. Hartley Bowen, Jr.

43. "War History of the Fourth Naval District," vol. 5, pt. 8, I 20 I 21, NDL; Manager, NAF, to Chief, BuAer, 6 June 1938, A1-3 (2251), box 4028, vol. 15, file NP 11, BuAer, Gen. Corresp., 1925–42, RG 72, NA; Manager, NAF, to Chief, BuAer, 21 Dec. 1936, N8-13/L5-2 (23469), box 4028, vol. 14, ibid.; Chief, BuAer, to Manager, NAF, 20 Dec. 1937, Aer-E-25-SG, EN 11, F49, box 4028, vol. 15, ibid.

44. *Air Scoop* 8 (16 Sept. 1960): 1; ibid. 3 (Dec. 1955): 1.

45. Memo, Hobbs to Ass't. Chief, BuAer, 13 Jan. 1938, F41-3, I12, box 4028, vol. 15, file NP 11, BuAer, Gen. Corresp., 1925–42, RG 72, NA; "War History of the Fourth Naval District," vol. 5, pt. 8, I-21, NDL.

46. "Historical Development of the Aeronautical Structures Laboratory, 1 January 1960"; "Aero Materials History" (1975), copies in files of J. Hartley Bowen, Jr., Haddonfield, N.J.

CHAPTER 8

1. Arpee, *From Frigates to Flat-Tops*, 98.
2. Crouch, *Dream of Wings*, 265–66; Small, "Catapults Come of Age," 1114.
3. Small, "Catapults Come of Age," 1114; memo, H. C. Richardson to SecNav, 5 Feb. 1926, Aer-M-1-AAM, S83-2, 601-1, box 4788, vol. 1, file S83-2, BuAer, Gen. Corresp., 1925–42, RG 72, NA; Swanborough and Bowers, *United States Navy Aircraft since 1911*, 92, 96; U.S. Navy Department, *United States Naval Aviation, 1910–1980*, 7.
4. Memo, Richardson to SecNav, 5 Feb. 1926, Aer-M-1-AAM, S83-2, 601-1, box 4788, vol. 1, file S83-2, BuAer, Gen. Corresp., 1925–42, RG 72, NA; "Brief of the Development of Airplane Launching Devices," 8 Feb. 1922, ibid.
5. Memo, Richardson to SecNav, 5 Feb. 1926, Aer-M-1-AAM, S83-2, 601-1, ibid.
6. Ibid.; Van Deurs, "Pete Mitscher and Armored Cruiser Aviation," 152–53.
7. "Brief of the Development of Airplane Launching Devices," 8 Feb. 1922, box 4788, vol. 1, file S83-2, BuAer, Gen. Corresp., 1925–42, RG 72, NA.
8. Ibid.; research data memo, R. S. Shreve (BuC&R), 14 Sept. 1920, ibid.; memo, Richardson to SecNav, 5 Feb. 1926, Aer-M-1-AAM, S83-2, 601-1, ibid.
9. "Brief of the Development of Airplane Launching Devices," 8 Feb. 1922, ibid.; SecNav to Acting Commandant, Phila. Navy Yard, 25 Oct. 1921, Aer-A-CCT, 51-3, 205-0, 205-5, box 4795, vol. 1, file S83-2 (AI), ibid.
10. "Brief of the Development of Airplane Launching Devices," 8 Feb. 1922, box 4788, vol. 1, file S83-2, ibid.
11. Wheeler, *Admiral William Veazie Pratt*, 201–3; Turnbull and Lord, *History of United States Naval Aviation*, 208–9; "Brief of the Development of Airplane Launching Devices," 8 Feb. 1922, box 4788, vol. 1, file S83-2, BuAer, Gen. Corresp., 1925–42, RG 72, NA.
12. "Brief of the Development of Airplane Launching Devices," 8 Feb. 1922, box 4788, vol. 1, file S83-2, BuAer, Gen. Corresp., 1925–42, RG 72, NA; *NAF Cavalcade of Aircraft*, 92, 94; Friedman, *U.S. Aircraft Carriers*, 378.
13. Memo, H. C. Richardson to SecNav, 5 Feb. 1926, Aer-M-1-AAM, S83-2, 601-1, box 4788, vol. 1, file S83-2, BuAer, Gen. Corresp., 1925–42, RG 72, NA; Mustin (by direction, Chief, BuAer) to Chief, BuOrd, 23 Nov. 1922, Aer-M-14-Wn, 51-3, 201-51, box 1425, file S83-2 (PIII, IV, IV-1), BuAer, Confid. Corresp., 1922–44, ibid.; memo, Lisle J. Maxson to Ass't. Chief, BuAer, 13 July 1933, Aer-D-111-BCP, box 1419, vol. 1, file S83-2, ibid.; Moffett to CinC, Battle Fleet, 2 Mar. 1928, Aer-M-111-AQ, box 4788, vol. 2, file S83-2, BuAer, Gen. Corresp., 1925–42, ibid.; Friedman, *U.S. Aircraft Carriers*, 379.
14. Joint letter, Chiefs BuAer, BuOrd, BuC&R to SecNav, 13 Mar. 1923, 51-3, 204-0, box 1425, file S83-2 (PIII, IV, IV-1), BuAer, Confid. Corresp., 1922–44, ibid.
15. *NAF Cavalcade of Aircraft*, 96; Capt. Emory S. Land (Acting Chief, BuAer) to Navy Yard Division, 28 Sept. 1927, Aer-M-111-MDJ, box 4788, vol. 1, file S83-2, BuAer, Gen. Corresp., 1925–42, RG 72, NA; Moffett to CinC, Battle Fleet, 2 Mar. 1928, Aer-M-111-AQ, box 4788, vol. 2, ibid.
16. Memo, Lt. Lisle J. Maxson to Ass't. Chief, BuAer, 13 July 1933, Aer-D-111-BCP, box 1419, vol. 1, file S83-2. BuAer, Confid. Corresp., 1922–44, RG 72, NA.
17. Moffett to SecNav, 26 Dec. 1928, Aer-2-111-MDB, box 4788, vol. 2, file S83-2, BuAer, Gen. Corresp., 1925–42, ibid.; Chief, BuOrd to BuAer, 12 Jan. 1929, S83(382) (T5-Ma8), ibid.

18. Maxson, memo for files, 11 May 1931, Aer-D-111-MJB, box 4789, vol. 4, file S83-2, ibid.; U.S. Navy Department, *United States Naval Aviation, 1910–1980,* 66.

19. Memo, Cdr. R. D. Weyerbacher (BuAer) to Plans Div., BuAer, 28 Dec. 1931, Aer-D-153-FAM, F83-2, box 4789, vol. 4, file S83-2, BuAer, Gen. Corresp., 1925–42, RG 72, NA; Weyerbacher to Ass't. Chief, BuAer, 26 Oct. 1932, Aer-D-111-MJB, box 4789, vol. 5, ibid.

20. Some of the technical problems presented by carrier catapults are covered in memo, M. R. Browning to Weyerbacher, 24 Oct. 1933, MRB:IE, box 1419, vol. 1, file S83-2, BuAer, Confid. Corresp., 1922–44, ibid.

21. Capt. A. B. Cook (Ass't. Chief, BuAer) to Manager, NAF, 13 Nov. 1933, Aer-D-111-BCP, S83-2, S83-2(AIV), ibid.; S. M. Kraus to Chief, BuAer, 13 Dec. 1933, S83 (17728), ibid.; Cook to Manager, NAF, 8 Mar. 1934, Aer-D-111-BCP, S83(XAV), file S83-2(XAV), box 1425, ibid.

22. Capt. S. J. Zeigler (Manager, NAF) to Chief, BuAer, 31 Oct. 1934, S83–2 (14628), box 1419, vol. 1, file S83-2, ibid.

23. U.S. Navy, BuAer, *Ten Year History,* 9:54.

24. Friedman, *U.S. Aircraft Carriers,* 44.

25. Memo, Lt. Cdr. C. A. Nicholson (Ship Installations, BuAer) to Plans Div., BuAer, 3 Sept. 1936, Aer-E-34-AMS, S83-2, CV, box 1419, vol. 1, file S83-2, BuAer, Confid. Corresp., 1922–44, RG 72, NA; *NAF Cavalcade of Aircraft,* 99. In a communication to the author of 20 July 1988, Richard K. Smith indicated the potential of explosion in high-pressure hydraulic units.

26. Memo, Lt. Cdr. C. A. Nicholson (Ship Installations, BuAer) to Plans Div., BuAer, 3 Sept. 1936, Aer-E-34-AMS, S83-2, CV, box 1419, vol. 1, file S83-2, BuAer, Confid. Corresp., 1922–44, RG 72, NA; memo, Lt. Cdr. C. A. Nicholson (Ship Installations, BuAer) to Procurement Branch, BuAer, 10 June 1937, Aer-E-344-AMS, box 4791, vol. 11, file S83-2, BuAer, Gen. Corresp., 1925–42, ibid.; *NAF Cavalcade of Aircraft,* 100.

27. Friedman, *U.S. Aircraft Carriers,* 70; Walter, "Hangar Deck Catapults," 10–11.

28. *NAF Cavalcade of Aircraft,* 108; Friedman, *U.S. Aircraft Carriers,* 379; Capt. W. W. Webster (by direction, Chief, BuAer) to John C. Smaltz, McKiernan-Terry Corp., 18 Dec. 1940, Aer-E-34-MEM, S83-2(HIV), S83-2(HV), box 1425, file S83-2 (HV), BuAer, Confid. Corresp., 1922–44, RG 72, NA.

29. Towers to Manager, NAF, 7 Sept. 1940, Aer-E-34-SL, box 4792, vol. 16, file S83-2, BuAer, Confid. Corresp., 1922–44, RG 72, NA; John C. Smaltz, McKiernan-Terry Corp., to Navy Yard, Philadelphia, 18 Sept. 1940, ibid.

30. Memo, C. M. Bolster to BuAer, 27 Feb. 1942, Aer-E-34-NJG, S83-2, box 1420, vol. 3, ibid.; memo, Sydney Kraus to Ass't. SecNav for Air, 18 Sept. 1942, Aer-E-34-MEN, S83-2, box 1420, vol. 4, ibid.; Friedman, *U.S. Aircraft Carriers,* 147, 379.

31. *NAF Cavalcade of Aircraft,* 106; memo report, Capt. John S. Mills and Maj. C. M. Cummings, Engineering Section, Air Corps Material Division, Wright Field, 9 Sept. 1939, box 1420, vol. 2, file S83-2, BuAer, Confid. Corresp., 1922–44, RG 72, NA.

32. Memo, Maxson to Ass't. Chief, BuAer, 13 July 1933, Aer-D-111-BCP, box 1419, vol. 1, file S83-2, BuAer, Confid. Corresp., 1922–44, RG 72, NA; Capt. A. B. Cook (Ass't. Chief, BuAer) to Manager, NAF, 1 Dec. 1933, box 1427, file S83-2(XS-1), ibid.; Lisle J. Maxson, "Description of Screw-Type Catapult," 3 Jan. 1934, box 4789, vol. 6, file S83-2, BuAer, Gen. Corresp., 1925–42, ibid.

33. Capt. W. W. Webster (Manager, NAF) to Chief, BuAer, 7 Jan. 1938, (2514), box 1419, vol. 1, file S83-2, BuAer, Confid. Corresp., 1922–44, ibid.

34. R. Adm. A. B. Cook to Manager, NAF, 16 Nov. 1937, Aer-E-34-CWA, S83-2(XH-III), box 1426, vol. 1, file S83-2(XH-III), ibid.

35. R. Adm. A. B. Cook to Chief, BuC&R, 14 Mar. 1938, Aer-E-34-AMS, S83-2 VP, box 1419, vol. 1, file S83-2, ibid.

36. Capt. A. C. Read to CNO, 18 May 1938, Aer-E-34-AMS, ibid.

37. Ibid.; actual performance data for the PBM are from Swanborough and Bowers, *United States Navy Aircraft since 1911*, 320.

38. Project orders, Type XH, Mark III Catapult, 8 Nov. 1938, box 1426, vol. 1, file S83–2(XH-III), BuAer, Confid. Corresp., 1922–44, RG 72, NA; R. Adm. A. B. Cook to Manager, NAF, 2 Dec. 1938, Aer-E-34-AMS, S83-2(XH-III), ibid.; Nicholson route slip comments, 28 Nov. 1938, on ibid.

39. Webster to Commandant, Phila. Navy Yard, 6 Mar. 1939, S83(XH3) (2367), ibid.; Capt. M. A. Mitscher (Ass't. Chief, BuAer) to Manager, NAF, 3 Sept. 1940, Aer-E-34-SL, S83-2(XIII), C67996, C70168, box 1426, vol. 2, ibid. Richard K. Smith provided data on the German catapults in a communication to the author, 20 July 1988.

40. Pace to Chief, BuAer, 27 Jan. 1941, S83-2 (6528), box 1426, vol. 2, file S83-2(XH-III), BuAer, Confid. Corresp., 1922–44, RG 72, NA.

41. Capt. W. W. Webster to Chief, BuAer, 27 Jan. 1942, S83(XH3) (1132), ibid.; Webster to Chief, BuAer, 7 June 1942, S83(XHIII) (30838), ibid.; J. Ross Allen (by direction, Manager, NAF) to Chief, BuAer, 28 Jan. 1943, S83(XH3) (1339) (E-4), ibid.; Stevens route slip comments, undated, on ibid.

42. Memo of conference, Cdr. L. C. Stevens, 12 March 1941, Aer-E-2-EP, S83-2, box 1420, vol. 2, file S83-2, ibid.; for information on the Boeing Model 344 (XPBB-1), see Bowers, *Boeing Aircraft since 1916*, 216–17.

43. Capt. E. M. Pace, Jr., to Chief, BuAer, 2 July 1941, S83 (19250), box 1426, file S83-2(XHVII), ibid.; R. Adm. J. H. Towers (Chief, BuAer) to Manager, NAF, 24 July 1942, Aer-E-3411-VF, S83-2(XHIII), AVC, box 1426, vol. 2, file S83-2(XHIII), ibid.

44. Melhorn, *Two-Block Fox*, 78–79, elucidates the dimensions of the problems of recovering aircraft on carriers at sea.

45. R. Adm. D. W. Taylor, memo of conference, 8 Dec. 1920, box 4814, vol. 1, file S83-3, BuAer, Gen. Corresp., 1925–42, RG 72, NA; Taylor to SecNav, 6 Jan. 1921, O-ZS-44(A), O-ZA-35, 201-Z-30, ibid.; Hunsaker to CO, NAS, Hampton Roads, 16 May 1921, 201-Z-30(A), O-Z8-44, ibid.; Westervelt (Manager, NAF) to Chief, BuC&R, 1 Aug. 1921, (11703), ibid.; "Arresting Gear for Naval Aircraft Carriers," 201–2. See also Rausa, "Turntables and Traps," 8–18.

46. Lt. Carl B. Harper, Scientific Group, BuAer, memo for files, 8 Aug. 1922, Aer-M-15-WZ, 201-30, 203-2, box 4814, vol. 1, file S83-3, BuAer, Gen. Corresp., 1925–42, RG 72, NA; Carl L. Norden to BuAer, 16 May 1925, box 4814, vol. 2, ibid.; Swanborough and Bowers, *United States Navy Aircraft since 1911*, 37.

47. Memo, Lt. Cdr. L. C. Stevens to Moffett, 10 May 1929, Aer-D-111-MDB, box 4814, vol. 3, file S83-3, BuAer, Gen. Corresp., 1925–42, RG 72, NA.

48. *NAF Cavalcade of Aircraft*, 128; Melhorn, *Two-Block Fox*, 81, 147.

49. Capt. Emory S. Land (Ass't. Chief, BuAer) to Manager, NAF, 3 Feb. 1927, Aer-M-111-AAM-RP, VF603/F13-2, VD604-F13-2, box 4814, vol. 3, file S83-3, BuAer, Gen. Corresp., 1925–42, RG 72, NA; see also misc. documents in file S83-3, ibid.

50. Capt. A. B. Cook (Ass't. Chief, BuAer) to Manager, NAF, 8 Nov. 1933, Aer-D-111-BCP, box 4815, vol. 5, ibid.; E. M. Pace, Jr. (Acting Manager, NAF) to Chief, BuAer, 1 Dec. 1933, S83-3 (18058), ibid.; Capt. A. B. Cook (Acting Chief, BuAer) to Manager, NAF, 7 Feb. 1934, Aer-D-111-BCP, ibid.; Capt. S. J. Zeigler, Jr.

(Acting Manager, NAF) to Chief, BuAer, 26 Apr. 1934, S83-3 (3751), box 1429, vol. 3, file S83-3, BuAer, Confid. Corresp., 1922–44, ibid.; Capt. F. R. McCrary (Ass't. Chief, BuAer) to Manager, NAF, 20 Nov. 1934, Aer-E-34-BCP, S83-3, CV5&6, box 4815, vol. 6, file S83-3, BuAer, Gen. Corresp., 1925–42, ibid.

51. Lt. P. E. Pihl (BuAer) to Public Works, 8 Mar. 1934, box 4815, vol. 5, BuAer, Gen. Corresp., 1925–42, ibid.; Capt. S. J. Zeigler, Jr., to BuAer, 29 Aug. 1934, A1-3 (12031), box 4027, vol. 11, file NP 11, ibid.; R. Adm. A. B. Cook (Chief, BuAer) to CO, NAS, Norfolk, 29 June 1937, Aer-E-34-AMS, N10-13, S83-3, box 1430, vol. 5, file S83-3, BuAer, Confid. Corresp., 1922–44, ibid.

52. Capt. A. C. Read (Acting Chief, BuAer) to Manager, NAF, 20 May 1938, Aer-E-343-AMS, CV2&3/S83-3, box 1430, vol. 5, file S83-3, BuAer, Confid. Corresp., 1922–44, ibid.; *NAF Cavalcade of Aircraft*, 128.

CHAPTER 9

1. Low, "First Guided Missile," 436–38; Gardner, "Automatic Flight," 477–81; Werrell, *Evolution of the Cruise Missile*, 8, 17–18.

2. Hughes, *Sperry*, 173–200, 243–70; Pearson, "Developing the Flying Bomb," 70–73.

3. Hughes, *Sperry*, 271–73.

4. Fahrney, "History of Pilotless Aircraft and Guided Missiles," 149–74, OANHC.

5. Gardner, "Automatic Flight," 482–88.

6. Memo, A. D. Bernhard to Chief, BuAer, 19 Aug. 1935, Aer-PL-3-EMN, vol. 1, box 639, file F31-1(43), BuAer, Confid. Corresp., 1922–44, RG 72, NA; Fahrney, "History of Pilotless Aircraft and Guided Missiles," 190-92, OANHC.

7. J. K. Taussig (acting CNO) to Chiefs, BuAer and Bureau of Engineering, 1 May 1936, Op-22-B(SC) QT Serial 3389, vol. 1, box 639, file F31-1(43), BuAer, Confid. Corresp., 1922–44, RG 72, NA; Fahrney, "History of Pilotless Aircraft and Guided Missiles," 195–96, OANHC; Fahrney, "Guided Missiles," 28.

8. Memo, Fahrney to Chief, BuAer, 6 Aug. 1936, Aer-E-17-EP, vol. 1, box 639, file F31-1(43), BuAer, Confid. Corresp., 1922–44, RG 72, NA.

9. Ibid.

10. Fahrney to Manager, NAF, 9 Sept. 1936, vol. 1, ibid.; Fahrney, "Guided Missiles," 17.

11. Fahrney, "Target Drone Development," 39; Fahrney, "History of Pilotless Aircraft and Guided Missiles," 200–206, 215–16, OANHC.

12. Fahrney, "Target Drone Development," 39.

13. Fahrney, "History of Pilotless Aircraft and Guided Missiles," 207, OANHC.

14. Ibid.; Fahrney to Chief, BuAer, 13 Oct. 1937, monthly progress report, F32 (16529), vol. 2, box 639, file F31-1(43), BuAer, Confid. Corresp., 1922–44, RG 72, NA; Fahrney to Chief, BuAer, 15 Nov. 1937, monthly progress report, ibid.

15. Fahrney, "History of Pilotless Aircraft and Guided Missiles," 208, 213–14, OANHC; Fahrney to Chief, BuAer, 13 Oct. 1937, monthly progress report, F32 (16529), vol. 2, box 639, file F31-1(43), BuAer, Confid. Corresp., 1922–44, RG 72, NA; Fahrney to Chief, BuAer, 4 Jan. 1938, Radio Control of Aircraft—Semi-Annual Report of Progress, ibid.

16. Fahrney to Chief, BuAer, 4 Jan. 1938, Radio Control of Aircraft—Semi-Annual Report of Progress, vol. 2, box 639, file F31-1(43), BuAer, Confid. Corresp., 1922–44, RG 72, NA; Fahrney to Chief, BuAer, 10 Feb. 1938, monthly progress report, ibid.;

Cook to Manager, NAF, 15 Dec. 1937, Aer-E-10-EP, ibid.; Webster to Chief, BuAer, 25 Feb. 1938, F32(2990), ibid.

17. Lt. Cdr. L. C. Stevens, memo for files, 14 Mar. 1938, Aer-E-10-LID, ibid.; Webster to CNO, 11 Mar. 1938, F32(8), ibid.; Cluverius to CNO, 14 Mar. 1938, A6-8, ibid.

18. Fahrney, "History of Pilotless Aircraft and Guided Missiles," 225–75, OANHC.

19. Fahrney to Chief, BuAer, 10 Aug. 1938, monthly progress report, F32-1, vol. 2, box 639, file F31-1(43), BuAer, Confid. Corresp., 1922–44, RG 72, NA; Cook to Manager, NAF, 7 Oct. 1938, Aer-E-13-EP, F42-1, VN2C2/F1-1, vol. 3, box 640, ibid.; Fahrney to Chief, BuAer, 16 Dec. 1938, monthly progress report, ibid.; C. T. Durgin, CO, Utility Wing, U.S. Fleet Base Force, NAS, San Diego, memo to Chief, BuAer, 20 Jan. 1940, CUW/F41-10, vol. 5, box 641, ibid.

20. Webster to Chief, BuAer, 7 Oct. 1938, F32 (19151), vol. 3, box 640, ibid.; Cook to Manager, NAF, 26 Oct. 1938, Aer-PL-4EMN, ibid.; Fahrney to Chief, BuAer, 18 May 1939, monthly progress report, vol. 4, ibid.; Towers to Manager, NAF, 14 June 1939, Aer-E-16-MVG, L8-3(1-40), ibid.; Towers to Manager, NAF, 26 Dec. 1939, Aer-E-16-MVG, VO3U6/A4, vol. 5, box 641, ibid.; Capt. E. M. Pace, Jr., to Chief, BuAer, 9 May 1941 F32 (16323), vol. 2, box 2117, file F31-1(43), BuAer, Gen. Corresp., 1925–42, ibid.

21. The risks of vertical dive tests are related in Hallion, *Test Pilots*, 128–38. Cook to Manager, NAF, 27 Oct. 1937, Aer-E-24-FAM/EP, VBF201/F1-1, vol. 2, box 639, BuAer, Confid. Corresp., 1922–44, RG 72, NA. For the background of telemetry, see Mayo-Wells, "Origins of Space Telemetry," 253–68.

22. Fahrney to Chief, BuAer, 4 Jan. 1938, Radio Control of Aircraft—Semi-Annual Report of Progress, vol. 2, box 639, file F31-1(43), BuAer, Confid. Corresp., 1922–44, RG 72, NA; Webster to Chief, BuAer, 5 Jan. 1938, F32 (22820), ibid.

23. Bilby, *The General*, 120–25; Fahrney, "History of Pilotless Aircraft and Guided Missiles," 304, 318.

24. Memo, MacCart to Manager, NAF, 10 Mar 1938, on conference, 4 Mar. 1938, no. 7366, vol. 2, box 639, file F31-1(43), BuAer, Confid. Corresp., 1922–44, RG 72, NA.

25. Mitscher to Manager, NAF, 9 Aug. 1939, Aer-E-24-FAM, vol. 4, box 640, ibid.; Webster to Chief, BuAer, 29 Sept. 1939, F32 (17098), ibid.

26. J. M. Lane, memo on television, 13 Oct. 1939, Aer-PL-31-EMN, ibid.; memo, MacCart to Manager, NAF, 10 Mar. 1938, on conference, 4 Mar. 1938, no. 7366, ibid.; Fahrney, "History of Pilotless Aircraft and Guided Missiles," 314–17, OANHC.

27. Fahrney, "History of Pilotless Aircraft and Guided Missiles," 319, OANHC; William Nelson (Acting Manager, NAF) to Chief, BuAer, 13 June 1940, VJO3/F32 (11497), vol. 7, box 642, file F31-1(43), BuAer, Confid. Corresp., 1922–44, RG 72, NA.

28. W. R. Furlong to CNO, 19 Feb. 1940, F42/F32/L5-2(134), vol. 6, box 641, file F31–1(43), BuAer, Confid. Corresp., 1922–44, RG 72, NA; H. F. Leary (by direction, CNO) to Chief, BuAer, 28 Feb. 1940, Op-22-B5(SC) QT Serial 023622, ibid.; Fahrney, "History of Pilotless Aircraft and Guided Missiles," 322, OANHC.

29. Jones to Chief, BuAer, 12 Oct. 1939, VJ-3/F41-1(134), vol. 7, box 642, file F31-1(43), BuAer, Confid. Corresp., 1922–44, RG 72, NA; Jones to CO, Aircraft Battle Force, 17 Apr. 1940, VJ-3/F41-10/F13-1(270), vol. 6, ibid.; Fahrney, "History of Pilotless Aircraft and Guided Missiles," 331–34, OANHC.

30. W. R. Furlong to CNO, 11 June 1940, F42-1(F32/45-2), vol. 7, box 642, file

F31-1(43), BuAer, Confid. Corresp., 1922–44, RG 72, NA; Richardson to Chief, BuAer, 19 Sept. 1940, ibid.

31. Mitscher to CNO, 30 Oct. 1940, Aer-E-15-RMN/EX, ibid.; Fahrney route slip comments, ibid.

32. William Nelson (Acting Manager, NAF) to Chief, BuAer, 19 Mar. 1940, F32 (1968), vol. 6, ibid.; Fahrney, "History of Pilotless Aircraft and Guided Missiles," 323, OANHC; Swanborough and Bowers, *United States Navy Aircraft since 1914*, 41.

33. Memo, Fahrney to engineering section, BuAer, 16 Dec. 1940, Aer-E-15-EP, vol. 7, box 642, file F31-1(43), BuAer, Confid. Corresp., 1922–44, RG 72, NA. For more information on the Kettering-GM flying bomb, see Werrell, *Evolution of the Cruise Missile*, 26–30, and Fahrney, "History of Pilotless Aircraft and Guided Missiles," 774–77, OANHC.

34. Towers to Manager, NAF, 17 Jan. 1941, Aer-E-15-LHM, vol. 7, box 642, file F31-1(43), BuAer, Confid. Corresp., 1922–44, RG 72, NA.

35. Towers to CNO, 18 Apr. 1941, Aer-E-15-EP, vol. 8, ibid.

36. J. Ross Allen (by direction, Manager NAF) to Chief, BuAer, 22 Aug. 1941, F32 (28565), vol. 9, box 643, ibid.; memo, CO, Utility Squadron 5 to CNO, 5 Sept. 1941, VJ5/F41-10/(156), (c-28-41), ibid.

37. Ralph S. Barnaby (by direction, Manager NAF) to Chief, BuAer, 27 Feb. 1941, F32 (2196), vol. 7, ibid.; Fahrney, "History of Pilotless Aircraft and Guided Missiles," 326–28, OANHC.

38. Fahrney, "History of Pilotless Aircraft and Guided Missiles," 321, OANHC; Fahrney, "Guided Missiles," 23.

39. Pace to Chief, BuAer, 21 Apr. 1941, F32 (16329), vol. 8, box 642, file F31-1(43), BuAer, Confid. Corresp., 1922–44, RG 72, NA; Mitscher to Manager, NAF, 16 May 1941, Aer-E-15-EP, ibid.; Fahrney route slip comments, ibid.

40. Fahrney, "History of Pilotless Aircraft and Guided Missiles," 330, OANHC; Pace to Chief, BuAer, 8 Oct. 1941, F32 (36249), vol. 9, box 643, file F31-1(43), BuAer, Confid. Corresp., 1922–44, RG 72, NA.

41. Fahrney, "History of Pilotless Aircraft and Guided Missiles," 336–37, OANHC; W. A. Lee, Jr. (by direction, CNO) to Chief, BuAer, 28 Oct. 1941, Op-22-B5(SC), F42-1/VX QT, Serial 0118722, vol. 9, box 643, file F31-1(43), BuAer, Confid. Corresp., 1922–44, RG 72, NA.

CHAPTER 10

1. Turnbull and Lord, *History of United States Naval Aviation*, 308–15; Holley, *Buying Aircraft*, 229 67.

2. Holley, *Buying Aircraft*, 276–89; U.S., Cong., *Statutes at Large, 1939–1941*, vol. 54, pt. 1, 676–83.

3. For perspectives on the employment of engineers in the NACA, see Roland, *Model Research*, 1:121–23; and Hansen, *Engineer in Charge*, 50–53.

4. Interview with J. Hartley Bowen, Jr., Haddonfield, N.J., 13 Oct. 1983; interview with William J. Cox, Lakehurst, N.J., 11 Oct. 1983.

5. Memo on adequacy of Naval Aircraft Factory, A. E. Watson (Commandant, Phila. Navy Yard) to Chief, BuAer, 21 May 1940, box 56, file NP 11, BuAer, Gen. Corresp., Secret, 1939–42, RG 72, NA; memo, William H. Miller for head, Engineering Division, BuAer, 26 May 1941, Aer-E-241-FAM, LL/NP11, box 4029, vol. 18, file NP 11, BuAer, Gen. Corresp., 1925–42, ibid.

6. N. S. Harzenstein, survey on plant protection, NAF, FBI file no. 99-18, 17 Apr. 1940, box 1206, file NP 11, BuAer, Confid. Corresp., 1922–44, RG 72, NA; memo on adequacy of Naval Aircraft Factory, A. E. Watson to Chief, BuAer, 21 May 1940, box 56, file NP 11, BuAer, Gen. Corresp., Secret, 1939–42, ibid.

7. N. S. Harzenstein, survey on plant protection, NAF, FBI file 99-18, 17 Apr. 1940, box 1206, file NP 11, BuAer, Confid. Corresp., 1922–44, ibid.

8. Capt. E. M. Pace, Jr., to Chief, BuAer, 2 Sept. 1941 (15620), box 4029, vol. 18, file NP 11, BuAer, Gen. Corresp., 1925–42, ibid.; "History of the Naval Air Material Center," Appendixes 12 and 13, OANHC.

9. "War History of the Fourth Naval District," vol. 5, pt. 8, III-1–III-2, NDL.

10. Ibid., III-2-III–15, III-17; *Air Scoop* 1 (Dec. 1944): 11.

11. "War History of the Fourth Naval District," vol. 5, pt. 8, III-19–III-31, NDL.

12. N. S. Harzenstein, survey on plant protection, NAF, FBI file 99-18, 17 Apr. 1940, box 1206, file NP 11, BuAer, Confid. Corresp., 1922–44, RG 72, NA.

13. Ralph A. Bard (Ass't. SecNav) to Commandant, Phila. Navy Yard, 20 Nov. 1942, SOSED-O-CRC-11/20, box 4029, vol. 19, file NP 11, BuAer, Gen. Corresp., 1925–42, ibid.; "History of the Naval Air Material Center," 75–77, OANHC; Cox interview, 11 Oct. 1983.

14. Lichtenstein, *Labor's War at Home*, 124; *Air Scoop* 1 (June 1944): 7, 15; ibid. 1 (Dec. 1944): 7; ibid. 2 (June 1945): 4; ibid. 2 (Sept. 1945): 12; Shumway, "Naval Aircraft Factory," 44–45, 188.

15. *Air Scoop* 1 (Aug. 1944): 4; "Where Designs Come to Life," ibid. 2 (June 1945): 2–4; Bowen interview, 13 Oct. 1983.

16. "Winning Waves," 2–3, 8.

17. Lichtenstein, *Labor's War at Home*, 124–25; *Air Scoop* 1 (Apr. 1944): 13; ibid. 1 (June 1944): 4; Ralph A. Bard (Ass't. SecNav) to Commandant, Phila. Navy Yard, 20 Nov. 1942, box 4029, vol. 19, file NP 11, BuAer, Gen. Corresp., 1925–42, RG 72, NA.

18. Case dockets are in the Records of the Fair Employment Practices Committee, Philadelphia Regional Office, Record Group 225, Federal Archives and Records Center, Philadelphia.

19. Draemel to G. James Fleming (Regional Director, FEPC), 12 Feb. 1944, in Docket 3-GR-420, Records of the FEPC, RG 225, Federal Archives and Records Center, Philadelphia. See also Docket 3-GR-435, and Hugh D. McDonald to Lawrence W. Cramer (Secretary, FEPC), 9 Feb. 1942, ibid.

20. "History of the Naval Air Material Center," 76, OANHC; *Air Scoop* 1 (Apr. 1944): 14; ibid. 1 (July 1944): 15; ibid. 1 (Nov. 1944): 20; ibid. 1 (Sept. 1944).

21. Asimov, "Airplane Torture Chamber," 6–7; Asimov, "When Powder Means Life," 8; *Air Scoop* 1 (Aug. 1944): 11; Asimov, *In Memory Yet Green*, 337, 356–57.

22. Asimov, *In Memory Yet Green*, 362, 397, 416–17, 432; Bowen interview, 13 Oct. 1983.

23. Barnaby interview, 12 Oct. 1983; Bowen interview, 13 Oct. 1983; *American Aviation* 4 (June 1, 1940): 4.

24. Pace, "Naval Aircraft Factory," 128.

25. *Philadelphia Inquirer*, 17 Mar. 1943; Barnaby interview, 12 Oct. 1983; Bowen interview, 13 Oct. 1983.

26. *Philadelphia Inquirer*, 19 Mar. 1943; "History of the Naval Air Material Center," n.p., OANHC; U.S. Navy Department, *United States Naval Aviation, 1910–1980*, 467–68.

27. *Air Scoop* 1 (Nov. 1944): 5.

28. "The History of the Aviation Supply Office to June 1944," 1–4, Philadelphia—Naval Aviation Supply Office file, Aviation History File, OANHC.

29. Ibid., 4–5.

30. Ibid., 6–7, 10–11.

31. "Naval Aviation's Storehouse," 166; William C. Russell to SecNav, 26 Mar. 1942, box 4029, vol. 18, file NP 11, BuAer, Gen. Corresp., 1925–42, RG 72, NA.

32. "History of the Naval Air Material Center," 4, Appendix 1, OANHC; "History of ASO-NASD, 1 Oct. 1945–30 Sep. 1946," Aviation History File, Air/Ground Establishments, OANHC; "Naval Aviation's Storehouse," 166; "ASO," 12.

33. Memo, Pace to Director of Planning, BuAer, 17 Aug. 1943, Aer-M-BB, box 4029, vol. 19, file NP 11, BuAer, Gen. Corresp., 1925–42, RG 72, NA.

34. Ibid.

35. Memo endorsement, J. H. Towers to Vice-Chief of Naval Operations, 3 Oct. 1942, Aer-PL-11-ES A4-1(1) A3-1, box 4029, vol. 19, file NP 11, BuAer, Gen. Corresp., 1925–42, RG 72, NA.

36. "History of the Naval Air Material Center," 71, OANHC; "War History of the Fourth Naval District," vol. 5, pt. 8, II-2- II-3, NDL.

37. "History of the Naval Air Material Center," 71–73, OANHC.

38. "War History of the Fourth Naval District," vol. 5, pt. 8, II-4-II-5, NDL.

39. *Air Scoop* 1 (Nov. 1944): 5; Capt. J. B. Pearson, Jr., to CNO (History Unit), 20 Sept. 1945, Aviation History File, Air/Ground Establishments, Philadelphia—Naval Air Material Center, OANHC.

40. Fahrney, "History of Pilotless Aircraft and Guided Missiles," 444–46, OANHC; memo, Fahrney to BuAer, 23 Apr. 1943, Aer-E-15-AK, box 644, vol. 14, file F31-1(43), BuAer, Confid. Corresp., 1922–44, RG 72, NA; R. Adm. John S. McCain (Chief, BuAer) to Chief, Bu Y&D, 1 July 1943, Aer-MA-315-HM, box 3471, vol. 23, file NP 11, BuAer, Gen. Corresp., 1943–45, ibid.

41. Maas, "Fall from Grace," 127, 131–32; Misa and Todd, *History of the Naval Air Development Center*, 5.

42. Zeigler to BuAer, 1 Jan. 1944, C-HS F32, box 645, vol. 1 (1944), file F31-1(43), BuAer, Confid. Corresp., 1922–44, RG 72, NA.

43. "War History of the Fourth Naval District," vol. 5, pt. 8, I-16–I-18, NDL; *Aviation News* 3 (23 Apr. 1945): 10.

44. Webster to Chief, BuAer, 5 June 1942, A1-3 (22056), box 4029, vol. 19, file NP 11, BuAer, Gen. Corresp., 1925–42, RG 72, NA; Chief, BuY&D, to Commandant, Phila. Navy Yard, 28 Oct. 1942, box 3472, file NP 11/NOY 5870, BuAer, Gen. Corresp., 1943–45, ibid.

CHAPTER 11

1. U.S., Cong., House, *Investigation into Status of Naval Defense Program*, 304–5.

2. D. C. Ramsey, Plans Division, BuAer, to Chief, BuAer (no date, but probably Nov. 1940), Aer-PL-4-AF, box 4029, vol. 17, file NP 11, BuAer, Gen. Corresp., 1925–42, RG 72, NA.

3. Swanborough and Bowers, *United States Navy Aircraft since 1911*, 401.

4. Project Order 269–41, dated 30 Jan. 1941, Aer-PR-21-AB VOS2N1/F1-1 L8-3(1-AD) box 5153, vol. 1, file VOS2N/F1-1, BuAer, Gen. Corresp., 1925–42, RG 72, NA; Mitscher to Manager, NAF, 4 Feb. 1941, Aer-PR-2-EMR, ibid.

5. Memo, Pace to all department heads, 20 Feb. 1941, ibid.

6. Pace to Chief, BuAer, 29 May 1941, VOS2N1/F1-1 (188), ibid.; Pace to Chief, BuAer, 12 Dec. 1941, VOS2N1/F1-1 (7492), ibid.

7. Towers to Manager, NAF, 23 Dec. 1941, Aer-M-BB C76493, ibid.

8. J. Ross Allen (by direction, Manager, NAF) to Chief, BuAer, 11 Mar. 1942, VOS2N1/F8 (5735), box 5153, vol. 1, ibid.; files VOS2N1/F49 and VOS2N1/L11, box 5155, ibid., contain information on OS2N-1 deliveries.

9. H. T. Stanley (by direction, CO, NAS, New York) to Manager, NAF, 9 Sept. 1942, 15/RJG/rww, box 5154, vol. 2, file VOS2N1/F1-1, BuAer, Gen. Corresp., 1925–42, RG 72, NA; Capt. L. A. Pope (by direction, Chief, BuAer) to CO, NAS, New York, and Manager, NAF, 28 Sept. 1942, Aer-F-11-R10, ibid.

10. Ens. P. A. Brady, USNR, to Chief, BuAer, 22 June 1942, VS1-D10/F8-1, ibid.; Capt. H. B. Sallada to CO, VS1D15, 1 Aug. 1942, Aer-E-13LSP, ibid.

11. R. S. Barnaby (by direction, Manager, NAF) to Chief, BuAer, 6 Nov. 1942, VOS2N1/F1-1 (62463) E-3, ibid.

12. For the PBY, see Swanborough and Bowers, *United States Navy Aircraft since 1911*, 80–81; and Creed, *PBY*, esp. 24–53.

13. Creed, *PBY*, 49; "Naval Aircraft Material Center's PBN-1," 89.

14. Capt. M. A. Mitscher to Manager, NAF, 5 Apr. 1941, Aer-PR-21-KH, box 5232, vol. 1, file VPBN1/F1-1, BuAer, Gen. Corresp., 1925–42, RG 72, NA; Pace to Chief, BuAer, 21 Apr. 1941, VPBN1/F1-1(170), ibid.

15. R. Adm. J. H. Towers to Manager, NAF, 2 May 1941, Aer-PRO20EMR, VPBN1/F1-1, box 5232, vol. 1, file VPBN1/F1-1, ibid.; "War History of the Fourth Naval District," vol. 5, pt. 8, I-8, NDL.

16. Cox interview, 11 Oct. 1983; Pace to Chief, BuAer, 16 June 1941, A2-14(5) (199), box 5232, vol. 1, file VPBN1/F1-1, BuAer, Gen. Corresp., 1925–42, RG 72, NA; Pace to Chief, BuAer, 18 Sept., 1941, VPBN1/VPBY5/F1-1 (37111), ibid.; Capt. W. W. Webster (Director of Material, BuAer) to Chief, BuAer, 27 Nov. 1941, Aer-M-AQ, VPBN1/F1-1, box 4029, vol. 18, file NP 11, ibid.

17. "Naval Aircraft Material Center's PBN-1," 89–94. Technical data for the PBN and PBY-5 differ from publication to publication. Those quoted here appear in Wagner, *Story of the PBY Catalina*.

18. Ramsey to Manager, NAF, 31 Oct. 1941, Aer-M-AQ, VPBN1/F1-1, NP 11, box 5232, vol. 1, file VPBN1/F1-1, BuAer, Gen. Corresp., 1925–42, RG 72, NA; Pace to Chief, BuAer, 8 Nov. 1941, VPBN1/F1-1 (7476), ibid.

19. Route slip comments on Pace to Chief, BuAer, 8 Nov. 1941, VPBN1/F1-1 (7476), ibid.; memo, Webster to Chief, BuAer, 27 Nov. 1941, Aer-M-AQ, VPBN1/F1-1, NP 11, ibid.

20. Memo, Webster to Chief, BuAer, 27 Nov. 1941, Aer-M-AQ, VPBN1/F1-1, NP 11, ibid.; Webster to Chief, BuAer, 12 June 1942, 26168, ibid.

21. Memo for Director of Material, BuAer, 8 Dec. 1941, Aer-Pl-6-KHK, VPBN1/F1-1, box 4029, vol. 18, file NP 11, ibid.; Capt. D. C. Ramsey to Manager, NAF, 17 Dec. 1941, Aer-PRD-GF, VPBN1/F1-1, ibid.; Capt. D. Ketcham, BuAer, to various divisions, 18 Nov. 1942, Aer-PL-62-EK, box 5233, file VPBN1/L4, ibid.

22. TWX, Manager, NAF, to BuAer, 16 Oct. 1942, box 5233, vol. 2, file VPBN1/F1-1, ibid.; memo for files, R. W. Mackert, 15 Nov. 1942, ibid.; Webster to Chief, BuAer, 18 Dec. 1942, VPBN1/F1-1 (64494) (E-3), box 5232, vol. 1, file VPBN1/A4, ibid.

23. Creed, *PBY*, 37; Barnaby interview, 12 Oct. 1983.

24. Memo for files, R. W. Mackert, 15 Nov. 1942, box 5233, vol. 2, file VPBN1/F1-1, BuAer, Gen. Corresp., 1925–42, RG 72, NA.

25. Webster to Chief, BuAer, 18 Dec. 1942, VPBN1/F1-1 (64494) (E-3), box 5232, vol. 1, file VPBN1/A4, ibid.

26. Telegram, NAF to BuAer, 11 Feb. 1943, box 4771, vol. 3, file VPBN1/F1-1, BuAer, Gen. Corresp., 1943–45, ibid.; memo, Capt. J. Ross Allen to Manager, NAF, 13 Mar. 1943, (1012) (E-2), ibid.; route slip comments on memo, Capt. T. R. Frederick to Planning, BuAer, 13 Mar. 1943, Aer-E-143-VF, ibid.

27. Memo, Capt. T. R. Frederick re. PBN-1 Airplane Conference on Directional Stability Troubles, 19 Mar. 1943, Aer-E-145-MS, ibid.

28. Memo, Capt. J. Ross Allen to Manager, NAF, 27 Apr. 1943, (850) (E-1), ibid.; memo, Capt. J. Ross Allen to Manager, NAF, 29 Apr. 1943, (852) (E-1), ibid.

29. Interview with V. Adm. Herbert Riley, no date, Oral History Collection, United States Naval Institute, 169.

30. Memo, Capt. J. Ross Allen for Chief, BuAer, 14 May 1943, (859) (E-1), box 4771, vol. 3, file VPBN1/F1-1, BuAer, Gen. Corresp., 1943–45, RG 72, NA.

31. Memo, Harrison to Manager, NAF, 1 June 1943, box 4771, vol. 4, ibid.; TWX, Manager, NAF to BuAer, 25 June 1943, ibid.; Lt. Cdr. L. D. Coates (by direction, Chief, BuAer) to CO, NAS, Patuxent River, 21 July 1943, Aer-E-143-VF, ibid.

32. Capt. Lloyd Harrison to BuAer, 28 July 1943, VPBN1/F8 (1840), ibid.

33. Capt. Lloyd Harrison to prospective CO, NAMC (Capt. S. J. Zeigler), 11 Aug. 1943, PP-MIA L9-3(9) (15537), box 4771, vol. 4, file VPBN1/F1-1, ibid.; memo, John W. Meader to CO, NAMC, 15 Sept. 1943, ibid.; Zeigler to BuAer, 14 Oct. 1943, C-MB, ibid.

34. Memo, John W. Meader to CO, NAMC, 15 Sept. 1943, ibid.; U.S. Department of Commerce, Civil Aeronautics Administration, *U. S. Military Aircraft Acceptances, 1940–1945*, 48, 53.

35. Capt. R. S. Barnaby to BuAer, 14 Dec. 1943, PE-2.16-ASK, ibid.; Riley interview, 170–72.

36. Riley interview, 172–77.

37. Ibid., 177–78; Powell, *Ferryman*, 106–7; Col. I. P. Kramarenko to Capt. C. J. Parrish, Office of the CNO, 5 Aug. 1944, box 4770, vol. 2, file VPBN1/F1-1, BuAer, Gen. Corresp., 1943–45, RG 72, NA; Capt. C. M. Huntington (Manager, NAF) to BuAer, 26 Aug. 1944, PE-2.16-BLR, ibid.

38. Royce to BuAer, 20 Mar. 1945, C-MB box 4770, vol. 2, file VPBN1/F1-1, BuAer, Gen. Corresp., 1943–45, RG 72, NA.

39. Teletype, Ramsey to CO, NAMC, 23 Mar. 1945, ibid.

40. Cdr. L. C. Stevens to Capt. E. M. Pace, 26 June 1940, box 5048, vol. 2, file VN5N1/F1-1, BuAer, Gen. Corresp., 1925–42, RG 72, NA.

41. Pace to Chief, BuAer, 23 July 1941, F1-1 (869), box 4029, vol. 17, ibid.

42. Ramsey to Manager, NAF, 7 Aug. 1941, Aer-E-LIIM VPB, box 4029, vol. 17, file NP 11, ibid.

43. Memo, Ivan H. Driggs to Cdr. L. C. Stevens, BuAer, 9 Jan. 1942, Aer-E-210-EM VPB F1, box 1206, file NP 11, BuAer, Confid. Corresp., 1922–44, ibid.

44. Memo, Towers to directors, all divisions, BuAer, 23 Dec. 1941, Aer-E-2-HYC, box 4029, vol. 18, file NP 11, BuAer, Gen. Corresp., 1925–42, ibid.

45. Webster to Chief, BuAer, 20 Feb. 1942, F1-1 (10623), ibid.; comments in BuAer survey of possible design projects for NAF, 26 Mar. 1942, ibid.

46. Comments in BuAer survey of possible design projects for NAF, 26 Mar. 1942, ibid.

47. Ibid.; Towers to Manager, NAF, 7 May 1942, Aer-E-2-EP A3-1, box 4029, vol. 18, file NP 11, ibid.

48. J. Ross Allen (by direction, Manager, NAF), to Chief, BuAer, 27 Jan. 1943, L9-3(9) (12605) (E-2), box 3472, vol. 21, file NP 11, BuAer, Gen. Corresp., 1943–45, ibid.; Webster to R. Adm. Ralph E. Davison, BuAer, 3 Feb. 1943, ibid.; Pace (by direction, Chief, BuAer) to Manager, NAF, 22 Feb. 1943, Aer-E-2-EP, ibid.
49. Memo, J. H. Stevenson (Planning Superintendent, NAF), to Zeigler, 12 Nov. 1943, box 4771, vol. 4, file VPBN1/F1-1, ibid.
50. "War History of the Fourth Naval District," vol. 5, pt. 8, I-15, NDL; route slip comments on memo, Capt. Robert S. Hatcher, BuAer, to Capt. Edward W. Clexton, BuAer, 8 Dec. 1944, Aer-E-20-HA, box 3471, vol. 24, file NP 11, BuAer, Gen. Corresp., 1943–45, RG 72, NA; memo, Clexton to Hatcher, 3 Jan. 1945, Aer-MA-151-AFO (AOS), box 3470, vol. 23, ibid.
51. Memo, Lt. Cdr. G. Chapman to Ass't. Head, Shore Establishments Group, 18 Jan. 1945, Aer-MA-315-GC, box 3471, vol. 24, file NP 11, ibid.
52. Ibid.
53. "War History of the Fourth Naval District," vol. 5, pt. 8, I-9–I-14, NDL.

CHAPTER 12

1. R. Adm. J. H. Towers to CNO, 4 Nov. 1941, Aer-E-15-EP, box 643, vol. 9, file F31-1(43), BuAer, Confid. Corresp., 1922–44, RG 72, NA; Capt. D. C. Ramsey to Manager, NAF, 29 Nov. 1941, Aer-E-151-LHM, ibid.
2. Webster to Chief, BuAer, 15 Jan. 1942, F1-1 (1115), vol. 10, ibid.; Project Order no. 518-42, 21 Jan. 1942, Aer-PR-47-EB, L8-3(1-42), box 2118, vol. 3, file F31-1(43), BuAer, Gen. Corresp., 1925–42, ibid.
3. Capt. J. E. Ostrander (by direction, Chief, BuAer) to Manager, NAF, 14 Feb. 1942, Aer-E-210-MMC, box 643, vol. 10, file F31-1(43), BuAer, Confid. Corresp., 1922–44, ibid.
4. Fahrney, "History of Pilotless Aircraft and Guided Missiles," 339, OANHC; Capt. D. C. Ramsey to Manager, NAF, 30 Mar. 1942, Aer-E-15-EP, box 643, vol. 10, file F31-1(43), BuAer, Confid. Corresp., 1922–44, RG 72, NA.
5. Fahrney, "History of Pilotless Aircraft and Guided Missiles," 339–41, OANHC.
6. Memo, Lt. (j.g.) M. B. Taylor, 28 Jan. 1942, box 643, vol. 10, file F31-1(43), BuAer, Confid. Corresp., 1922–44, RG 72, NA; Webster to Chief, BuAer, 3 Feb. 1942, F42(R) (1346), ibid.
7. Webster to COMINCH, 22 Mar. 1942, F42-1 (5277), ibid.
8. Ostrander, Stevens, and Fahrney route slip comments on ibid.
9. Fahrney, "Guided Missiles," 24; Fahrney, "History of Pilotless Aircraft and Guided Missiles," 347–49, OANHC.
10. Fahrney, "History of Pilotless Aircraft and Guided Missiles," 370–71, OANHC.
11. Webster to Chief, BuAer, 2 May 1942, VTDN1/F1-1, box 643, vol. 10, file F31-1(43), BuAer, Confid. Corresp., 1922–44, RG 72, NA; Webster to Chief, BuAer, 6 May 1942, VTDN1/F1-1 (2144), ibid.; Air Scoop 8 (28 Oct. 1960): 1.
12. Capt. E. M. Pace, Jr. (by direction, Chief, BuAer) to Manager, NAF, 9 May 1942, Aer-E-15-AK, box 643, vol. 10, file F31-1(43), BuAer, Confid. Corresp., 1922–44; Webster to Chief, BuAer, 14 May 1942, VTDN1/F1-1 (2891), ibid.
13. Fahrney, "History of Pilotless Aircraft and Guided Missiles," 351, 372–76, OANHC.
14. Memo, E. M. Pace to Plans Div., BuAer, 3 June 1942, Aer-E-15-AK, box 643, vol. 11, file F31-1(43), BuAer, Confid. Corresp., 1922–44, RG 72, NA.

15. Cdr. Ralph Barnaby (by direction, Manager, NAF) to Chief, BuAer, 24 Mar. 1942, VTDN/F8 (20115), box 1711, vol. 1, file VTDN1/F1-1, BuAer, Confid. Corresp., 1922–44, RG 72, NA; J. Ross Allen (by direction, Manager, NAF) to Chief, BuAer, 6 May 1942, VTDN1/F1-1 (20175), ibid.; Mock-up Inspection Report of the XTDN-1 Airplane at the Naval Aircraft Factory, 1 July 1942, Aer-E-15-AK, VTDN1/F1-1, ibid.

16. C. C. Sorgen, memo of visit to Naval Aircraft Factory, 6 May, 1942, Aer-E-443-LHC, box 643, vol. 10, file F31-1(43), ibid.; Fahrney to Chief, BuAer, 7 Oct. 1942, Aer-E-47-VC, box 5531, vol. 1, file VTDN1/F1-1, ibid.; Webster to Chief, BuAer, 14 Oct. 1942, VTDN1/F1-1/F23-1 (47098) (E-3), ibid.; Fahrney (by direction, Chief, BuAer) to Manager, NAF, 16 Oct. 1942, Aer-E-15-AK, VTDN1/F42-1, F31-1(43), VTDN1/F21, box 1712, file VTDN1/F42-1, ibid.

17. Telegram, NAF to BuAer, 16 Nov. 1942, box 5531, vol. 1, file VTDN1/F1-1, ibid.; memo, Capt. Oscar Smith to Capt. A. M. Pride, 17 Dec. 1942, box 1711, ibid.; *NAF Cavalcade of Aircraft*, 78.

18. Progress Report, Manager, NAF, to Chief, BuAer, 30 Nov. 1942, box 2118, vol. 4, file F31-1(43), BuAer, Confid. Corresp., 1922–44, RG 72, NA; Report, Board of Inspection and Survey to SecNav, 29 Mar. 1943, VXTDN1/F8 (947-S), Serial 05121, box 1712, vol. 2, file VTDN1/F1-1, ibid.

19. Webster to Chief, BuAer, 4 Dec. 1942, VTDN1/F1-1 (15828) (P-2), box 1711, vol. 1, file VTDN1/F1-1, ibid.; Webster to Chief, BuAer, in reference to 26 Dec. 1942 conference at NAF, VPTDN1/F1-1 (27961), ibid.; TDN Airplanes Disposition and Acceptance, 30 Apr. 1943, box 5224, vol. 2, file VTDN1/F1-1, BuAer, Gen. Corresp., 1943–45, ibid.; Capt. Hugh H. Goodwin (by direction, Chief, BuAer), to Board of Inspection and Survey, 9 Aug. 1943, Aer-E-211-RJ, VTDN1/F1-1, box 1712, vol. 2, file VTDN1/F1-1, BuAer, Confid. Corresp., 1922–44, ibid.

20. J. A. Smith to Chief, BuAer, 29 Jan. 1943, VJ6/F41-10/X02029 (C-515-43), box 644, vol. 13, file F31-1(43), BuAer, Confid. Corresp., 1922–44, ibid.; Ralph S. Barnaby (by direction, Manager, NAF) to Chief, BuAer, 17 June 1943, VTDN1/F1-1 (42941) E-3, box 1712, file VTDN1/F13-2, ibid.

21. For detailed information on the operational use of assault drones, see Fahrney, "History of Pilotless Aircraft and Guided Missiles," 416–32, OANHC, and Fahrney, "Guided Missiles," 26.

22. Fahrney, "History of Pilotless Aircraft and Guided Missiles," 952, OANHC.

23. Ibid., 435–37.

24. Ibid., 437–38; Barnaby interview, 12 Oct. 1983.

25. Fahrney, "History of Pilotless Aircraft and Guided Missiles," 438, 450–53, OANHC; J. Ross Allen (by direction, Manager, NAF) to Chief, BuAer, 3 June 1942, F32 (25687), box 643, file F31-1(43), BuAer, Confid. Corresp., 1922–44, RG 72, NA.

26. Fahrney, "History of Pilotless Aircraft and Guided Missiles," 454–55, 459–61, OANHC.

27. Ibid., 457, 459, 462; Cdr. J. W. Davison (by direction, CO, NAMU) to BuAer, 14 Nov. 1944, ME-21-DS, F45(G), box 1524, file VLNT2/F1-1, BuAer, Confid. Corresp., 1922–44, RG 72, NA.

28. Fahrney, "History of Pilotless Aircraft and Guided Missiles," 464–65, OANHC; "Taylorcraft Tid-Bits" (Jan., Feb. 1981), courtesy of Forrest Barber, Alliance, Ohio.

29. Barnaby interview, 27 Aug. 1969, OANHC; E. M. Pace, Jr., to Chief, BuAer, 12 Aug. 1941, F13-3 (27535), box 1524, file VLR, BuAer, Confid. Corresp., 1922–44, RG 72, NA; R. S. Barnaby (by direction, Manager, NAF) to Chief, BuAer, 10 Oct. 1941,

F1-1 (892), ibid.; Swanborough and Bowers, *United States Navy Aircraft since 1911*, 501.

30. Section Directive no. 1-43, 24 July 1942, box 1524, file VLR, BuAer, Confid. Corresp., 1922–44, RG 72, NA; Progress Report, Manager, NAF, to Chief, BuAer, 28 July 1942, ibid.; Fahrney, "History of Pilotless Aircraft and Guided Missiles," 457–58, OANHC.

31. Merrill to Chief, BuAer, 25 Oct. 1943, Aer-E-18-JBM, box 1524, file VLRN1/F1-1, BuAer, Confid. Corresp., 1922–44, RG 72, NA.

32. Barnaby interview, 27 Aug. 1969, OANHC; Fahrney, "History of Pilotless Aircraft and Guided Missiles," 458–59, OANHC; W. W. Pearl to Chief Engineer, NAMU, 14 Nov. 1944, box 1524, file VLRN1/F1-1 (1944), BuAer, Confid. Corresp., 1922–44, RG 72, NA; "XLRN-1 Glider Status as of 11/25/44," 25 Nov. 1944, ibid.; Capt. R. S. Barnaby to BuAer, 30 Nov. 1944, ME:mdt VLRN1/F1-1, ibid.

33. Fahrney, "History of Pilotless Aircraft and Guided Missiles," 465–67, OANHC.

34. Barnaby interview, 27 Aug. 1969, OANHC; Barnaby to BuAer, 30 Nov. 1944, ME:mdt VLRN1/F1-1, box 1524, file VLRN1/F1-1, BuAer, Confid. Corresp., 1922–44, RG 72, NA.

35. Fahrney, "History of Pilotless Aircraft and Guided Missiles," 468–70, OANHC.

36. Ibid., 477–78; Driggs to BuAer, 7 Aug. 1943, Aer-E-22-BMS, box 644, vol. 14, file F31-1(43), BuAer, Confid. Corresp., 1922–44, RG 72, NA.

37. Fahrney, "History of Pilotless Aircraft and Guided Missiles," 478–79, OANHC; Capt. S. J. Zeigler to BuAer, 25 Oct. 1943, C-MB F32, box 644, vol. 14, file F31-1(43), BuAer, Confid. Corresp., 1922–44, RG 72, NA.

38. Capt. R. S. Barnaby to BuAer, 3 Nov. 1943, PE-BLR F32, box 644, vol. 14, file F31-1(43), BuAer, Confid. Corresp., 1922–44, RG 72, NA.

39. Memo, William H. Miller to Special Design Branch, BuAer, 5 Jan. 1944, Aer-E-2412-BR, box 645, vol. 1 (1944), ibid.

40. Telegram, NAF to BuAer, 21 Feb. 1944, ibid.; memo, Lt. Cdr. R. F. Farrington to Special Design Desk, BuAer, 22 Mar. 1944, Aer-R-10-RFF, F31-1(43), box 645, vol. 2 (1944), ibid.; Chief, BuAer, to CO, NAMC, 25 Mar. 1944, Aer-E-18-RMF, F31-1(43), ibid.; Barnaby to BuAer, 1 Apr. 1944, PE-2.18/FGT, F32(G), ibid.; Fahrney, "History of Pilotless Aircraft and Guided Missiles," 480, OANHC.

41. Capt. R. S. Barnaby to BuAer, 15 Feb. 1944, PE-2.18-ASK, F32-G, box 645, vol. 2 (1944), file F31-1(43), BuAer, Confid. Corresp., 1922–44, RG 72, NA; G. W. Lewis (Director of Aeronautical Research, NACA) to Chief, BuAer, 3 Aug. 1944, box 645, vol. 4 (1944), ibid.; Fahrney, "History of Pilotless Aircraft and Guided Missiles," 481–82, OANHC.

42. Fahrney, "History of Pilotless Aircraft and Guided Missiles," 481–82, OANHC; Capt. Lloyd Harrison (Manager, NAF) to BuAer, 1 May 1944, PP-MIA, F32(G), box 645, vol. 3 (1944), file F31-1 (43), BuAer, Confid. Corresp., 1922–44, RG 72, NA; memo, Lt. Cdr. Norman E. Knapp (by direction, Chief, BuAer) to Head, Ship Installations Branch, BuAer, 26 Sept. 1944, Aer-E-18-PEA, box 646, vol. 5 (1944), ibid.

43. Memo, Lt. Cdr. M. B. Taylor to Chief Engineer, NAMU, 23 Jan. 1945, ME-2.1, MJS, F32, box 149, vol. 9 (1945), file F31-1 (43), BuAer, Confid. Corresp., 1945, RG 72, NA.

44. Memo report, Lt. Cdr. M. B. Taylor to CO, NAMU, ME-2.1-BW, F32(G), box 150, vol. 10 (1945), ibid.; memo report, Lt. Cdr. M. B. Taylor to CO, NAMU, ME-2.1: mdt, F32(G), ibid.

45. Memo report, Lt. Cdr. M. B. Taylor to CO, NAMU, 22 Mar. 1945, ME-2.1: mdt, F32(G), box 150, vol. 10 (1945), ibid.

46. Richardson to CO, NAMU, 2 Apr. 1945, Aer-E-18-KAH, F31-1(43), box 150, vol. 11 (1945), ibid.; Shortal, *A New Dimension*, 123–24.

47. Telegram, CO, NAMU, to BuAer, 5 Dec. 1944, box 5217, file VTD2N1/F1-1, BuAer, Gen. Corresp., 1943–45, RG 72, NA; memo, Cdr. Grayson Merrill to Power Plant Design Branch, BuAer, 4 Jan. 1945, Aer-E-18-PEA, box 149, vol. 8 (1945), file F31-1(43), BuAer, Confid. Corresp., 1945, ibid.; Cdr. Grayson Merrill to CO, NAMU, 8 Jan. 1945, Aer-E-18-PEA, F31-1(43), F13-4 (1-TJ), ibid.

48. Ramsey to CO, NAMC, 17 Apr. 1945, Aer-E-18-PEA, F31-1(43), box 150, vol. 11 (1945), file F31-1(43), BuAer, Confid. Corresp., 1945, RG 72, NA.

49. Memo, Taylor to CO, NAMU, 12 May 1945, Weekly Report on Special Weapons Activities, box 150, vol. 12 (1945), ibid.; Fahrney, "History of Pilotless Aircraft and Guided Missiles," 492, 503, OANHC; Fahrney, "Genesis of the Cruise Missile," 39.

50. Fahrney, "History of Pilotless Aircraft and Guided Missiles," 493, OANHC.

51. Memo, Taylor to CO, NAMU, 23 June 1945, Weekly Report on Special Weapons Activities, ME-2.1: mdt, box 151, vol. 14 (1945), file F31-1(43), BuAer, Confid. Corresp., 1945, RG 72, NA; R. Adm. H. B. Sallada (Chief, BuAer) to all sections and divisions, BuAer, 6 Aug. 1945, Aer-F1-4-WAK, box 153, vol. 19 (1945), ibid.; Capt. Ralph S. Barnaby to BuAer, 20 Sept. 1945, Weekly Report on Special Weapons Activities, ME-2.1: rem, A9/L9-3 (15), box 152, vol. 18 (1945), ibid.; Fahrney, "Genesis of the Cruise Missile," 39.

52. Lt. Cdr. N. E. Knapp (by direction, CO, NAMU), to BuAer, 27 Aug. 1945, ME-2.25: MM, F32(G), box 152, vol. 17 (1945), file F31-1(43), BuAer, Confid. Corresp., 1945, RG 72, NA.

53. Lt. Cdr. N. E. Knapp (by direction, CO, NAMU) to BuAer, 8 Nov. 1945, ME 2:20: rdf, F32/VTDN-1/F8, box 5217, file VTDN1/F1-1, BuAer, Gen. Corresp., 1943–45, ibid.; Fahrney, "History of Pilotless Aircraft and Guided Missiles," 496–97, OANHC; U.S. Navy Department, *United States Naval Aviation, 1910–1980*, 163.

54. Fahrney, "History of Pilotless Aircraft and Guided Missiles," 567–71, OANHC; memo, Cdr. Grayson Merrill to Ass't. Chief, BuAer, 27 July 1945, Aer-E-18-GM, box 151, vol. 16 (1945), file F31-1(43), BuAer, Confid. Corresp., 1945, RG 72, NA.

55. Fahrney, "History of Pilotless Aircraft and Guided Missiles," 530–31, OANHC.

56. Ibid., 531–35.

57. Memo, Cdr. Grayson Merrill to Ass't. Chief, BuAer, 27 July 1945, Aer-E-18-GM, box 151, vol. 16 (1945), file F31-1(43), BuAer, Confid. Corresp., 1945, RG 72, NA; Fahrney, "History of Pilotless Aircraft and Guided Missiles," 533–36, OANHC.

58. U.S. Navy Department, *United States Naval Aviation, 1910–1980*, 163.

59. Taylor comments in biographical sketches of key personnel, box 86, History of Pilotless Aircraft and Guided Missiles, BuAer, Gen. Records, RG 72, NA.

CHAPTER 13

1. Richardson (Ass't. Chief, BuAer) to CO, NAMC, 26 Feb. 1944, Aer-E-18-JBM, F31-1(43), box 645, vol. 1 (1944), file F31-1(43), BuAer, Confid. Corresp., 1922–44, RG 72, NA.

2. For the development and employment of the catapult ships by the British, see Bishop, *Hurricane*, 68–74. See also information in box 1420, vol. 4, file S83-2, BuAer, Confid. Corresp., 1922–44, RG 72, NA.

3. *NAF Cavalcade of Aircraft*, 112; Ramsey (Ass't. Chief, BuAer) to Chief, BuOrd, 11 Aug. 1941, Aer-E-352-MEN, S83-2, box 1420, vol. 3, file S83-2, BuAer, Confid. Corresp., 1922–44, RG 72, NA; R. Adm. W. H. P. Blandy (Chief, BuOrd) to National Defense Research Committee, 18 Aug. 1941, S78/S83-2(166) (Re2), ibid.; L. J. Maxson (by direction, Manager, NAF) to Chief, BuAer, 15 Jan. 1942 (1116), ibid.; Capt. C. M. Bolster (by direction, Chief, BuAer) to CO, NAMC, 29 Sept. 1944, Aer-E-341-RD, S83-2, F13-4(1), box 1422, vol. 3, file S83-2(44), ibid.

4. *NAF Cavalcade of Aircraft*, 114; Col. C. L. Fike, USMC (by direction, Chief, BuAer) to CO, NAMC, 27 Mar. 1944, Aer-E-341-RD, S83-2, box 1422, vol. 1, file S83-2 (44), BuAer, Confid. Corresp., 1922–1944, RG 72, NA; NAMC, NAF, Ship Installations Div., "News Bulletin No. 14," 5 July 1944, box 1422, vol. 2, ibid.; memo, Cdr. A. E. Paddock to Ass't. Chief Engineer, Ship Installations Div., NAF, 14 Oct. 1944, PESC-3-AES, box 1425, file S83-2 (J-2), ibid.

5. Capt. J. E. Ostrander (by direction, Chief, BuAer) to Manager, NAF, 6 June 1942, Aer-E-3411-MEN, S83-2, box 1420, vol. 4, file S83-2, BuAer, Confid. Corresp., 1922–44, RG 72, NA; R. Adm. D. C. Ramsey (Chief, BuAer) to CO, NAMC, 10 June 1944, Aer-E-341-RD, S83-2(XEE), box 1425, file S83-2(XEE), ibid.; R. Adm. D. C. Ramsey (Chief, BuAer) to SecNav, 9 Nov. 1944, Aer-MA-315-RH, box 1427, file S83-2/NA83(44), ibid.

6. Lt. Cdr. Harold Allen (by direction, Chief, BuAer) to CO, NAMC, 21 Dec. 1944, Aer-E-341-RD, S83-2, box 1423, vol. 4, file S83-2(44), ibid.; *NAF Cavalcade of Aircraft*, 116; U.S. Navy, BuAer, *Ten Year History*, 9:67.

7. Capt. H. B. Sallada (by direction, Chief, BuAer) to Manager, NAF, 27 June 1942, Aer-E-3411-MEN, S83-2, box 1420, vol. 4, file S83-2, BuAer, Confid. Corresp., 1922–44, RG 72, NA; Sallada (by direction, Chief, BuAer) to Manager, NAF, 3 Aug. 1942, Aer-E-3411-VF, ibid.; Capt. E. M. Pace, Jr., (by direction, Chief, BuAer) to Manager, NAF, 29 Sept. 1942, Aer-E-3411-VF, S83-2, ibid.

8. U.S. Navy, BuAer, *Ten Year History*, 9:45-48; for the P-47 and P-51 kits, see project orders in box 1422, vol. 1, file S83-2(44), BuAer, Confid. Corresp., 1922–44, RG 72, NA.

9. Capt. J. E. Ostrander (by direction, Chief, BuAer) to Manager, NAF, 5 Feb. 1942, Aer-E-342-FE, S83-3, box 1431, vol. 7, file S83-3, BuAer, Confid. Corresp., 1922–44, RG 72, NA; NAMC, NAF, Ship Installations Div., "News Bulletin No. 18," 5 Nov. 1944, box 1423, vol. 4, file S83-2(44), ibid.; *NAF Cavalcade of Aircraft*, 130.

10. Capt. E. M. Pace, Jr. (by direction, Chief, BuAer) to Manager, NAF, 10 Jan. 1942, Aer-E-344-MEN, S83-2, BAVG, box 1420, vol. 3, file S83-2, BuAer, Confid. Corresp., 1922–44, RG 72, NA.

11. Webster to Chief, BuAer, 16 Jan. 1942 (1121), ibid.; Cdr. C. M. Bolster, "Ships' Installations Comment," 22 Jan. 1942, ibid.; Ramsey to Chief, Bureau of Navigation, 4 Feb. 1942, Aer-Pe-14-DMN, S83-2, S83-3, LL/NP11, ibid.

12. H. S. Sease (by direction, Manager, NAF) to Chief, BuAer, 19 Apr. 1942, S83-3, BAVG-2 (23009), box 1431, vol. 7, ibid.

13. NAMC, NAF, Ship Installations Div., "News Bulletin No. 7," 5 Dec. 1943, box 1421, vol. 6, file S83-2, ibid.

14. "History of the Naval Air Material Center," 24–25, OANHC; "Annual Report of Naval Air Experimental Station, Naval Air Material Center, Philadelphia, Pa., 30 June 1944," 1–2, copy in files of J. Hartley Bowen, Jr., Haddonfield, N.J.; memo, Lt.

Cdr. Morris Duane (by direction, Chief, BuAer) to BAMO, Eastern Procurement District, New York City, 24 Mar. 1944, Aer-PRD-314, HFG, S83-2, S83-3, box 1422, vol. 1, file S83-2(44), BuAer, Confid. Corresp., 1922–44, RG 72, NA.

15. Ramsey to CO, NAMC, 3 Jan. 1944, Aer-E-341-JAH, S83-2, S83-3, box 1422, vol. 1, file S83-2(44), BuAer, Confid. Corresp., 1922–44, RG 72, NA.

16. Zeigler to Chief, BuAer, 2 Feb. 1944, PES-AES, S83-2, S83-3, ibid.

17. Richardson (Acting Chief, BuAer) to CO, NAMC, 25 Feb. 1944, Aer-E-341-FBG, S83-2, S83-3, ibid.

18. An excellent study of the development of radar in the United States Navy is Allison, *New Eye for the Navy*.

19. Fahrney, "History of Pilotless Aircraft and Guided Missiles," 357–58, 624–25, OANHC.

20. Ibid., 625–26; "War History of the Fourth Naval District," vol. 5, pt. 8, I-22, NDL.

21. Capt. D. C. Ramsey (Chief, BuAer) to Manager, NAF, 7 Feb. 1942, Aer-PR-47-EM, F42-1, box 4029, vol. 18, file NP 11, BuAer, Gen. Corresp., 1925–42, RG 72, NA; Capt. W. W. Webster to Chief, BuAer, 3 Feb. 1942, F42(R) (1346), box 643, vol. 10, file F31-1(43), BuAer, Confid. Corresp., 1922–44, ibid.; memo, V. H. Soucek (Ass't. Chief Engineer, Radio Control) to Manager, NAF, 4 Feb. 1943, (1271[E-7]), box 644, vol. 13, ibid.; Capt. L. C. Stevens (by direction, Chief, BuAer) to CO, NAMC, 8 Oct. 1943, Aer-E-18-GM, box 644, vol. 14, ibid.

22. Fahrney, "History of Pilotless Aircraft and Guided Missiles," 640–46, 650, OANHC.

23. Ibid., 641–42, 658–59.

24. Ibid., 659–61.

25. Ibid., 666–69; G. F. Hussey, Jr. (BuOrd) to Chief, BuAer, 26 Oct. 1944 (Re 4g), box 646, vol. 6, file F31-1(43), BuAer, Confid. Corresp., 1922–44, RG 72, NA.

26. Fahrney, "History of Pilotless Aircraft and Guided Missiles," 676–89, OANHC.

27. Swanborough and Bowers, *United States Navy Aircraft since 1911*, 405; Capt. M. A. Mitscher (Ass't. Chief, BuAer) to Manager, NAF, 21 Mar. 1940, Aer-PL-4-EMN, box 641, vol. 6, file F31-1(43), BuAer, Confid. Corresp., 1922–44, RG 72, NA; Capt. W. W. Webster to Chief, BuAer, 1 May 1940, F32 (8472), ibid.; Webster to Chief, BuAer, 7 July 1942, F32 (244), box 643, vol. 11, ibid.; R. Adm. D. C. Ramsey to CO, NAMC, Work Plan for NAMU for Calendar Year 1944 (no date), Aer-E-18-GM, F3H(43), C29908, box 645, vol. 1, file F31-1(43) (1944), ibid.

28. Fahrney, "History of Pilotless Aircraft and Guided Missiles," 405–7, OANHC.

29. Ibid., 407–8.

30. Olsen, *Aphrodite*, 20–26; Fahrney, "History of Pilotless Aircraft and Guided Missiles," 408–9, OANHC.

31. Fahrney, "History of Pilotless Aircraft and Guided Missiles," 409–11, OANHC.

32. Ibid., 411–12; Lt. Hugh P. Lyon, report, 14 Aug. 1944, in memo, Capt. John M. Sande (Operations Officer) to 3d Bombardment Div., AAF, 14 Aug. 1944, Aphrodite Mission No. 3 (Navy), 12 Aug. 1944, vol. 3, file 527.431 A-7, U.S. Air Force Historical Research Center, Maxwell Air Force Base, Alabama (hereafter cited as Lyon report, 14 Aug. 1944).

33. For accounts of SAU operations, see Fahrney, "History of Pilotless Aircraft and Guided Missiles," 412–17, OANHC, and the reports of missions 3 and 7 in file 527.431 A, U.S. Air Force Historical Research Center, Maxwell Air Force Base,

Alabama. For Olsen and Simpson's reservations about the ordnance control panel, see Olsen, *Aphrodite*, 196–211.

34. Olsen, *Aphrodite*, 199; Lyon report, 14 Aug. 1944.

35. Lyon report, 14 Aug. 1944; Fahrney, "History of Pilotless Aircraft and Guided Missiles," 414–17, OANHC.

36. Searls, *Lost Prince*, 296–99, 318.

37. Capt. M. A. Mitscher (Ass't. Chief, BuAer) to Manager, NAF, 1 July 1941, Aer-PL-2-AFW, S76, box 70, file S76, BuAer, Gen. Corresp., Secret, 1939–42, RG 72, NA; Stevens route slip comments on ibid.

38. Preliminary Report on Proposed Coil Design, Electrical Installation and Magnetic Tests, Instrument Development Section, NAF, Report No. IDS-10-41 (no date), ibid.

39. Pace to Chief, BuAer, 3 Sept. 1941, F31-1 (17184), ibid.

40. Capt. Ralph E. Davison (by direction, Chief, BuAer) to Manager, NAF, 19 Sept. 1941, Aer-Pt-22-ES, S76, EF 13-1/S76, NP 11, ibid.

41. Capt. E. M. Pace, Jr., to Chief, BuAer, 14 Oct. 1941, F31-1 (41102), ibid.; Capt. D. C. Ramsey (Ass't. Chief, BuAer) to Manager, NAF, 15 Nov. 1941, Aer-E-3101-VBT, S76, EF13-1/S76, NP 11, ibid.; E. W. Sylvester (by direction, SecNav) to Irwin Stewart, NDRC, 26 Nov. 1941, (SC) 881-1 (SONRD), ibid.

42. G. Ross Allen (by direction, Manager, NAF) to Chief, BuAer, 20 July 1942, F41-6 (29621), ibid.

43. Stevens route slip comments in ibid.; Capt. H. B. Sallada (by direction, Chief, BuAer) to Manager, NAF, 24 Dec. 1942, Aer-E-31532-JTK, S76, ibid.

44. "Annual Report of Naval Air Experimental Station, Naval Air Material Center, Philadelphia, Pa., 30 June 1944," 7–13, copy in files of J. Hartley Bowen, Jr., Haddonfield, N.J.; "War History of the Fourth Naval District," vol. 5, pt. 8, I-21–I-22, NDL.

45. "War History of the Fourth Naval District," vol. 5, pt. 8, I-20–I-21, NDL; "Chemistry and Naval Aviation," lecture by J. Hartley Bowen, Jr., 6-8; Capt. J. E. Ostrander, Jr. (by direction, Chief, BuAer), to Manager, NAF, 13 June 1942, Aer-E-256-RP, JJ32L1, box 4029, vol. 19, file NP 11, BuAer, Gen. Corresp., 1925–42, RG 72, NA.

46. Bowen interview, 13 Oct. 1983.

47. Webster to Chief, BuAer, 24 Feb. 1942, F32 (14910), box 643, vol. 10, file F31-1(43), BuAer, Confid. Corresp., 1922–44, RG 72, NA.

48. Capt. L. C. Stevens (by direction, Chief, BuAer) to Manager, NAF, 23 Dec. 1942, Aer-E-2453-KR, F31-4, box 2118, vol. 4, file F31-1(43), BuAer, Gen. Corresp., 1925–42, ibid.

49. Capt. D. Ketcham (by direction, Chief, BuAer) to CO, Marine Corps Air Station, Cherry Point, N.C., 16 Feb. 1943, Aer-E-2453-CG, box 644, vol. 13, file F31-1(43), BuAer, Confid. Corresp., 1922–44, ibid.; memo, Lt. Cdr. Sheldon W. Brown to Contracts Div., BuAer, 4 Aug. 1943, Aer-E-2450-RP, box 644, vol. 14, ibid. See also Fahrney, "History of Pilotless Aircraft and Guided Missiles," 444, OANHC.

50. Semi-Monthly News Report of Projects, Aeronautical Materials Section, Engineering Dept., NAF, 5 May 1943, box 3471, vol. 22, file NP 11, BuAer, Gen. Corresp., 1943–45, RG 72, NA.

51. "Annual Report of Naval Air Experimental Station, Naval Air Material Center, Philadelphia, Pa., 30 June 1944," 7-11, copy in files of J. Hartley Bowen, Jr., Haddonfield, N.J.; project orders, 28 June 1940, 9 June 1941, 25 Oct. 1941, 7 Mar. 1942, in vols. 2, 3, file NP 12, BuAer, Gen. Corresp., 1925–42, RG 72, NA; Webster

to Chief, BuAer, 5 Mar. 1943, N19 (E-5) (16660), box 3471, vol. 22, file NP 11, BuAer, Gen. Corresp., 1943–45, ibid.; D. M. Patterson, BuY&D, to Public Works Officer, Phila. Navy Yard, 5 June 1943, NOy-6537, NP11/N8-11, C5J, box 3471, vol. 23, ibid.
52. R. Adm. D. C. Ramsey (Chief, BuAer) to CO, NAMC, 24 Dec. 1943, Aer-E-4-SBS, box 3472, vol. 4, file NP 12, BuAer, Gen. Corresp., 1943–45, RG 72, NA.
53. R. Adm. D. C. Ramsey (Chief, BuAer) to CO, NAMC, 3 Mar. 1945, Aer-E-425-FKS, N8/NP11, box 3470, file NP 11, ibid.
54. "War History of the Fourth Naval District," vol. 5, pt. 8, appendix, NDL; information on explosive decompression tests from J. Hartley Bowen, Jr., to author, 23 June 1988.

EPILOGUE

1. War Diary for October 1945, 28 Nov. 1945, Philadelphia—NAMC file, Aviation History File, Air/Ground Establishments, OANHC; Weigley, *American Way of War*, 408–9.
2. War Diary for October 1945, 28 Nov. 1945, Philadelphia—NAMC file, Aviation History File, Air/Ground Establishments, OANHC; War Diary for June 1946, 31 July 1946, Aviation History File, Air/Ground Establishments, OANHC; NAMC Quarterly History, 1 July 1946 to 30 Sept. 1946, inclusive, ibid.; NAMC Quarterly History, 30 Sept. 1946 to 31 Dec. 1946, inclusive, ibid.
3. NAMC Quarterly History, 1 July 1946 to 30 Sept. 1946, inclusive, ibid.; NAMC Quarterly History, 30 Sept. 1946 to 31 Dec. 1946, inclusive, ibid.
4. NAMC Quarterly History, 30 Sept. 1946 to 31 Dec. 1946, inclusive, ibid.
5. Historical Report for Aviation Medical Acceleration Laboratory, ibid.; War Diary for May 1946, 15 July 1946, ibid.; NAMC Quarterly History, 1 July 1946 to 30 Sept. 1946, inclusive, ibid.; NAMC Quarterly History, 1 Apr. 1947 to 30 June 1947, inclusive, ibid.
6. NAMC Quarterly History, 1 July 1947 to 30 Sept. 1947, inclusive, ibid.; Historical Report for Aviation Medical Acceleration Laboratory, ibid.; Misa and Todd, *History of the Naval Air Development Center*, 9.
7. NAMC Quarterly History, 1 July 1947 to 30 Sept. 1947, ibid.
8. For the condition of the aircraft manufacturing industry in 1946–47, see Rae, *Climb to Greatness*, 173–74. The postwar climate in regard to a national aviation policy is summarized in Wilson, *Turbulence Aloft*, 193–94.
9. *Congressional Record*, House, 79th Cong., 2d sess., vol. 92, pt. 1, 490.
10. U.S., Cong., House, *Subcommittee Hearings on H.R. 3051 to Amend the Act . . . of March 27, 1934*, 3171, 3173–74.
11. Ibid., 3172–73.
12. *Congressional Record*, House, 80th Cong., 1st sess., vol. 93, pt. 6, 7522; ibid., vol. 93, pt. 7, 8337; ibid., Senate, 80th Cong., 1st sess., vol. 93, pt. 7, 9346; ibid., Senate, 80th Cong., 2d sess., vol. 94, pt. 3, 2933–35, 2992.
13. Wilson, *Turbulence Aloft*, 207; U.S., President's Air Policy Commission, *Survival in the Air Age*, 158, 160–61; U.S., President's Air Policy Commission, "Unclassified Testimony," 2:849.
14. Capt. L. Harrison, BuAer Presentation to the Presidential Air Policy Commission, 18 Sept. 1947, box 23, Finletter Commission, BuAer, Gen. Corresp., 1947–48, Military Archives Division, Washington National Records Center, Suitland, Md.
15. R. Adm. A. M. Pride, Statement before the President's Air Policy Commission, 28 Oct. 1947, ibid.

16. U.S., President's Air Policy Commission, _Survival in the Air Age_, 64–67.

17. _NAF Cavalcade of Aircraft_, 122, 124, 126; Friedman, _U.S. Aircraft Carriers_, 259, 380.

18. Twenty-first Supplement to Naval Air Material Center History, NAMATCEN Semi-Annual History for Period 31 Dec. 1951 to 30 June 1952, 6 Aug. 1952, OANHC; Friedman, _U.S. Aircraft Carriers_, 265, 296, 380.

19. Cox interview, 11 Oct. 1983; _Air Scoop_ 5 (15 June 1956): 1.

20. _NAF Cavalcade of Aircraft_, 136, 138; Friedman, _U.S. Aircraft Carriers_, 397.

21. _NAF Cavalcade of Aircraft_, 132, 134.

22. "Jet Engine Icing Tests," 8; "No Job Too Big and No Job Too Small," 5.

23. _Air Scoop_ 3 (30 July 1954): 1; Director, NAES to Chief, BuAer, 3 Aug. 1951, XM-55-FWH:rmcg (1536); Director, NAES to Chief, BuAer, 29 Nov. 1951, XM-41-MK:rmcg (3815); misc. AML reports; all in files of J. Hartley Bowen, U.S. Naval Aviation Museum, Pensacola, Florida.

24. "No Job Too Big and No Job Too Small," 5–6; U.S. Navy Department, _United States Naval Aviation, 1910–1980_, 185; _Air Scoop_ 1 (6 June 1952): 3; "Naval Air Experimental Station History," 1 Dec. 1954, copy in files of J. Hartley Bowen, Jr., Haddonfield, N.J.

25. "Mammoth Test Machine," 19; "No Job Too Big and No Job Too Small," 6–7; "Naval Air Experimental Station History," 1 Dec. 1954, copy in files of J. Hartley Bowen, Jr., Haddonfield, N. J.

26. "Naval Air Experimental Station History," 1 Dec. 1954, copy in files of J. Hartley Bowen, Jr., Haddonfield, N.J.; "No Job Too Big and No Job Too Small," 6; "Navy's Space Suit," 15.

27. "No Job Too Big and No Job Too Small," 7; "Naval Air Experimental Station History," 1 Dec. 1954, copy in files of J. Hartley Bowen, Jr., Haddonfield, N.J.

28. U.S. Naval Air Research and Development Activities Command, Johnsville, Pennsylvania, "Command History, 1 January 1960 to 31 December 1960," Aviation History Files, OANHC; Misa and Todd, _History of the Naval Air Development Center_, 11; Sapolsky, _Polaris System Development_, 51, 145.

29. _Air Scoop_ 5 (24 Feb. 1956): 1, 3; ibid. 5 (18 May 1956): 1, 3.

30. Ibid. 6 (8 Feb. 1957): 1.

31. Ibid. (21 Mar. 1958): 1, 3;

32. Sapolsky, _Polaris System Development_, 145; _Air Scoop_ 7 (13 Mar. 1959): 7; Czaplicki, "Half Century of Service to the Fleet," 23; _Naval Aviation News_, Nov. 1960, 35.

33. _Symposium on Elevated Temperature Strain Gages_; _Air Scoop_ 7 (13 Mar. 1959): 3–5; Swenson, Grimwood, and Alexander, _This New Ocean_, 228–31.

34. "Sortie into Space," 1–5; "Research to Reality," 4–5.

35. Swenson, Grimwood, and Alexander, _This New Ocean_, 96, 239, 288; Hacker and Grimwood, _On the Shoulders of Titans_, 223.

36. "Proof of Quality," 1–7.

37. U.S. Navy Department, _United States Naval Aviation, 1910–1980_, 248; "Command History—U.S. Naval Air Engineering Center, Philadelphia" (1962), Aviation History Files, OANHC.

38. "Command History—U.S. Naval Air Engineering Center, Philadelphia" (1964), Aviation History Files, OANHC; ibid. (1966); ibid. (1969).

39. "Installations Survey of the Naval Air Engineering Center, Philadelphia, Pennsylvania, 1964," Appendix D, 11–12, copy in files of J. Hartley Bowen, Jr.,

Haddonfield, N.J.; Czaplicki, "Half Century of Service to the Fleet," 22–23; Friedman, *U.S. Aircraft Carriers*, 380, 382; *Air Scoop* 11 (1 Feb. 1963): 1.

40. "Command History—U.S. Naval Air Engineering Center, Philadelphia" (1973), OANHC; Winkel, "LAMPS," 114–17; Cody, "RAST," 104–7.

41. Mulquin, "ARAPAHO Goes to Sea," 33; Mulquin, "ARAPAHO Update," 103–6; Mulquin, "ARAPAHO Update," 20–23.

42. "Installations Survey of the Naval Air Engineering Center, Philadelphia, Pennsylvania, 1964," Appendix D, 1–2, copy in files of J. Hartley Bowen, Jr., Haddonfield, N.J.; Czaplicki, "Half Century of Service to the Fleet," 23; "Power Plant Facilities Are Merged," 25; "In Search of Power," 9.

43. "Installations Survey of the Naval Air Engineering Center, Philadelphia, Pennsylvania, 1964," Appendix D, 6–7, copy in files of J. Hartley Bowen, Jr., Haddonfield, N.J.; Czaplicki, "Half Century of Service to the Fleet," 24–25.

44. "Installations Survey of the Naval Air Engineering Center, Philadelphia, Pennsylvania, 1964," Appendix D, 2–5, copy in files of J. Hartley Bowen, Jr., Haddonfield, N.J.; Czaplicki, "Half Century of Service to the Fleet," 23–24.

45. "Installations Survey of the Naval Air Engineering Center, Philadelphia, Pennsylvania, 1964," Appendix D, 8–9, copy in files of J. Hartley Bowen, Jr., Haddonfield, N.J.; Czaplicki, "Half Century of Service to the Fleet," 25.

46. Misa and Todd, *History of the Naval Air Development Center*, 12; *Aircraft and Crew Systems Technology Directorate, Naval Air Development Center*, 2–3.

47. U.S. Navy Department, *United States Naval Aviation, 1910–1980*, 305.

Bibliography

MANUSCRIPT AND ARCHIVAL MATERIAL

Bowen, J. Hartley, Jr. Files. U.S. Naval Aviation Museum, Pensacola, Fla.
Bowen, J. Hartley, Jr. Files. Haddonfield, N.J.
"Aero Materials History." 1975.
"Annual Report of Naval Air Experimental Station, Naval Air Material Center, Philadelphia, Pa., 30 June 1944."
"Chemistry and Naval Aviation." Lecture by J. Hartley Bowen, Jr., 1961.
"Historical Development of the Aeronautical Structures Laboratory, 1 January 1960."
"Installations Survey of the Naval Air Engineering Center, Philadelphia, Pennsylvania, 1964."
"Naval Air Experimental Station History," 1 December 1954.
Bristol, Mark L. Papers. Manuscript Division, Library of Congress.
Daniels, Josephus. Papers. Manuscript Division, Library of Congress.
Federal Archives and Records Center. Philadelphia.
Fair Employment Practices Committee, Philadelphia Regional Office. Records. Record Group 225.
Howe, Louis M. Papers. Franklin D. Roosevelt Library, Hyde Park, N.Y.
Moffett, William Adger. Papers. Nimitz Library, U.S. Naval Academy, Annapolis, Md.
National Archives and Records Administration. Washington, D.C.
Bureau of Aeronautics. Confidential Correspondence, 1922–44. Record Group 72.
Bureau of Aeronautics. Confidential Correspondence, 1945. Record Group 72.
Bureau of Aeronautics. General Correspondence Initiated in the Bureau of Construction and Repair, 1917–25. Record Group 72.

389

Bureau of Aeronautics. General Correspondence, 1925–42. Record Group 72.

Bureau of Aeronautics. General Correspondence, 1943–45. Record Group 72.

Bureau of Aeronautics. General Correspondence, 1947–48. Military Archives Division, Washington National Records Center, Suitland, Md.

Bureau of Aeronautics. General Correspondence, Secret, 1939–42. Record Group 72.

Bureau of Aeronautics. General Records. Record Group 72.

Secretary of the Navy. General Correspondence, 1897–1915. General Records of the Navy Department. Record Group 80.

Secretary of the Navy. General Correspondence, 1916–26. General Records of the Navy Department. Record Group 80.

Secretary of the Navy. General Correspondence, 1926–42. General Records of the Navy Department. Record Group 80.

Naval Aircraft Factory Log. Historian's Office, Naval Air Systems Command Headquarters, Washington, D.C.

Operational Archives Division. Naval Historical Center. Washington, D.C.

"Command History—U.S. Naval Air Engineering Center, Philadelphia." 1962, 1964, 1966, 1969, 1973.

Fahrney, Rear Adm. D. S. "The History of Pilotless Aircraft and Guided Missiles." Undated MS., probably 1958.

General Board Records (since transferred to National Archives).

Historical Report for Aviation Medical Acceleration Laboratory.

"The History of the Aviation Supply Office to June 1944." Philadelphia—Naval Aviation Supply Office file, Aviation History File.

"History of ASO-NASD, 1 Oct. 1945–30 Sep. 1946." Aviation History File, Air/Ground Establishments.

"History of the Naval Air Material Center, Philadelphia, Pa. 31 Dec. 44." Aviation History File, Air/Ground Establishments, Philadelphia—Naval Air Material Center.

NAMC Quarterly Histories: 1 July 1946 to 30 Sept. 1946, inclusive; 30 Sept. 1946 to 31 Dec. 1946, inclusive; 1 April 1947 to 30 June 1947, inclusive; 1 July 1947 to 30 Sept. 1947. Aviation History File, Air/Ground Establishments, Philadelphia—Naval Air Material Center.

NAMC War Diaries: October 1945, 28 November 1945, May 1946, June 1946, 15 July 1946, 31 July 1946. Aviation History File, Air/Ground Establishments, Philadelphia—Naval Air Material Center.

Twenty-first Supplement to Naval Air Material Center History. NAMAT-CEN Semi-Annual History for Period 31 December 1951 to 30 June 1952, 6 August 1952, Aviation History File, Air/Ground Establishments, Philadelphia—Naval Air Material Center.

Sims, William S. Papers. Manuscript Division, Library of Congress.

U.S. Air Force Historical Research Center, Maxwell Air Force Base, Ala.

Aphrodite Mission No. 3 (Navy), 12 August 1944, vol. 3, file 527.431 A-7.

U.S. President's Air Policy Commission. "Unclassified Testimony before the President's Air Policy Commission." 6 vols. 1948.

PUBLIC DOCUMENTS

Congressional Record. House. 73d Cong., 2d sess., vol. 78, pts. 1, 5.
Congressional Record. House. 79th Cong., 2d sess., vol. 92, pt. 1.
Congressional Record. House. 80th Cong., 1st sess., vol. 93, pts. 6, 7.
Congressional Record. Senate. 73d Cong., 2d sess., vol. 78, pts. 3, 4.
Congressional Record. Senate. 80th Cong., 1st sess., vol. 93, pt. 7.
Congressional Record. Senate. 80th Cong., 2d sess., vol. 94. pt. 3.
U.S. Congress. *The Statutes at Large of the United States of America.* 73d Cong., 2d sess., vol. 48, pt. 1. Washington, D.C.: U.S. Government Printing Office, 1934.
———. *United States Statutes at Large . . . 1939–1941.* 76th Cong., 2d and 3d sess., vol. 54, pt. 1. Washington, D.C.: U.S. Government Printing Office, 1941.
U.S. Congress, House. *Hearings before the Committee on Naval Affairs, House of Representatives, on Estimates Submitted by the Secretary of the Navy, 1915,* 63d Cong., 3d sess. Washington, D.C.: U.S. Government Printing Office, 1915.
———. *Hearings before the Committee on Naval Affairs, House of Representatives, on Estimates Submitted by the Secretary of the Navy, 1916.* 2 vols. 64th Cong., 1st sess. Washington, D.C.: U.S. Government Printing Office, 1916.
———. *Hearings before the Committee on Naval Affairs . . . on Estimates Submitted by the Secretary of the Navy, 1919.* 65th Cong., 3d sess. Washington, D.C.: U.S. Government Printing Office, 1919.
———. *Hearings before the Committee on Naval Affairs . . . on Estimates Submitted by the Secretary of the Navy, 1920.* 2 vols. 66th Cong., 2d sess. Washington, D.C.: U.S. Government Printing Office, 1920.
———. *Hearings before the Committee on Naval Affairs . . . on Sundry Legislation Affecting the Naval Establishment, 1920–1921.* 66th Cong., 3d sess. Washington, D.C.: U.S. Government Printing Office, 1921.
———. *Hearings before the Committee on Naval Affairs . . . on Sundry Legislation Affecting the Naval Establishment, 1921.* 67th Cong., 1st sess. Washington, D.C.: U.S. Government Printing Office, 1922.
———. *Hearings before the Committee on Naval Affairs . . . on Sundry Legislation Affecting the Naval Establishment, 1933–1934.* 73d Cong., 1st and 2d sess. Washington, D.C.: U.S. Government Printing Office, 1934.
———. *Hearings before Subcommittee of Committee on Appropriations . . . on Navy Department Appropriation Bill for 1938.* 75th Cong., 1st sess. Washington, D.C.: U.S. Government Printing Office, 1937.

———. *Hearings before the Subcommittee of the Committee on Appropriations on the Navy Department Appropriation Bill for 1940.* 76th Cong., 1st sess. Washington, D.C.: U.S. Government Printing Office, 1939.

———. *Hearings before the Subcommittee on Aeronautics Making an Investigation into Certain Phases of the Manufacture of Aircraft and Aeronautical Accessories as They Refer to the Navy Department.* In *Hearings before the Committee on Naval Affairs . . . on Sundry Legislation Affecting the Naval Establishment, 1933–1934.* 73d Cong., 1st and 2d sess. Washington, D.C.: U.S. Government Printing Office, 1934.

———. *Inquiry into Operations of the United States Air Services, Hearings on Matters Relating to Operations of United States Air Services.* 68th Cong. Washington, D.C.: U.S. Government Printing Office, 1925.

———. *Report of the Select Committee of Inquiry into Operations of the United States Air Services.* House Report No. 1653, 68th Cong., 2d sess. Washington, D.C.: U.S. Government Printing Office, 1925.

———. *Subcommittee of the Committee on Naval Affairs for Investigation of Conduct and Administration of Naval Affairs.* 65th Cong., 2d sess. Washington, D.C.: U.S. Government Printing Office, 1918.

———. *To Amend . . . the Act of March 27, 1934. . . .* House Report 102, 80th Cong., 1st sess. Washington, D.C.: U.S. Government Printing Office, 1947.

———. Committee on Armed Services. *Subcommittee Hearings on H.R. 3051 to Amend the Act . . . of March 27, 1934 . . . Relating to the Construction of Vessels and Aircraft.* House Report 158, 80th Cong., 1st sess. Washington, D.C.: U.S. Government Printing Office, 1947.

———. Committee on Naval Affairs. *Investigation into Status of Naval Defense Program.* 76th Cong., 2d sess. Washington, D.C.: U.S. Government Printing Office, 1941.

U.S. Congress, Senate. *Hearings before a Special Committee Investigating the National Defense Program.* 78th Cong., 2d sess. Washington, D.C.: U.S. Government Printing Office, 1944.

———. Subcommittee of the Committee on Naval Affairs. *Lieut. Alford J. Williams, Jr.—Fast Pursuit and Bombing Planes, Hearings.* 71st Cong., 2d sess. Washington, D.C.: U.S. Government Printing Office, 1930.

U.S. Department of Commerce. Civil Aeronautics Administration. *U.S. Military Aircraft Acceptances, 1940–1945: Aircraft, Engine and Propeller Production.* Washington, D.C.: Civil Aeronautics Administration, 1946.

U.S. Department of Labor. Women's Bureau. *The New Position of Women in American Industry.* Washington, D.C.: U.S. Government Printing Office, 1920.

U.S. National Advisory Committee for Aeronautics. *Sixth Annual Report of the National Advisory Committee for Aeronautics, 1920.* Washington, D.C.: U.S. Government Printing Office, 1921.

———. *Eleventh Annual Report of the National Advisory Committee for Aeronautics, 1925.* Washington, D.C.: U.S. Government Printing Office, 1925.

U.S. Navy. Bureau of Aeronautics. *Ten Year History and Program of Future Research and Development.* Vol. 9. *Naval Aircraft, Equipment and Support Facilities: Ship Installations.* Washington, D.C.: Bureau of Aeronautics, Navy Department, 1945.

U.S. Navy Department. *United States Naval Aviation, 1910–1970.* Washington, D.C.: U.S. Government Printing Office, 1970.

———. *United States Naval Aviation, 1910–1980.* Washington, D.C.: Naval Air Systems Command, 1981.

U.S. President's Aircraft Board. *Aircraft in National Defense: A Message from the President of the United States Transmitting the Report of the Board . . . to Make a Study of the Best Means of Developing and Applying Aircraft in National Defense.* Washington, D.C.: U.S. Government Printing Office, 1925.

———. *Hearings before the President's Aircraft Board.* 4 vols. Washington, D.C.: U.S. Government Printing Office, 1925.

U.S. President's Air Policy Commission. *Survival in the Air Age: A Report by the President's Air Policy Commission.* Washington, D.C.: U.S. Government Printing Office, 1948.

PERIODICALS

Aero Club of America Bulletin
Aeroplane
Air Scoop
American Aviation
American Society of Mechanical Engineers, Transactions
Aviation
Aviation News
Bureau of Aeronautics, *Daily Aviation News Bulletin*
Bureau of Aeronautics, *News Letter*
Hook
Journal of the American Society of Automotive Engineers
New York Times
Philadelphia Inquirer
Pittsburgh Dispatch
Society of Automotive Engineers, Transactions
U.S. Air Services

BOOKS

Aircraft and Crew Systems Technology Directorate, Naval Air Development Center. Warminster, Pa.: Naval Air Development Center, 1983.

Aircraft Year Book, 1920. New York: Manufacturers Aircraft Association, 1920.

The Aircraft Year Book for 1934. New York: Aeronautical Chamber of Commerce of America, 1934.

Albion, Robert Greenhalgh. *Makers of Naval Policy, 1798–1947.* Annapolis: Naval Institute Press, 1980.

Allison, David Kite. *New Eye for the Navy: The Origin of Radar at the Naval Research Laboratory.* Washington, D.C.: Naval Research Laboratory, 1981.

Andrade, John M. *U.S. Military Aircraft Designations and Serials since 1909.* Leicester, Eng.: Midland Counties Publications, 1979.

Arpee, Edward. *From Frigates to Flat-Tops: The Story of the Life and Achievements of Rear Admiral William Adger Moffett, U.S.N.* Chicago: Lakeside Press, 1953.

Asimov, Isaac. *In Memory Yet Green: The Autobiography of Isaac Asimov, 1920–1954.* Garden City, N.Y.: Doubleday, 1979.

Barker, Ralph. *The Schneider Trophy Races.* Shrewsbury, Eng.: Airlife Publishing, 1981.

Bilby, Kenneth. *The General: David Sarnoff and the Rise of the Communications Industry.* New York: Harper & Row, 1986.

Bishop, Edward. *Hurricane.* Shrewsbury, Eng.: Airlife Publishing, 1986.

Bowers, Peter M. *Boeing Aircraft since 1916.* London: Putnam, 1968.

Buell, Thomas B. *Master of Sea Power: A Biography of Fleet Admiral Ernest J. King.* Boston: Little, Brown, 1980.

Coletta, Paolo E. *Admiral Bradley A. Fiske and the American Navy.* Lawrence: Regents Press of Kansas, 1979.

Cooling, Benjamin Franklin. *Gray Steel and Blue Water Navy: The Formative Years of America's Military-Industrial Complex, 1881–1917.* Hamden, Conn.: Archon Books, 1979.

———, ed. *War, Business, and American Society: Historical Perspectives on the Military-Industrial Complex.* Port Washington, N.Y.: Kennikat Press, 1977.

Creed, Roscoe. *PBY: The Catalina Flying Boat.* Annapolis: Naval Institute Press, 1985.

Crouch, Tom D. *A Dream of Wings: Americans and the Airplane, 1875–1905.* New York: Norton, 1981.

———. *The Eagle Aloft: Two Centuries of the Balloon in America.* Washington, D.C.: Smithsonian Institution Press, 1983.

Cuff, Robert D. *The War Industries Board: Business-Government Relations during World War I.* Baltimore: Johns Hopkins University Press, 1973.

Daniels, Josephus. *The Wilson Era: Years of War and After, 1917–1923.* Chapel Hill: University of North Carolina Press, 1946.

Davies, R. E. G. *Airlines of Latin America since 1919.* Washington, D.C.: Smithsonian Institution Press, 1984.

Davis, George T. *A Navy Second to None: The Development of Modern American Naval Policy.* New York: Harcourt, Brace, 1940.

Emme, Eugene M., ed. *The History of Rocket Technology: Essays on Research, Development, and Utility.* Detroit: Wayne State University Press, 1964.

Freudenthal, Elsbeth E. *The Aviation Business: From Kitty Hawk to Wall Street.* New York: Vanguard Press, 1940.

Friedman, Norman. *U.S. Aircraft Carriers: An Illustrated Design History.* Annapolis: Naval Institute Press, 1983.

Gerber, Larry G. *The Limits of Liberalism: Josephus Daniels, Henry Stimson, Bernard Baruch, Donald Richberg, Felix Frankfurter and the Development of the Modern American Political Economy.* New York: New York University Press, 1983.

Greenwald, Maurine Weiner. *Women, War, and Work: The Impact of World War I on Women Workers in the United States.* Westport, Conn.: Greenwood Press, 1980.

Hacker, Barton C., and James M. Grimwood. *On the Shoulders of Titans: A History of Project Gemini.* Washington, D.C.: National Aeronautics and Space Administration, 1977.

Hallion, Richard P. *Test Pilots: The Frontiersmen of Flight.* Rev. ed. Washington, D.C.: Smithsonian Institution Press, 1988.

Hansen, James R. *Engineer in Charge: A History of the Langley Aeronautical Laboratory, 1917–1958.* Washington, D.C.: National Aeronautics and Space Administration, 1987.

Holley, Irving Brinton, Jr. *Buying Aircraft: Matériel Procurement for the Army Air Forces.* Washington, D.C.: Department of the Army, Office of the Chief of Military History, 1964.

———. *Ideas and Weapons: Exploitation of the Aerial Weapon by the United States during World War I.* New Haven: Yale University Press, 1953.

Hughes, Thomas Parke. *Elmer Sperry: Inventor and Engineer.* Baltimore: Johns Hopkins Press, 1971.

Johnson, Edward C. *Marine Corps Aviation: The Early Years, 1912–1940.* Washington, D.C.: History and Museums Division, Headquarters, U.S. Marine Corps, 1977.

Leary, William M. *The Dragon's Wings: The China National Aviation Corporation and the Development of Commercial Aviation in China.* Athens: University of Georgia Press, 1976.

Lichtenstein, Nelson. *Labor's War at Home: The CIO in World War II.* Cambridge: Cambridge University Press, 1982.

McClure, John. *The Logbook of the Naval Aircraft Association of Philadelphia.* Philadelphia: Naval Aircraft Association, 1919.

McCraw, Thomas K. *TVA and the Power Fight, 1933–1939.* Philadelphia: Lippincott, 1971.

Melhorn, Charles M. *Two-Block Fox: The Rise of the Aircraft Carrier, 1911–1929.* Annapolis: Naval Institute Press, 1974.

Messimer, Dwight R. *No Margin for Error: The U.S. Navy's Transpacific Flight of 1925.* Annapolis: Naval Institute Press, 1981.

Misa, Thomas, and Ed Todd. *History of the Naval Air Development Center.* Report No. NADC-82251-09, 15 September 1982. Warminster, Pa.: Naval Air Development Center, 1982.

Morison, Elting E. *Admiral Sims and the Modern American Navy.* Boston: Houghton Mifflin, 1942.

Morrison, Joseph L. *Josephus Daniels, the Small-d Democrat.* Chapel Hill: University of North Carolina Press, 1966.

NAF Cavalcade of Aircraft. Philadelphia: Naval Air Material Center, 1948.

Naval Aircraft Factory, Philadelphia, Manual Prepared by Lt. R. S. Barnaby, 1920–1921. Copy in Historian's Office, Naval Air Systems Command Headquarters, Washington, D.C.

Olsen, Jack. *Aphrodite: Desperate Mission.* New York: G. P. Putnam's Sons, 1970.

Page, Victor W. *Modern Aviation Engines: Design—Construction—Operation and Repair.* 2 vols. New York: Norman W. Henley, 1929.

Powell, Griffith. *Ferryman: From Ferry Command to Silver City.* Shrewsbury, Eng.: Airlife Publishing, 1982.

Rae, John B. *Climb to Greatness: The American Aircraft Industry, 1920–1960.* Cambridge, Mass.: MIT Press, 1968.

Rea, Robert R., and Wesley Phillips Newton. *Wings of Gold: An Account of Naval Aviation Training in World War II.* Tuscaloosa: University of Alabama Press, 1987.

Register of Commissioned and Warrant Officers of the United States Navy and Marine Corps, January 1, 1930. Washington, D.C.: U.S. Government Printing Office, 1930.

Robinson, Douglas H., and Charles L. Keller. *Up Ship! U.S. Navy Rigid Airships, 1919–1935.* Annapolis: Naval Institute Press, 1982.

Roland, Alex. *Model Research: The National Advisory Committee for Aeronautics, 1915–1958.* 2 vols. Washington, D.C.: National Aeronautics and Space Administration, 1985.

Sapolsky, Harvey M. *The Polaris System Development: Bureaucratic and Programmatic Success in Government.* Cambridge, Mass.: Harvard University Press, 1972.

Searls, Hank. *The Lost Prince: Young Joe, the Forgotten Kennedy.* New York: World, 1969.

Shortal, Joseph Adams. *A New Dimension: Wallops Island Flight Test Range, the First Fifteen Years.* NASA Reference Publication 1028. Washington, D.C.: National Aeronautics and Space Administration, 1978.

Shrader, Welman A. *Fifty Years of Flight: A Chronicle of the Aviation Industry in America, 1903–1953.* Cleveland: Eaton Manufacturing Company, 1953.

Simonson, G. R., ed. *The History of the American Aircraft Industry: An Anthology.* Cambridge, Mass.: MIT Press, 1968.

Smith, Henry Ladd. *Airways: The History of Commercial Aviation in the United States.* New York: Knopf, 1942.

Smith, Herschel. *Aircraft Piston Engines: From the Manly Baltzer to the Continental Tiara*. New York: McGraw-Hill, 1981.

Smith, Richard K. *The Airships Akron and Macon: Flying Aircraft Carriers of the United States Navy*. Annapolis: Naval Institute Press, 1965.

———. *First Across! The U.S. Navy's Transatlantic Flight of 1919*. Annapolis: Naval Institute Press, 1973.

Souvenir program. *20th Anniversary Naval Aircraft Factory, 1917–1937*.

Starr, Harris E., ed. *Dictionary of American Biography, Supplement One*. Vol. 21. New York: Scribner's, 1944.

Swanborough, Gordon, and Peter M. Bowers. *United States Navy Aircraft since 1911*. 1968. Rev. ed. Annapolis: Naval Institute Press, 1976.

Swenson, Loyd S., James M. Grimwood, and Charles C. Alexander. *This New Ocean: A History of Project Mercury*. Washington, D.C.: National Aeronautics and Space Administration, 1966.

Symposium on Elevated Temperature Strain Gages. ASTM Special Technical Publication 230. Philadelphia: American Society for Testing Materials, 1958.

Thetford, Owen. *British Naval Aircraft since 1912*. London: Putnam, 1982.

Trimble, William F. *High Frontier: A History of Aeronautics in Pennsylvania*. Pittsburgh: University of Pittsburgh Press, 1982.

Turnbull, Archibald D., and Clifford L. Lord. *History of United States Naval Aviation*. New Haven: Yale University Press, 1949.

Wagner, Ray. *American Combat Planes*. 3d ed. Garden City, N.Y.: Doubleday, 1982.

———. *The Story of the PBY Catalina*. San Diego: Flight Classics, 1972.

Weigley, Russell F. *The American Way of War: A History of United States Military Strategy and Policy*. Bloomington: Indiana University Press, 1973.

———, ed. *Philadelphia: A 300-Year History*. New York: Norton, 1982.

Werrell, Kenneth P. *The Evolution of the Cruise Missile*. Montgomery, Ala.: Air University Press, Maxwell Air Force Base, 1985.

Wheeler, Gerald E. *Admiral William Veazie Pratt, U.S. Navy: A Sailor's Life*. Washington, D.C.: Naval History Division, Department of the Navy, 1974.

Wilson, John R. M. *Turbulence Aloft: The Civil Aeronautics Administration Amid Wars and Rumors of Wars, 1938–1953*. Washington, D.C.: U.S. Department of Transportation, Federal Aviation Administration, 1979.

ARTICLES

"Activities at the Philadelphia Naval Aircraft Factory." *Aerial Age Weekly* 8 (9 December 1918): 666–67, 681.

Andrews, Harold. "Yellow Bird Goes Out to Pasture." *Naval Aviation News*, December 1959, pp. 24–25.

Armstrong, William J. "Dick Richardson: His Life in Aeronautics." *Naval Aviation News*, April 1977, pp. 32–39.

———. "Henry C. Mustin: A Clear Voice for Naval Aviation." *Naval Aviation Museum Foundation Journal* 2 (September 1981): 29–33.

"Arresting Gear for Naval Aircraft Carriers." *Aviation* 12 (13 February 1922): 201–2.

Asimov, Isaac. "Airplane Torture Chamber." *Air Scoop* 1 (November 1944): 6–7.

———. "When Powder Means Life." *Air Scoop* 2 (January 1945): 8.

"ASO: Supply, Support, Success." *Naval Aviation News*, April 1966, pp. 12–13.

Coburn, F. G. "Modern Management Applied to Navy Yards." *USNIP* 43 (May 1917): 955–72.

———. "Problems of the Naval Aircraft Factory during the War." *Society of Automotive Engineers, Transactions* 14, pt. 1 (1919): 304–32.

Cocklin, Henry S. "Development of Navy Patrol Planes." *Aero Digest* 6 (May 1925): 242–44, 280.

Cody, Lt. Cdr. John M. "RAST Helps Get LAMPS III on Small Combatants." *USNIP* 108 (January 1982): 104–7.

Czaplicki, Hilary S. "Half Century of Service to the Fleet." *Naval Aviation News*, July 1966, p. 23.

Daniels, R. W. "Duralumin." *Society of Automotive Engineers, Transactions* 17, pt. 2 (1922): 751–58.

D'Orcy, Ladislas. "The Curtiss Marine Flying Trophy Race." *Aviation* 13 (16 October 1922): 490–92.

"The Dornier 'Falke' Fighter." *Aeronautical Engineering* (Supplement to *Aeroplane*) 26 (13 December 1922): 451–52.

Fahrney, Delmar S. "The Genesis of the Cruise Missile." *Astronautics and Aeronautics* 20 (January 1982): 34–39, 53.

———. "Guided Missiles: U.S. Navy the Pioneer." *American Aviation Historical Society Journal* 27 (Spring 1982): 15–28.

———. "Target Drone Development." *Naval Aviation Museum Foundation Journal* 3 (March 1982): 36–43.

Featherston, Frank H. "AEDO: A History and a Heritage." *USNIP* 94 (February 1968): 33–45.

Feeley, J. J. "Some Aspects of Airplane Inspection." *Journal of the Society of Automotive Engineers* 17 (November 1925): 441–47.

Freeman, Roger M. "The Armor-Plate and Gun-Forging Plant of the U.S. Navy Department at South Charleston, W. Va." *American Society of Mechanical Engineers, Transactions* 42 (1920): 983–1032.

"Gallaudet Multiple Drive Tested." *Aviation* 11 (5 September 1921): 279.

Gardner, G. W. H. "Automatic Flight—The British Story." *Journal of the Royal Aeronautical Society* 62 (July 1958): 477–96.

Gordon, Robert A. "Naval Aircraft Factory Giant Boat." *W.W.I Aero: The Journal of the Early Aeroplane*, no. 98 (February 1984): 12–37

Hunsaker, J. C. "Progress in Naval Aircraft." *Society of Automotive Engineers, Transactions* 14, pt. 2 (1919): 236–77.

"In Search of Power." *Naval Aviation News*, April 1982, pp. 6–11.

"Jet Engine Icing Tests." *Naval Aviation News*, January 1949, p. 8.

Kraus, Captain S. M. "The Naval Aircraft Factory." *Aero Digest* 36 (February 1940): 46–47, 159.

"Large All-Metal Seaplanes." *Aeroplane* 28 (22 October 1924): 396–97.

Low, A. M. "The First Guided Missile." *Flight* 62 (3 October 1952): 436–38.

McCarthy, Charles J. "Notes on Metal Wing Construction." *U.S. Air Services* 10 (March 1925): 9–16.

McCord, Charles G. "The Aeronautical Engine Laboratory, Naval Aircraft Factory, Philadelphia, Penna." *Journal of the Society of Naval Engineers* 37 (May 1925): 279–305.

Maas, Jim. "Fall from Grace: The Brewster Aeronautical Corporation, 1932–42." *Journal of the American Aviation Historical Society* 30 (Summer 1985): 118–35.

"Mammoth Test Machine." *Naval Aviation News*, December 1948, p. 19.

Mayo-Wells, Wilfrid J. "The Origins of Space Telemetry." In Eugene M. Emme, ed., *The History of Rocket Technology: Essays on Research, Development, and Utility*, 253–68. Detroit: Wayne State University Press, 1964.

Miller, Roy G. "Metal Aircraft." *Journal of the American Society of Naval Engineers* 39 (August 1927): 584–85.

Miller, Roy G., and F. E. Seiler, Jr. "The Design of Metal Airplanes." *Aviation* 14 (19 February 1923): 210–14.

Mingos, Howard. "Birth of an Industry." In G. R. Simonson, ed., *The History of the American Aircraft Industry: An Anthology*, 25–69. Cambridge, Mass.: MIT Press, 1968.

Mulquin, James J. "ARAPAHO Goes to Sea." *Naval Aviation News*, February 1983, pp. 30–33.

———. "ARAPAHO Update." *Naval Aviation News*, April 1982, pp. 20–23.

———. "ARAPAHO Update." *USNIP* 109 (January 1983): 103–6.

"The Naval Aircraft Factory." *Aviation* 6 (1 February 1919): 28–30.

"Naval Aircraft Material Center's PBN-1." *Aero Digest* 44 (January 15, 1944): 88–94.

"Naval Aviation's Storehouse." *Flying* 34 (April 1944): 166.

"Navy's Space Suit." *Naval Aviation News*, April 1953, p. 15.

"No Job Too Big and No Job Too Small." *Naval Aviation News*, November 1951, pp. 1–7.

Pace, E. M., Jr. "The Naval Aircraft Factory." *Flying* 30 (January 1942): 128–32.

Paullin, Charles Oscar. "Early Naval Administration under the Constitution." *USNIP* 32 (1906): 1001–30.

Pearson, Lee. "Developing the Flying Bomb." In Adrien O. Van Wyen, ed., *Naval Aviation in World War I*, 70–73. Washington, D.C.: Chief of Naval Operations, 1969.

"Power Plant Facilities Are Merged." *Naval Aviation News*, July 1967, p. 25.

"Proof of Quality: Tested at Trenton." *Naval Aviation News*, April 1958, pp. 1–7.

"Properties and Uses of Light Alloys." *Journal of the Society of Automotive Engineers* 25 (September 1929): 315.

"Radio Robots." *Naval Aviation News*, July 1951; pp. 1–5.

Rausa, Cdr. Rosario. "Turntables and Traps." *Naval Aviation News*, August 1976, pp. 8–18.

"Research to Reality." *Naval Aviation News*, November 1955, pp. 1–7.

Richardson, H. C. "Development in Naval Aeronautics." *Society of Automotive Engineers, Transactions* 19, pt. 2 (1924): 661–92.

Richardson, Lt. Cdr. L. B. "Prevention of Corrosion in Duralumin Aircraft Structures." *Journal of the Society of Automotive Engineers* 24 (January 1929): 24–29.

———. "Progress at the Naval Aircraft Factory." *Your Navy* (1936): 40.

Robb, Izetta Winter. "The Navy Builds an Aircraft Factory." In Adrian O. Van Wyen, ed., *Naval Aviation in World War I*, 34–37. Washington, D.C.: Chief of Naval Operations, 1969.

Shumway, George N. "Naval Aircraft Factory." *Flying* 33 (December 1943): 44–45, 188.

Small, Dorothy L. "Catapults Come of Age." *USNIP* 80 (October 1954): 1113–21.

Smith, Richard K. "The Intercontinental Airliner and the Essence of Airplane Performance, 1929–1939." *Technology and Culture* 24 (July 1983): 428–49.

"Sortie into Space: The NADC Story." *Naval Aviation News*, March 1958, pp. 1–5.

Stout, W. B. "Duralumin All-Metal Airplane Construction." *Journal of the American Society of Automotive Engineers* 22 (April 1928): 430–36.

"Successful Design of Light Weight Metal Wings." *Aviation* 14 (8 January 1923): 38–41.

"Taylorcraft Tid-Bits" (Newsletter), January, February 1981.

Tillman, Barrett. "The N3N Story." *Journal of the American Aviation Historical Society* 13 (Winter 1968): 288–90.

Trimble, William F. "The Naval Aircraft Factory, the American Aviation Industry, and Government Competition, 1919–1928." *Business History Review* 60 (Summer 1986): 175–98.

Van Deurs, George. "Pete Mitscher and Armored Cruiser Aviation." *USNIP* 95 (November 1969): 152–53.

Walter, H. J. ("Walt"). "Hangar Deck Catapults." *Hook* 13 (Summer 1985): 10–13.

Warner, Edward P. "Notes on a Great Confusion." *Aviation* 33 (April 1934): 116.

Webster, W. W. "The Navy PN-12 Seaplane." *Aviation* 24 (14 May 1928): 1366, 1404.

Weyerbacher, R. D. "Metal Construction of Aircraft." *Journal of the Society of Automotive Engineers* 21 (November 1927): 489–93.

———. "Proposed Functions of the Naval Aircraft Factory." *USNIP* 52 (December 1926): 2428–36.

"Where Designs Come to Life." *Air Scoop* 2 (June 1945): 2–4.

Winkel, R. Adm. Raymond M. "LAMPS: The Ship System with Wings." *USNIP* 106 (March 1980): 114–17.

"Winning Waves." *Air Scoop* 1 (15 May 1944): 2–3, 8.

Zeigler, S. J., Jr. "The Naval Aircraft Factory." *Aero Digest* 7 (September 1925): 465–69.

———. "The Naval Aircraft Factory," *USNIP* 52 (January 1926): 83–94.

INTERVIEWS

Capt. Ralph S. Barnaby, Philadelphia, Pa., 12 October 1983.

Capt. Ralph S. Barnaby by John T. Mason, Jr., U.S. Naval Institute, 27 August 1969, in OANHC.

J. Hartley Bowen, Jr., Haddonfield, N.J., 13 October 1983.

William J. Cox, Lakehurst, N.J., 11 October 1983.

Vice-Adm. Herbert Riley, no date, Oral History Collection, U.S. Naval Institute.

THESES, DISSERTATIONS, AND UNPUBLISHED PAPERS

Bowman, Chester Grainger. "The Philadelphia Naval Aircraft Factory and the Emerging American Aircraft Industry, 1917–1927: A Case Study of Business-Government Relations." Senior thesis, Princeton University, 1969.

Commandant, Fourth Naval District. "The War History of the Fourth Naval District." 6 vols., vol. 5, pt. 8. Philadelphia, 1946. Copy in Navy Department Library, Washington, D.C.

Dix, E. H., Jr. "Alclad: A New Corrosion Resistant Aluminum Product." NACA Technical Note 259, 24 May 1927.

Jenkins, Innis LaRoche. "Josephus Daniels and the Navy Department, 1913–1916: A Study in Military Administration." Ph.D. dissertation, University of Maryland, 1960.

Kean, John S. "Looking Backward, or Forty Years on League Island, 27 October 1960." Copy in files of J. Hartley Bowen, Haddonfield, N.J.

Pearson, Lee M. "Notes on the History of the Naval Aircraft Factory." Undated MS. in Historian's Office, Naval Air Systems Command Headquarters, Washington, D.C.

Rawdon, Henry S. "Corrosion Embrittlement of Duralumin." NACA Technical Note 282, April 1928.

Schatzberg, Eric. "In Defense of the Wooden Airplane: Choice of Materials in American Transport Airplanes between the World Wars." Paper submitted for the Newcomen Society Prize in the History of Technology, 6 May 1988.

Index

About the Author

William Trimble is a military and naval historian who teaches at Auburn University in Alabama. He is the author of several articles and books on the history of aeronautics in Pennsylvania.

The **Naval Institute Press** is the book-publishing arm of the U.S. Naval Institute, a private, nonprofit professional society for members of the sea services and civilians who share an interest in naval and maritime affairs. Established in 1873 at the U.S. Naval Academy in Annapolis, Maryland, where its offices remain today, the Naval Institute has more than 100,000 members worldwide.

Members of the Naval Institute receive the influential monthly magazine *Proceedings* and discounts on fine nautical prints, ship and aircraft photos, and subscriptions to the quarterly *Naval History* magazine. They also have access to the transcripts of the Institute's Oral History Program and get discounted admission to any of the Institute-sponsored seminars regularly offered around the country.

The Naval Institute's book-publishing program, begun in 1898 with basic guides to naval practices, has broadened its scope in recent years to include books of more general interest. Now the Naval Institute Press publishes more than forty new titles each year, ranging from how-to books on boating and navigation to battle histories, biographies, ship and aircraft guides, and novels. Institute members receive discounts on the Press's more than 375 books.

Full-time students are eligible for special half-price membership rates. Life memberships are also available.

For a free catalog describing the Naval Institute Press books currently available, and for further information about U.S. Naval Institute membership, please write to:

Membership & Communications Department
U.S. Naval Institute
Annapolis, Maryland 21402
or call, toll-free, (800) 233-USNI. In Maryland, call (301) 224-3378.

THE NAVAL INSTITUTE PRESS
WINGS FOR THE NAVY
A History of the Naval Aircraft Factory, 1917–1956
Designed by Alan Carter

Set in Trump (text) and Eras Bold (display)
by Byrd Data Imaging Group, Richmond, Virginia

Printed on 60-lb. Eggshell Cream, 392 ppi,
bound in Holliston Roxite A 49249, vellum finish,
with 80-lb., Rainbow FD endsheets,
and stamped in aluminum gloss
by Maple-Vail, Inc., York, Pennsylvania